Media and Participation in Post-Migrant Societies

Media and Participation in Post-Migrant Societies

Edited by
Tanja Thomas, Merle-Marie Kruse
and Miriam Stehling

ROWMAN &
LITTLEFIELD
INTERNATIONAL
Lanham • New York

Published by Rowman & Littlefield International Ltd
6 Tinworth Street, London, SE11 4AB, U.K.
www.rowmaninternational.com

Rowman & Littlefield International Ltd.is an affiliate of Rowman & Littlefield
4501 Forbes Boulevard, Suite 200, Lanham, Maryland 20706, USA
With additional offices in Boulder, New York, Toronto (Canada), and Plymouth (UK)
www.rowman.com

British Library Cataloguing in Publication Information Available

A catalogue record for this book is available from the British Library

ISBN: HB 978-1-78660-725-6 | PBK 978-1-78660-727-0

Library of Congress Cataloging-in-Publication Data

Names: Thomas, Tanja, editor. | Kruse, Merle-Marie, editor. | Stehling,
   Miriam, editor.
Title: Media and participation in post-migrant societies / edited by Tanja
   Thomas, Merle-Marie Kruse and Miriam Stehling.
Description: London ; New York : Rowman & Littlefield International, [2019] |
   Includes bibliographical references and index.
Identifiers: LCCN 2018059065 (print) | LCCN 2019002464 (ebook) | ISBN
   9781786607263 (Electronic) | ISBN 9781786607256 (cloth)
   ISBN 9781786607270 (pbk)
Subjects: LCSH: Immigrants—Cultural assimilation. | Mass media and
   immigrants. | Immigrants—Politcal activity. | Citizenship. | Social
   participation.
Classification: LCC JV6342 (ebook) | LCC JV6342 .M427 2019 (print) | DDC
   305.9/06912—dc23
LC record available at https://lccn.loc.gov/2018059065

Contents

Figures and Tables

CHAPTER 4

CHAPTER 6

CHAPTER 12

CHAPTER 13

Foreword

Arjun Appadurai

It is three years since the wave of migration to European shores which produced a crisis of public security, an avalanche of media images, multiple debates in the political and civil sectors of different countries, and generated acts of heroism as well as of rage among both migrants and their places of movement and arrival. That first wave of responses, frequently worded in the language of crisis, has now receded, and what has been left behind is a slower but more worrisome struggle in many European countries, as well as in the European Union as a whole.

At first glance, the main result appears to be a deepening of nationalist populism across Europe, in which scepticism about the EU is combined with opposition to migrants, especially those that arrive with full and proper vetting by their hosts. This might be called the Orban model, most successfully deployed in Hungary by Victor Orban, who has consolidated his power in Hungary largely around his negative views of the EU and of most migrants. Similar politicians, parties, and processes are rising in Scandinavia, Austria, Italy, and Poland. Germany and France still have a vigorous liberal centre, but they are witnessing a notable rise in right-wing forces, both in official politics and on the streets.

Media play a critical role in the construction of the migrant archive since circulation, instability, and the disjunctures of movement always cast doubt on the 'accidental' trace through which archives are sometimes assumed to emerge. In the effort to seek resources for the building of archives, migrants thus often turn to the media for images, narratives, models, and scripts of their own story, partly because the diasporic story is always understood to be one of breaks and gaps. Nor is this only a consumer relationship, for in the age of the internet, literate migrants have begun to explore social media, chat rooms, and other interactive spaces in which to find, debate, and consolidate their own memory traces and stories into a more widely plausible narrative. This task, never free of contest and debate, sometimes does take the form of what Benedict Anderson disparagingly called 'long-distance nationalism.' But long-distance nationalism is a complex matter, which usually produces many sorts of politics and many sorts of interest. In the age in which electronic mediation has begun to supplement and sometimes even supplant print mediation and older forms of communication, imagined communities are sometimes much more deeply real to migrants than natural ones.

Interactive media thus play a special role in the construction of what we may call the diasporic public sphere (an idea I proposed in *Modernity at Large* to extend the insights of Habermas, Anderson, and others about national public spheres), for they allow new forms of agency in the building of imagined communities. The act of reading together (which Anderson brilliantly identified in regard to newspapers and novels in the new nationalisms of the colonial world) is now enriched by the technologies of the web, Facebook, Twitter, and Google, creating a world in which the simultaneity of reading is complemented by the interactivity of messaging, searching, and posting. Thus, what we may call the 'diasporic archive' or 'migrant archive' is increasingly characterized by the presence of voice, agency, and debate, rather than of mere reading, reception, and interpellation.

But the migrant archive operates under another constraint, for it has to relate to the presence of one or more narratives of public memory in the new home of the migrant, where the migrant is frequently seen as a person with only one story to tell—the story of abject loss and need. In his or her new society, the migrant has to contend with the minority of the migrant archive, of the embarrassment of its remote references, and of the poverty of its claims on the official 'places of memory' in the new site. Thus, the electronic archive becomes a doubly valuable space for migrants, for, in this space, some of the indignity of being minor or contemptible in the new society can be compensated, and the vulnerability of the migrant narrative can be protected in the relative safety of cyberspace.

What is more, both new electronic media as well as traditional print media among migrant communities allow complex new debates to occur between the memory of the old home and the demands of public narrative in the new setting. Migrant newspapers in many communities become explicit sites for debate between microcommunities, between generations, and between different forms of nationalism. In this sense, the migrant archive is highly active and interactive, as it is the main site of negotiation between collective memory and desire. As the principal resource in which migrants can define the terms of their own identities and identity-building, outside the strictures of their new homes, the diasporic archive is an intensified form of what characterizes all popular archives: it is a place to sort out the meaning of memory in relationship to the demands of cultural reproduction. Operating outside the official spheres of both the home society and the new society, the migrant archive cannot afford the illusion that traces are accidents, that documents arrive on their own, and that archives are repositories of the luck of material survival. Rather, the migrant archive is a continuous and conscious work of the imagination, seeking in collective memory an ethical basis for the sustainable reproduction of cultural identities in the new society. For migrants, more than for others, the archive is a map. It is a guide to the uncertainties of identity-building under adverse conditions. The archive is a search for the memories that count and not a home for memories with a preordained significance. This living, aspirational archive could become a vital source for the challenge of narratability and identity in contemporary times. The interaction of migration, memory, and media is today played out mostly at the national border, or in the borders of camps, prisons, and temporary shelters where refugees and undocumented aliens are frequently forced to live. This brings me back to the issue of borders in today's world.

The central issues of our times are today being played out in borders. The crisis of the nation-state is nowhere clearer than on its borders. The border is no longer an edge, a limit, or a container for the modern nation-state. It is the very site of the struggles over the future of sovereignty in the era of globalization. I have elsewhere argued that the time has come for a deep look at the architecture of sovereignty that we have inherited from the treaty of Westphalia. Its time is up, and we have no replacement for it. So, it is on life-support, and we are all its hostages. Many of us wish to think of the planet, of the city, of the region, and of humanity, but the nation-state makes this hard because it has captured our imaginations by linking sovereignty, citizenship, and territory in a single envelope, and we are hostage to this design.

The dramas that are taking place on today's borders bring together all the central challenges of the nation-state in the era of globalization. Drugs and arms move freely across borders. Humans are trafficked across borders. Illicit money from the world of high finance knows no boundaries. Storms and hurricanes sweep from nation to nation, as do diseases, terrorists, and global mafiosi. There is no border for these things. But borders can show their significance when people from the poorer countries of the world seek to escape tyranny, state failure, climate change, and persecution in their own homes. They are pushed out of their borders, and they land on our borders. The border is their purgatory, sometimes a permanent one.

Take the Rohingya from Myanmar, who have recently been the targets of the most brutal ethnocide of the twenty-first century, stigmatized, hunted, raped, and killed by the Burmese army and accepted with only the greatest reluctance by other South-East Asian countries, and by Bangladesh, India, and Nepal. They have become permanent citizens of a world made up only of borders. Wherever they are, they are in a border zone because they have no rights, no security, no dignity, and no future. The world has become a border zone for them, since no nation-state where they live or to which they come wants to have them. They are too poor, too abject, too voiceless, and too closely connected to the delicate political relationships between India, Burma, Bangladesh, China, and many other countries. They are dispensable, a kind of human waste.

Borders are certainly the markers of the physical boundaries between nation-states. But borders have also become a brutal life-world, where millions of people are living in a permanent state of insecurity, precarity, and indignity. They are the leading symptoms of the larger crisis of the nation-state in the era of globalization, a sign that soon the nation-state will become no more than a series of borders, boundaries, barriers, and edges with no secure spaces in between. So, I want to propose that migrants are not simply sites at the edges of our nations but are signs of the spreading of borders into the very heart of our societies, as sites of violence, suffering, fear, and exclusion, redeemed occasionally by acts of passion, compassion, and care.

In this outstanding volume, I believe we see ample evidence of the complexities of the migrant predicament in an age of media saturation. The essays document the race between narratives and images *of* migrants and those *by* migrants. The authors cover a remarkable range of countries, technologies, practices, and dilemmas that characterize the migrant order in today's world. I urge you to read these essays carefully because they show, beyond the shadow of a doubt, that the migrant predicament is at the heart of our collective political futures.

Arjun Appadurai
Berlin
7 October 2018

Introduction

Creating New Pathways for Convivial Futures: Media and Participation in Post-Migrant Societies

Merle-Marie Kruse, Miriam Stehling, and Tanja Thomas

[A]s mass mediation becomes increasingly dominated by electronic media [. . .], and as such media increasingly link producers and audiences across national boundaries, and as these audiences themselves start new conversations between those who move and those who stay, we find a growing number of diasporic public spheres. [. . .] Diasporic public spheres, diverse among themselves, are the crucibles of a postnational political order. (Appadurai 1996, 22)

The links between (digital) media communication, migration, and participation in a globalizing world have been described and analysed by Arjun Appadurai as early as 1996. Even more, his ideas in *Modernity at Large* showcase how migration becomes not only an object of study, but also the starting point for new ways of theorizing and developing epistemologies, as in conceptualizing mediated diasporic public spheres as cradles of a postnational political order. Similarly, by introducing the concepts of post-migrant societies and convivialism, this volume aims at further developing and intervening into recent debates and discourses in two distinct, but connected areas of media and communication research: (digital) migration studies on the one hand, and research on participation in media cultures on the other.

By focusing on media and participation in heterogeneous, post-migrant societies (for the concept see Foroutan 2015; Römhild 2017), this book addresses socio-political contexts where migration has been acknowledged by state institutions and the public as inevitable and 'real.' The term 'post-migrant' originated within the performing arts scene (introduced by the Berlin-based theatre maker and artistic director Şermin Langhoff, who named her theatre *Ballhaus Naunynstraße* 'post-migrant theatre'). Meanwhile, it has been taken up by social scientists to analyse the conflicts and processes of identity construction as well as the social, political, and cultural transformations within societies, which are characterized by a history of different forms of migration (e.g., postcolonial migration, migrant work/itinerant labour, and forced migration). The prefix 'post-' introduces a temporal dimension, which—similar to the 'post-' in 'postcolonial'—not simply denotes a state *after* migration, but rather refers to the consequences and repercussions of migration for individuals and society (Yıldız 2015). However, this does not mean that societal negotiation processes over migration and participation have come to an end; they actually continue and expand to conditions after migration has occurred. Therefore, post-migrant societies are considered to be fundamentally defined by tension-ridden processes where forms of (forced) togetherness are negotiated on different social and political levels. On the one hand, this involves new structural challenges for participation and new formations of racist inclusions and exclusions (Espahangizi et al. 2016; Tsianos and Karakayalı 2014). On the other hand, this bears the potential for postnational transformations and convivial futures, allowing for a renegotiation of voice and listening, visibility and recognition, as well as collaboration in the light of migration (for these and other post-migrant visions, see Hill and Yıldız 2018). The contributions to this volume capture the productivity that the concept of post-migrant societies offers, as well as the ambivalences it entails. They suggest different, but complementary approaches to an analysis of post-migrant societies, which resonate with recent ideas brought forward by Naika Foroutan (2018a, see also Foroutan 2018b). According to her, the concept of post-migrant societies includes three approaches: First, an *empirical-analytical approach* focuses on how societies are changing after migration has occurred. Here, the socially structuring forces of decades of migration, as well as the ambiguous negotiation processes within post-migrant societies are in question, which among others can be characterized by a dissonance between cognitive acceptance and emotional rejection of pluralism and heterogeneity. Second, a *critical-deconstructivist approach* aims at critically challenging established bodies of knowledge and presuppositions with regard to migration and hyper-real notions of nationally-ethnically-culturally homogeneous societies, which contribute to a reproduction of unequal power relations and binary oppositions such as 'migrants' and 'natives.' Furthermore, the analytical purpose of such an approach is to understand how the omnipresence of migration in public discourse obscures other social conflicts and structural inequalities. Finally, it also aims at recognizing possibilities for new solidarities, alliances, and resistive practices. Third, a *normative-ontological approach* addresses the challenge of systematically pointing beyond the 'migrant condition,' and instead focusing on the complexity of dynamics and transformations in societies, which are constituted on norms of equality and justice. This involves asking questions about economically, gender-specific, culturally and racially legitimized inequalities, and ultimately entails the normative key question of 'how we want to live together in increasingly plural societies' (Foroutan 2018a, 286; translation by authors)—a question which is also at the core of ideas about 'convivialism.'

The concept of 'convivialism' has gained growing importance within the debate on new forms of living together in increasingly plural and heterogeneous societies. As Elke Grittmann and Tanja Thomas (2017) argue, this debate had already started in the late 1990s, when increased mobility and forced migration boosted the interconnectedness and increased 'proximity' (Tomlinson 1999) of formerly distant others and the encounter of migrants and non-migrants became a common experience as well as a challenge in everyday life, which was highly shaped by (digital) media cultures. In reference to intensive debates about options and constraints of intercultural and transcultural communication among individuals and groups of different cultural, ethnical, and religious background, at first it was the concept of 'cosmopolitanism' that has experienced some revival across various disciplines (Appiah 2006; Beck 2002; Breckenridge et al. 2002; Held 2010; Tomlinson 1999; Vertovec and Cohen 2002), and also had been taken up in media and communication studies. The rise of transnational broadcasting news and worldwide news networks had created new forms of interconnectedness and globalized public spheres, thus raising new questions of responsibility and hospitality towards 'distant others' (Silverstone 2013). Therefore, some scholars argued that particular media aesthetics (Chouliaraki 2008a, 2008b) and/or modes of representation (e.g., Cottle and Lester 2009; Robertson 2010) have the potential to evoke cosmopolitan obligations and dispositions in (Western) audiences (e.g., Kyriakidou 2009; Lindell 2014; Corpus Ong 2009).

Later on, some scholars preferred the term 'another' (Benhabib 2006), 'new' (Strand 2010), or 'critical cosmopolitanism' (Delanty 2006) or even replaced the term with the concept of 'convivality' (Gilroy 2004; Nowicka and Vertovec 2014) in order to overcome some of the cosmopolitan heritage, such as its Eurocentric bias. By now, some authors, like the ones of the 'Convivialist Manifesto' (Käte Hamburger Kolleg/Centre for Global Cooperation Research 2014), mention a wide variety of different initiatives that 'point towards an alternative to the current organization of the world' (Les Convivialistes 2014) and describe their activities as 'a quest for *convivialism*. [. . .] By convivialism we mean a mode of living together (*con-vivere*) that values human relationships and cooperation and enables us to challenge one another without resorting to mutual slaughter and in a way that ensures consideration for others and for nature' (Käte Hamburger Kolleg/Centre for Global Cooperation Research 2014, 24–25; italics in original). Importantly, from our perspective, the concept of convivialism values conflict as a legitimate and 'necessary [. . .] part of every society' (ibid., 25), which corresponds with our argument about conflictual negotiation processes around participation in post-migrant media cultures. With this volume, we aim at presenting contributions that refer to the ideas of post-migrant societies and convivial futures, thereby enhancing the research in (digital) migration studies and on participation in media cultures.

FROM CONNECTED MIGRANTS TO PARTICIPATION AND COLLABORATION IN POST-MIGRANT MEDIA CULTURES

For the field of *(digital) migration studies*, this focus on post-migrant conditions and challenges for convivial futures implies an epistemological turn: first and foremost, it means a shift from doing research *about* migration to concentrating on society's *negotiations over* migration (Römhild 2017, 72). Such a perspective acknowledges the figure of the 'connected migrant' (Diminescu 2008), and 'connected refugees' (Leurs and Ponzanesi 2018), as well as ideas such as 'digital migrant connectivity' (ibid., 5), 'mobile commons,' and 'migrant digitalities' (Trimikliniotis, Parsanoglou, and Tsianos 2015) as important concepts for rethinking power struggles, processes of identity construction, and inclusions/exclusions around (forced) migration in the current era of mediatization and digitalization. At the same time, we argue with Koen Leurs and Kevin Smets for a 'reflexive politics of knowledge production on digital migration' (Leurs and Smets 2018, 1), which commits itself towards equity and social justice while being aware of the complexity and contextuality of migration in contemporary media cultures. It is our firm belief that focusing on struggles for participation and collaboration in and through media, as well as on potentials for convivial futures in post-migrant media cultures, is a good starting point for this new pathway. Hence, drawing on the concept of post-migrant media cultures, this volume introduces a perspective that not only analyses media representations and media use of diasporic communities and migrants—a perspective always in danger of 'othering' certain groups and reproducing essentialist notions of 'the migrant'; it also explicitly examines from a transmedia perspective the (im)possibilities for participation and collaboration of different social actors within 'arrival societies' and addresses the challenges and conflicts that come along with this type of analytical work on multiple levels. With regard to emerging theories and concepts, the contribution by Tanja Dreher and Poppy de Souza discusses how the term 'post-migrant society' has a different meaning in settler colonial states such as Australia than in Western European countries, while Viktorija Ratković argues how speaking of 'post-migrant media' instead of 'ethnic minority media' intervenes in problematic essentialist discourses on migration within the field of media production. With regard to the (im)possibilities of convivial futures in post-migrant societies, Brigitte Hipfl explores film as a resource to intervene in the remediation of racist and colonial tropes within the Austrian context, while the contributions by Fabian Virchow and Radha Hegde analyse different forms of nativist and xenophobic attacks on aspirations towards convivialism.

As far as research on *participation in media cultures* is concerned, this volume addresses an important shortcoming in this field by situating struggles around participation in social conditions characterized by people coming, going, and staying. It thereby introduces the concept of post-migrant societies both in terms of conceptual refinements and empirical studies to this area of research. The contributions of this book provide diverse analyses of the possibilities, but also constraints for participation and the role that media communication plays in the reshaping of civic culture in post-migrant societies. While Peter Dahlgren's contribution offers an application of his 'Civic Culture' model to post-migrant societies and thereby develops a theoretical framework to understand the dynamics that can facilitate as well as hinder participation in these conditions, the chapter by Nico Carpentier promotes a political studies approach towards participation in post-migrant societies and conceptualizes participation as an entanglement of discourses and materials. Furthermore, the book contributes novel perspectives to the flourishing field of media and participation research by providing theoretical tools and instruments to further develop a conceptualization of participation—for example by introducing concepts from the fields of critical migration studies and feminist participation research to the discussion, as proposed by Miriam Stehling, Tanja Thomas, and Merle-Marie Kruse in this volume—and by examining ambivalent negotiations over migration and togetherness as 'modality of connectivity' (Tomlinson 1999, 157) in post-migrant societies within a wide range of media forms and diverse media practices in a variety of ways. These contributions range from representations of migrants in European broadsheet press, as analysed in the chapter by Rafal Zaborowski, and the discussion of film and other artistic media as an intervention into discourses of the current 'refugee crisis' in the contributions by Brigitte Hipfl and Katarzyna Marciniak, to the manifold uses of social media as tools for refugees' agency and participation (see Arnold and Görland in this volume), for doing memory on right-wing violence (see Rudolph, Thomas, and Virchow in this volume), for organizing volunteer activities in post-migrant societies (see Kaun and Uldam in this volume), and for amplifying marginalized voices and promoting a politics of listening as media participation (see Dreher and de Souza in this volume), as well as for the articulation of anti-refugee sentiments (see Virchow in this volume). With all these varied and rich contributions, the volume advances an empirical differentiation of the concept of participation and meets the challenge of researching and analysing participation within the context of media appropriation, a research gap that different authors have previously identified in media and participation research (Cammaerts, Mattoni, and McCurdy 2013, 15–16; Carpentier and Dahlgren 2011).

KEY THEMES AND STRUCTURE OF THE VOLUME

Integral to the volume are multi-faceted analytical perspectives of how media communication is currently shaping and transforming participation and convivialism in post-migrant societies. The book is divided into four parts.

Part I: Conceptual Perspectives on Media and Participation in Post-Migrant Societies presents different theoretical perspectives by addressing questions such as: How can the interrelations of participation and media be (re-)conceptualized in increasingly diverse, post-migration societies? Is there a 'right' to participate and to not participate, and how are norms of participation negotiated in and via different media? How is participation linked to concepts such as voice and listening, visibility and recognition, as well as collaboration? Which resources (both material and symbolic) and competences are prerequisites for participation? Which ambiguities, dilemmas, and challenges arise for participation in post-migrant media cultures?

Chapter 1: *Media, Participation, and Collaboration in Post-Migrant Societies* by Miriam Stehling, Tanja Thomas, and Merle-Marie Kruse is dedicated to a (re)conceptualization of the relationship between media and participation from a perspective from and within post-migrant societies. The authors critically discuss existing conceptualizations and models of media and participation and suggest broadening these with a perspective of post-migration. It is argued that models of participation can be fruitfully enhanced by referring to (feminist) research that critically reflects on the meaning of voice and listening, visibility, and recognition as conditions and requirements for participation. Understanding collaboration as encounter and foundation for convivial democratic societies, the chapter argues to better link studies of digital migration with insights from participation research and presents a list of questions as a heuristic tool in order to critically investigate and interrogate projects of media and participation in post-migrant societies.

In chapter 2: *Immigrants, Social Media, and Participation: The Long and Winding Road via Integration*, Peter Dahlgren schematically looks at the arduous passage to participation, via integration, that newly arrived immigrants face, attempting to specify the contingencies that shape this democratic ideal and highlight the role of social media in the process. In doing so, he focuses on recent immigration—mostly by refugees—to Europe, with a few examples from Sweden. The chapter establishes a theoretical framework for understanding the dynamics that can facilitate as well as hinder the development of civic cultures in post-migrant societies; this framework will help guiding further empirical studies.

Chapter 3: *Dangerous Precarity: Sexual Politics, Migrant Bodies, and the Limits of Participation* by Radha S. Hegde argues that the mediated circulation of nativist ideologies reproduces visions of homogeneity by criminalizing migrants and classifying them as pathologically inclined to sexual deviance and violence. Drawing, among others, on the discourse generated in the post-migrant context of the United States about the dangerous pathologies of the precariat, this chapter theorizes how the xenophobic imagination's historical preoccupation with race and sexuality has been renewed and fortified. As a result, the chapter demonstrates how complex transnational politics of global migration produce exclusionary boundaries that determine the eligibility of migrants and the limits of their legitimate participation in the national polity—thus showing that in many cases, normative post-migrant visions of equality and justice are by no means achieved.

Part II: Visibilities and Vulnerabilities of Refugees and Migrants in Media and Art explores how refugees, migrants, and (post-)migratory conditions in societies are represented in media and how art reacts to the current 'refugee crisis.' The chapters of this part cover different media formats, ranging from press coverage to film to artistic media images.

In chapter 4: *Between the Vulnerable and the Dangerous: Representations of Refugees in British Press*, Rafal Zaborowski discusses the findings of a long-term research project about media representations of migrants and refugees in European broadsheet press in 2015 in order to analyse which representations of migrants were allowed and disallowed, legitimized and discarded, in the British press and to what extent these structures and representations enabled the European community to meaningfully engage with the distant other, enabling participation between the citizens and new arrivals. Specifically, he focuses on refugee representations in four British quality newspapers (*The Guardian, The Times, The Independent,* and the *Daily Telegraph*), while contextualizing the findings within a broader analytical framework, including systematic content analysis of quality press in eight European countries and two main Arabic-language European newspapers. The chapter argues that while the representations differed across time and across editorial stances of the British press, the framing of refugees and asylum seekers positioned them as either vulnerable or dangerous, but always as the

'Other' to the presumed 'Us,' thus leading to an exclusion of diverse voices, as well as the impossibility of dialogue and equal participation of refugees in post-migrant societies.

Chapter 5: *Exploring Films' Potential for Convivial Civic Culture* by Brigitte Hipfl focuses on the potential of film to address and intervene in the re-mediation of racist and colonial tropes, images, and discourses in the Austrian public realm. This is contextualized in the broader question about the ability of film to make migrants feel being part of society, not being positioned as the 'Other,' as a first step towards extending the possibilities for participation in post-migrant societies and establishing more diverse representations of post-migrant experiences. It proposes that films are a means to crystallize and condense collective feelings, to give insights in the banality of togetherness in everyday life, and to illustrate what can emerge from new, unexpected encounters. The four films discussed in this chapter all engage with issues of migration. The discussion is grounded in a cartography of media and migration that explores the power relations expressed in the entanglement of regimes of representation and affects.

Chapter 6: *Art and Refugeeism: Speaking-with and Speaking-from-within* by Katarzyna Marciniak showcases artists who have contributed particularly provocative and compelling commentaries on the current 'refugee crisis.' Collectively, the chapter argues, their politically engaged and participatory art offers an eloquent audio-visual and material resistance to xenophobic and racist responses to global migrations. Starting with artistic interventions by Chinese dissident artist Ai Weiwei, London-based rapper M.I.A., and Crocheted Olek, a Polish-American installation artist, as examples of speaking-with, or being-with refugees, the chapter then moves on to discuss the experimental video art of Another Kind of Girl Collective, authored by young Syrian women living in Jordan's Za'atari refugee camp, as examples of what speaking-from-within might look and feel like.

Part III: Ambiguities and Contestation in Social Media concentrates on digital and social media and how this media is used for participation in post-migrant societies. The different chapters investigate different aspects of social media use by refugees or volunteer-led initiatives, but also by right-wing populist movements.

In chapter 7: *Participatory Logistics from Below: The Role of Smartphones for Syrian Refugees*, Sina Arnold and Stephan Görland contribute to an understanding of the role that smartphones played for Syrian refugees during and after their process of migration to Germany. Based on qualitative and quantitative data, they shed light on specific forms of mobile-mediated self-empowerment that enable different forms of participation. In that sense, the smartphone is analysed as a local object that expresses and, at the same time, shapes global relations and transnational migratory movements both into and within Europe. This chapter suggests that smartphones are digital tools that facilitate self-organization, greater autonomy, and increased participation among forced migrants in several ways.

Chapter 8: *'It Only Takes Two Minutes'—The So-Called Migration Crisis and Facebook as Civic Infrastructure* by Anne Kaun and Julie Uldam examines the role of social media for civic participation by studying Swedish volunteer initiatives that emerged in the context of the so-called migration crisis that reached a peak in 2015 as a case study. Theoretically, the chapter draws on an analytical framework for civic engagement and participation in social media, combining questions of power relations, technological affordances, practices, and discourses. Furthermore, it relates the discussion of civic engagement, participation, and social media to insights from infrastructure studies to theorize the role of Facebook and its implications for volunteer activities. The analysis focuses particularly on temporal affordances of social media in coordinating volunteer work and critically questions the emerging position of Facebook as civic infrastructure in volunteer organizing. It thus explores forms of negotiating the implications of post-migrant societies, namely, the development of ways of living together from bottom up rather than top down.

Chapter 9: *Sentiment-Driven Demands and Scenarios for Political Participation in Nativist SNS* by Fabian Virchow explores the social media use of the nativist PEGIDA movement in post-migrant Germany. Specifically, it focuses on the ways that the people who used the PEGIDA Facebook page as the movement's main channel of communication, in order to comment on the latest political developments and events, speak out about political decisions by state actors and by political parties. Furthermore, the analysis examines how these comments frame the need for and the proposed ways of political participation and intervention that might stop what these commentators are calling 'evil' (e.g., Chancellor Merkel's decisions in asylum policies). In doing so, the chapter also seeks to understand what place emotions and sentiment have in the way of demanding particular kinds of political action.

Part IV: Voice and Agency of Marginalized Actors in Post-Migrant Societies includes examples in which voice is given to or taken by subaltern groups in post-migrant societies. The chapters examine the (often conflictual) negotiations within communities and (media) institutions that come along with processes of participation in and through the media. The authors discuss necessary changes to tap into the full potential of participation and collaboration in post-migrant societies.

Chapter 10: *From Niche to Mainstream? Post-Migrant Media Production as a Means of Fostering Participation* by Viktorija Ratković elaborates on the media's role in fostering civic cultures by presenting the Austrian magazine *biber* as an example of post-migrant media, as a type of media that highlights ways of combatting marginalization of migrants in media production as well as in non-mainstream media. The main focus is post-migrant media production as experienced by the producers of *biber*. By discussing *biber*'s efforts to enable marginalized groups to participate in and through media, the need for and the challenges of incorporating post-migrant perspectives in all media are highlighted.

In chapter 11: *Beyond Marginalized Voices: Listening as Participation in Multicultural Media*, Tanja Dreher and Poppy de Souza analyse 'listening' as a crucial mode of media participation for the privileged in response to marginalized voices. The empirical example is Indigenous Health May Day (#IHMayDay), an annual Twitter event that privileges and amplifies First Nations' voices in settler colonial Australia. During this event, non-Indigenous people are invited to participate by listening and amplifying. The chapter extends an interest in media, voice, and participation to focus on the politics of listening as a necessary and undervalued practice for media participation and transformation.

Chapter 12: *Doing Memory and Contentious Participation: Remembering the Victims of Right-Wing Violence in German Political Culture* by Steffen Rudolph, Tanja Thomas, and Fabian Virchow discusses the relevance of remembering as part of political culture and as a potential way of contentious participation around issues of belonging and recognition. The chapter uses the case of contested memory with regard to the deadly arson attack against migrants in Mölln as a case study and argues that forms of collaboration between the victims of right-wing violence and activists vitally rely on the use of digital media to foster solidary bonds and connections. By addressing resource-based hierarchies as well as by listening to the voices of the victims and the marginalized, this collaboration is quintessential for shaping the future of a post-migrant society that is aware of racist violence.

Chapter 13: *Memorialization, Participation, and Self-Representation. Remembering Refugeedom in the Cypriot Village of Dasaki Achnas* by Nico Carpentier focuses on the negotiations of memoralization in the Cypriot village Achnas concerning the commemoration of the villagers' displacement in August 1974. More particularly, the case study analyses the participatory components of the construction of a memorial where the community, represented by the mayor and the community council, engaged in negotiations with the artist Pampos Mihlis and resisted the critical suggestions of the Cypriot Advisory Monuments' Committee. Theoretically, the chapter is positioned in a political-studies approach towards participation, which defines participation as the equalization of power relations. Moreover, inspired by a combination of discourse theory, new materialism, and assemblage theory, participation is seen as an entanglement of discourses and materials.

The discussions, ideas, and contributions to our project could not have materialized into this book without great participation and support on various levels. First of all, a heartfelt thank-you goes to all the authors for their commitment and contributions to this project. We are especially grateful to Anne Kaun for taking the time to discuss an early version of the proposal for this book with us and for her helpful advice on many aspects, not least on our search for a suitable publisher. A very special thank-you is dedicated to Arjun Appadurai and Nick Couldry, whose preface and afterword, respectively, frame this volume with crucial impetuses for engaging with participation in post-migrant media cultures. Also, we would sincerely like to thank Isabell May for copyediting the chapters to this volume. Her great sense of language and her instructive comments and suggestions have definitely enriched the contributions. Many thanks as well to Lennart Stock, whose careful proofreading, formatting, indexing, and keeping track of all the formalities was a huge help to us. Furthermore, we would like to thank the publisher Rowman & Littlefield International for trusting in this project, especially Natalie Linh Bolderston, Holly Tyler, and Gurdeep Mattu for their kind and productive collaboration.

Part I

CONCEPTUAL PERSPECTIVES ON MEDIA AND PARTICIPATION IN POST-MIGRANT SOCIETIES

Chapter One

Media, Participation, and Collaboration in Post-Migrant Societies

Miriam Stehling, Tanja Thomas, and Merle-Marie Kruse

Participation has become a crucial buzzword in discussions about migration, integration, and living together in current (Western) societies. While the relationship between media and participation in general has been examined quite exhaustively (see, e.g., Carpentier 2011; Carpentier and Dahlgren 2011; Dahlgren 2013), the discussion about how this relationship is relevant in post-migrant realities has just begun. As recent studies have shown, digital and social media play an important, but ambivalent role in participation-related issues for refugees (see, e.g., Kutscher and Kreß 2018). Therefore, we dedicate this chapter to a (re)conceptualization of the relationship between media and participation from a perspective from and within post-migrant societies. Convivial togetherness and participation have become crucial topics in the debate about the future of these (mediatized) post-migrant societies. Therefore, and as a matter of principle, our chapter seeks to contribute to what Koen Leurs and Kevin Smets (2018, 1) called a 'plea for non-digital-media-centric-ness and a commitment toward social change, equity and social justice.'

Such commitments have to be put into practice repeatedly. For example, in the summer of 2018, Ali Can, a twenty-five-year-old Turkish-German activist, posted a video in which he called for a #MeTwo hashtag for people to share their experiences of racism in Germany. In his video, he explains that he was inspired by the #MeToo campaign against sexism. 'I have more than one identity,' he said, hence #MeTwo.[1] Meanwhile, thousands of people in Germany with migrant backgrounds started sharing stories of everyday discrimination under the hashtag #MeTwo. Some may have felt inspired by soccer star Mesut Özil's resignation from Germany's national team. Özil announced via social media that he would no longer play for Germany after he faced racist abuse for posing for a picture alongside Turkish President Recep

Tayyip Erdoğan. 'I have two hearts, one German and one Turkish,' wrote Özil, who accused the German Football Federation (DFB) of failing to stand up for him after critics questioned his patriotism and singled him out to be blamed after Germany's World Cup flop.[2] Özil's resignation and #MeTwo triggered a heated debate not only on Twitter, but also in the national news in German media about racism. Obviously, in post-migrant Germany, people of different social backgrounds have access to media; they interact, they are visible, and they raise their voices. Yet Myria Georgiou's (2018, 45) question comes to mind when considering participation of people with migration backgrounds in post-migrant societies: 'When do they become, if at all, agentive participants in European mediascapes?'

This chapter aims at shedding light on the relationship between media and participation in post-migrant societies. First, we will critically discuss existing conceptualizations and models of media and participation and suggest broadening these with a perspective of post-migration. In the second section, we will argue that models of participation can be enhanced by referring to work on participation that 'uses and extents the insights of critical feminist, postcolonial, queer, anti-racist, and other approaches attentive to power' (Hasinoff 2014, 270). In particular, we will refer to (feminist) research that critically reflects on the meaning of voice and listening, visibility, and recognition as conditions and requirements for participation. In the third section, we suggest integrating concepts of collaboration and participation into research on digital migration and understanding collaboration as encounter and foundation for convivial democratic societies. We will then argue to more directly link studies of digital migration with insights from participation research and present a list of questions as a heuristic tool in order to critically investigate and interrogate projects of media and participation in post-migrant societies. We conclude the chapter by stressing the undeniable truth that plurality is a fact in post-migrant societies and that a collaborative and convivialist perspective is important in order to shape better futures for everyone.

1. CONCEPTUAL APPROACHES TO MEDIA AND PARTICIPATION IN POST-MIGRANT SOCIETIES

Many authors have been working hard to define and systematize the concept of participation. A variety of different approaches exists particularly in terms of the relationship between participation and media. There have been conversations between well-known scholars in the field (Jenkins and Carpentier 2013) as well as special-issue publications (Carpentier and Dahlgren 2011) and books (Carpentier 2011; Dahlgren 2009; 2013) about the concept of participation and its relationship with media. All have contributed important perspectives, and some have created helpful models and theoretical approaches to better understand the relationship between media and participation. Due to the range of conceptualizations of participation in the research area on media and participation, we first want to derive and justify our broad understanding of participation, one that is nevertheless characterized by its political resonance. Second, we briefly refer to those models that seem to be particularly suitable for investigating participation in post-migrant societies.

Dahlgren (2013, 11) points out that although most scholars agree that democracy needs people's participation, views on what forms this participation should take and how much of it is desirable can vary significantly. This is important because it also explains the variety of approaches around participation. In the context of post-migrant societies, we need to remember that democracies offer certain 'structures of opportunity for participation' (ibid., 11) rather than automatically guaranteeing that citizens participate extensively. That means that there are different obstacles for different groups in societies; this is especially true when we consider the living conditions of newly arrived refugees and migrants. The agency of citizens themselves, as well as of non-citizens who are temporary or long-term residents of a nation state, is always contingent on the circumstances that a democracy gives to them. Thus, the lack of participation must not solely be seen as civic apathy, but must be understood more generally in the context of the dynamics and dilemmas of late modern democracy (ibid., 11). The spectrum in which participation is seen as ideal varies from participation being realized in regular political elections to approaches in which an active role of citizens in all decision-making processes is seen as fundamental to participation (Geißel 2004).

In terms of the relationship between media and participation in particular, we can observe an omnipresence of the concept of media participation in academic and public debates as well as in everyday life. As Carpentier and Dahlgren (2011, 7) argue, this omnipresence, however, has not helped in developing a clearer concept of participation. On the contrary, they even diagnose a 'black boxing of the meaning(s) of the concept of participation' (ibid., 7). As Carpentier and Dahlgren (ibid., 8) continue to note, participation is not a fixed notion, but is deeply embedded within our political realities and thus the object of long-lasting and intense ideological struggles. Labelling all social processes as participatory makes it difficult to analyse different social practices in different contexts as well as in terms of different types of power relations and imbalances; however, we still advocate for a broad definition of participation, mainly inspired by feminist interventions into concepts of political participation, to which we return later. In reference to Wimmer et al. (2018, 3), we understand participation as an appropriation of public communication that can take different forms across different levels of organizational complexity and activity, ranging from the discussion and interaction between citizens in online forums or social media through social and protest movements to more general debates in the political public sphere. Ekman and Amnå (2012, 289), for example, suggest a typology of participation that distinguishes between latent and manifest forms of participation, as well as between individual and collective forms of engagement and participation. This typology also allows us to consider forms of nonparticipation and disengagement in its individual and collective forms (ranging from nonvoting and non-political lifestyles to acts of violence and civil disobedience), as well as forms of latent civil participation, such as social and civic engagement, and forms of manifest political participation (ibid., 295). With this typology, a variety of forms of participation emerge, while other forms of social practices are clearly distinguished from being participatory. In this chapter, we therefore follow an approach to participation that includes the idea that all action, no matter how small and seemingly random, can be termed 'participatory' as far as it adopts a political meaning—be it purposefully or not (Kaase 1992, 146 cited after Geißel 2004, 5). This idea of participation comes close and possesses many links to the notion of civic culture and civic agency that Peter Dahlgren proposed. He argues that the notion of civic culture points to those features of the socio-cultural world that constitute everyday preconditions for all democratic participation: in the institutions of civil society, engagement in the public sphere, and involvement in political activity broadly understood (Dahlgren 2000, 336). He further distinguishes between four and, later, six dimensions of civic culture, which are relevant: knowledge, values, trust, spaces, practices, and identities (Dahlgren 2009, 108). The dimension of identities can be seen as the centrepiece of civic cultures and is understood in plural form, emphasizing the heterogeneity of multiple identities (ibid., 109). Identity as a subjective view of people, as members and participants of a society, is seen as a foundation for agency and also includes forms of non-formal, cultural citizenship. Overall, these six dimensions should be seen as a circuit, mutually reinforcing each other, and as conditions under which participation and civic engagement flourish, or not (Dahlgren 2000, 339).

Furthermore, the distinction between participation in and through media, based on Carpentier (2011, 67), is helpful to us. Building on Wasko and Mosco's distinction between democratization in and through the media, Carpentier (ibid., 67) distinguishes between two interrelated forms of participation: participation through the media and participation in the media. Participation through the media refers to the opportunities for mediated participation in public debates and for self-representation in different public spaces that characterize the social (ibid., 67). Media then can serve as a location where citizens can voice their opinions and experiences, and where they can interact with other voices. At the same time, we need to take into account that the structures and cultures of the media sphere itself, and the ideological-democratic environment, have a strong impact on the intensity of participation (ibid., 67).

Participation in the media, on the other hand, means participation in the production of media output or content, as well as in media-related organizational decision making (ibid., 68). These forms of media participation allow citizens to be active in one of the numerous spheres relevant to everyday life and to put their right to communicate into practice. Here, community and alternative media are especially important and possess a strong link to participation. They offer many participatory opportunities at the levels of both self-representation and self-management, which positions them close to the logics of direct, delegative, and participatory democracy (ibid., 68). However, we need to take into account that such opportunities might not be equal for every person in a society, as, for example, the gender-oriented perspective on participation points out (Geißel 2004).

In order to grasp this idea of participation in a more concrete form and to relate the concept of participation to media, Carpentier (2011, 129–30) introduced the AIP model that connects the three concepts of *access*, *interaction*, and *participation* to each other; at the same time, this model allows us to highlight the distinctions between them. These distinctions help one to more clearly understand which practices constitute participation when it comes to media. First, access means having access to media technologies and ICTs (information and communication technologies) and being present in media production. Second, interaction points to the socio-communicative relationships that are established via media and asks about how and under which circumstances these relationships are established. Third, participation as such, then, is different from the former two concepts as participation refers to decision-making processes in, for example, media production companies or in editorial departments, where power plays a key role.

This differentiation is important when we think about post-migrant societies that are, as we argue, fundamentally characterized by conflicts that, following Chantal Mouffe (2013), people in pluralistic societies have to negotiate in agonistic struggles. From our view, the concept of collaboration can play a central role towards convivial futures in post-migrant societies that we also strive for as researchers. For this reason, the next sections discuss prerequisites of participation and collaboration, namely, the concepts of voice and listening, as well as visibility and recognition (Section 2) and collaboration (Section 3).

2. AMPLIFYING THE CONCEPTUALIZATIONS OF MEDIA AND PARTICIPATION IN POST-MIGRANT SOCIETIES

The section above discusses different substantial approaches to the concept of participation and demonstrates how participation is connected to power. In order to find ways to develop nuanced studies of participation that prioritize hierarchies and power relations, Hasinoff (2014) suggests that we should be sceptical of the promises of participation; instead, we should carefully attend to how participation can reproduce power structures even while it promises to destabilize them. In order to meet such challenges, Tanja Dreher (2017a) argues with Carpentier (2011b) and Couldry (2010) for greater engagement with political theory in order to develop a normative–critical framework for evaluating participation 'defined as the equalization of power relations between privileged and non-privileged actors in formal or informal decision-making processes' (Dreher 2017a, 24). In line with this argument, we additionally propose to consider ideas mainly from feminist and postcolonial political theory in order to put more emphasis on the (un)equal power relations in participation processes.

Feminist research expanded the notion of participation, applied it to social and private activities, and developed a critique of the categorization and hierarchization of various forms and practices of participation. In feminist thought, activities with clear political intent are not the only ones that are considered political. Instead, the transformative power and social change of an action is called 'political' (Geißel 2004). In consequence, 'when studying and assessing political participation, we therefore need to consider both parliamentarian as well as extra-parliamentarian political participation to understand their interrelations' (Uldam and Kaun 2017, 183), and participation is not limited to so called 'rational' forms of participation.

Furthermore, feminist interventions into political theory criticize the binary thinking within (liberal/mainstream) political theory, stating that 'dichotomies like public/private, mind/body, reason/emotion, etc. are not neutral and innocent but imply powerful and exclusionary hierarchies' (Bargetz 2009, paragraph 9). Hence, much work within this field has attempted to deconstruct these dichotomies and the exclusionary hierarchies they imply. We agree with Amy Adele Hasinoff (2014, 270) when she writes, 'there is plenty of work (on participation) that uses and extends the insights of critical feminist, postcolonial, queer, anti-racist, and other approaches attentive to power,' but such work is still marginalized in the general field. Yet, she argues, this work is more than suitable for answering questions such as: 'Who gets to participate and on what terms? What are the implications of this participation? And what forms of privilege are necessary to be viewed as capable of participating at all?' (ibid., 271). In line with Hasinoff's plea to de-centre media technologies and to focus on power and context, we suggest asking for these kinds of inherent privileges in more detail. The postcolonial debate of feminist scholars influenced some work on media and participation. For instance, in her journal article on migrant voices in Europe, Myria Georgiou (2018) uses Gayatri Chakravorty Spivak's well-known question 'Can the subaltern speak' for the title of her paper and puts an emphasis on the fact that 'what needs attention is not just listening of poor people, but listening to them' (ibid., 47). By following Gayatri Spivak's basic dictum of 'unlearn one's privilege,' Trinh T. Minh-ha introduces the notion 'speaking nearby' for speaking and listening at eye level and in coexistence. Her book *Woman Native Other* (1989) was ground-breaking in its concern to combine postcolonial theory and feminism. It explored the entanglements of seeing, speaking, listening, and power; her many theoretical writings on documentary film and, most recently, on digitalization make her a significant media theorist who, despite her meaningful contributions, still finds herself at the margins of mainstream media theory discourses (see also Marciniak's chapter in this volume).

In what follows, we will address the interrelatedness of 'voice' and 'listening' in post-migrant media cultures as another means to think beyond the hierarchical conceptualizations of participation and politics. While concepts of voice are quite well established within media and participation research, listening as 'the "other side" of participation and voice' (Dreher 2017a, 26) has only quite recently been taken up in discussions around participation in media studies and political theory (ibid., 25). One of the reasons for this 'privileging of voice, and particularly voice-as-democratic-participation' (Crawford 2009, 526) is that voice is 'closely tied to the libertarian model of online democracy' (ibid.), which rests on a hierarchical relationship of voice as an allegedly 'active' form of participation over listening as a supposedly 'passive' mode. In this narrow context, voice is connected to claims and acts of speaking in public discourse and political processes. However, drawing on the work towards a politics of listening by authors such as Nick Couldry (2009; 2010), Leah Bassel (2017), Tanja Dreher (2009; 2010; 2017a; see also the contributions in O'Donnell, Lloyd, and Dreher 2009), and Elke Grittmann and Tanja Thomas (2018), we argue for 'rethinking the politics of voice' (Couldry 2009) and broadening our perspective to focus on the 'mutual interweaving of the concepts of listening and voice' (ibid., 580). In the context of social change, equity, and social justice in post-migrant media cultures, which we are interested in, as we expressed earlier, questions of the repercussions of voice, of 'receptivity and responsiveness' (Dreher 2017a, 26) come to the fore, asking which voices can be heard and are recognized as intelligible subject positions. In that sense, 'an effective process of voice *always* means more than just being able to speak. Voice as a social process involves, from the start, both speaking *and listening*' (Couldry 2010, 8–9, italics in original). An analysis of the possibilities provided by social media for 'diverse and previously marginalized voices' to 'speak up, have a voice and share stories' makes apparent that this will not ensure that 'a greater range of voices will actually be heard' (Dreher 2017a, 25).

By asking 'what comes after listening,' Dreher (2009, 454) suggests linking listening and recognition (see also Bassel 2017, 8–9; Couldry 2009, 579–80), and we will suggest using that connection for researching media and participation in post-migrant societies. We also propose learning from Nancy Fraser's (2003) and Judith Butler's (2010) concepts of recognition that are connected to redistribution, but also to representation or visibility, respectively.

According to Fraser, social justice demands focusing on redistribution, representation, and recognition. New kinds of questions arise from framing the issue of participation in media cultures in relation to redistribution, representation, and recognition. In a more general take, Uldam and Kaun (2017, 185) emphasize the fact that multinational media corporations such as Google and Facebook dominate the majority of social media platforms (van Dijck 2013; Dahlberg 2014). Several studies on political participation in social media demonstrate that technologies are embedded in unequal power relations that privilege government and male-dominated corporate elites (Dahlgren 2013). Therefore, political participation should be analysed from a perspective of intersectionality in order to describe the ways in which oppressive institutions (racism, sexism, homophobia, transphobia, ableism, xenophobia, classism, etc.) are interconnected and cannot be examined separately from one another. We can illustrate this with reference to Gajjalla's (2014) work. She helps us to better understand the relevance of gender relations when studying access to media, interaction, and participation by pointing out that we still have to consider that the gender divide in media (and participation) maps onto ways that technology use is described. While male internet technology users are often described as the ones with knowledge of code, descriptions of women's engagement with online technologies often focuses on social media, characterized as casual and social. Furthermore, 'the image of the westernized women of leisure is placed hierarchially above the image of the oppressed women of color or the rural women from the Global south' (Gajjala 2014, 288). Thus, these images continue the idea of two different kinds of women:

> One is the individual agent—the self-empowered, mostly western(ized) and urban woman who will form global networks through activities of leisure, pleasure, consumption, caretaking, philanthropy, and women-centered entrepreneurship. The other is the subaltern woman—most often a woman of color, of lower class and caste, and/or a rural third-world woman—who is

empowered by the self-empowered woman and by various NGO-sponsored development programs. (ibid., 289)

Thus, access, interaction, and participation have to be discussed as an outcome of structural as well as cultural dimensions of patriarchal, neoliberal, and post-colonial social order and knowledge production. The underlying interests and conditions of unequal power relations, as we would like to emphasize with Uldam and Kaun (2017, 186), further spur asymmetrical,—and this means, for example, gendered, racialized, and class related—(in)visibilities of monitoring and being watched (see Hedge's chapter in this volume).

Finally, Butler's (2009) concept of social visibilities and recognition is promising in order to analyse the preconditions for access, interaction, and participation. For Butler, interaction demands visibility. This visibility is only enabled by coming into existence as a recognizable subject, which depends on being able to pass norms and schemes of recognition that determine who will be regarded as a subject worthy of recognition. Consequently, visibility cannot be equated with recognition. Even more, to become visible is a highly ambivalent process, as open to recognition as it is to misrecognition and disrespect.

The conditions for passing as a recognizable subject are structured by power and embedded in discourse, practices, and apparatuses. This way, recognition can be described as interaction-theoretical. Power relations interfere with recognition that may become a problem for those who have been expelled from the structures and vocabularies of political representation. According to Carleheden, Heidegren, and Willig (2012, 2), recognition can be theorized in terms of social order. Institutionalized recognition orders, practices and institutions determine who can interact and participate. As a result, the authors ask: 'What does the recognition order of contemporary Western societies look like? To what extent do multicultural societies run the risk of harboring recognition orders that conflict with one another?' (ibid., 2). And we would like to add one more question: How can people not only participate in but also collaborate on creating recognition orders that enable convivial futures in post-migrant societies?

3. FROM CONNECTED MIGRANTS TO CIVIC COLLABORATION? NEW PERSPECTIVES ON POST-MIGRANT REALITIES AND FUTURES

According to Terkessidis (2015), a society of diversity can only work when many voices are being heard and different people work together. For Terkessidis, collaboration thus means a form of teamwork through which involved actors realize that they are being transformed within this process and they are welcoming this change. Similarly, Noveck (2009) emphasizes the idea of teamwork behind collaboration, although she does not consider post-migrant societies in particular. She defines collaboration as a collective solution to social (and political) challenges. Other definitions point out that collaboration, defined/understood as work on shared interests, can be distinguished from coordination, which means teamwork on an operational level, and from cooperation, which means a shared work distribution. While collaboration is often driven by mutual self-interest, cooperation is often driven by a directive and is done out of a certain need to achieve a certain business or, in our case, political goal (The Economist Intelligence Unit 2008). In this context, digital technologies offer the potential to realize democracy as collective problem solving (Gohl 2015, 218).

We want to use collaboration in Terkessidis's sense to critically discuss existing studies and concepts from what Leurs and Smets (2018) call 'digital migration studies.' Already during the 1990s, Arjun Appadurai has described the phenomenon of human mobility and digital mediation in his popular book *Modernity at Large* (1996) and has renewed his analysis with a paper on migrant narratives and imagined future citizenship (2016) during the so-called European refugee crisis. Appadurai's brilliant work raises questions of how refugees can imagine and articulate their future in the new country and how citizenship needs to be challenged and rethought in post-migrant societies. In line with our argument, Appadurai suggests some ways to think about convivial futures by stressing the important role media can play in creating a migrant archive. He writes:

> Both new electronic media as well as traditional print media among migrant communities allow complex new debates to occur between the memory of the old home and the demands of public narrative in the new setting. Migrant newspapers in many communities become explicit sites for debate between microcommunities, between generations and between different forms of nationalism. In this sense, the migrant archive is highly active and interactive, as it is the main site of negotiation between collective memory and desire' (ibid., 7).

When we consider digital migration studies that have emerged before and during the so-called refugee crisis, we have observed that such studies emphasize that connected migrants and refugees are considered an active part of post-migrant societies, equipped with digital media that allow them to cultivate connections and bonds. For example, Dana Diminescu (2008) has shaped the term 'connected migrant' with the intention to 'conceive and prove the continuum, in space and in time, as perceived in the multiple movements that are accumulated and articulated in people's lives' (ibid.,

570). Another term similar to 'connected migrant' is the term 'mobile commons'; it describes 'an essential acquisition resulting from the collective power to reshape the world of people on the move' (Trimikliniotis, Parsanoglou, and Tsianos 2015, 9). According to the authors, mobile commons use the vital organizing force of digitality and new knowledge forms to revolutionize and transform the world. While this perspective emphasizes the agency and competencies that refugees and migrants possess and also bring with them to the new country, we suggest combining this perspective with our discussions and concerns presented above about participation and collaboration. This would allow us to systematically interrogate unequal power relations with regards to gender and other social and cultural categories for processes to achieve and realize agency.

In a special issue, 'Connected Migrants: Encapsulation and Cosmopolitanization' for the journal *Popular Communication*, Ponzanesi and Leurs (2018, 5) follow up on the idea of the connected migrant and address social, cultural, and political implications of everyday practices of mediation among migrants. Articles in this special issue stress that the two constructs in the context of digital migrant connectivity—that of the cosmopolitan and the encapsulated self—are not mutually exclusive but can operate simultaneously (ibid., 5). They use the term 'digital migration' to refer to the 'expanding and intensifying roles digital technology play in migration processes, ranging from top-down governmentality and bottom-up practices of everyday meaning-making' (ibid., 13). Up to this point, a variety of studies have been published (for a very informative overview on this see Leurs and Smets 2018, 3–4) that critically investigate the relationship between migration and digital media technologies. While most of the studies about digital migration and connected migrants emphasize the connectivity and the potential of digital media to put democracy into practice, we conclude from our arguments elaborated in section 2 of this chapter that neither access (meaning presence of digital media), nor interaction (meaning communication between actors), nor participation alone can fulfil this potential, mainly because of unequal conditions and an uneven distribution of resources, especially in post-migrant societies. Having said this, we argue that participation in post-migrant societies should focus on bringing people together in truly collaborative practices. People with different backgrounds need to use participation as a space of encounter, not because of their heterogeneous identities, but on the basis of their interest of shaping desirable convivial futures (see also Grittmann and Thomas 2018).

Thus, we suggest combining the perspective of participation and collaboration with the perspective of digital migration studies and wish to introduce a list of questions as a heuristic tool to analyse and critically interrogate processes of access, interaction, participation, and collaboration in post-migrant societies. This tool emphasizes the relevance of conditions and consequences of how participation plays out in post-migrant societies. Based on Carpentier's AIP model, we suggest using the following questions as a heuristic tool to analyse conditions of participation in post-migrant societies:

Access: Who has access to which resources and conditions essential for participation and collaboration? Who can articulate oneself how, in which channels? Who can represent oneself how, in which channels?

Interaction: Who interacts how with whom? Who is visible, and who is recognized? Who can speak, and who is heard by whom?

Participation: Who participates in which decision-making processes? Who is making which decisions in the end? What resources are needed and what conditions need to be fulfilled to make decisions?

Collaboration: Who collaborates how with whom in and through digital public spheres? Who shapes and realizes which forms of living together?

With this, we aim to provide a map of how mediated participation and collaboration can be successfully analysed, realized, and fostered and how it can contribute to better living together in post-migrant societies. We developed these questions as an interrogation tool for analysing participatory projects in post-migrant societies. They can be used to identify the different points of departure that people face in post-migrant societies due to their ascribed status as refugees or migrants. Furthermore, the questions enable us to analyse what resources and conditions are needed to have access, interaction, participation, and collaboration in post-migrant societies. Ultimately, these are questions that often have been neglected in concepts of participation, as we have argued in Section 2 of this chapter.

4. TOWARDS CONVIVIAL FUTURES?
INTERROGATING FORMS OF PARTICIPATION
AND COLLABORATION IN POST-MIGRANT SOCIETIES

In post-migrant societies, encounters between migrants and non-migrants have become a common experience as well as a challenge in everyday life, often shaped by digital media cultures. Ideas of new or critical 'cosmopolitanism' (Delanty and He 2008; for cosmopolitan media studies see Silverstone 2006; Roberston 2010; Christensen and Jansson 2015), 'convivialism' (Käte Hamburger Kolleg/Centre for Global Cooperation Research 2014, Les Convivialistes 2014), and 'cohabitation' (Butler 2012) demonstrate that plurality is the sine qua non of human existence. Scholars of cosmopolitanism insist on the recognition of otherness, while 'Les Convivialistes' (2014) search 'for an art of living together (con-vivere) that would allow humans to take care of each other and of Nature, without denying the legitimacy of conflict, yet by using it as a dynamizing and creativity-sparking force.' And in Butler's (2012) view, 'cohabitation' entails obligations: 'we must actively preserve and affirm the unchosen character of inclusive and plural cohabitation: we not only live with those we never chose and to whom we may feel no social sense of belonging, but we are also obligated to preserve those lives and the plurality of which they form a part' (ibid., 125). Undoubtedly, these approaches differ considerably. Nevertheless, all of them insist that plurality is a fact in societies. Furthermore, all approaches can be discussed in the context of political ethics, as questioning global/national social orders on ethical, political, economic, and ecological levels. All of them address not only the responsibilities of (supra)national policies, but also civil societies and the need for participation and collaboration.

In this chapter, we have discussed participation and collaboration in post-migrant societies in order to broaden analytical approaches for researching media and participation in post-migrant societies. In line with Carpentier (2015, 24), we argue that democratic participation should be distinguished from access and interaction as this 'allows emphasizing the importance of equal power positions in decision making processes for the definition of participation,' and that research on participation has to consider material and symbolic dimensions equally. Nevertheless, in our view, we need to deepen our understandings of preconditions of participation. Additionally, we need research on collaboration that does not rest on identity and exclusionary solidarities, in order to allow us to find new opportunities to offer and promote them. Thus, we would like to encourage research that aims at capturing these two directions and promoting what we have termed 'convivial futures' in post-migrant societies.

NOTES

1. See Ali Can's video '#MeTwo' on Perspective Daily's Facebook page. Accessed 6 October 2018. https://www.facebook.com/PerspectiveDailyMedia/videos/metwo/1881267988844852.

2. See Mesut Özil's statement 'Meeting president Erdogan' on Twitter. Accessed 6 October 2018. https://twitter.com/mesutozil1088/status/1020984884431638528?lang=de.

Chapter Two

Immigrants, Social Media, and Participation

The Long and Winding Road via Integration

Peter Dahlgren

Upon arrival in the country of destination, migrants are slotted into various (and at times evolving) legal categories (e.g., asylum seeker, refugee, economic migrant), and their handling within the 'immigration bureaucracy' and the struggles towards integration begins—for them and for the host society. From here, it can be another long journey before immigrants become reasonably settled in the new country, and even longer before they can actually begin to 'participate' in some way within their new environment. Meanwhile, the host population also undergoes change, and the interplay between the groups further engenders the post-migrant society.

Over the last few years, the use of mobile phones and social media has profoundly reformatted the various phases of migration and integration. As researchers soon began to demonstrate, this has permitted migrants to, among other things, keep in touch with family and friends, keep up with the changing information about immigrant policies in various countries, have access to many kinds of unofficial, insider knowledge, and maintain social networks in their new country (Diker 2017; Dekker and Engbersen 2012); even insightful journalism has probed this development (*The Economist* 2017). A helpful overview of the literature is found in McGregor and Siegel, 2013.

In this chapter, I schematically examine the arduous passage to participation, via integration, that newly arrived immigrants face, In so doing, I attempt to specify the contingencies that shape the democratic ideal of participation and to highlight the role of social media in the process. My focus will be on recent immigration, mostly by refugees, to Europe, with a few examples from Sweden, the country I know best. The aim is to establish a general framework to understand the dynamics that facilitate as well as hinder the development of a post-migrant society; hopefully, this can help guide further empirical studies.

This framework has four major elements that follow a conceptual sequence. I begin my analysis with what I call the 'existing discursive crosscurrents of the host country,' the first element. Each of the European host countries (even those that have essentially refused to be hosts) experiences, at the time of arrival of any migrant, a pre-existing political climate with regard to immigration. Such a climate consists of a variety of discourses, often conflicting ones. Key concepts such as integration, multiculturalism, interculturalism, and assimilation contribute to the discourses; these four terms are contested, and I will very briefly discuss each. The second element relates to the notion of participation itself. As a key concept/element of the democratic ideal, participation is often treated as obvious and taken for granted, but is in fact multivalent. In the context of this chapter, I highlight three different meanings. The third element, integration, points to the long-term process that precedes and conditions the nature and degree of participation among immigrants. I explore its dynamics and parameters as well as the role of social media, making use of a model of four domains of integration that has gained prominence in the literature (Ager and Strang 2008; Alencar 2017). The fourth element addresses the more specific resources that may promote and/or hinder democratic participation, for both immigrants as well as the host society's citizens. I call this element 'civic cultures' and briefly discuss several of its dimensions. I conclude with some short reflections on the longterm perspective on integration and participation.

ARRIVAL SETTINGS: DISCURSIVE CROSS-CURRENTS

New arrivals to any country obviously do not encounter a tabula rasa in terms of how immigration is perceived. Each country has its own history of managing immigration and has developed a legal framework, embodied in policies, to address immigration. Moreover, previous as well as current discussions and debates on this topic are a part of a country's collective memory, circulating in mass and social media as well as in everyday conversations. Together, such discussions and debates shape an overall discursive-political climate with regard to immigration.

Analytically, various discourses composing such a climate are identifiable. In this chapter, I draw loosely on Laclau and Mouffe's (2001) discourse theory. Briefly, the notion of *discourse* points to structures of relatively fixed meanings that arise as communicative and material practices. Yet discourses are never permanently fixed; they shift and evolve, and the boundaries between different discourses may not always be fully clear. Discourses are embedded in power relations and manifested in speech, images, and sounds that circulate within particular societal contexts. In discourses, meaning derives not just from the content but also from the taken-for-granted framing and filtering of thought and perception that discourses accomplish. Some discourses, in relation to others, have hegemonic positions; that is, they offer preferred or dominant meanings. These can be challenged by counter-hegemonic discourses, or—I would add—modifying discourses that in some way complicate the dominant ones. In both cases, meaning becomes less stable. Discourses also contain definitive signs, key terms that serve as the core concepts or vocabulary of a discourse.

From this perspective, an analysis of discourses around immigration and related themes will usually show that not one unified discourse exists, but often several hegemonic ones, which are challenged by varying counter- or modifying discourses. Identifying and examining foundational (and mostly very positive) discourses about the nation and collective identity (Who are we as a society?) is usually a good place to start (for the Swedish case, see Emilsson 2009). In Sweden, for example, we have basic discourses about the country and its people being fair, honest, generous, and so on, with a strong commitment to democracy, equality, and welfare. In the post-war era, Sweden's discourses about immigration have strengthened its self-perception as open and welcoming, and they have been a source of pride. In addition to this self-perception, a robust moral discourse of civic engagement, a readiness to assist refugees, and, moreover, a business and policy-based positive discourse on Sweden's need of immigrants for the labour market have affected Sweden's discourse on immigration. There has also been a very strong anti-racist discourse in the post-war era—so strong, in fact, that it has stifled much-needed public discussion about immigration policies, problems, and limits.

In recent decades, another modifying discourse has emerged regarding the difficulties of the welfare state. Over the past years, dramatic reports about the public sectors' declining capacities to deliver quality services have filled the media. The reports have particularly focused on healthcare, day care, schools, and homes for the elderly; among the issues have been the debates on whether the neoliberal trend towards privatization in the public sector has been a positive or negative development. Domestic politics has, to a great extent, centred on these problems. While mostly not linked at the start to the so-called refugee crisis in 2015, these difficulties were soon evoked, as logistical and financial problems around the refugee question began to materialize, thereby connecting 'refugees' and 'immigrants' with 'social problems.'

After large numbers of refugees arrived in Sweden in the autumn of 2015, policies as well as public discourses changed quickly (Dahlgren 2016). The populist anti-immigration discourse of the extreme right-wing Sweden Democrat Party gained momentum. There were also many incidents of violence, including the firebombing of several dozen refugee centres, but such practices were only defended on neo-Nazi websites. At the same time, the mainstream moral discourse of responsibility began to shift towards defining this new situation of increasing refugee numbers in terms of administrative challenges and the rise of 'responsible restrictions.'

During 2015, several EU member states explicitly stated that they would refuse to take in refugees. With reference to this lack of solidarity within the EU, Sweden announced in early 2016 that it was now forced to close its doors, leading to much internal protest from many sides. A new discourse was taking form. It emphasized that Sweden, compared to all EU member states, had taken in the largest number of refugees per capita, and this should be seen as a moral triumph, even though the policy of taking in refugees was changing. Yet, some counter-discourses challenged this, claiming that Sweden had now abandoned a core element of its political-moral identity. The Swedish collective identity had clearly taken a serious blow. In the interim, support for the nationalist Sweden Democrats had grown; now, they had become the third largest party in the parliament, a fact that many Swedes find hard to accommodate with their national identity underscoring values such as equality, fairness, and generosity.

I offer this Swedish example to illustrate the contestation and rapid changes that can take place in public discourse. One can find coexisting views that range from emphasis on our humanitarian responsibility towards the Other, to racist scapegoating in the name of 'the nation.' In these discursive cross-currents, a few key terms, whose meanings have often been contested, have been prominent over the years: *assimilation, multiculturalism*, and *integration*. More recently, the concept of interculturalism has gained prominence (Meer, Modood, and Zapata-Barrero 2016). Interculturalism underscores the importance of a two-way accommodation between host country and migrants; the concept is gaining traction, and is increasingly seen in some circles as the key to successful integration (Alencar 2017).

These terms reflect both policies or governmental practices and ideational conceptions that are in social circulation; the two domains of concrete policies and broad ideals may not always be congruent. Assimilation, in the sense that new arrivals essentially abandon their old culture and become indistinguishable from the majoritarian dominant culture, has largely been dropped as a formal policy platform in Sweden (see Wickström 2013 for a history of this policy change in Sweden). Yet it can well linger on as a popular sentiment, resulting in conflict, for example in the clash of codes of interaction in everyday life (e.g., some Muslim men refusing on religious grounds to shake hands with women in professional encounters [Kirkwood, McKinlay, and McVittie 2013 describe a situation in Scotland]).

MULTICULTURALISM AND BEYOND

In the post-war era, multiculturalism gradually emerged in many Swedish policy quarters as the philosophy to follow, and a good deal of academic work has pursued this trajectory as well. Its core principles have a democratic resonance: immigrants should be able to retain basic features of their own cultures, and the host society would become ever more diverse, with people of many different cultural backgrounds living side by side. By the 1970s, this policy was in place in Sweden, with generous conditions for new arrivals (Wickström 2013). The hybridization of identities was also part of this vision. Indeed, in Sweden, for example, many people would come to call themselves Greek-Swedes, Turk-Swedes, and so on. Yet, as recent scholarship argues (Chin 2017; Rattansi 2011), such policy initiatives were often insufficient to truly achieve such genuine diversity in many countries, not least knowing that there was often considerable popular resistance and even a substantial backlash (Vertovec and Wessendorff 2010). In 2010, the political leaders of Britain, France, and Germany pronounced multiculturalism a failure, and other European leaders followed suit—even if for some academics and activists, it still remains an inspiration, despite its difficulties (Modood 2013).

One major practical dilemma about multiculturalism is that it can indirectly promote and legitimize self-segregation, thereby facilitating enclaves (Weinstock 2007) where practices emerge that may collide with national law and cultural patterns. This has been observed not least with regard to the freedom of some immigrant women who may be caught between traditional customs and the secular laws and values of their new society—an issue that has been observed and much debated in the Swedish press and social media. Moreover, in immigrant-dense neighbourhoods, one often finds that the social problems of poor schools, unemployment, crime, drugs, and others reinforce one another. At the same time, overt racism can be quite visible among the host population, driven by extreme right-wing groups, as is discrimination in the areas of employment and housing, for example. Discrimination is often discreet, almost covert, yet remains a serious mechanism of exclusion.

Thus, if we today hear little about multiculturalism or cultural diversity in policy circles or in dominant popular discourses, and if the idea of interculturalism is still in somewhat of an embryonic state, it is because the notion of 'integration' has become the dominant theme. A recent and massive twenty-seven-country study jointly carried out by the OECD and the EU (OECD/ European Union 2015) shows considerable variation in degree of success of immigrant integration. One optimistic finding is that there appears to be no correlation between the proportion of immigrants in the total population and the success of integration processes; if anything, countries with a higher proportion of immigrants demonstrate better integration outcomes. With regard to discrimination, which is seen as an obstacle to 'social cohesion,' the study found that there was a large range among these countries. For example, among immigrants between fifteen and sixty-four years of age coming from 'low income countries,' those who consider themselves members of groups that experience discrimination ranged from 35 percent in Greece, to 14 percent in Norway, at the lower end.

Yet this newer turn towards a seemingly more practical vision of integration has also raised questions. In the wake of right-wing populism, 'culture' has increasingly become framed in terms of 'the nation,' with immigrants being faced with monolithic conceptions of national culture and its canons. In some countries, these are even incorporated into citizenship tests, as in Denmark and the Netherlands (for the Dutch case, see de Leeuw and van Wichelen 2012). This constricts room for diversity. More importantly, it raises the question of whether the vision of interculturalism can take hold of mainstream political discourses, or if governments are surreptitiously resurrecting policies of assimilation.

Thus, the circumstances of host countries for receiving immigrants can vary greatly in terms of policies and shifting hegemonic and counter-discourses among political elites, the media, and the population. Moreover, the stability of the key terms within these discourses cannot be taken for granted. Any rendering of the situation in any given country requires an up-to-date empirical analysis.

PARTICIPATION AS A DEMOCRATIC CHALLENGE

The concept of participation derives from several different fields in the social sciences, and thus remains somewhat of a fluid notion, not least within media and communication studies.

I propose that we can productively distinguish between three modes of participation, which correspond to three different social fields: socio-cultural, civic, and political participation (see Dahlgren 2009 for a fuller treatment; see also Carpentier 2011). The boundaries separating these modes of participation are not rigid because the social fields themselves easily blur into each other and are ultimately mutually dependent. However, even if empirical realities can be messy, retaining these distinctions is analytically useful.

Socio-cultural participation is the broadest category; it focuses on 'taking part' in many kinds of human interplay, face-to-face as well as mediated. It encompasses consumption; in its broadest understanding, the whole field of consumption is on offer here—the consumption of things, products, events, and spectator activities, for example sports and concerts. Socio-cultural participation can also involve sharing lived routines and even rituals, which can provide a sense of fellowship and belonging. In the realm of popular culture, Hermes (2005) argues forcefully that mediated entertainment can often be experienced as shared and 'participatory,' fostering what she calls 'cultural citizenship.' Thus, in post-migrant society, watching the same television programmes and films, engaging in the same social media sites, and so on, are participatory in the socio-cultural sense. Playing sports together can certainly be included here. Such participatory activities promote a sense of belonging, facilitating socio-cultural integration.

In *civic participation*, the term 'civic' resonates with the notions of 'citizen' as well as with 'public,' in the sense of being visible and in some way accessible to many people (i.e., outside the private, intimate domain). 'Civic' thus implies engagement in public life—a cornerstone of democracy. There is also the obvious etymological link between 'civic' and the notion of 'civil society.' The concept of civil society is a somewhat slippery one (for a contemporary overview see Edwards 2014; for a modern Habermasian rendering, see Cohen and Arato 1992). At the general level, civil society is seen by many writers as the societal terrain between the state and the economy, the realm of free association, where citizens can interact to pursue their shared interests.

Even if it may at times be difficult to classify which of the many forms of collective activity and organization should be considered part of civil society, there is a dominant trajectory of thought here that suggests that healthy democracy needs a robust, public domain of associational interaction. This requires social cohesion, as the OECD/EU (2015) report underscores. Consequently, marginalized populations not only signal unsuccessful interactions but also democratic failures of the post-migrant society. It is not difficult to see how civic participation is to a great extent predicated on socio-cultural participation—and how involvement in both fields enhances 'social capital' among participants (e.g., expanding their social networks and communicative competencies).

Political participation, in turn, is dependent on a foundation of both socio-cultural and civic participation. A starting point is found in the notion of 'the political' itself. This refers to the ever-present potential for collective antagonisms and conflicts of interest inherent in all social relations and settings (Mouffe 2013). This is a broader notion than that of politics, which most often refers to more formalized institutional contexts. Thus, we can say that political participation means involvement with power relations, however remote (or mediated) in both parliamentarian and extra-parliamentarian contexts. 'Power relations,' in turn, refers not only to such obvious manifestations as the state, with its legal system, military, and police, or the corporate sector, with its political economic power, but also to contestable hierarchies based on gender, ethnicities, and other markers of (social/individual/collective) identity.

The political can thus arise discursively and appear in any domain of social and cultural activity, even within consumption and entertainment (and we can find innumerable examples of that on social media). Political participation of any kind can in itself be seen as an expression of some degree of (enabled) power, however modest. This is important from the standpoint of a post-migrant society: while some groups may have more limited formal political means than citizens of the dominant society, they may still be able to find alternative ways to participate politically.

This was illustrated in Sweden in the summer of 2017. On August 6, a sit-down strike began next to Riksdagshuset—the parliament house—in Stockholm. Coordinated by a loose social movement among youth, the main participants were young, newly arrived Afghans, many of whom were facing deportation. The Swedish government had hardened its criteria for admittance of refugees and had recently defined Afghanistan as sufficiently 'safe' for refugees to be returned there. However, many of the young Afghans had spent years in Iraq or Pakistan and had little or no connection with Afghanistan. Some of the strike's participants had learned sufficient Swedish to articulate their demands to reporters. The movement spread to other parts of the country, coordinated with the help of Facebook and Twitter. Despite the hardships, including attacks by neo-Nazis, the protest continued for fifty-five days, into October 2017, and succeeded in triggering extensive public debate in the Swedish mainstream media over the handling of these refugees.

SOCIAL MEDIA AND INTEGRATION

The three modes of participation have a variety of contingencies that make possible, as well as delimit, their character and extent. From an analytic angle, one can say that much pivots on the processes of integration. Integration has been theorized extensively over the years (see chapter 2 of Schunck 2014 for an overview). Recently, a new framework has emerged (Ager and Strang 2008; Strang and Ager 2010) that emphasizes four core domains of integration and offers a useful point of entry for analysis. Also, this framework has been extended to incorporate a perspective on social media (Alencar 2017). This framework's four core domains are:

- markers and means: this has to do with basic aspects of immigrants' social reality, such as employment, housing, education, and health;

- social connection: this is conceptualized into three areas: social bridges, social bonds, and social links;
- facilitators: here, the emphasis is on language and cultural knowledge, safety and stability;
- foundation: this category essentially addresses rights and citizenship.

The *markers and means* involve vast and complex social challenges that are shaped largely by government services and bureaucratic administration, although the private sector actors can be involved at certain points. With *social connections*, the second domain, we enter the domain that is central to shaping migrant identities in post-migrant societies (Ager and Strang 2008). Drawing on several social theorists, the authors distinguish between three forms of social connections. First, *social bridges* have to do with interactions with other communities, often from the host culture—and this points us towards the theme of interculturalism. Establishing such bridges becomes imperative for participating in the new society. Secondly, *social bonds* refer to relations with family and co-ethnic, co-national, co-religious, or intra-group members. These are crucial since this proximity allows immigrants to share cultural practices, maintain familiar patterns of relationships, and use their native language. Such connections are very important in helping them feel 'settled.' Thirdly, *social links* refer to the contacts that immigrants have with the state and the administrative bureaucracies; these are indispensable for the pragmatics of everyday life. The third domain, that of *facilitators*—linguistic and culture competence in the new society—clearly plays a mutually reciprocal role with social connections, each reinforcing the other in the process of integration. Both, in turn, conceptually overlap to a great extent with the discussion above with regard to socio-cultural participation. Ultimately, all these concepts have to do with evolution of subjectivity, identity, and competencies that promote integration.

Lastly, the *foundation* domain ushers us into the realm of citizenship, rights, and obligations. As a large body of literature has underscored, 'citizenship' is a concept whose definition is often contested, even by political philosophers, and whose practices vary considerably (see Dahlgren 2009 for an overview). Cultural understandings of 'nation' and 'nationhood' embody different sets of values and conceptions of belonging. Thus, some traditions of citizenship, understood as national political cultures, are more inclusionary (see Strang and Agar 2010; they use France as an example), others more exclusionary, that is, 'membership' in the new society presents more obstacles (e.g., in Germany). Similarly, some notions of citizenship and its relation to integration emphasize responsibilities on the part of the immigrants, others less so. In the Swedish case, for example, critics have noted the debilitating consequences of treating immigrants as 'semi-adults' and not demanding much in terms of responsibility.

When examining social media use in connection with these four domains of integration, Alencar (2017) found that the immigrants she interviewed used Facebook, YouTube, LinkedIn, Twitter, Instagram, WhatsApp, Viber, and Google; among Syrian refugees, Line, a variant of Skype, was also important. She highlights that such networking sites play an important role, but that their significance varies between the domains. Social connections, the second domain, are immensely facilitated. Social bonding with fellow immigrants, social bridging with people from the host society, and social links with governmental agencies and services are all enhanced. Also, acquiring language and cultural competencies, which are at the core of the third domain, are greatly facilitated by social media. Particularly in this domain, social media helps immigrants' social and cultural capital to grow.

However, with regard to accessing practical information for such markers and means as employment, housing, and health, the first domain, Alencar (2017) notes (and as Dekker and Engbersen (2014) also observe) that offline, face-to-face contact with civil society actors and local organizations is seen as more helpful than social media. In terms of the fourth domain, that of citizenship, social media use was not very significant; it consisted mainly of bureaucratic contact with government agencies. We can note that for recent immigrants, their circumstances, for the most part, unsurprisingly render participation in the political sense difficult, despite access to social media.

These authors also share the observation that immigrants experience integration largely in the context of their local environment, their neighbourhood, rather than at the abstract level of the nation. Social media use facilitates social encounters in these environments, with organizations, groups, and individuals. Importantly, Alencar (2017) underscores that it is the interplay of three sets of actors—government, the host society, and the immigrants themselves—that determine the ways in which immigrants make use of social media. This points us again in the direction of the importance of the two-way model of integration, of interculturalism, in the post-migrant society.

It has become an important truism that media use is always shaped by social, economic, and cultural factors, and at least indirectly by power relations. Alencar (2017) thus finds that immigrants' use of social media platforms is also influenced to a great extent by their own attitudes towards integration in the host society, which can vary according to group and individual background. These attitudes, in turn, derive partly from how governments and host societies handle the integration process, the kinds of possibilities offered, and constraints imposed. Notably, what governments and host societies make available on social media is significant.

In sum, we can say that social media play an important role in the integration process; yet, as a large body of research over the years has concluded, media use and its consequences are shaped by social contingencies. There is no one-size-fits-all, and no quick fix for societal challenges. Users can produce, upload, remix, link, and share materials in complex and collaborative ways on social media. Therefore, social media certainly offer many spectacular opportunities and can be used in all three modes of participation; these electronic tools, both as soft- and hardware, have become more effective, less expensive, easier to use. Social media have become a central terrain of our social lives and impact the strategies and tactics of everyday reality (Baym 2015). They can link people and organizations horizontally for organizing civil society activities, sharing information and affect, providing mutual support, and organizing, mobilizing, or solidifying collective identities. Notably, they can give voice to people and issues, which is highly relevant in terms of integration. This makes them well suited as civic media; under suitable circumstances, they can even foster democratic social relations and facilitate participation. Additionally, social media can help to promote a subjective sense of social agency and empowerment (Dahlgren 2013).

At the same time, research has shown that the online environment generally, and social media in particular, are not merely neutral, free-floating communicative spaces. These media are embedded in broader society, with its prevailing patterns of power, hierarchy, and discursive ideological currents. In the mediated digital world, ownership of major corporate entities is globally more concentrated than it ever was in the era of mass media communication (Fuchs 2014). A few large corporate actors such as Google, Microsoft, Facebook, and YouTube dominate the internet environment. This political economy situates the user in a very subordinate position. The role of Google, for example, in shaping how the web functions can hardly be exaggerated. This company has become the largest holder of information in world history, structuring not only how we search for information, but also what information is available, and how we organize, store, and use it.

All of us are strewing personal electronic traces online daily; these are gathered up, stored, sold, and used for commercial purposes by a variety of actors (van Dijck 2013). The lack of privacy is furthered by governments who can also gather our private information. There is particular danger for immigrants with a political past, in that they might be tracked down by agents of the regimes they have fled. Further, in this era of 'post-truth,' the online environment is filled with misinformation, deception, propaganda, fake news, financial traps, and so on—one has to be critically alert (Phillips and Milner 2017). Also, social media can at times be a rather nasty place, with many small counter-public spheres spewing out hate, harassment, racism, and so forth. These and other issues certainly do not suggest that social media should be avoided in the context of integration, but they do warn us that we all should proceed with caution.

CIVIC CULTURES, INTEGRATION, PARTICIPATION

The more the processes of integration continue, the more the potential for participation grows. This is particularly obvious with regard to the domains of social connection/facilitators and socio-cultural participation. As discussed above, however, the step towards civic participation is often greater, and even more so towards political participation. How can we conceptualize the contingencies that impact such participation? A starting point is the notion of civic cultures (the following discussion is adapted from Dahlgren 2009), which addresses the question of citizens' participation in the life of democracy generally, and can be adapted for the situation of post-migrant societies specifically.

The question of citizens' participation—and non-participation—in democracy has been on the research agenda for decades. In the approach taken here, I start with the premise that participation consists of visible, empirical behaviour, that is, action, usually in the form of some kind of communication. Behind this observable action lies engagement, a subjective disposition with an emotional investment in some issue or cause. Thus, engagement is the subjective precondition for participation. The basic argument is that for people to act as citizens, to participate in civic and political agency, they have to be able to see themselves as such agents. They need to develop something we can call 'civic identities,' a perception of agency sufficiently empowered to facilitate meaningful engagement. There is an important constructionist perspective here that tries to take into account *how* people actually self-create as citizens.

In emphasizing identity as a key element in civic agency, we need to ask which cultural factors can impinge on this identity and can promote (or hinder) such perceptions of their civic selves. Civic identities do not hover in a vacuum; they develop and evolve in an on-going interplay with the cultural environments in which they are operative. This is what I term 'civic cultures.' *Civic cultures* refers to cultural patterns that are available as accessible resources—albeit very vulnerable ones—that can support democratic civic and political agency. To the extent that they are compelling, civic cultures operate at the level of citizens' taken-for-granted perceptions in everyday reality. From a Bourdieu perspective, one might speak of 'civic habitus.'

And it is more accurate to speak of civic cultures—in the plural—since in the late-modern world, there are many ways in which civic agency can be accomplished and enacted, in other words, many ways of 'doing' democracy.

Civic cultures comprise several dimensions. Among the key dimensions are *knowledge, values, trust,* and *practices.* That citizens need *knowledge* in order to participate politically is obvious and basic. People must have access to reliable reports, analyses, discussions, and debates about current affairs and society in general. This can be accomplished in many ways; however, in the modern world, the media play a key, if problematic, role in this regard. Knowledge is always evolving in its forms; today digital forms have become dominant and offer new ways of knowing, as well as new obstacles to knowing, as noted above. Further, democracy will not function if such *values* as tolerance and willingness to follow democratic principles and procedures are not grounded in everyday life. Yet it must be seen as a sign of democratic health that debates abound about which are the 'best' or 'real' democratic values, especially with regard to immigration. Additionally, a minimal degree of *trust* in the institutions, procedures, and representatives of democracy is essential, as is a degree of trust among or between groups of citizens, even between political opponents. The lack of trust towards groups seen as 'strangers,' as 'others,' obviously undercuts civic cultures, and ultimately democracy.

A viable democracy must be embodied in citizens' concrete, recurring *practices*—individual, group, and collective—relevant for diverse situations. Such practices must have an element of the taken-for-granted about them; they must be seen as accessible. Participating in elections is usually defined as the paramount concrete democratic practice; yet civic cultures require many other practices as well in order to deal with varied forms of political conflict. New practices and traditions can and must evolve in new situations to ensure that democracy does not stagnate. Practices require specific skills, especially communicative competencies. Thus, reading, writing, speaking, working a computer, and navigating the internet are all important competencies for democratic practices, especially in post-migrant societies. Skills can develop through practices and thereby foster a sense of empowerment.

In terms of viability, civic cultures are both strong and vulnerable. They are shaped by an array of factors; family and schools certainly lay a sort of foundation. From there, social relations of power, economics, the legal system, and organizational possibilities can have their impact. Power centres can constrict the flow of information/knowledge, undermine trust, and hinder practices; the resources that citizens can draw upon tend to be more abundant among the more privileged. The media, both the traditional mass media and social media, in particular, directly and routinely impact the character of civic cultures via their form, content, specific logics, and modes of use, furthering and/or impeding a sense of empowerment. It is a question of navigating existing civic cultures as optimally as possible, while at the same time developing new ones, suitable for specific communities and interests.

THE LONG-TERM PERSPECTIVE

Ultimately, the issues around integration and participation have to do with how we conceive the nation and citizenship. In the present climate in much of Europe, with the voices of right-wing populism on the ascent, discursive cross-currents in many host countries are not encouraging for immigration. All three modes of participation are curtailed to various degrees, either deliberately or as the inadvertent consequence of short-sighted policies. Social media are an important resource in the process of integration, despite the issues they raise; yet they cannot offer a techno-solution to deep-rooted problems and policy shortcomings when it comes to integration. At the same time, it must be recognized that even with genuine governmental good will and favourable policies, integration presents a challenge in areas such as housing, employment, and social services, especially at the level of everyday life in institutions where members of host societies and immigrants meet.

Lazaridis (2015) underscores the complexities and contradictions at work in the dynamics of inclusion and exclusion, and in the negotiation of the boundaries between 'us' and 'them.' She concludes that such problems in post-migrant societies render new arrivals vulnerable to many risks. While acknowledging the diversity of policies within the EU, she sees what she calls the 'transcultural subject' (i.e., the immigrant who is often transformed from a legal subject into a 'legal abject') marginalized from the host society. Similarly, Chin (2017) argues that in renouncing the core principles of diversity, European countries pay a high social cost; the continent must find new initiatives to deal fruitfully with cultural difference in post-migrant society.

In highlighting the differences in policies between the UK and Scottish governments, Mulvey (2013) critically accentuates the former's unwillingness to take into account the evidence that considerable research has provided. UK policy statements ignore much relevant research, while the Scottish government, on the other hand, makes use of relevant studies, especially Ager and Strang's (2008) framework with its domains of integration, to develop strategic policies. It addresses integration in a more innovative manner, treating it as a genuinely multifaceted phenomenon. The Scottish government has mobilized broad engagement with public and voluntary sectors, building on open meetings, which seems to signal a useful approach on how to perceive, contextualize, consult, and address integration in a holistic manner.

Interestingly, Mulvey (2013) also finds that refuges are quite aware of the differences in policy between the two governments, and they also understand how the mainstream media construct them as a 'social problem,' something to be 'controlled.' This insight seems to result in a stronger focus on intra-community social bonds than on social bridging with the host society, thereby further hindering integration.

The approach in Scotland is encouraging, and positive experiences with various models and measures around integration can undoubtedly be gleaned from other countries. For example, Gillespie and her colleagues (2016) ana-lysed media and informational resources that refugees from Syria and Iraq used on their journeys to the UK. They targeted especially the perceived gaps and misinformation and drew several conclusions. These were presented to the EU Commission, European member states, and their state-funded interna-tional news organizations, and focused on what resources could be offered to assist migrants in making decisions, but also to offer protection as stipulated by the UN Refugee Convention of 1951.

While the perspective here was on the pre-settlement phase of migration, some of the proposals are still relevant for integration. First, the authors note that the lack of initiative from the government seems at least in part driven by the fear of attracting more immigrants. Further, the authors urge that states and news organizations cooperate with NGOs, technology corporations, and other stakeholders to develop sustainable partnerships that can engender coherent, coordinated news and information strategies for and with refugees at different times, in their country of origin, during their journeys, and upon their arrival in Europe. They also suggest that such resources be easily acces-sible in terms of technological use, cost, language, and literacy. Moreover, the authors advocate planning such strategies and providing necessary resources so that such initiatives are sustainable in the long term.

All of these proposals are promising, and surely more can be devised. The problem is not a lack of imagination but rather of political will. Immigration and integration are among the most politically divisive, indeed infected issues in Europe today. As Chin (2017) contends, merely declaring multiculturalism dead is not helpful; large immigrant populations will still be around, and post-migrant societies must find satisfactory ways to live together. This involves a larger project of making democracy more responsive and inclusive. As Chin clearly states, 'Whether or not we choose to call these blueprints multicultur-alism is ultimately far less important than that we engage in the democratic struggle to produce new ways of thinking about European diversity, instead of settling for denial, demonization or disavowal' (Chin 2017, 305). A long and winding road of piecemeal struggles and (hopefully) gains lies ahead before we can speak of immigrant participation as a robust reality.

Chapter Three

Dangerous Precarity

Sexual Politics, Migrant Bodies, and the Limits of Participation

Radha S. Hegde

> The immigrant presence is always marked by its incompleteness: it is an at-fault presence that is in itself guilty. It is a *displaced* presence in every sense of the term (Sayad 2004, 283).

Nationalist ideologies have historically fired up claims about the proclivity of certain groups to dangerous and deviant behaviour. While the nature of these claims and the groups targeted have shifted over time, their role in securing the vision of a homogenous national community has endured. Across spatial and temporal contexts, the sexualized and racialized body of the migrant is often evoked in order to mark the outsider as the one who disrupts the national equilibrium by unsettling the ideological balance of hegemonic structures. Nation-states, as well as hard-line nationalist groups, strategically deploy arguments about race and sexuality to naturalize the connection between immigrant pathologies and criminality. Stories about the sexual crimes committed by migrants circulate in public discourse, contributing to the production of moral panics about their seemingly dangerous presence.

This sustained focus on the undesirable alien, who stands in sharp contradistinction from the rightful native, plays a significant role in maintaining a coherent normative script of national identity and citizenship. The terms and conditions of who rightfully belongs and who can claim legitimacy to be seen, to be heard, and to participate in political discourse have become a focal point of national contestation, especially with the widespread resurgence of populist anti-immigrant resistance. With immigration being easily the most divisive subject on national agendas in the West at the present moment, the manner in which this subject comes into public view impacts how migrants can position themselves in order to participate in the societies to which they

have relocated. The forms of visibility or hyper-visibility thrust on this subject define the conditions under which the civic participation of immigrants
is enabled, disrupted, or curbed. While geopolitical instabilities and economic
imperatives continue to be the engines that drive and necessitate global mobility and migration, the on-going perception of migrants and migration in
crisis mode 'deepens the gap between the citizen, who has the birthright to
determine the composition of the national family, and the alien, who threatens
the polity' (Behdad 2005, 166).

The subject of migrant sexuality is one that further stirs nativist rage
and forges fiercely patriarchal nationalistic solidarities. It also makes for
sensational media coverage and serves as a contested site on which debates
about immigration are played out. For instance, media coverage of specific
crimes committed by migrants incriminates communities at large and adds
fuel to the already existing anti-immigrant panic. Not only do sexual crimes
attributed to migrant men and perpetrated against white women gain intense
media scrutiny, but so too do highly charged and contested cultural practices
such as honour killings within diasporic communities. From the regularity of
coverage and high visibility around these stories, it is clear, as Ticktin (2008)
writes, that sexuality is most often recognized only through 'the framework
of racial, cultural and religious difference; in other words, sexual violence is
noted primarily when it is attached to other types of difference' (865). The
body of the migrant as sexually dangerous fortifies the argument about the
violence that inheres to the migrant body and its enduring quality of unassimilable Otherness. The point here is not to check the veracity of the claims
about the perpetrators of sexual crime, but rather to show how sexual politics
is inserted into the material practices, meanings, and politics of bordering in
order to disqualify the migrant from the national polity.

The right to participate in the civic structures of the nation is premised
upon membership within the imagined community and the expectation of
adherence to a set of values associated with the nation. Participation is a
nebulous term, one that in its various manifestations is central to any democratic society, whether defined in terms of access to digital infrastructures
or membership in the polity or recognition in the public sphere. Developments in the area of digital media and new technologies have redirected the
attention of media scholars on the concept of participation, often linking it
to questions of access, visibility, and connectivity. With the renewed importance and attention received, however, there is also a noticeable tendency to
decontextualize and depoliticize the term. As Carpentier (2009) notes, the
theoretical tendency to isolate the concept disconnects it from a necessary
articulation with democracy and ignores the power dynamics that frame the
uneven terrain of participatory practice.[1] Imbued with normative stipulations

about citizenship and voice, *participation*, while variously defined, remains a politically charged and contested term that is tightly secured by logics of sovereign power and nationalist ideologies.

Relevant to the subject of migration is the fact that participation is highly dependent on the manner in which populations are culturally sorted and legitimized. In the context of migration in particular, any discussion of the right and the ability to participate must also attend to parallel processes of disqualification and thus to the discrediting of the imagined prerequisites deemed necessary to claim voice, visibility, or eligibility. Sexuality is one of the key sites where an agenda of discreditation enforced on the migrant body is mobilized to secure public consensus about hegemonic notions of citizenship. Bodies become culturally intelligible only within frameworks that classify and contain the normative and legitimate sexual citizen.[2] The complex pathways of the global precariat have fuelled the xenophobic imaginary and renewed its preoccupation with the intersection of race and sexuality. As Sabsay (2012) notes, we need to pay attention to how bodies become the locus of political practices of citizenship beyond liberal and Orientalist presumptions. In addition, media technologies have intensified modes of communication and accelerated the circulation of populist ideologies that promote racialized visions of bodies and geographies through the logic of deviant sexualities (Puar 2007; Hegde, 2011). The mediated circulation of nativist ideologies reproduces visions of an injured nation by criminalizing migrants and classifying them as pathologically inclined to sexual deviance and violence. This marking of the migrant body, mobilized and aggressively circulated in anti-immigration discourse, works to progressively limit, exclude, and ultimately erase the presence of migrants and their potential to participate in any manner. For critical media scholars, the challenge is to grapple with the complex ways in which communication technologies and the infrastructures of information reinforce racial and sexual construction of the legitimate national subject.

Informed by feminist and postcolonial theoretical perspectives, this chapter advances a discussion of how the image of the migrant body as a site of unrestrained and dangerous sexuality is reproduced in order to fortify exclusionary boundaries and undermine the eligibility of migrants deemed to be worthy of participating in the national community. With the global growth of nationalist movements and the rise of anti-immigrant politics, we need to engage with the manner in which media technologies actively reproduce exclusionary paradigms of citizenship. The term *post-migrant* foregrounded in this collection signals the need to pay attention to the presence of migrants and the limits of what constitutes democratic participation. Responding to the challenge, this chapter, organized in four sections, elaborates on (1) bordering practices as racial regimes of exclusion that instrumentalize migrant sexuality; (2) national discourses of protection and the reproduction of heteronormative modalities of belonging; (3) mediated visibility of the migrant body and the crisis of informationalization; and (4) implications to rethink mediated politics, the representation of migrant sexualities, and the limits of participation in the context of global migration.

BODIES AND BORDERING REGIMES

Borders have historically represented sites of regulation where nations display their symbolic and material power. While geopolitical and economic instabilities have led to complex patterns and pathways of global migration, nations have also redoubled efforts to police and secure their bordering practices. The politics of the border extend beyond cartographic lines that demarcate the space of nations. Borders are better described as complicated sets of processes involving dense assemblages of assumptions, institutions, actors, and technologies. There have been compelling scholarly arguments to think about borders as social institutions or finely tuned instruments that manage, calibrate, and govern (Mezzadra and Neilson 2013, 3) or to shift the focus of study from borders as territorial markers to bordering practices in the everyday that factor in the role of ordinary people in the making, shifting, and erasing of borders (Cooper, Perkins, and Rumford 2014). This expansive approach to viewing the border is critical in the contemporary context when barriers to the movement of refugees and migrants are becoming ever more impenetrable precisely because practices of bordering are becoming diffuse and ubiquitous as they are reimagined and assembled as techno-affective practices (Chouliaraki and Musarò 2017).

At the same time, the perception of migration as threat and risk to the nation is becoming the singular logic, shaping modalities of immigration control at the edge of territorial borders. Technologies of surveillance and modes of securitization identify, profile, and mark individuals and communities as bearers of risk who have the potential to contaminate and destroy. Consider, for example, the lines and processes at border control and the complex bureaucracies of immigration applications. This, no doubt, leads to sharply differentiated classed and raced experiences at the border, where the nation clearly codes the recognizability of the native and the insider. These practices at the border force immigrants and refugees into a vulnerable role, awaiting recognition through the ultimate gift of national access and documentation. Balibar (2002) attributes the politics of these experiences to the polysemic nature of borders in that they are designed to differentiate and exclude identities while, at the same time, reduce from them all complexity. In this calculated production of minority identities, migrants are turned into one-dimensional figures, inherently regressive, barbaric, and dangerous. The restrictions and the biopolitics of the border ultimately consolidate the racialized dominant mythology of the nation, its rightful insiders, and its expendable outsiders.

At the edge and within state territories, bordering regimes and mythologies of nationalism mutually sustain each other by connecting scripts of citizenship, race, gender, and morality. Borders, as Khosravi (2010) writes, are not only racialized; they are also pre-eminently gendered and sexualized. Border crossers have been subject to sexual violence in various parts of the world in flagrant demonstration of masculinist exceptionalism (see Luibhéid 2002). These experiences of terror and trauma have become banal realities within the colossal spectrum of migration regimes, where individuals are rendered vulnerable as they seek entry into national spaces. However, this part of the narrative does not gain as much publicity as the imagined danger that lurks in the fleeing body of the migrant. As Haddad (2007) writes, things that cross the border are frequently imagined to have the capacity to 'pollute' the inside, undermine the border's authority, and weaken national identity. In this discursive logic, the racialized migrant subject is now the dangerous outsider who does not subscribe to nationally upheld values, is further perceived to be incapable of assuming those values, but rather has the potential to destroy or contaminate the nation.

Bodies perceived to be high risk and dangerous to the nation are made visible as objects of scrutiny that need to be contained and excluded. Part of the border security operation's strategy is to maintain, produce, and renew a state of ongoing anxiety and a pervasive culture of fear. The trope of over-sexualized black and brown men from whom white women must be saved has served as the grounds to legitimize imperial projects of expansion, justify racial segregation and colonial projects, and, in the past as well as in the present, the invasion of nations (see Hegde 2011). The racial profiling of perpetrators of sexual crime has existed across nations and time periods, and the fear gets seemingly more intense with each new group. Stereotypical media representations of the sexual aggression of particular immigrant groups and exaggerated crime statistics have also contributed over the years to reinforcing the image of the uncontrolled sexual body of migrant men, whether they are South Asians, North Africans, Middle Eastern, or Latinos.

In the United States, Donald Trump evokes the subject of sexual crime, extremism, and migrant men repeatedly in different contexts. This was most flagrantly expressed in his infamous ban on Muslims entering the United States, but has been common to his rhetoric on the campaign trail and in the Oval Office. For instance, in a political rally in 2016 in Minnesota, where there is a visible Somali immigrant community, Trump commiserated with the locals that they had 'suffered enough' due to taking in Somali refugees (Jacobs and Yuhas 2016). Earlier in 2015, Donald Trump launched his presidential campaign with the promise to construct a wall between the US and Mexico because, he asserted, Mexico is 'not sending its best' (*Washington Post* 2015). He made the claim that Mexico is sending drug dealers, criminals, and rapists and that the wall will keep these immigrants from crossing.

Although his sweeping claims have been challenged and refuted by scholarly and policy sources, his tactic of racializing fear and demonizing immigrants is less about facts than a means of redeploying a familiar script. The migrant body as lurking, dangerous, and capable of forcefully penetrating the body of the nation is established as received knowledge by mobilizing the isomorphism between race, sexuality, modernity, morality, and citizenship. As Soguk (2007, 284) argues 'culture, race, class, gender are all appropriated as camouflage in the reproduction of borders, creatively and resourcefully in unexpected places and surprising forms. Cultural fences, class walls, and gender ditches emerge as new and powerful borders even as they never announce themselves as borders.' Put differently, the body of the migrant is rendered visible and eligible only as a stereotype contained within an indeterminate zone of the border. The migrant's status is already conferred as always already within the border and outside of all eligible modes of public recognition or participation.

RACIALIZATION, PROTECTION AND SEXUALITY

Across global border locations, the flow of migrants is increasingly regulated from the standpoint of security where the meanings of what constitutes internal and external threats to the nation are entangled. This convergence of national and global levels is significant since it directly impacts who is defined and recognized as an immigrant. This, in turn, spreads fear and anxiety about Otherness among a wider assemblage of actors and institutions (Bigo 2002). Such securitization procedures are focused on determining and classifying bodies that are deemed to possess the potential to endanger the community at large or siphon off jobs and other resources from the nation. Mobilizing these cultural anxieties about displacement and change, a well-worn political strategy, continues to have alarming results worldwide in terms of aggressively igniting social uncertainty. Nativist movements, for example, stir up fear scenarios about global migration by evoking a lost homogeneity and igniting speculations about the dangers of migrants infecting the nation and its polity. The rise of global populist nativism rests on the antagonistic animation of this uncertainty and creates profound doubts, as Appadurai (2006, 5) writes, about 'who exactly are among the "we" and who are among the "they"' (and how many of them are there now among us?).

The figure of the violent migrant has been revived in public discourse in order to maintain a populist focus on the deviancy of bodies that desire entry into the exclusivity of the national domain. Regimes of border control define the conditions and terms under which citizens are constituted within very rigid assumptions about race, gender, and sexuality. In the name of securitization, however, raced bodies and social identities are selectively evicted from the possibility of citizenship and inclusion. This highly stratified bordering creates what Balibar (2002, 82) terms 'a world apartheid, or a dual regime for the circulation of individuals.' This colour bar, Balibar (2002) argues, no longer now merely separates "centre" from "periphery," or North from South, but runs through all societies, reinforcing the racialization of national insecurity.

While border regimes employ elaborate procedures to surveil the inclusion of migrants and other noncitizens, they also, as De Genova (2013) argues, almost universally impose a susceptibility for deportation as a defining horizon for migrant status. This serves to make the spectacle of border enforcement 'a persistent and pernicious reminder of the extraordinary vulnerabilities that suffuse the migrant predicament' (1188), long after terrestrial borders have been crossed. As we have witnessed recently with the increase in refugees and asylum seekers, the media and the state continue to frame the subject of migration as a crisis and an economic and security threat that needs to be contained, halted, and evicted. It is also an intensely heated subject that is used to gain political clout and following in both the United States and Europe. In this production of state vigilance at the border, the politics of citizenship is embedded within a disciplinary calculus of race and gender. Sexuality is the site where citizenship, hegemonic visions of racial homogeneity, and morality are firmly interconnected and where the criminalization of raced bodies is justified. A plot line is created, and the victims and criminals are arranged while allegorically pitting good against evil, purity against danger, in predictable sequences of purported common sense.

These narratives and discursive structures are particularly well evidenced in Donald Trump's electoral rhetoric. In a 2016 campaign speech on immigration delivered in Phoenix, Arizona, Trump made the case for securing the border between the United States and Mexico by raising the spectre of what a reduction in immigration enforcement would lead the country to in his view: 'The result will be millions more illegal immigrants, thousands of more violent, horrible crimes, and total chaos and lawlessness. That's what's going to happen, as sure as you're standing there' (*New York Times* 2017). In these comments, Trump capitalized on the shooting of a woman on a pier in San Francisco by an undocumented immigrant who later was acquitted when it was proved that it was an unintentional ricochet shot that killed the woman. Immigration or legal status was not an issue in the trial, but in Trump's use of this crime, it served to conjure the animalistic impulses of brown migrants and the victimization of innocent, beautiful, white women. Ironically, academics and media sources have widely reported that while crime by undocumented migrants does indeed exist, it is not the social epidemic that Trump makes it out to be.[3]

In this speech, Trump further shared the stage with a group of mothers, the 'Angel Moms,' whose children or close relatives had been killed by undocumented immigrants. The Angel Moms provide the human-interest angle to support the case that migrants violate the sacred familial space of the nation. The conservative media cashed in on the plight of these families, framing migration explicitly in reference to the coherence and safety of white domestic forms (Golshan 2016).

The argument that the body of the nation is violated by undocumented migrants, and that stronger immigration control will restore a law-abiding country where citizens can be safe, is the simple yet often used narrative employed by nationalist groups and politicians like Trump. In this narrativized account, the white female victim is the sign for the endangered nation that needs to be protected, thereby legitimating the masculinist impulse and heteronormativity of the nation. This is not new; political ideas about gender, race, and sovereignty have always influenced the ways in which sexual violence is perceived and defined. Definitions of the rapist have been linked strongly to prejudicial perceptions of class and race, as the stark examples from the African American experience reveal (Freedman 2015). While the political trajectory of these examples is distinct, reductive and essentialist accounts of the pathological lust of dark-skinned men for white women has frequently provided the rationale and legitimacy for the civilizing mission of the colonial project (Sharpe 1991). Today, in the context of neoliberal globalization, the discourse of national sovereignty continues to evoke the inherent violence and dangerous sexuality of migrants of colour. As Bhattacharyya (2008) argues, 'such developments collapse immigration, terrorism and criminality into one multi-headed demon, a monster that demands that the protections of law and a fair hearing are curtailed for the greater good' (79). Represented within a sexualized and racialized matrix of terror, racialized Others are made visible as bodies that neither belong nor have the moral acumen to participate in the social and political fabric of the nation.

CRISIS OF INFORMATIONALIZATION

As the surveillance of social environments for suspicious individuals is being promoted as civic responsibility, everyday life begins to mimic the zones of border policing and securitization. Fears about changing demographic and racial compositions of the nation are also being digitally reignited with the speed and volatility of media technologies. The rapid transfer of information via social media fires up xenophobic rage and rescripts the performance of a strident patriotism. Conservative media outlets and websites go into high gear, inciting fear about migrants. For instance, alt-right news sites track crimes by undocumented migrants, seeking to find connections between local crime, global connections, and ideological affiliations. For example, after the 2013 bombing at the Boston Marathon, the police solicited the help of the public to identify suspects from surveillance video. A hysteric reaction spread among networked publics, whose highly active but faulty detective work reinforced the stark divide between citizens and noncitizens. In the discussions and viral flow of information that followed, the binary separating of those who belong and those who do not qualify to belong were reiterated (Hegde 2016, 43). Then, and now still, the digitally isolated and decontextualized figure of the dangerous migrant serves as the provocation for public vigilantism against the unworthy and undesirable.

These narratives of the dangerous Other abound in small towns in the United States where the news of one crime can lead to the rapid cascading flow of negativity about immigrant groups. The presence of refugees and migrants is changing the social dynamics in formerly insular communities, often sparking rumours and scapegoating techniques that brand migrants as potentially violent or as rapists. Their beliefs, behaviours, activities, rituals, and morality are fitted into a racialized narrative about unwelcome outsiders. For example, this trajectory has played out in numerous small towns including most recently Hazelton, Pennsylvania, with Latino immigrants, and in Lewiston, Maine, with Somali immigrants (see Finnegan 2006; Longazel 2016). Such rage about the arrival of newcomers includes and relies on the belief that these migrants diminish the national culture. This incendiary politics of Othering has taken some new global and mediated turns, reinvigorating the strategic production and circulation of the inherently violent thesis about certain migrant groups.

A very recent event in Idaho exemplifies this coming together of social media, networked publics, refugees, and the role that sexual politics plays in the framing of immigration. In June 2016, the quiet, peaceful town of Twin Falls was reeling with news about the alleged assault of a young girl by 'foreign' perpetrators. This occurred during the U.S. presidential election, when immigration and national borders were being vigorously debated on the political arena. News began to fly around Twin Falls that three juvenile Syrian refugees had raped a five-year-old girl at knifepoint and had urinated on her naked body. It was also rumoured that the attackers' parents had celebrated the event, even high-fiving the boys. The circulating stories also claimed that city police were covering up and downplaying this incident. Angry citizens at a City Council meeting spoke vehemently about a perceived Islamic invasion, a war that is being waged on the American people, warnings about a global Jihad, the basic incompatibility of Muslims with American culture, and the urgent need to take the country back. The story of the rape gathered momentum as the disinformation about Muslim violence spread like wildfire on right-wing websites, news feeds, YouTube channels, Facebook sites, and the blogosphere. City officials clarified that while a young girl was assaulted, no knife was used, and there was no gang rape. The children charged with lewd and lascivious behaviour, moreover, were not Syrian refugees. It turned out that there were two boys from Sudan and one from Iraq (Dickerson 2017).

An unfortunate incident happened in Twin Falls, and there is no denying that fact. However, what is of interest here is the spiralling story, its predictable plot, and the dramatic detours that criminalize migrants and evict the possibility of any alternate subject position in the public imaginary. In the case described here, the spectre of a Muslim invasion held by anti-immigrant activists was reinforced by the fallout from incidents in Europe. In Cologne, Germany, on New Year's Eve in 2015, groups of asylum seekers had groped women in a public space; the German police had been cautious and slow to acknowledge the details for fear of inciting a racist backlash. According to Dickerson (2017), this incident provided the contours of a narrative script that right-wing bloggers and activists used when blaming the local police department and law enforcement for concealing the crime or looking the other way. Circuits of information and outrage transformed the isolated incidents into viral capital resounding across digital echo chambers. The fear that migration will deplete the country economically and physically is one that runs deep. A generic script linking migrants to invasions, the spread of disease, and uncontrollable violence is replayed in various locations by populist groups with nativist agendas. The flow of information takes multiple turns and detours, linking a spectrum of issues, places, actors, and events.

Earlier in Idaho, there was further manufactured controversy concerning Hamdi Ulukaya, a Turkish immigrant of Kurdish descent and owner of the Greek-yogurt company Chobani. Ulukaya, sites such as Breitbart alleged, sought to take jobs away from locals and instead hire refugees at his large Idaho plant, or as the conspiracy theorists described it, 'choke the U.S. with Muslims' (Kirchick 2016). Conservative media groups not only condemned Chobani for hiring refugees, but along with racist name calling also made false claims, blaming the yogurt company for the increase in rape cases and for a spike in tuberculosis cases in Idaho (Gelles 2016).

When embedded within a social media ecosystem, such story lines are rapidly transformed into campaigns of fake news and conspiracy theories. The immediacy and circulatory reach of these intense exchanges of resentment serve to forge a strong group identity in opposition to immigrants. The networking constructed along these affective lines leads to the formation of ideologically connected groups that further reinforce the white gaze and perspective that rape is typical of less civilized cultures (Block 2001). These digital networks become in turn mobile infrastructures that materialize informational borders that contain, classify, and exclude racialized migrant bodies from the national polity.

PARTICIPATION AND THE POLITICS OF LIMITS

Migration is a touchstone of national debate, a controversial subject that stirs dissent and intense affect. Every day, there is news about some crisis erupting about migration, migrants, and the pathways and politics of their journeys and destinations. Framing the migrant presence as a threat is becoming a well-rehearsed global response. The accompanying and unceasing focus on sexuality magnifies local anxieties and, in turn, reinforces racist, patriarchal, and heterosexist assumptions of the nation. As the discussion in this chapter observes, the image of migrants as rapists is one that seems to travel across time and space. For instance, only recently, a centre-left politician in Italy was at the middle of a controversy when she said that sexual violence is especially reprehensible when it is committed by people who had been granted asylum in Italy (Rome 2017). The granting of status to migrants is regarded here as an act of benevolent sovereign power that requires the gratitude of the recipient. Immigration is the site of exceptional sovereign power where the vulnerability of the precariat is made 'spectacularly visible' (De Genova 2013, 1181). When the migrant precariat becomes the object of the state's disciplinary gaze and moral repugnance directed at entire communities, the very basis of articulating a civic identity and negotiating terms of participation is foreclosed. Marking groups of people as being inherently violent sets them apart from the rightful citizens who deserve protection from the state. The excessive visibility from these skewed angles effectively makes the more structural and transnational instabilities of migrant life invisible to public view. The media play a major role in this oscillation from visibility to invisibility. As Bigo (2002, 81) writes, 'giving a face to crime is therefore giving the migrant a face.' In turn, such discourse also serves to give the nation a face—one with a racialized and sexualized identity that clearly demarcates those deemed worthy and those who do not factor into the national community.

While the discussion in this chapter has rested mainly on events and incidents that have taken place in the United States, it is clear that these issues and the implications are relevant worldwide, of course within the specificity of their political and social contexts. The global spread of populist movements and the circulatory speed of communication technologies are two significant backdrops whose intersections must be factored into any theorization of migration and society. In this space, sexuality and sexual crime are domains where aggressive claims on the nation, primal forms of identity, and gendered politics of citizenship emerge. Singling out certain groups of migrant men as sexual predators cannot be considered an isolated act of prejudice. This move to castigate all migrants for the crimes of a few reflects broader operation of hegemonic power relations and the creation of a newly intensified underclass.

The stigmatization of refugees and migrants as rapists and child molesters turns them into objects of derision and delivers them into the ranks of the precariat. Criminalized for their very presence, the bodies of migrants are rendered unintelligible by the imagined civic and sexual standards of Euro-American modernity. When Donald Trump publicly announces that the United States needs more immigrants from Norway and fewer immigrants from 'shithole' countries like Haiti or those of Africa (Libell and Porter 2018), the racist fantasy of a white nation is once again normalized. It also plays into the received notion that the West is the site of all progressive sexual politics and that other countries such as the ones Trump censured are mired in an anachronistic past at least in terms of gender relations. Marking migrant men as sexual predators also identifies them as unassimilable to an imagined set of Western values. For example, the sexual assaults by migrant men in Cologne led to the widespread idea that misogyny had been overcome in Germany and has been rekindled by racialized Others (Boulila and Carri 2017). Or in the case of the Islamophobic imagination, as Horsti (2017a) argues, the fear of Muslims converges with fears of feminism and multiculturalism. The sexualization of racism only serves to fortify patriarchy, heteronormativity, and whiteness as the ideological bases for national cohesion.

Participation, one of the central concepts examined in this book, is premised politically on the idea of national belonging, citizenship, and the ability to have agency in the public sphere. Focussing on the manner in which issues of race and gender surface within discussions of migrants and refugees reveals the logics of exclusion that define nationalist politics. It captures the insidious ways in which the body of the Other is rendered unintelligible and undeserving of recognition or voice. In these conservative responses to race and gender described in this chapter, national, cultural, racial, and sexual identities serve as the fulcrum or, as Gilroy (2005) writes, supply 'the single homogenous and unchanging centre of social life and moralized community' (124). The claims of migrants in global locations are real, demand imminent political attention, and are a serious alert for scholars to rethink the politics and conditions under which bodies that matter are marked and registered. Concepts like participation, while capacious, are highly charged and circulate within a matrix of assumptions about the conditions of belonging to the nation. When dominant visions of community are narrow and insular, the criminalized migrant body is denied recognition and hence permanently assigned the precarious and devalued status of outsider. In the cases discussed here, the distance between rightful citizens and the precariat is maintained and surveiled through sexual and racial boundaries that work together with territorial boundaries. As Butler (2009a, ii) writes, precarity designates a 'politically induced condition of maximized vulnerability and exposure for populations exposed to arbitrary state violence and to other forms of aggression that are not enacted by states and against which states do not offer adequate protection.' Once seen as flawed, the body of the migrant merits no protection but only constant exposure as an invasive and unwelcome Other, an identity that then is mobilized to demarcate the limits or even the impossibility of participation.

The reiteration, reproduction, and normalizing of these limits and exclusions reveal that while we might term societies *post-migrant*, we are neither in a post-feminist nor post-racist world. Media technologies today add familiar and sometimes new creases to the narrative of migration and its complex intersections with race, gender, and nationalism. On a hopeful note, communication technologies and digital platform do offer the potential for migrant voices to be heard. To media scholars, the challenge is to generate innovative questions about the enactments of power and the mediated structures of complicity through which the social and political vulnerability of the precariat is perpetuated.

NOTES

1. See Jenkins and Carpentier (2013); Pateman (1970).
2. See Butler (1993) on the idea of cultural intelligibility.
3. For information that refutes Trump's claims regarding Mexican immigrants and crime, see https://cis.org/Report/Immigration-and-Crime; https://www.nytimes.com/2017/01/26/us/trump-illegal-immigrants-crime.html.

Part II

VISIBILITIES AND VULNERABILITIES OF REFUGEES AND MIGRANTS IN MEDIA AND ART

Chapter Four

Between the Vulnerable and the Dangerous

Representations of Refugees in the British Press

Rafal Zaborowski

In 2015, over a million refugees and migrants arrived at European shores, predominantly from the Middle East and Africa. Many fled war and poverty, risking their lives during the dangerous passage across the Mediterranean Sea. In April and May of that year, the European public learned just how deadly the trip might be, through highly mediated reports of shipwrecks that proved tragic for thousands of asylum seekers. These were neither the first nor the last humanitarian tragedies involving refugees and migrants on the Mediterranean, but in terms of media discourse, they were a start of a journalistic focus on the situation and the beginning of the media frame of the 'refugee crisis.'[1]

The arrivals were received by representatives of local and European structures, the coast guard and volunteers, officials and citizens, whose actions, on the regional, national, and EU level, represented in many ways the framework in which the European community attempted to balance humanitarian efforts towards refugees against protective measures prioritizing citizens (Vaughan-Williams 2015; Chouliaraki and Zaborowski 2017). Symbolically, however, these encounters between 'us,' the presumed European (Western) community, and 'them,' the distant others, were mediated by European press coverage throughout 2015. Media continued to report on the unfolding situation and its aftermath, representing the complex and nuanced situation in a simplified way: as a 'crisis' that required solving. The UK press played a crucial role in such framing for British and European audiences and policy makers, as the dynamically evolving situation required citizens and politicians alike to rely on journalistic coverage in order to stay informed. The press representations of the 'crisis' in 2015 were uneven and fluctuating, moving from stories of anxiety and hope in late spring and early summer, through avid expressions of humanitarianism in early autumn, to narratives of fear and negativity in early winter.

A quick look at the headlines after the tragic death of the little Syrian boy Alan Kurdi reveals a range of emotional responses. *The Guardian* (4 September) reported '[s]hocking images of drowned Syrian boy' that demonstrate the 'tragic plight of refugees.' The *Daily Telegraph* (3 September) talked about Alan '[w]ashed up on the beach' as 'the symbol of despair.' *The Independent* (3 September) referred to 'humanity washed ashore,' a phrase circulating in press and on social media, and asserted that Alan's 'life was full of fear.' 'Europe divided,' proclaimed *The Times* on the first page on 3 September, linking '[b]odies of infants washed up on beaches' and '[p]olitical leaders paralysed by crisis over migrant quotas.' Indeed, the photograph of Alan became the mediated symbol of the crisis, and the iconic image was spread virally across traditional and new media, as comprehensively analysed by Vis and Goriunova (2015). This powerful visual shaped the overarching narrative in the press, accruing particular meanings with outlet-specific by-lines, positioning, and editing.

However, not even three months later, the humanitarian call for action was replaced by suspicion, fear, and anger. 'Public abandons support for Syrian refugees coming to Britain,' proclaimed *The Times* (18 November), while *The Independent* spoke about '[t]his crumbling continent' (17 November). *The Guardian* warned that the 'Paris attacks changed our compassion equation—and not for the better' (25 November), and the *Daily Telegraph* assured that 'refugees will be vetted' in order to 'address fears that extremists will infiltrate Britain' (16 November).

In light of these drastic changes in representation, two types of questions emerge about the British media landscape participating in the crisis. Firstly, which representations of migrants were allowed and disallowed, legitimized and discarded in the British press? And secondly, to what extent did these structures and representations enable the European community to meaningfully engage with the distant other, enabling participation between the citizens and new arrivals? To answer these two questions, I discuss the findings of a long-term research project concerning media representations of migrants and refugees in European broadsheet press in 2015 in this chapter. Specifically, I will focus on refugee representations in four British quality newspapers (*The Guardian*, *The Times*, *The Independent*, and the *Daily Telegraph*), while contextualizing the findings within a broader analytical framework, including systematic content analysis of quality press in eight European countries and of two main Arabic-language European newspapers.

REPRESENTATION OF MIGRANTS AND REFUGEES

Critical scholarship on migration locates the tension between humanitarianism and securitization as a key aspect of the framework in which European structures respond to migrant reception. This tension, defined as 'humanitarian securitisation' (Vaughan-Williams 2015), is characterized by how humanitarian efforts do not necessarily impede, but often go hand in hand with securitizing logics, with the consequence being that the protection of some lives remains contingent on the deterrence of others. Humanitarian securitization, then, goes beyond static structural measures, but rather constitutes 'an active process of bifurcation that does not simply divide once and for all, but continuously redirects flows of people and things across or away from itself' (Nail 2016, 4). In this approach, securitization and humanitarianism are not situated on opposite ends, but as coevolving practices of classification operating through the symbolic (Squire 2015; Walters 2011). Following this conceptualization, it becomes crucial to then analyse and deconstruct the interplay between the symbolic forces of 'bordering' mediated through national and European media.

The concept of humanitarian securitization can be observed in action through concrete practices of border governance in Europe and within national boundaries. For instance, the transformation of the island of Lampedusa into a mediated spectacle of 'bare life' informed the migration discourse and policy in Italy and in Europe (Dines, Montagna, and Ruggiero 2015). De Genova's concept of the 'border spectacle' (2013) further highlights the tension between legality and illegality, fuelling anti-migrant initiatives. The concept of a humanitarian border becomes crucial to the overarching categorization of subjects into legitimate citizens and illegitimate aliens, the legals and the illegals, those who meaningfully participate in the public sphere and those who operate outside of it. An understanding of the symbolic practices of bordering during the refugee crisis is essential to uncovering the complexities and consequences of the public debate that shapes national and global imaginaries. The evident complexities embedded in humanitarian securitization manifest themselves through the paradoxical figure of the migrant, who is constructed through contradicting standpoints as a victim and passive recipient of our help, on the one hand, and as a dangerous perpetrator, on the other (Nail 2015; 2016).

Of course, the link between mediated representations of migrants in Europe and discourses of civic participation and inclusion has been covered by international scholarship before 2015. National and cross-national studies have empirically investigated cases from France (Benson 2002; 2013),

Germany (Bauder 2008), Italy (Campani 2001), and The Netherlands (Vliegenthart and Roggeband 2007). Notably, Caviedes's (2015) comparative analysis of newspaper articles in the UK, France, and Italy explored the salience of a European securitization narrative, finding that differences among national media are ideologically prominent, and this significance reflects varied economic and socio-political interests. Still, it is the highly mediated refugee inflow to Europe in 2014/2015 that has been a focus of critical journalism and academic scholarship. For example, the European Journalism Observatory (2015) analysed newspapers in eight countries (Czech Republic, Germany, Italy, Latvia, Poland, Portugal, the UK, and Ukraine) centred on three media events in September 2015. It concluded that Western European media were more compassionate towards the refugees than the press in Eastern Europe. Regarding the UK press, the report highlighted the short-lived attention given to the refugee issue following the drowning of Alan Kurdi. Berry, Garcia-Blanco, and Moore (2015) also compared media coverage in five European countries (Spain, Italy, Germany, the UK, and Sweden) and found significant differences in journalistic sources used, language employed, and solutions suggested in the press of each of the countries. Among the five, it was the UK media that Berry, Garcia-Blanco, and Moore found the most polarized and negative about migrants and refugees, with a particular emphasis on the anti-refugee aggression of the British right-wing media. In addition, the report by the Ethical Journalism Network (White 2015) raised the dangers of simple narratives of migration, and in its chapter devoted to the UK, specifically warns that 'where fear often frames the story deceptive handling of the facts, political bias and a rush to publish without sufficient thought as to the impact on the audience provide traps for all journalists' (Suffee 2015, 43). Similar findings expressing a mix of hope and concern in journalistic coverage can be seen in studies more focused in methodological scope, such as in Somaini's (2018) investigation of by-lines in Italy and the US, in Pantti and Ojala's (2018) research on the Finnish press, or in Franquet Dos Santos Silva, Brurås, and Bañares's (2018) investigation of newsrooms in Spain and Norway.

It is in this context that the presence or absence of different voices as well as their qualities and characterizations become crucial to understand the narratives surrounding the crisis. In a globalized world without a universal ethic, these narratives, depending on their qualities and context, may increase or decrease the distance between audiences and sufferers (Linklater 2007) and raise the profile of international developments, but also result in compassion fatigue (Sontag 2003, see also Moeller 1999). This becomes critically salient in late modernity, as we are increasingly encountering the inevitable clashes between national or regional communities and cosmopolitan values.

In post-migrant societies in particular, voice and representation, their me-diations and re-mediations, closely relate to meaningful and inclusive citizen participation. We can link research investigating the quality of voice and representation with contemporary debates on societal diversity, diaspora, and multiculturalism, the last of which seems to have been in perpetual crisis for at least a decade (cf. Turner 2006). For Turner, tragic European events in the 2000s, such as the 7/7 bombing in London in 2005 or the March 2004 bomb-ing in Madrid, reduced trust within local communities, which, at least in the UK, were already challenged by the vulnerable institutions of citizenship, dating back to the complex historical circumstances of migration to Britain in the late nineteenth century. As alluded to in the beginning of this chapter, we should see crisis as a permanent fixture underlying modern discussions of migration and participation, even before its 2015 mediated iteration.

The intricacies of citizenship and participation in post-migrant societies need to be seen in the context of competing voices and representations sur-rounding migrants and refugees. While we can observe that the global reach and speed of the media highlights the scale of migrant tragedies more than ever before, it does not necessarily result in more nuanced narratives or di-verse frames. As the International Centre for Migration Policy Development's report (2017) shows, journalists often lack time and resources necessary to reach such contextual nuances, and a hostile environment of structural pres-sure on reporters is aggravating the situation. This is certainly not limited to press, as demonstrated, for instance, by Horsti's (2016) study of the BBC on-line news of the migration crisis in Spain, in which media coverage may have contributed to the reach of global witnessing and compassion, but ultimately resulted in limited and unbalanced accounts of the situation. However, these processes emerge as particularly crucial to broadsheet newspapers, which remain the source of quality information for general and specialist audiences.

This brings to the fore the critical role that the media and journalists play in the process of recognition. Couldry (2010) refers to this broadly as 'voice as value,' in which the context and quality of narratives renders recognition potentially viable. The act of allowing people to speak for themselves goes beyond just legitimizing their claims; it is also an act of humanizing them and including them in a community of belonging. Recognition as a symbolic act of humanization may involve respect for individual human entities, but also acknowledges their moral dimensions and their potential to valuably contribute to a community (cf. Honneth 2007). Consequently, the discourse of differentiation between refugees who are allowed entry to Europe and those who are not (being sent back or existing in a transitional limbo) is pre-constituted by conditions of voice and representation. This brings back Butler's concept of 'hierarchies of grief,' where grievability of human life and the amount of protection attributed to it depend on each other, resulting in some lives being 'regarded as lives worth saving and defending' (2009b, 38) and some not qualifying as such. Names, personal histories, and social contexts become markers of recognition and, through that, vehicles of public acknowledgement (Butler 2004). Here we are reminded of Alan Kurdi, whose tragic death and its mediated aftermath connected global audiences in grief and solidarity. And yet, that humanitarian moment was extremely short-lived and in strong contrast to the lack of recognition of thousands of anonymous migrants and refugees drowning in the Mediterranean Sea in 2015. The mediated representation of Alan's tragedy was an exception rather than a rule. Similarly, young migrants in the UK are faced with what Back, Sinha, and Bryan call 'neo-imperial hierarchies of belonging' (2012, 151), which negatively impact social recognition and preclude humanization. Broadly speaking, then, this chapter takes on the 2015 migration crisis in British and European press coverage in order to look closely at how 'hierarchies of place and human life' (Chouliaraki 2006, 8) are reproduced though mediated discourse of news, and what consequences this might have for meaningful participation in post-migrant societies.

METHODOLOGY

The findings discussed in this chapter are drawn from data collected as part of a long-term and multi-stage research project 'Migration and the Media' at the Department of Media and Communications at the London School of Economics and Political Science.[2] In order to understand the European press narratives (but also local and regional trends) surrounding the refugee crisis, twenty newspapers across the continent, including eight European countries (Czech Republic, France, Germany, Greece, Hungary, Ireland, Serbia, and the UK) as well as two Arabic-language European outlets, were systematically analysed across three time periods in 2015. The periods were selected to correspond to three key and internationally mediated events during the crisis: Hungary erecting a physical barrier along its Serbian border in July, the drowning of the Syrian boy Alan Kurdi in the Mediterranean in September, and the Paris terror attacks in November. For a comparison of editorial stances of the press, where possible, a sample for each country was composed of articles in the largest left-leaning newspaper and the largest right-leaning newspaper.

Specifically, the data corpus consisted of most prominent press articles in each media outlet, systematically sampled across ten days after the event (Chouliaraki, Georgiou, and Zaborowski 2017). This resulted in a total of

1,200 articles, including 240 articles in the UK sample from the *The Daily Telegraph* (conservative), *The Guardian* (left/centre-left), *The Independent* (liberal), and *The Times* (generally centre-right). The focus on broadsheet newspapers reflects the study's aim of investigating quality press as, firstly, particularly influential in framing of news (Entman 1993) and, secondly, as an important resource through which national and European stakeholders often understand fast-changing developments on the ground.

After the data collection, the sampled articles were coded using quantitative content analysis. The codebook was driven by the study's conceptual framework and the overarching research question of the patterns in which migration reporting in the press reflects certain practices of representation. Following Entman (1993, 52), framing was understood in the study as calling attention to 'some aspects of a perceived reality' in a text, while directing attention from others, 'as to promote a particular problem definition, causal interpretation, moral evaluation, and/or treatment recommendation.' Thus, the coding categories were devised to investigate narratives surrounding agents (refugees, migrants, politicians, but also NGO representatives, activists, or citizens), causes (different dimensions of reasons behind the refugee influx), judgements (positive and negative evaluations of the situation), and suggested remedies, both on a national and European scale. A pilot coding exercise was used to calculate intercoder reliability between independent researchers. Based on the results, the codebook was revised, and items that did not meet reliability criteria were removed before the main coding of the whole sample was completed.

FROM THE VULNERABLE TO THE DANGEROUS

The analysis of the articles was focused on markers of causes and consequences of the refugee crisis. In reference to the former, the study examined how the road to European shores was framed with regard to refugees' aims and motivations. In reference to the latter, the study was driven by how the consequences (either national or European) of the crisis, understood primarily in the press through the inflow of refugees, were depicted in the articles. These consequences could entail narratives of economy, geopolitics, culture, or morality, and each of these could be positive or negative. The study also focused on the quality of refugee representations, including both their personal and collective characteristics and the amount of voice attributed to them in the press.

The analysis shows that there was a gradual shift in the press from empathetic representations of refugees and migrants between July and September

2015, towards securitization and fear in the coverage in November 2015. The paradoxical narrative of Europe as both protective of its borders and caring for the refugees also emerged in the analysis. At the same time, the chapter argues that while the representations differed across time and across editorial stances of the British press, the limited framing of refugees and asylum seekers positioned them as either vulnerable or dangerous, but always as the other to the presumed 'us.' Finally, I will discuss the different dimensions (including the presence/absence of refugee voices, the amount of contextual cues, and personal information about the refugees) in which the press (de) humanized refugees and (de)legitimized their plight.

What emerges from the analysis of the British press articles is an overall focus on negative consequences of refugee arrivals. The UK articles mentioned negative economic consequences in 32 percent of all articles in the sample, and negative cultural consequences in 31 percent of articles in the sample (see figure 4.1). These are high figures, especially in comparison with the other countries included in the study—in fact, the UK press was the only one in the European sample with negative-consequence frequencies in three areas (economic, geopolitical, and cultural) at over 30 percent.

Reporting on the reasons behind refugee arrivals was present in 59 percent of all British articles. The composition of the types of reasons, however, was highly uneven. The UK press reported geopolitical reasons behind the refugee influx in 51 percent of all articles, with other reasons placing far

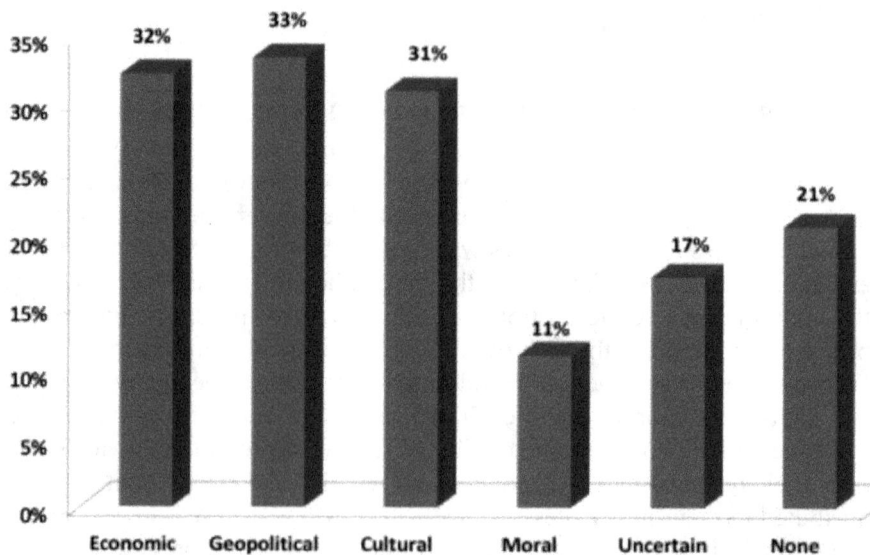

Figure 4.1.   Negative framing of consequences of refugee arrivals in the UK press. Figure constructed by author.

behind (economic 17 percent, moral 11 percent, cultural 10 percent). The percentage representing geopolitical reasons in British media was the second highest among all countries, second only to Greek media (64.1 percent). However, while this figure was high across the European sample in general, it still invites the question of the other 41 percent of the articles in the British press which did not mention any reasons. This is particularly crucial, as the UK was also one of only three countries in Europe where reported security measures dominated reported humanitarian measures. This, combined with the fact that the effects of the refugee inflow in the UK were specified in 75 percent of the articles, shifts the discourse from the plight of refugees understood in a global context of historical, social, and geopolitical nuances towards the figure of refugee masses as agents of change, defined either by their potential to contribute to the British and European communities, or by the level of danger they bring with them.

THE VOICELESS AND THE NAMELESS

Another focus of the press analysis was on the specific representation of migrants and refugees. Across the European sample, despite the strong presence of refugees and migrants as subjects of news stories, their voices were more often than not invisible, and their representations homogenous. The analysis of British press articles in particular confirms these trends, albeit with some deviations.

The analysis of the data makes clear whose voices are legitimized to appear in the symbolic sphere. In the British sample, refugees were quoted only in 23 percent of all articles, while this figure for politicians (national or EU) was more than three times higher, at 75 percent. This finding speaks to the divide between the European community understood as driven by the interest of stakeholders and the external arrivals, who are without a platform to plead their case. The tragic and complex reality of human life becomes but a policy affair; the refugees are not here to speak, they are spoken about.

The gap between 'us' and 'them' in the symbolic sphere becomes even more severe with the former constituted by politicians and not the general public. UK citizens were only quoted in 6 percent of the articles in the British press, despite frequent journalistic descriptions referring to the sentiments of 'the people' about the situation. Consequently, what emerges from the texts is a double narrative of humanitarian and securitization efforts, through which the encounter between British citizens and incoming refugees takes place, but the terms of this encounter are being shaped without the voices of either collective. A dialogue with the symbolic other had been muted before it even began.

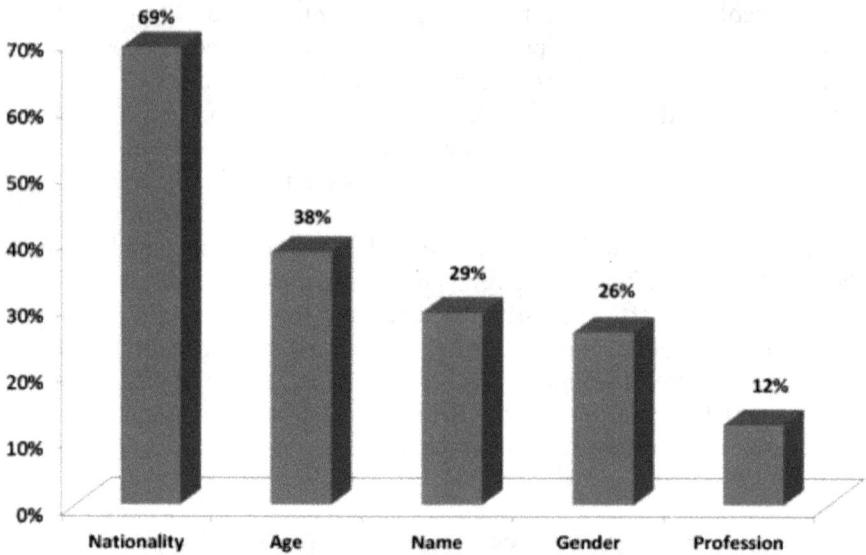

Figure 4.2.   Refugee characteristics in the UK press. Figure constructed by author.

This marginalization of voice becomes particularly impactful when paired with the lack of nuance in the descriptions of refugees in the press (see figure 4.2). In the British articles, names of refugees featured in 29 percent of all articles, their age in 38 percent, and their profession in only 12 percent. The refugees were predominantly characterized through their nationality (69 percent). This narrow characterization furthers the gap between British civil society and newcomers. Without their individual characteristics, the mediated refugee remains a stranger—the dehumanizing narrative prioritizes collective (nationality) to individual attributes (profession, name). A gendered dimension of these representations manifests itself through the overall emphasis on (loud, demanding, dangerous) male refugees in comparison to refugee women, who remain either invisible or silent in the press. The faceless persona of a refugee becomes either an object of pity, characterized by their precarious condition and lack of skills, or an object of fear, as their symbolic massification aids the popular framing of 'mostly young men chancing their luck.'[3]

Overall, then, the general lack of complexity and diversity in journalistic reporting places the narratives on one of two extremes, pity or fear, neither of which attributes agency to refugees themselves. The lack of narratives depicting personal histories or nuanced accounts of aims and motivations with refugees as actors, not subjects, contributes to framing the unknown arrivals either as an anonymous, dangerous collective that needs regulation, or as pitiful, passive victims of an obscure tragedy, looking for noble compassion and aid from the national and European community. In this way, the grand narrative of the crisis in the press simplifies (at best) or altogether omits the complex social and historical dimensions of migration and the geopolitical realities of war and conflict in the origin regions. The discursive momentum is shifted instead towards the refugees' 'deservingness' (cf. Holzberg, Kolbe, and Zaborowski 2018) and the ways in which their presence might be beneficial—or not—for the UK and the EU.

THE END OF 'THE CRISIS'

In November 2016, Myria Georgiou and I observed that while migrant stories from the Mediterranean stopped dominating the news, the reality for refugees trying to reach Europe by sea is even more tragic than it was in 2015 (Zaborowski and Georgiou 2016). After the Paris attacks in 2015, the discourse on European migrants moved towards security and border control, soon to gradually disappear from the broadsheets' first (and, eventually, most) pages. This was, by no means, a sign of resolution. Humanitarian tragedies were bound to continue, securitizing policies, and refugee quotas were still being negotiated. But the mediated spectacle had, seemingly, concluded.

In the light of the ephemerality of the media spectacle, it is crucial to recognize the role of the press in framing these dynamic events for British stakeholders and publics. Precisely because press coverage has been increasingly challenged by newer forms of media and journalism, the press must be responsible for providing fairness in representation and diversity of viewpoints, while remaining critical and curious about structural and political realities. To what extent this remains feasible in the current news cycle, with the deepening precarity of journalistic resources, is another question.

I return then to the question of voice as a necessity for a meaningful dialogue, a prerequisite to humanity (Couldry 2010). Voice here is strongly linked to political participation, with the quality and possibilities of voice correlating with inequalities in terms of participation in the public sphere. The tensions between communitarian and cosmopolitan logics manifest themselves through acts of recognition between us and the other. Following that, the role of media is critical in legitimizing certain voices and denying others, and through that, underlining the conditions of humanity through processes of recognition or misrecognition.

Our national imaginations, and ideas of who we are, are directly linked to the portrayal of others, and the more limited their representations are, the more confined to stereotypes we become. The coverage of migrants and refugees is, in this matter, certainly just a part of a larger picture of the mediated civic landscape in the United Kingdom. However, the findings from studies analysing press coverage on the EU Referendum campaign in the UK (Moore and Ramsay 2017), young people and Brexit (Mejias and Banaji 2017), or journalistic representations of Jeremy Corbyn[4] (Cammaerts et al. 2016) leave little room to speculate that the concerns outlined in this chapter are unique to the subject of refugees. British press reporting emerges from the analysis as, at best, problematic and, at worst, ideologically biased and unethical.

At the same time, in these difficult times of discursive and structural ruptures, the responsibility of the media is particularly high. The decisions of who speaks in the news, how issues are framed, and what actions are highlighted regulate not only the quality of representations and the amount of agency attributed to the vulnerable, but also shape public recognition of the refugees, indicating which policy options are viable or desirable. Since meaningful participation and the quality of civic engagement depends on the inclusion of diverse voices in the public debate, we should require journalism to transcend the easy framings, to legitimize and include misrecognized voices, and finally, to provide complexity necessary to cultivate informed, participatory publics.

NOTES

1. The use of the term 'crisis' throughout the chapter should not be understood as the author's view of the situation surrounding the refugee arrivals to Europe in 2015. I remain critical of the Eurocentric use of the term, which ignores structural and historical dimensions of the situation and, as discussed by Mazzara (2016), limits refugee narratives to a spectacle of misery and grief. Rather, I use the term in referring to 'crisis' as the framing device used frequently in public and media debates surrounding refugees.

2. The Migration and the Media project (2015–2017) was coordinated by Professor Lilie Chouliaraki, Dr Myria Georgiou, and Dr Rafal Zaborowski and funded by the Department of Media and Communications at the London School of Economics and Political Science. Whereas the project report focused mainly on overall trends of migrant and refugee representation in Europe, this chapter is concerned with how the press of a particular country (UK) mediated the 'crisis' in the context of contemporary British society and its place in the European community.

3. As exemplified by the words of a Welsh MP David Davies speaking to BBC Radio Wales on 2 September 2015 (available at http://www.bbc.co.uk/news/uk-wales -34126247).

4. Jeremy Corbyn has been the Leader of the Labour Party and Leader of the Opposition in the UK since 2015. His strongly left-wing political stance has brought him much critical attention from the British press.

Chapter Five

Exploring Films' Potential for Convivial Civic Culture

Brigitte Hipfl

This chapter focuses on how film can address and intervene in the reme-diation of racist and colonial tropes, images, and discourses in the Austrian public realm. The context for this analysis has to do with the broader question of what films can do to make migrants feel part of society, not the 'Other.' I will propose that films are a means to crystallize and condense collective feelings, to give insights in the banality of conviviality of everyday life, and to illustrate what can emerge from new, unexpected encounters. The four films discussed all address issues of migration and are produced by the Riahi brothers in Vienna, Austria. The discussion is grounded in a cartography of media and migration, which explores the power relations expressed in the entanglement of regimes of representation and affects. On the one hand, the chapter examines the ways in which these films deploy and undermine certain repertoires of media representations of migrants. On the other hand, a strong focus is placed on the films' potential to affect the audience through a dif-ferent imaginary of migrants and the expression of 'convivencia.' I propose that it is these aspects of films that are shaping and transforming participation under current social and political conditions.

POST-MIGRANT AUSTRIA

The current public discourse on refugees and migration in Austria is fuelled by an ambivalence from two divergent positions. There is a broad general understanding of what makes Austria a historically grown assemblage of different ethnicities and groups of migrants. Contemporary Austria's predecessor,[1] the Habsburg monarchy, was a 'Vielvölkerstaat' (a 'multi-ethnic' state), where internal migration was commonplace. After World War II, Austria was one of the countries of destination for different refugee movements. These were ethnic Germans who were expelled from Eastern Europe after the Second World War; refugees from Hungary in 1956 and Czechoslovakia in 1968, followed by refugees from Yugoslavia later in the 1990s. The Austrian population's openness to and support of these refugees is engrained in its collective memory. State-sponsored immigration began in the 1960s when the Austrian government developed recruitment agreements with Spain, Turkey, and Yugoslavia to bring in 'guest workers,' intended to rotate out and only stay temporarily, but who nevertheless settled in (see Rupnow 2017, 39–42). It is quite obvious 'that Austria has long been a country of immigration,' and has always been diverse and pluralistic, as Dirk Rupnow (2017, 41) points out.

Conservative and right-wing politicians' current rhetoric, however, of the negative effects of the so-called 'refugee crisis' is based on the construction of Austria as a rather homogenous state, contrary to the understanding of Austria as a 'country of immigrants.' That rhetoric denies the fact that societies in general, and Austria in particular, are defined by movements of people and migratory culture (Bal and Hernández-Navarro 2011); instead, it suggests that the 'refugee crisis' makes Austria a 'migrant society.' Austrian collective memory that reproduces a romanticized notion of diversity in the Habsburgian Empire supports this idea, while ignoring the history of recent labour migrants and their significant contribution to Austria's post-war prosperity (see also Rupnow 2017, 47–48; Hipfl 2016, 197–98).

Official and public discourses, as well as Austrian migration laws, support the tendency to differentiate between 'real' Austrians and those who migrated into Austria over the last decades. Statistical data from 2016 show that about 22 percent of Austrian residents have a so-called 'migration background,'[2] with the highest percentage, about 43 percent, residing in Austria's capital Vienna (Statistik Austria 2017). The common use of the term 'migration background' has been criticized because it covers such a diverse range of living conditions, and also implies not being a 'real' Austrian. Hyphenated identities are only used in Austria when someone has achieved something of importance for Austria, for example, Canadian ice hockey players who were offered Austrian citizenship, so that they could play on Austria's national team, and were then addressed as Austro-Canadians. Regular migrants have to follow strict rules and have to prove legal residence in Austria for ten years before they are eligible to apply for Austrian citizenship. Dual citizenship is only possible in exceptional cases. Children born in Austria acquire Austrian citizenship according to *ius sanguinis*, when the parents (or at least the father) are Austrian citizens (HELP-Service for Foreign Citizens, Bundeskanzleramt n.d.).

When it comes to Austrian public opinion on the 'refugee crisis,' Manfred Kohler (2017), in his analysis of various surveys conducted in Austria in 2016 about the increased number of refugees that entered Austria in 2015, draws a complex picture. Asked about the handling of the refugee issue, almost two-thirds of the interviewees rated mayors' and federal-state levels' handling of refugees as excellent and fairly good, whereas fewer than half of the survey respondents felt that the Austrian national government was doing a good job in handling the issue. Similarly, the respondents were slightly more optimistic regarding the assistance and integration of refugees on the municipal level than on the national level (ibid., 260f.). A poll taken of Austrian mayors and municipalities who host refugees shows that mayors did not find national institutions helpful, but they were highly appreciative of the voluntary support by municipal residents and Caritas, a faith-based organization (ibid., 264f.). Overall, these results do not support the consistent negative attitude towards refugees as represented in the tabloid *Kronen Zeitung*, Austria's daily newspaper with the highest circulation.

Based on this socio-political context in Austria in terms of refugees, I propose that Austrian films about refugees and migrants can contribute to what, according to Rupnow (2017, 44), can be defined as a requirement for a post-migrant society, namely, a 'polyphonic history from multiple perspectives in order to come to terms with itself, with its development through the past, but also with its future.' Films can be a place where migrants can tell their stories and retell their memories, so that the plurality that defines Austria becomes palpable. Films can help fill what Rupnow (2017, 39) calls a 'blank space in hegemonic memory,' which is materialized in museums, public spaces, and schoolbooks, for example. He also finds it problematic that the public realm is dominated by polemic statements, racism, and, when more informed, social analysis while 'historical knowledge and (hi)stories' are less present (ibid., 49). As a historian, Rupnow refers mostly to the classic institutions of collective memory, such as archives, museums, and exhibitions. Unfortunately, only a few exceptions to the above directly address Austria's recent migration history, like the 2004 exhibition Gastarbajteri: 40 Jahre Arbeitsmigration (Gastarbeiter: 40 Years of Labour Migration [Wien Museum 2004]) (*Gastarbajteri* is the Yugoslav derivate form of 'Gastarbeiter' [guest worker]). Even in media like newspapers, magazines, radio and television, as key institutions of storytelling, we find again only rare incidents where migrants can voice their stories and experiences (see also Ratković in this volume). These few incidents are not enough to make Austrian collective memory more inclusive regarding migrants' histories. Here, I find Michele Baricelli's (2013) plea to turn to 'collected memories' very helpful. He points towards the need to create spaces to bring forward different memories and make their various entanglements recognizable. It is my opinion that films are very well suited for these goals because of their potential to deeply engage with migrants' experiences, traumas, hopes, and pains, but also with their resilience, courage, creativity, survival, and coping techniques, all of which enrich Austrian society. With their capacity to express what migration feels like from within, films also intervene in and interrupt the clichéd and stereotypical mainstream media representations of migrants and refugees, which I will discuss in the next section.

MEDIA DEPICTIONS OF (FORCED) MIGRATION: REGIMES OF REPRESENTATION AND AFFECT

Following Stuart Hall (1997), 'regimes of representation' refers to the fact that media, again and again, use a specific repertoire when it comes to the representation of certain groups of migrants and refugees. In his well-known essay, 'The Spectacle of the Other,' Hall shows how racial differences are signified through racialized regimes of representing the 'Other.' He illustrates how current representations of 'Blacks' still bear traces of earlier racialized representations based on past ideas of racial hierarchies, with 'White' employing the top position in European race theories. These theories legitimized European colonization and slavery and resulted in stereotypical representations of 'Blacks' based on the binaries of civilized/uncivilized and culture/nature. One side of the binary represents 'White' and all the elements characteristic of so-called Enlightenment: intelligence, knowledge, rationality, formal institutions for the regulation of social life, self-control of emotions, and morally governed sexuality. The other side of the binary represents 'Black': nature, uncivilized, rituals, open expressions of emotions and feelings, and excessive sexuality instead of intelligence (also childishness and kind-heartedness, for example, in the novel *Uncle Tom's Cabin*). In this racialized regime of representation, 'Blacks' are reduced to nature, and the difference between 'Black' and 'White' becomes naturalized. As Hall points out, traces of this stereotypical regime of representation are found long after the end of slavery. Hall's analysis is exemplary for postcolonial critique; he makes us aware of racialized regimes of representation that are still at work, but he also stresses how difficult it is to contest and change racialized regimes of representation. Neither reversing stereotypical images nor substituting racialized images with positive images will undo such binaries. Such reversal is only possible by addressing the forms of racialized regimes of representation directly (as, for example, with comedy, which is a way of 'laughing with' instead of 'laughing at').

What are, then, the regimes of representation when it comes to migrants and refugees in Austria? Generally, we can see an overall trend of 'Othering' migrants and refugees that dominates main social discourses, despite the ideological differences that surface in different media. This process of 'Othering' materializes in two ways. On the one hand, refugees are shown as victims of war, terror, hunger, and traffickers, most strongly embodied by images of women and children who then become clients of the new humanitarianism (with governmental and nongovernmental organizations helping them). On the other hand, they are represented as a threat, as criminals and villains, who abuse the system with the help of others. They are connoted masculine (see Habring 2016; Scheibelhofer 2016). At the same time, there is also the trope of the illegal, undocumented refugee making the dangerous trip to Europe, in total despair, having nothing, being speechless, embodying what Giorgio Agamben (1998) refers to as 'bare life' (see Zaborowski's chapter in this volume).

In particular, Muslim migrants have been subjected to processes of 'Othering,' which reflect and reproduce patriarchal gender relations, as Birgit Sauer (2016) stresses. Muslim women are positioned as oppressed by patriarchal, violent Muslim men, an image that makes Western-liberal states responsible for protecting these women. As Sauer (2016, 9) argues, this resonates with Spivak's (1985) famous description of colonial power relations as 'white men saving brown women from brown men,' which not only refers to processes of 'Othering,' but, at the same time, to the affirmation of the colonial self. In this discourse, Muslim women do not have any agency, while male Muslim migrants are stigmatized as wrongdoers. This supports the idea that violence against women only takes place in patriarchal Muslim cultures, and that Western European societies are characterized by gender equality.

The moral panic after the sexual assaults of women by young men who were described as Arabic or North African looking during the New Year's Eve celebrations 2015/2016 in Cologne (and to a much smaller extent in other German and Austrian cities) shifted the focus on the 'sexually dangerous Muslim refugee.' It is no longer the 'Other' women that need to be saved, but it is now 'white men saving white women from brown men' (Sauer 2016, 9). In other words, no longer are minority groups at risk, but 'white' women are. With 'white' women as victims of migrant men, *society in general* is seen as threatened by 'brown' men (Sauer 2016, 9). For Gabriele Dietze (2016), the 'sexually dangerous Muslim' refugee is first and foremost a figure of defence against migrants and refugees. 'Rape-Fugees are not welcome' was one of the slogans of right-wing demonstrations against the sexual threat by male refugees. This understanding of the migrant can conveniently mobilize resentments that are already in place and articulated by nationalist politicians.

As these examples illustrate, addressing (forced) migration and media also requires taking into account the significant role that the imaginary and affects play in this context. Media narratives and images not only function as building blocks for imagined worlds that promise a safer life in other places, but media also produce collective imaginations of (national) communities (see, for example, Orgad 2012), raising the question of how migrants and refugees are positioned in relation to these imagined communities. Additionally, when we take into account what Brian Massumi (2015) stresses so forcefully, namely, that the dominant forms of power are performed through the modulation of affect under contemporary conditions of capitalism, we have to refocus our questions: What is the effect of the modulation of affects as directed towards (forced) migrants on the general tenor of everyday life? What kind of collective feelings are mobilized in relation to (forced) migration, and what do they *do*? It is important to stress that affects and feelings here are not understood as something that is personal and private; rather, they are cultural and social. For example, Austrian political scientist Monika Mokre (2015) points out that the focus in Austrian media on 'the wave of solidarity' of Austrians towards the refugees arriving in and travelling through Austria in 2015 generated a new national pride. However, it was a pride based on positioning the refugees as victims, either telling their stories of suffering or expressing their gratitude for the help and support they received. This makes Austrians feel good, without any danger of having to face changes. What is not part of the Austrian 'national consensus' of charity, as Mokre calls it, however, is the refugee as a political subject who demands human rights and self-organization, as, for example, expressed in the Refugee Protest Camp movement in Vienna in 2012.

How is it possible to intervene in such regimes of affect? For Massumi, an intervention or disruption is only possible on the same level—that is, through modulation of affect. In general, empathy and laughter are powerful means to interrupt the rhythms and intensities of certain affects, as I will illustrate later in my discussion of the four films. In Austrian news media, politicians, as well as various experts, mostly speak about migration; migrants and refugees are hardly ever given a chance to speak for themselves. Generally, migration is presented as a problem, connecting migrants and refugees with issues of criminality and/or violence, but also positioning them as victims that need help (see, for example, Drüeke and Fritsche 2015). These recurring patterns of attributing certain problems to migrants and refugees or positioning them as helpless modulate collective feelings, which can then be appropriated politically (a process explored in the British context by Ahmed 2004). The collective feelings generated in Austrian media both resonate and reproduce what Georg Seeßlen (2016, 2) outlined as a Europe split by the dispute between two opposed positions regarding (forced) migration and refugees. On the one hand, we have 'the humanist, accommodating civic society' that 'wants to take in refugees and equip them with human and civic rights.' On the other hand, there is an 'unthinkingly depreciative, racist and xenophobe movement, with a politics maneuvering between them' (author's translation). Seeßlen makes the claim that this is where cinema can make a difference because of film's potential to provide a much more detailed, humane, and touching approach than the usual selective and serial flow of hyped media images.

WHAT FILMS CAN DO

In my attempt to illustrate what films can do for a more inclusive approach towards migrants, I extend Seeßlen's claim that film can provide more nuanced representations than media images. I explore the kind of cultural work the four films I analyse perform and discuss the ways in which these films have the capacity to express and make palpable the complexities of migratory culture. The four films do not only address the various encounters the protagonists undergo, but they are themselves also spaces of encounter for the audience. As in any art, films in general, with their respective aesthetics, offer complex, embodied experiences of what migration feels like (see also Pollock 2006). With the focus on the incidental and the everyday, details often overlooked in mainstream media are focused upon in depth, potentially opening up new insights and connections that can undo hegemonic constructions of difference and processes of 'Othering.'

Through its specific aesthetics, film produces certain structures of feeling or affective atmospheres. Raymond Williams's concept of structures of feeling refers to 'a particular quality of social experience and relationship' (Williams 1978, 131) that gives us a sense of lived lives: 'What does it feel like to be in a particular situation?' (Sharma and Tygstrup 2015, 1). As Williams emphasizes, art is often expressive of structures of feeling that are emerging, thereby articulating new sensibilities. Notwithstanding, films are also expressive of structures of feeling that reinforce collective feelings already in place.

When it comes to films on migration, a single film cannot capture all the complexity of such a life-changing, dramatic experience, but it can focus on specific aspects. Loshitzky (2006) speaks of three evolving film genres about migration in European cinema. The focus is either on the migratory path and the hardships migrants and refugees experience, on the encounters between migrants and host societies, or on coping strategies of the second generation of migrants and beyond. Similarly, Seeßlen suggests thinking of the drama of refuge including five acts that films can explore: the unbearable situation in a particular place and its culmination that forces people to leave; parting; the dangers of refuge as an experience of tragedies and adventures; arrival; attempts to find a home, which are successful or fail. Whatever the focus of the film, films about the refugee experience not only give insights into what usually is unseen and overlooked, but they also make the audience feel what it is like being a refugee, with all its multifaceted, ambivalent, and vital aspects. Here, I discuss four films produced by Austrian brothers Arash T. Riahi and Arman Riahi to illustrate these films' potential to affect the audience through a different imaginary of migrants. Two of the films, *A Moment, Freedom* and *The Migrumpies*, were directed by Arash T. Riahi and Arman T. Riahi, respectively, while the third film, *Mama Illegal*, was directed by Ed Moschitz, and the fourth one, *Tomorrow We Will Leave*, was directed by Martin Nguyen. I present each film as exemplary of expressing different aspects of refuge and migration: from acts of survival and subversion to 'convivencia' as the ordinariness of living together and the interconnectedness of migrants' lives and our lives, and humour as 'convivial labour.' The film *Mama Illegal* is also an example of collaborative filmmaking.

THE RIAHIS FILMIC INTERVENTIONS

Arash T. Riahi was born in Iran and fled at the age of nine, with his parents, to Austria after the overthrow of Reza Shah Pahlavi by the Islamic Republic in 1979. At that time, his younger brother Arman and sister Azi had to stay in Iran, but escaped later to join the family in Austria. Arash T. Riahi's interest in making films started in high school, where he took part in short-film competitions. From the early1990s on, he documented his family's life on film. His brother Arman, who was also involved with film as a teenager, later became his partner in their film production company *Golden Girls.* The company's goal, according to its website, is to 'make films that make a change.'[3] The company's promotional clip characterizes the approach as follows: 'The imagination is not constrained. That ultimately the only way we can really fundamentally change the world we're in is to rethink it. And you can't re-think it if you think in old ways. . . .'[4] Quite a number of its films have a focus on issues of migration.

The Riahi brothers' films could be labelled 'accented cinema,' using Hamid Naficy's (2001) term; he is an Iranian-born American film scholar. Naficy claims that films made by exiles, displaced people, or members of a diaspora strongly reflect personal experiences and capture them in a certain style and form, what he calls 'accented.' Such films often have multilingual narratives, combine aesthetic styles of different cultures, and emphasize political agency. However, I prefer the term 'postcolonial cinema' in the way Ponzanesi and Berger (2016, 113) characterize it, as being able 'to foreground new forms of interventions by accounting for silenced or marginalized histories that might be de facto centre stage in the New Europe.' They refer to 'postcolonial cinema' as a *conceptual* space that allows us to make connections to what is occluded by national and colonial frames (see Ponzanesi and Waller 2012, 1). As Ponzanesi and Berger (2016, 111–12) stress, 'postcolonial' is a broader term than 'accented'; it also describes films by directors who were not personally forced to leave their country of birth. But, above all, 'postcolonial' denotes an analytical stance 'through which films emerge in engagement with and as contestations of colonial dynamics and their legacies in the present' (ibid., 112). Postcolonial cinema, with its focus on passages, encounters, and new figurations, can be understood as a new form of intervention that opens alternative visions and imaginaries (see Ponzanesi and Berger 2016, 113). This is where I locate the potential of such films to contribute to a reshaping of civic culture.

Since I discuss Austrian films, there is an obvious national framing. However, the ways in which these films address issues of migratory culture clearly undermine a traditional understanding of Austria as a homogenous and stable configuration and address instead (unexpected) encounters and everyday, banal examples of conviviality. The films mentioned and discussed in this chapter are by no means the only Austrian films exploring migration. In recent years, quite a number of documentaries and feature films have focused on issues of migration and integration.[5]

The films produced by the Riahi brothers, which I discuss, make visible some of the multifaceted, manifold, and complex realities of refugees and migrants, which are neither part of public discourse nor of Austrian collective memory. I see these movies as examples of 'collected memories,' showing migrants' pain and suffering, the obstructions and hindrances they have to face, as well as the resourceful, creative, imaginative, and joyful ways of dealing with everyday life. These movies clearly intervene in the mainstream ways migration is publicly talked about. At the same time, they are expressive of certain structures of feeling that resonate with the audience. The respective aesthetics of these films make it easy for the audience to deeply connect with protagonists' experiences. This phenomenon of being affected is also called 'prosthetic memory' (Landsberg 2004). According to Landsberg, technologies of mass culture, like films, make it possible for anyone to share collective memories because the filmic experiences become assimilated and memorized as the viewers' own personal memories.

COLLECTED MEMORIES—AUTONOMY OF MIGRATION

In his first feature film, *In a Moment, Freedom* (2008), Arash T. Riahi condensed his own family's experiences and the stories of other refugees into three exemplary stories based on three groups of protagonists. First, Ali and Merdad, two college-aged friends, try to bring their two young cousins Azi and Arman (representing the director's siblings) into their family, already granted asylum in Austria. Then there are Lale and Hassan, a couple, with their young son Kian, who try to escape political persecution. The final group consists of two men who became friends, a Kurdish happy-go-lucky sort of a fellow, Manu, and a political activist, Abbas. *In a Moment, Freedom* was well received and was awarded prizes in numerous film festivals. As Sylvain Richard (2009) remarks, 'in its genre, it ranks among the very best.'[6]

In this film, Arash T. Riahi's intention was to show the force of the desire to be with one's family and to live in freedom and peace. He emphasized how this desire can enable people to do what seems impossible, such as overcoming humiliation and failures and not giving up on dreams. According to Riahi, this desire to follow one's dreams is something that is part of everybody's life, not just refugees (Riahi in von Hilgers, n.d., 11). He further points out that the film is divided into three sections, which also refer to different temporalities. The first part captures the dangerous and arduous escape itself, with refugees fighting their way through rough mountains, moving towards an insecure future. The structure of feeling that is expressed is one of danger, and restlessness. The second part, when the refugees are caught up by bureaucratic procedures and are forced to wait, expresses stoppage and stagnancy, a feeling of 'in-betweenness,' interrupted by intense emotional outbursts by the characters, who have reached their limits when it comes to enduring their frustrations, fears, and feelings that all hope is lost. The last part focuses on the different routes that emerge for the three groups of protagonists, with the goal of eliciting feelings of deep empathy among viewers (ibid., 8).

In this film, all the protagonists are portrayed in complex and ambivalent ways, from showing their illusionary dreams, despair, and hopelessness to touching moments of feeling free. This portrayal is a pervasive theme throughout the film. Refugees are caught by a non-transparent bureaucracy; at the same time, they are also resourceful and inventive in their will to survive, and to become free from political persecution. This film shows some extreme and difficult situations that people experience in their pursuit of freedom. It is a film full of tears and laughter, a film that is, after all, according to Arash T. Riahi (Riahi in von Hilgers n.d., 12), 'a declaration of the love to life' (author's translation). Director Arash T. Riahi purposely uses a humorous angle as a way to affect the audience: 'When people start laughing, this opens the mind and increases the chance to also be affected by more unconventional contents' (ibid., 14) (author's translation). He further explains that 'the proximity of tragic and humorous elements is extremely important. I regard humor as a survival technique, and if you don't keep at least a minimum of humor when you are in such extreme situations as these refugees, you will be destroyed' (Riahi in Schiefer 2007, 1).

The film gives the audience an idea of the hardship, suffering, and distress of refugees escaping as well as when they are in transit. At the same time, the film addresses this in a way that relates to the so-called autonomy of migration perspective (Papadopoulos and Tsianos 2013). This perspective emphasizes the human agency involved and illustrates that migration has its own logics and trajectories, forms of negotiations, contestations, and refusals, despite state attempts to control and regulate migrant movements. Thus, the focus is put on the creativity of human agency, on everyday acts of survival and subversion, and on an understanding of migration as an inventive force, or, as Papadopoulos and Tsianos (2013, 185) point out, 'a gesture of freedom' that can lead to new, unexpected situations and 'new modes of being in the world' (Nyers 2015, 31).

COLLECTED MEMORIES—
THE EVERYDAYNESS OF CONVIVIALITY

Tomorrow You Will Leave (2012) is a documentary film by Martin Nguyen about his father, Quang, who ended up with his family in a small village in the Austrian countryside after he fled from Vietnam. The film shows the peaceful, hilly, green landscape where Quang lives and works. It is a laid-back life, characterized by his interactions with plants, his young granddaughter, and the villagers. In long interview excerpts, Quang talks about his life and his desire to find Ali, a soldier from the refugee camp in Malaysia who had helped him to escape thirty years ago, and whom he had promised to let know when he 'made it.' The second thread in this film is about the unobtrusive, everydayness of conviviality in a small rural village in Austria. When I use 'conviviality' in this context, I refer to Paul Gilroy's (2004) notion of convivial culture as a pattern that emerges in contact zones such as metropolitan areas characterized by the coexistence of diverse groups. In their everyday interaction, ethnic differences become ordinary and insignificant. However, conviviality should not be romanticized. Rather, it should be understood in a very specific way, as Amanda Wise and Greg Noble (2016, 424) suggest, namely, as 'a way that includes potential ambivalence at the heart of the everydayness of living together.'

Tomorrow You Will Leave introduces viewers to an example of the un-spectacular ways in which convivial culture exists in places where one would not expect it at first sight, like rural Austria. The film presents Quang's many mundane interactions with other people in the village. Martin Nguyen offers an explanation of what made this example of convivial culture possible:

> In the beginning, the people there did not quite know how to deal with him (his father Quang), so they treated him like everybody else. They spoke to him in their dialect and that was the way he learnt how to speak German; his is a German with strong dialect and a Vietnamese accent. I think it was pure luck, our luck, that under such circumstances where everybody knows everybody, anonymity is not possible, and so one inevitably gets to know and understand everybody. (Golden Girls Filmproduktion n.d. 5, author's translation)

However, conviviality does not automatically emerge in encounters involving members of different groups. As Les Back and Shamser Sinha (2016) argue, in their study on adolescent migrants in London, a certain toolkit needs to be utilized. What they describe as key elements is a kind of attentiveness to everyday multicultural life and the capacity to care for the life of the city (Back and Sinha 2016, 523).

Watching *Tomorrow You Will Leave,* the audience witnesses the ordinariness of living and working together, or in the words of Wise and Noble (2016, 425), the 'layers of "with-ness" that play through the space of interaction and coexistence.' All of this is presented in unspectacular ways. For example, it has become quite natural for the locals to eat Vietnamese dishes. At the same time, the film is also exemplary for what Wise and Noble (ibid.) suggest, following Gilroy's (2004) argument, that the Spanish term 'convivencia' is much more complex than the English 'conviviality.' 'Convivencia' connotes a sense of 'rubbing along,' a way of living together that is characterized by effort and negotiation, and also by dealing with conflict and friction. For Wise and Noble (ibid., 425), 'convivencia' puts the focus on practice and negotiation, that is, on what people *do* to make convivial culture happen, instead of referring to conviviality as an ethical imperative. In that sense, *Tomorrow You Will Leave* gives us some insights into the 'situated' nature of the practices that characterize 'convivencia' (ibid., 426).

COLLABORATIVE FILMMAKING— EXPOSING ENTANGLED LIVES

The documentary film *Mama Illegal* (2011), directed by Austrian investigative journalist Ed Moschitz, documents seven years in the lives of Aurica,

Raia, and Natasa, three women who left their family and children due to ex-treme poverty and lack of prospectives in their Moldavian village to become undocumented domestic workers in Austria and Italy. The women agreed to participate in the film project and make their experiences public despite the risks of exposing themselves to control regimes. For them, as Aurica, one of the three Moldovan women explains in an interview, this was a chance to let the people know what the situation was like in their home country, why they left their children back home, and why they were gone for such a long time (Pfoser 2012). This is the same concern expressed in the sans-papiers-movement and in immigrant protests where activists not only aim for legal status and justice, but also make themselves visible as human beings, counter-ing the hegemonic stereotypical images in mainstream media (see Marciniak and Tyler 2014, 7). The 'collaborative filmmaking' started with Moschitz's shock about his own ignorance regarding the fact that the babysitter he had hired, whom he, his partner, and their children fully embraced, actually was an undocumented worker in Austria, herself a mother of two small children living in Moldova. His intention was to make the public aware of the complex situation of women like Aurica, and how their lives and his were entangled. He also wanted to sensitize us to how we are complicit in the perpetuation of these unequal relations.

The aesthetics of *Mama Illegal* is defined by Moschitz's use of 'classi-cal' documentary modes, mixing the 'observational' with the 'participatory' mode (according to Nichols 2001). On the one hand, the camera documents situations from the three women's lives by observing lived experience, with-out any staging or arrangement. On the other hand, the film is also a product of the encounter between the filmmaker and the three women when they talk about their situation, the work they do, their dreams, hopes, anxieties, fears, and their longing to be with their own children. Those scenes are the result of the collaborative interactions of Ed Moschitz with Aurica, Raia, and Na-tasa. Throughout the film, these women talk about themselves. There is no voiceover. The audience hears only the voices of the three subjects, with Ger-man translations in subtitles. Emphatically, the film presents these undocu-mented female workers as subjected to oppressive and disabling structures and as courageous agents, developing their own survival tactics along with the help of their community of fellow undocumented workers.

The move of Aurica, Raia, and Natasha is also a move from one kind of precarity to another. *Mama Illegal* illustrates the interconnectedness and entanglement of mobility and immobility (see also Götz 2016, 10) that not only characterizes the precarious situation of many migrants and undocu-mented workers in particular, but also marks one of the key power relations deployed in the 'regimes of mobility' in general, following Nina Glick

Schiller and Noel Salazar's (2013, 188) argument. The film painstakingly confronts its audience with these relations by displaying how 'the labour of those whose movements are declared illicit and subversive . . . make(s) possible the easy mobility of those who seem to live in a borderless world of wealth and power" (ibid.).

Humour as 'Convivial Labour'

The Migrumpies (Riahi 2017) is a warm-hearted comedy situated in a fictive Viennese multi-ethnic district (represented by a grocery and fruit market) which puts the focus on the so-called 'migration background' and second-generation migrants. The main protagonists are best friends: Benny, the son of a judge with Egyptian roots and a trained actor, and the hipster-looking Marko, whose advertising agency's bankruptcy is looming. Marko's father, Mr. Bilic, moved to Austria from Yugoslavia when he was twenty years old. Ambitious television director Marlene Weizenhuber, who is planning to make a documentary TV series of this Viennese district, mistakenly takes Benny and Marko, who were transporting a sofa from Mr. Bilic's apartment, to be migrants living there. As a joke, they act as if they are migrants. They pretend to be called Omar and Tito and are hired by the TV director as key characters to represent and explain what it means to live in this Viennese quarter. Benny and Marko start studying the milieu in order to pass as someone with a 'migration background.' They even hire Juwel, a young Austrian with a Turkish background, who works at a fruit stand at the market, to get background information about what 'really is going on,' enabling them to portray 'realistic' characters. Without them realizing it, Juwel makes up stories that abound with stereotypes of criminal migrants who take advantage of Austria's welfare system. Omar and Tito pretend to be these petty crooks in Weizenhuber's documentary series; as a result, the series becomes very successful.

The film is, on the one hand, a kind of reconciliation story, where both Benny and Marko acknowledge and recognize their own 'migration background,' from which they have tried to distance themselves. In the beginning of the film, Benny refuses to audition for the role of the foreign taxi driver, hoping instead to be hired for the role as a 'real' Austrian. On the other hand, the film problematizes the media's logics with its continuous search for appealing stories to increase viewership, thereby spreading and reactivating stereotypical views of migrants. *The Migrumpies* illustrates what media can do as exemplified by the reactions of the people in the market, which is a contact zone where daily encounters of groups with different backgrounds take place. We can see how quickly convivial culture, as the established way to live and work together, turns into a place of tensions and conflicts, triggered by processes of 'Othering,' distrusting, and mutual scapegoating.

Humour is the central mode of *The Migrumpies*, and it plays out on different levels. Much 'playful' humour in the literal sense is at work. For example, the two main protagonists perform and play the stereotypical Austrians with 'migrant backgrounds,' while they themselves are 'being played' by Juwel, who is supposed to feed them 'authentic' stories. One could also say that Benny/Omar and Marko/Tito were unable to pick up Juwel's 'ironic racism,' a practice often performed by males in everyday multicultural contexts (see Wise 2016, 490). 'Ironic racism' refers to jokes and statements that come across as very offensive, but within a context of great familiarity are ways of both recognizing and undermining pejorative meanings and actually help to constitute convivial sociality and friendship (ibid., 491). The setup in a filmic comedy makes it possible to explicitly address all the negative attributions to people with 'migrant backgrounds,' thereby questioning this kind of categorization. This can also be understood as a variation of what Wise calls 'convivial labour,' in order to emphasize the fact that 'the everyday practice of living together takes work' (ibid., 496). To get along with one another in such contexts, like the market as a contact zone in the film, requires practices of negotiating differences in life. Humour and jokes are important means of doing that kind of convivial labour. Wise suggests speaking of convivial labour when somebody in a joking relationship realizes that he or she has gone too far. We see this at the end of the film, when Benny and Marko take responsibility for the problems their acting has caused and then take the initiative to rebuild convivial culture. In that sense, *The Migrumpies* addresses what Wise describes as the friendly and conflictual mode of interethnic encounters.

Towards the end of the film, convivial labour and convivial culture are explicitly addressed in the emotional statement of Mr. Bilic to his son Marko: 'You have no idea of the state this city would be in if there would not be people like me. What would these districts be like without us? The city would not be able to function, no city in the world would be able to function' (author's translation). This statement summarizes what could be described as one of the key interventions of *The Migrumpies*: to make the public aware of and acknowledge the contribution of migrants to Austrian culture and society.

THE FORCE OF A CONVIVIALIST POLITICS OF AFFECT

The overall argument of this chapter is that the films discussed here are capable of interfering with dominant narratives, especially with their stereotypical representations of migrants and refugees and their collective interconnected feelings. All these films break with ideas of a homogenous understanding of Austria under threat because of the recent 'refugee crisis.' They address, in particular, the differences that manifest within its borders and that are crucial to understanding the composition of contemporary Austria. In this way, these films also contribute to what historian Dirk Rupnow pursues in the research project 'Deprovincializing Contemporary Austrian History: Migration and the Transnational Challenges to National Historiographies,' which defines its most important task as linking the narratives and spaces of migrants with Austrian history.[7]

To summarize, these films, as I suggest, establish a different way of approaching migrants and dealing with differences. Firstly, these films are exemplary in their attempt to modulate collective feelings when it comes to migrants. All of them offer something that Frank Adloff (2015) understands as a requirement for conviviality; that is, 'emotional authenticity.' With their respective aesthetics—as exemplified by the 'observational' and 'participatory' mode used in the documentaries, the creation of 'prosthetic memory,' and humour that explicitly addresses prejudices and stereotypes in feature films—all four films create what can be called an 'affective proximity' (see Olivieri 2016). In other words, these films address and express what protagonists feel and desire, often through very intense outbursts, which also enables the audience to feel what it is like to be in their respective situations.

Secondly, the films express a structure of feeling that, following Adloff (2015), can be characterized as a 'convivialist politics of affect.' The films do not comply with the regimes of affect that dominate the public realm when it comes to migration and refugees. In that respect, they support what Adloff et al. (2016, n.p.) describe as the aim of convivialists to create 'a society in which the alliances of individual groups, and communities are visible in new ways, [where] people respect each other in their diversity and thereby cooperate for the benefit of all, through the constructive resolution of conflicts.' These films portray ways in which conviviality is practiced in everyday life, in the sense of 'convivencia' as 'rubbing along.'

Lastly, I suggest understanding these films as 'collected memories' that contribute to a polyphonic history of Austria and to an awareness of the entanglements of different histories. These films also help us understand 'how feelings of togetherness . . . [are] not given but actively produced through social practices, often in the face of change and conflict' (Wise and Noble 2016, 424).

Overall, this is where I see these films' potential contribution in shaping and transforming participation under current conditions.

NOTES

1. The Habsburg dynasty reigned for more than six centuries in most of the regions of contemporary Austria and parts of Central Europe. The Austrian Empire was founded in 1804. It became the dual monarchy of Austria-Hungary from 1867 and lasted until its collapse after the First World War in 1918. The surviving state of Austria was then proclaimed a republic. In 1938 the Anschluss to national socialist Germany took place. In 1945, after the Second World War, Austria became an independent republic, occupied by the Allied Forces of France, Great Britain, the Soviet Union, and the United States until 1955.

2. Someone has a migration background when he or she has foreign citizenship or was born to an Austrian parent in another country (MA 23, Wirtschaft, Arbeit, Statistik, Vienna, https://www.wien.gv.at/search?q=migrationshintergrund+definition& client=wien&proxystylesheet=wienres&tlen=250&ulang=de&oe=UTF-8&ie=UTF -8&getfields=*&entsp=a__wiengesamt&site=wiengesamt).

3. http://www.goldengirls.at/company-profile.

4. http://www.goldengirls.at.

5. See for example *Good News* (1990, Ulrich Seidl), *Northern Skirts* (1999, Barabara Albert), *Nachtreise* (2002, Kenan Kilic), *Welcome Home* (2004, Andreas Gruber), *The Arrangement* (2005, Nathalie Borgers), *Import Export* (2007, Ulrich Seidl), *Cash & Marry* (2008, Atanas Georgiev), *Bock for President* (2009, Houchang Allahyari), *Little Alien* (2009, Nina Kusturica), *The Crazy World of Ute Bock* (2010, Houchang Allahyari), *Black Brown White* (2010, Erwin Wagenhofer), *Arab Attraction* (2010, Andreas Horvath and Monika Muskala), *Spain* (2012, Anja Salomonowitz), *Kuma* (2012, Umut Dag), *Summer 1972* (2012, Wilma Calisir), *Deine Schönheit ist nichts wert* (2012, Hüseyin Tabak), *Evdeki Ses—22m2 Österreich* (2015, Ufuk Serbest), *Unten* (2016, Djordje Cenic and Hermann Peseckas), *Ciao Chérie* (2017, Nina Kusturica) (see http://medienservicestelle.at/migration_bewegt/2013/02/14/ migration-im-osterreichischen-mainstream-film.

6. *For a Moment, Freedom* ranked 3.8 out of 4 in the 2008 Montreal International World Film Festival.

7. https://www.uibk.ac.at/zeitgeschichte/aktuelles/deprovincializing_projekt.pdf.

Chapter Six

Art and Refugeeism

Speaking-with and Speaking-from-within

Katarzyna Marciniak

SPEAKING-WITH REFUGEES: AI WEIWEI

'Even at a celebrity art gala you can don an emergency blanket and feel good about yourself. Hard political questions, not required.' —Jerome Phelphs (2017)

Reflecting on the aesthetic usability of refugeeism and self-congratulatory apolitical engagement, Jerome Phelphs articulates this point on openDemocracy.net in May 2017 while grappling with Chinese dissident artist Ai Weiwei's recent art-activism, particularly with his enactment of the death of Aylan Kurdi, a Syrian toddler who drowned off the coast of Turkey in fall 2015. The image, produced in collaboration with photographer Rohit Chawla (figure 6.1), caused quite a stir among various critics who accused Ai of callousness, unethical appropriation, and self-promotion while treating his artistic experiment as 'careerist,' and even 'egotistical victim porn' (Ratnam, 2016; Steadman, 2016).[1]

Since then, Ai released his 2017 cine-essay, *Human Flow*, a self-reflective documentary commenting on the global dispossession and displacement of refugees from various parts of the world. The film offers an extraordinary scope of gathered materials. As viewers, through a panoramic overview, we are invited to contemplate the images of human movement, landscapes, animals, and objects, intertwined with interviews with refugees from different regions, NGO aid workers, politicians, and activists. While the narrative moves through twenty-three countries and regions such as Lebanon, Libya, Gaza, Kenya, Malaysia, Pakistan, Turkey, the US/Mexico border, and across Europe, Ai, again, inserts himself into the narrative, creating a participatory

Figure 6.1. Ai Weiwei on the Greek island of Lesbos. *Source:* Ai Weiwei.

diegetic mode. We see him present in various locations as he consoles refugees, jokes with them, interacts with children, visits graves, films with his phone, directs the crew, and even performs daily activities like cooking on a grill, buying fruit, or getting a haircut. His insistent presence thus introduces various emotionalities, and stresses the mode of being-with refugees, even though such a being-with is, necessarily, only temporary and provisional.[2]

It is provisional and fleeting because the artist's participation is temporal. As Ai himself acknowledges, 'You tell these people that you're the same as them. But you are lying because you are not the same. Your situation is different; you must leave them. And that's going to haunt me for the rest of my life' (Brooks 2017).

Human Flow is a film that, once again, has attracted much attention from art critics. While many praised the film for its representational sensitivity and dignity, *Human Flow,* like his other often controversial work,[3] has also received harsh criticism. Xan Brooks interviewing Ai for the *The Guardian* article summarizes these critiques: 'His critics view him rather differently: as a crude provocateur, trading in stereotypes and bankrolled by the west' (2017). And Ai's response to such critiques is quite pointed: 'All day long, the media ask me if I have shown the film to the refugees: "When are the refugees going to see the film?" But that's the wrong question. The purpose is to show it to people of influence; people who are in a position to help and

Figure 6.2. *Human Flow*. **Being-with refugees.** *Source:* **Ai Weiwei.**

who have a responsibility to help. The refugees who need help—they don't need to see the film. They need dry shoes. They need soup' (ibid., 2017).

I start with this example because Ai's comments open up questions about the usability of art-activist work and artists' participatory modes of filming, witnessing, or being-with refugees. But I believe that his response is not about whether art can be 'useful,' because of course it is. Rather, it is a point about spectatorship, reception, and the political afterlife of such art. It is about how various artistic efforts participate in shaping cultural consciousness and invite or dis-invite participatory action in the public sphere. It is about producing new perspectives and new knowledges that have the potential to make us think in novel ways about the need for contestation and action. While Ai's insistence that refugees need 'dry shoes' and 'soup' is indisputable, the point that refugees 'need' art as well is manifested in the fact that refugees make art themselves.

Developing this point, in what follows, I briefly look at varied artistic productions by rapper M.I.A., a Sri Lankan Tamil who came to London at the age of nine with her mother, and Crocheted Olek, a Polish American installation artist, to set a conceptual stage for the in-depth exploration of experimental shorts produced by Another Kind of Girl Collective, an initiative started in Jordan's Za'atari refugee camp. The arch of my analysis moves from artistic possibilities of speaking-with refugees to the idea of speaking-from-within in order to explore the capacity of artistic productions to challenge the images of victimhood that often dominate accounts of refugees' experiences. As an ethical inquiry into representational politics, my analysis shifts the focus from a politics of pity to a more nuanced understanding of art-activism as a form of audio-visual protest against xenophobic and racist responses to global migrations. This chapter thus contributes to the conceptual practice of thinking about politics through aesthetics, considering how various artists as well as refugees themselves experiment with different modes of artistic engagement to seek innovative modes of aesthetic expression.

SPEAKING-WITH REFUGEES: M.I.A. AND CROCHETED OLEK

As *Human Flow* demonstrates, speaking-with refugees is necessarily fraught with tension. At one point, we see Ai holding a piece of paper with words: '#standwithrefugees.' Seconds later the wind blows it away, metaphorically underscoring the transient nature of such artistic displays of 'being-with refugees' and pointing to both possibilities and limits of such endeavours. Offering a distressing view of the global refugee crisis, the film reminds us that already in 2014, as the result of the civil war in Syria, more than 53 million people were displaced around the world, the highest number since the end of World War II.

Aside from Ai, an exilic artist from China residing in Berlin, who, along with his family, was displaced within his own country,[4] another well-known example of a refugee artist advocating for refugee rights, for instance, is M.I.A., a songwriter who has always articulated her art and politics as someone intimately familiar with experiential refugeeism. Her 2016 video *Borders* conceptually rests on a repeated question: 'Borders: What's up with that?' 'Politics: What's up with that?' 'Police shots: What's up with that?' 'Your privilege: What's up with that?' 'Boat people: What's up with that?' She also subtly ridicules hashtag activism by singing: 'Slaying it: What's up with that?' 'Love wins: What's up with that?' Most importantly for my discussion, she counters the current demonization of the male refugee figure of colour and purposefully screens out female refugees and children whose images often readily evoke feelings of empathy in the context of humanitarian crises. This tactic created an unusual visual landscape for her music by shrewdly engaging only dark-skinned men.[5] And M.I.A.'s being-with refugees is carefully composed: the initial shots of men are long takes, which block the viewer's potential intimacy, eventually moving us closer to their bodies and revealing their faces. As figure 6.3, for example, demonstrates, the men's faces appear expressionless and look away, and their gaze does not address the viewers directly, thus pushing away the possibility of the voyeurism of gratuitous and racist spectatorship. Considering such art-activism, I am

Figure 6.3. *Borders.* **M.I.A.'s being-with-refugees.** *Source:* **M.I.A.**

interested in these kinds of strategic engagements that allow us to consider various modes of speaking-with, or being-with refugees as *Human Flow* and *Borders* advocate with them as well.[6]

Speaking-with, rather than 'speaking about,' or 'speaking for' refugees— troubling concepts in feminist explorations—might be thought of as performative and ethically inclined tactics that allow various artists to resist the inherent mode of patronization or 'capture' of subjectivities that have experienced all kinds of vulnerabilities and traumas. In this respect, Agata Olesiak, known as Crocheted Olek, a Polish American installation artist, offers us another compelling example of participatory art making with a political purpose. It is, again, a politics through aesthetics. Crocheted Olek, known for her provocative crocheted street art and for covering all kinds of bodies and objects with crochet, collaborated with Syrian and Ukrainian refugees in 2016, creating an unusual installation: The Pink Houses project. According to *W* magazine, Olek was commissioned to recreate a home made entirely of yarn for the Verket museum in Avesta, Sweden:

> When I first came to install a work of art at the Verket museum, I had originally intended to recreate a traditional home. And I did. However, when the Syrian and Ukrainian refugees who helped me install my piece started telling me the candid stories of their recent experiences and horrors of their home countries, I decided to blow up my crocheted house to illustrate the current unfortunate

situation worldwide where hundred of thousands of people are displaced. After I exploded the house I wanted to create a positive ending for them as a symbol of a brighter future for all people, especially the ones who have been displaced against their own will. Women have the ability to recreate themselves. (Munzenrieder 2016).

As Olek explains, the project changed its tonality and purpose when she teamed up with refugee women. Motivated by the refugees' stories of displacement and dispossession, she subsequently blew up one of the crocheted houses (figure 6.4) to symbolize the horrors these women had experienced, while leaving two houses of hope, one in Avesta, Sweden, and one in Kerava, Finland to advocate the possibility of a future for displaced people[7] (figure 6.5). Olek's experiment is explicitly participatory, involving collaboration with the refugee community and showing us how aesthetic projects can change their political and emotive articulation when refugees themselves are involved (figure 6.6).

While artists such as Ai, M.I.A, and Crocheted Olek experiment with such evocative modes of artistic engagement and seek novel ways to create art by employing the mode of speaking-with refugees, their politically engaged art collectively offers an eloquent audio-visual and material resistance to the perpetual guarding of real and imagined borders, practices that continually discipline those who, arriving from various elsewheres, are implicitly perceived as unwanted intruders. Their work provides a meta-commentary on the collusion

Figure 6.4.   Crocheted Olek's exploded installation. *Source:* **Crocheted Olek.**

Figure 6.5.   Crocheted Olek. The Pink House as a symbol of hope. *Source:* Crocheted Olek.

Figure 6.6.   Olek crocheting with refugee women in Sweden. *Source:* Crocheted Olek.

of current border regimes in the violent death of refugees seeking aid, acceptance, and inclusion. Such art, I would argue, offers an aesthetic opposition-
ality to waves of Islamophobia, which single out specifically the figure of a
dark-skinned man as a site of national panic, spearheading what Imogen Tyler
calls 'epidemics of racial stigma,' epidemics that recast the 'refugee crisis'
as a 'racial crisis' (2017, 4). It shows the power of alternative aesthetics and
political visions created by artists committed to counter-hegemonic representations of forced human mobility.

Considering the potential power of speaking-with, the main portion of this
chapter focuses on Another Kind of Girl Collective and experimental shorts
produced by young women in Jordan's Za'atari refugee camp. In contrast to
Ai, M.I.A., and Crocheted Olek, Another Kind of Girl Collective is an opportunity to consider not just the transformative power of art—in this case
video making—but also a participation-from-within in remarkable ways. The
Collective's works engage with the questions of legibility, audibility, and
visibility that pertain to refugees' lives through very different audio-visual
tonalities and through a different treatment of diegetic space. Their work also
brings into focus the inside/outside dynamic, as they are creating from within
the refugee camp, hoping to communicate their complex experiences to the
outside. Through their experimental video art, Another Kind of Girl Collective showcases what speaking-from-within might look and feel like.

WEIRD ANGLES IN REFUGEE CAMP:
SPEAKING-FROM-WITHIN

'Condemned by history, as Marxists were fond of saying, perhaps belonging to a wrong class, wrong ethnic group, wrong religion—what
have you—they [refugees] were and continue to be an unpleasant
reminder of all the philosophical and nationalist utopias gone wrong.'
—Charles Simic, "Refugees" (1999)

Charles Simic, a US-based poet from post–World War II Yugoslavia, offered
this reflection on the precarious status of refugees while commenting on massive displacements of people at that time. And he added sarcastically, 'My
family, like so many others, got to see the world for free thanks to Hitler's
wars and Stalin's takeover of Eastern Europe' (1999, 120). I bring up his
point to signal both the history and historicity[8] of refugeeism, which remind
us that national uprootings and dispossessions are not new phenomena; as
Simic writes, '"displaced persons" is the name they had for us back in 1945'
(ibid., 119). He also articulates a seemingly suspicious status of refugees
who, as his family, were subjected to endless scrutiny and humiliation: 'Ev-

ery passport office, every police station, every consulate had a desk with a wary and bad-tempered official who suspected us of not being what we claimed to be. No one likes refugees. The ambiguous status of being called a DP made it even worse' (ibid.,123). Similarly, as Ai's *Human Flow* demonstrates, xenophobic tendencies and the turmoil of dislocation are rooted in what Simic calls 'nationalist utopias gone wrong.' Studying Another Kind of Girl Collective's art, we can see how the young women's experiments offer a counter-visuality to typical documentation of war upheavals, speaking in the first person to the idea of what it might mean to be 'condemned by history.'

'Another Kind of Girl Collective is envisioning and developing a new model of alternative education for refugee girls that values creativity and experimentation'—this is the Collective's mission statement. It signals the importance of individual voice and artistic self-expression. Keeping their mission in mind, I approach Another Kind of Girl Collective by focusing on some of the video work produced by the Collective while also thinking about the politics and aesthetics of refugeeism and larger meanings surrounding the idea of a refugee camp.[9] Zooming in on specific imagery, I will also privilege the notions of weird angles and touch, and think about their conceptual relation to the configuration of a refugee camp. The young women's video art, overwhelmingly privileging the trope of touching and thus offering the touch as the primary visual language, compels various questions: How do representations of the phenomenology of touch engender the spectatorial possibilities and limits of 'being touched' by various visual intimacies? What does a politics of touch reveal about the knowability of a refugee camp? What does it reveal about participation-from-within?

The Collective's shorts I am focusing on speak to the tactility of bodies and the relationship between the tactility of bodies and the tactility of cinema, making us consider the affective potential of cinema, in other words, the medium's sensory power. This relationship has a theoretical history. In 2000, Laura Marks introduced the discussion of hapticity into film studies. Hapticity, in the sense she uses the term, describes cinema's capacity to evoke the sense of touch through audio-visual means: 'a visuality that functions like a sense of touch' (Marks 2000, 22). She uses the metaphor of 'the skin of the film' as a way of drawing attention to film's materiality, and she argues that 'vision itself can be tactile, as though one were touching a film with one's eyes: I term this *haptic visuality*' (ibid., xi). She also emphasizes what she calls 'the tactile and contagious quality of cinema as something we viewers brush up against like another body' (ibid., xii). A similar concept is present in Trinh T. Minh-ha's *Elsewhere, within Here: Immigration, Refugeeism and the Boundary Event* in which she claims that 'the eye hears, the ear sees' (2011, 2). She writes: 'the question is not so much to choose between sight and speech, as *to see what the eye hears, and hear what the ear sees*' (ibid.).

While Trinh appeals to the complexity of the senses, Vivian Sobchack, in turn, demands that we consider embodied spectatorship and 'the carnal sensuality of the film experience' (2004, 56), thereby inviting us to think about 'the capacity of films to physically arouse us to meaning' (idid. 57). Yet Laura McMahon, using Jean-Luc Nancy's philosophy of touch, argues for an apprehension of cinema as 'a privileged space for understanding touch as a figure of withdrawal, discontinuity, and separation rather than under its more traditional guise as a marker of immediacy, continuity, and presence' (2012, 2). Considering these various theoretical approaches, I want to tease out how the conflictual trope of touching can 'arouse us to meaning' and how representations of the senses are related to the figurations of the refugee camp as a border zone. Perhaps a heightened desire for a sense of touch, a tactile feeling, might be related to bodily reconfigurations that one experiences when one *becomes* a refugee? After all, as Ai's *Human Flow* demonstrates, no one just *is* a refugee; one becomes one, through experiences of dispossession, war violence, or postcolonial upheavals.

The shorts I am analysing are authored by young Syrian women living in Jordan's Za'atari refugee camp and are the result of the work of the Another Kind of Girl Collective, an initiative founded in 2014 by Laura Doggett, a US community artist and educator, in response to the Syrian refugee crisis. Together with documentary animator and educator Tasneem Toghoj, her co-facilitator and translator, Doggett, on a postgraduate fellowship from Duke University, organized a series of workshops in partnership with several organizations such as the International Rescue Committee, Save the Children International, and WomenOne.[10] Together, they worked with about twenty-five teenage girls to develop their media and storytelling skills. Acting as the Collective's creative director, Doggett explains:

> My desire for the films is what the girls' desires are for their films as they are being shown around the world. They are smart, creative young women who have a unique perspective and a lot to say. They are not passive or tragic beings, as mainstream media often present them. They are . . . *creative visionaries*. They also want their stories to encourage other girls and young women in difficult circumstances to express their most important stories. (Enrado 2017, my emphasis)

These are great points, of course, but, given that the films are the pedagogical afterlife of the workshops, one also has to wonder how much of the imagery was actually curated by Doggett.

The Collective has equipped teenage girls living as refugees with cameras and has offered them technical training in visual literacy so that they can tell their often turbulent stories in the first person. For example, Khaldiya,[11] a seventeen-year-old girl from Syria, explains: 'I live in the camp, I am within the camp, and I know the camp. An outsider will miss a lot of the deeper meanings because they haven't *felt* what it's like to live here'[12] (my emphasis). Indeed, the young women engaged in these projects reveal, through their short films, the images and the sounds, in a deeply affective aesthetic project, that form the reality of their lives in the refugee camp. Their experimental productions have already reached international audiences, as they have been screened at festivals in Cannes, London, Los Angeles, Sundance, Sydney, and Toronto, among others.

In light of the proliferation of recent artistic-activist efforts in support of refugees—and, as I have already argued, of such efforts always raising questions of ethical responsibility vis-à-vis appropriation and speaking on behalf of—it is crucial, of course, that the Collective's video art is produced by the refugee women themselves. The ethics of art making in a humanitarian disaster are complex, especially when refugees' bodies are often mobilized to feed 'hungry Western eyes,' as Slavoj Žižek once put it in the context of the Balkan wars (1994, 2). There are eyes that are eager to see, whether they see sensationalized images of suffering, or celebratory images of human endurance. It is hard, no doubt, to produce art that self-consciously seeks to resist the aesthetization and sublimation of what Tyler, for example, calls 'social abjection'—'abjection as a lived social process' (2013, 4). Furthermore, if speaking for the other, or giving voice to the other, as many feminist critics have already successfully argued, is a deeply flawed tactic of representation and a patronizing way of conceptualizing the filmic space, then how can a film offer the speaker an enunciative space of agency and integrity? Trinh T. Minh-ha, grappling with such issues, coined the well-known term 'speaking nearby' (1983) in her film *Reassemblage*, but the shorts offered by the refugee women do more than speak nearby; they speak-from-within.

'Whenever I'm angry, I go out and start filming. However it comes out doesn't matter. What is important is that I'm filming. *Especially when I take the shots from weird angles* (my emphasis). When I film I feel I am someone very important.' This is how Khaldiya describes her motivation for her documentary short, *Another Kind of Girl*. It is interesting, no doubt, that her motivation for filming is anger, an emotion that is discursively risky for different precarious subjects and certainly for Arab refugee women for whom the prohibition against anger is especially intense because of the converging axes of gender, race, and national (un)belonging. An angry refugee—and specifically an angry female refugee—is a defiant figure, an anxiety-inducing figure, and Khaldiya's short is strategically devoid of anger either visually or through narration; anger only serves as an affective motivator for her filming.

The shots she chooses oscillate between close-ups (of her siblings, of various objects, of dirt, of her own hand) and long shots showing us the shacks where families live, thereby revealing the camp's landscape. Similarly to Ai's *Human Flow*, which intertwines drone photography with close-ups on the ground, we thus get a glimpse of the immediate and the distant. Her camera is at times intrusive, getting close to the bodies of her siblings, for example, and at times it appears neutral, as if just observing, witnessing. It also moves up and down, showing us images of the sky and the flying birds, and at other moments, being positioned close to the ground. The aesthetic feel is decidedly exploratory, as Khaldiya is commenting on her discovery of filmmaking that offers her a sense of newly found agency amidst reflections on how it feels to inhabit the camp. There is no non-diegetic sound to manipulate spectatorial emotions, and her voiceover offers us guidance, marking her short film as an intimate and personal exploration without inviting sentimentalization, thereby blocking the potential evocation of the politics of pity, a term Luc Boltanski, for example, uses to discuss what he terms the rhetoric of distant suffering (1999).

The opening of *Another Kind of Girl* speaks to the shifts in Khaldiya's subject-position that she felt upon arriving at the camp: 'There were a lot of thoughts I couldn't understand going through my head. It was a feeling I can't describe. From that moment, I felt I had changed and become a different person.' In many ways, Khaldiya describes her move into the experience of alterity—what it is like to *feel* uprooted, displaced, defamiliarized, what it is like to be placed in the space of otherness as a young female, what it is like to experience what Judith Butler calls 'social intelligibility' (2007, 15). Khaldiya describes the social intelligibility of a refugee as an indescribable *feeling*, an elusive and personal feeling related to drastic identity shifts and to being placed-into-refugeeism and ejected beyond the limits of knowability of one's national space. 'The refugee,' Giorgio Agamben writes, 'is a border concept that radically calls into question the principles of the nation-state' (1995, 117). Following this line of thinking, we could understand the refugee camp as a noncitizen space offered to those whose subject-position moves from that of endangered citizen to that of refugee. It is this shift that Khaldiya vocalizes, finding herself inhabiting such a 'border concept.'

If we think about the refugee camp as the liminal space of otherness, a heterotopic space, to use Michel Foucault's term, we begin to see how Khaldiya marks it visually (heterotopias etymologically mean 'other places'; Foucault theorizes heterotopias as spaces 'outside of all spaces' [1986, 24]). In her film, we often see lines—vertical and horizontal ones (bars, electricity wires, window frames, clotheslines, poles) (figure 6.7)—that draw the spectatorial gaze and signal tropes of enclosure, division, and also potential rupture or breakage. This breakage materializes at the very end when her hand appears between the sheets of a white material, signalling a fissure, a crack, wanting to touch and

Figure 6.7. Khaldiya. *Lines.*

catch the moon into her palm. Shortly before the conclusion, when she mentions the weird angles, we see her camera moving along the floor and peeking
under the bed. Earlier in the film, through a subjective point of view, Khaldiya
is peeking at her siblings though a crack between her fingers (figure 6.8). The
'weird' angles she offers are thus tied to her perception, her attempt to record
how she *sees* her life in the camp and how that life is *felt*. And, as spectators,
we can deduce that it is felt askew—angled and lopsided—while the often-
visible lines (figure 6.7) point to the separation from the outside.

Figure 6.8. Khaldiya. *Cracks.*

We see the imagery of the moon also evoked in Walaa's short film *The Girl, Whose Shadow Reflects the Moon*. Sixteen-year-old Walaa tells her viewers about traumatic events she experienced when she still lived in Syria. She recreates the past predominantly through the imagery of shadows, flickering light, the sky, and the close-ups of her own hand. We see her hand touching various surfaces as her voiceover reveals fragmented stories of violence and dispossession. In contrast to Khaldiya's short, which reveals her exploration of the camp and shows us her siblings and her friends, Walaa's film is more conceptual. Its opening privileges her voiceover narrative about witnessing her friends' deaths from bullets in Syria while showing us her hand touching an unidentifiable surface (figure 6.9). This surface has a bright opening, and Walaa's hand appears to want to *feel* it, perhaps metaphorizing the falling bomb, or her friends' wounds. Her voice narrates: 'There was a bomb right over us but we were used to them coming from above us.'

These short experimental films produced in the camp might be described as video diaries that stand in opposition to media coverage by Western reporters who, as the young women claim, cannot capture their reality. Filming her siblings playing in the dirt, Khaldiya remembers that although they used to play with toys in Syria, they now can play only with their hands. In one of the shots featuring a starry sky, Walaa's hand touches a windowpane as if she were trying to touch the moon. Khaldiya's hand too is shown touching the windowpane marked by vertical frames. In yet another short by sixteen-year-old Syrian Muna, *Dreams Without Borders*, we see her hand touching water in the opening scene, showing us, yet again, a desire for a tactile experience

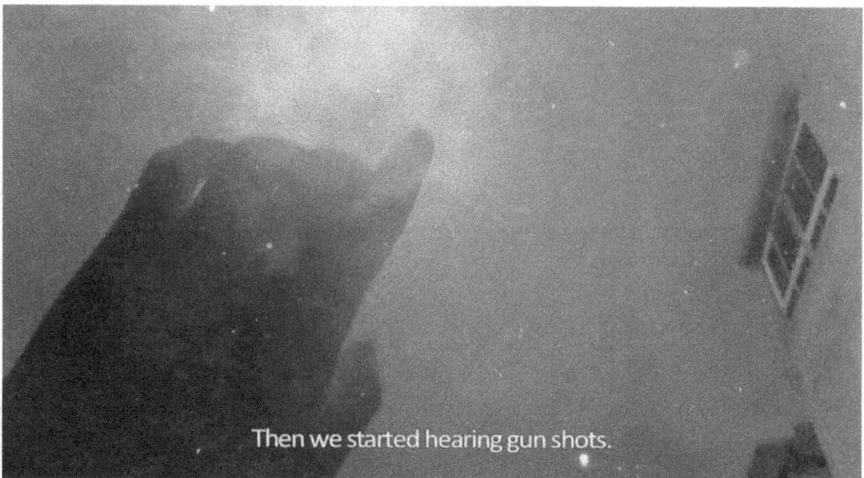

Figure 6.9. Walaa. *The Trope of Touching.*

Figure 6.10. Muna. *The Trope of Touching.*

(figure 6.10). She is filming on the rooftop (figure 6.11) and draws our attention to her own audibility. Her hand in water produces splashing sounds, her stomping feet in water offer more splashing sounds, and the repeated movement of her bracelets on her wrist produce rhythmic vibrations. We may think of those sounds as a need for being heard, being vocal, since moments later, Muna explains that she yearns for education and for camaraderie with her friends: 'At this point I don't share anything with any one. I just keep everything to myself.' 'When I was in Syria I had a drawing pad. When I would get mad I would just want to draw and then all my anger would go away,' narrates Muna. Much like Khaldiya's evocation of anger, in this short we also hear about female anger and its translation into art. As her hand above water illustrates (figure 6.10), tactility is not only about the sensation of feeling, but about an audible experience as well.

Indeed, fingers, hands, and touching—a desire for contact—form a compelling trope in these video diaries, asking the audience to contemplate the complexities of speaking from the inside to the outside. 'Since I started class all I can think of is filming. I started going outside just so I could film. I love to film on the roof. For example, when I am bothered and I want to just breathe, really, I just feel at peace,' claims Muna. As Walaa says: 'It's important for girls to bring things from inside to the outside. So many girls are afraid of speaking up. I hope that each young woman is able to express her inner self directly and indirectly, and that she can just break the world. It doesn't matter, just break it all over the place.'[13]

I don't know,
sometimes I like to dance by myself.

Figure 6.11.   Muna. *Dancing Hands*.

It is interesting that filmmaking, always already mediated, of course, is used here to 'break the world,' and 'break it all over the place.' Filmmaking functions metaphorically as a window (an object we see in *Another Kind of Girl* and in *The Girl, Whose Shadow Reflects the Moon* multiple times) to break through to the outside while also drawing our attention to the fact that windows are barriers, like the filmic screen itself. Considering both the imagery of the windows being touched and the moon 'being touched' as well (figure 6.12), we can see how touchability emerges as permissible and not

Figure 6.12.   Walaa. *Moon Touching*.

permissible, possible and not possible; windows are touchable and the moon is not. Touchability is thus represented as conflicted, aporetic, as a trope commenting on being inside, of the need to transfer tactility to the outside and the difficulties of doing just that. The repeated touching in these various shorts highlights the importance of hapticity—sensuous proximity, contiguity, contact, but also a profound separation—all commenting on the tactile experience of the refugee camp and the way it reconfigures and reshapes one's subjectivity. In the end, I would argue that touching points to the limits of knowability. As viewers, we might be moved, indeed 'touched' by the images and sounds, but the repeated emphasis on hands and touching reminds us of the epistemological limits of our *feeling* the camp. Perhaps, as viewers, all we are left with is *com-passion,* the way Jean-Luc Nancy envisioned it while talking about refugees—not altruism, not pity, not an identification even, but 'the disturbance of violent relatedness' (2000, xiii).

CODA: ON ANGER AND REFUGEEISM

'My fear of anger taught me nothing. Your fear of that anger will teach you nothing, also.' —Audre Lorde, *Sister Outsider* (1984)

Even though Khaldiya and Muna evoke anger indirectly, their comments prompt a reflection on the troubled intersection of refugeeism and anger, conjuring, as I have argued, the figure of an angry female refugee. Why should we even contemplate this uneasy intersection? And what does it have to do with artistic creation, participatory politics, and speaking-from-within, considering that anger is most often directed *at* refugees who, in many countries, are apprehended as unwanted and burdensome intruders while the figure of an angry refugee is typically conflated with terrorism? Is anger perhaps a viable emotionality—or a necessary impetus—to speak-from-within? Especially now, when the intense nationalistic and xenophobic logics shape social attitudes and public policies, should we, again, contemplate Judith Halberstam's question: 'When and why and how did rage disappear from the vocabulary of organized political activism?' (1993, 189). This question returns us to Audre Lorde's words, who, as a lesbian of colour, famously reflected on how anger can be a potent source of oppositional energy that could bring about radical change when facing racism. So many years later, despite various cultural prohibitions that cast anger as unhealthy, dangerous, and pathological, especially for women (and the stereotype of the angry black woman is particularly historically potent and hurtful), Lorde's words still resonate powerfully, reminding us that anger is a tool that women should utilize to create heightened awareness, to consider the value of a politicized anger and critical contestation. As she wrote, reclaiming anger: 'Black women are expected to use our anger only in the service of other people's salvation or learning. But that time is over' (Lorde 1984, 132).

Since Lorde's publication, other feminist critics have added their voices (Gay 2016, Halberstam 1993, hooks 1995, Lesage 1988, Marcus 1988), contributing to a history of a feminist discourse on anger. However, if feminist rage is something feared and often mocked (in order to belittle its power), then feminist immigrant rage is definitely a hard-core offense. We know that an immigrant is expected to be quiet and grateful, barely visible and barely audible but, at the same time, a hardworking body that pays off her debt to the host nation (Marciniak 2006). This unspoken but deeply ingrained mandate is especially applicable to immigrant or refugee women—and non-white foreign women are particularly vulnerable in this respect.

Despite the fact that Khaldiya and Muna acknowledge anger seemingly only in passing, they tap into this critical emotionality, which, as Lorde claimed, when 'focused with precision [. . .] can become a powerful source of energy serving progress and change' (1984, 127). We could certainly think of the video diaries I analysed as examples of such 'focused' anger, offering a 'powerful source of energy.' Being 'creative visionaries,' as Doggett calls them, they utilize their anger to offer deeply affective and intimate projects that take the viewers to the embodied insides of a refugee camp, albeit also conveying certain limits of intimacy between the camp and the viewer. Is anger then a potential motivator for participating in oppositional politics? As a scholar who, over the years, invested intellectual energies in validating various modalities of immigrant rage in different border zones, my answer is definitely yes.[14] Politicized anger allows us to comprehend the ethics of refugeeism differently—outside of the paradigm of a grateful and quiet refugee, who is expected to offer heart-warming stories of survival (see Nayeri 2017) and palatable narratives of gratitude.

In conclusion, it would be perhaps easy to argue that speaking-from-within is a more compelling mode of artistic expression then speaking-with because we hear the mediated voices of refugees themselves from the inside of the camp. While this is certainly a valid point, ultimately, these two different aesthetic tactics of speaking emerge as not easily comparable. The tension between these two modes in art-activist work registers as incommensurable, pointing to the difficulties and complexities of representing an ontological weight of refugeeism. Ultimately, it is the cumulative afterlife effects of such art and their relation to social protests that perhaps matter the most. As Jane Marcus aptly writes: 'Anger is *not* an anathema in art; it is a primary source of creative energy. Rage and savage indignation sear the hearts of female poets and female critics. . . . Out with it' (1988, 153). We could think of these various modes of speaking as 'outing' such aesthetically politicized rage through different modalities of representation. We could also think of such rage as a political category of intervention, which can influence our sensibilities and open us up to new ways of thinking about resistance to oppressive forms of phobic nationalisms and exclusionary practices of citizenship.

NOTES

1. See Marciniak 2017. I explored Ai's performative quality of the photograph further, placing it in the context of other contemporary artistic explorations of refugeeism, arguing that Ai's image can be apprehended as a powerful instantiation of a politics of mourning and a performance enunciating what Judith Butler calls 'grievability' (2009).

2. See Marciniak and Bennett 2018 for an analysis of *Human Flow*.

3. For a compelling overview of his work, see, for example, Klayman's 2012 documentary about Ai's life and work.

4. This is how Ai reflects on his internal displacement: 'I was born in 1957, the same year China purged more than 300,000 intellectuals, including writers, teachers, journalists and whoever dared to criticize the newly established communist government. As part of a series of campaigns led by what was known as the anti-rightist movement, these intellectuals were sent to labour camps for 're-education.' Because my father, Ai Qing, was the most renowned poet in China then, the government made a symbolic example of him. In 1958, my family was forced from our home in Beijing and banished to the most remote area of the country—we had no idea that this was the beginning of a very dark, long journey that would last for two decades' (Ai 2018).

5. Such issues of ethical utility of art involving the figure of the refugee often cause various controversies around identity politics (who has the moral 'right' to produce such art) and around the usability of refugees' stories for the advancement of artists' careers. M.I.A., for example, received criticism for exploiting the men she engaged in 'Borders,' for utilizing them as 'props for her art.' See, for example, Tom Murphy (2015).

6. For a scholarly mode of such engagements, see, for example, Horsti 2017b. She brings to light the mode of *seeing with* refugees: 'Film critics and film studies scholars rarely discuss the settings in which they watch a film and usually do not mention audience members other than themselves. In this article, I consider the context of watching a film and the conversations I had with my co-viewers, making this ethnographic encounter visible to the reader as I proceed with the film analysis. This experiment suggests that the practice of *seeing with* is important in the practice of listening to "unimaginable" experiences, including the silences that are part of the telling' (Horsti 2017b).

7. As Thompson explains, the Kerava house was itself a survivor of war: 'During the Winter War—a military conflict between the Soviet Union and Finland from 1939 to 1940—bombs fell into the property's garden, but the house and the family living there survived' (Thompson 2016).

8. I follow Frantz Fanon's notion of historicity here as 'details, anecdotes, stories' (1952, 91).

9. I approach the realm of experimental Arab video art not as a specialist of Arab media, but as a scholar and pedagogue of transnational cinema. In my work, I am invested in the aesthetics and politics of transnational cinema, particularly in representations of foreignness, immigration, exile, and refugeeism. I have been interested in the issues pertaining to national belonging or unbelonging, border crossings, liminality, and the construction of border zones as sites of contention.

10. http://anotherkindofgirl.com/about-the-workshops.

11. The young women typically use only their first names to protect their identities.

12. http://anotherkindofgirl.com/about-the-workshops.

13. http://anotherkindofgirl.com/about-the-workshops.

14. See Marciniak 2006, 2013, 2014.

Part III

AMBIGUITIES AND CONTESTATION IN SOCIAL MEDIA

Chapter Seven

Participatory Logistics from Below

The Role of Smartphones for Syrian Refugees

Sina Arnold and Stephan Görland

Since the summer of 2015, more than one million refugees have come to Germany, most of them from Syria.[1] Along with their histories, dreams, and future plans, almost all of them brought along one item: a smartphone. In public debates and the media, right-wing populist voices soon commented on this omnipresence, taking it as an indicator that refugees are not as needy as they claim to be. 'Weird . . . allegedly they are sooooo poor but have a mobile and money for their "escape,"' a Facebook user comments.[2] 'Now it's happenin' now the refugees are ringing the doorbell an demant money thenn they leave an get out the newst mobile [*sic*],' another complains.[3] Challenging these stereotypes, refugees and their supporters have pointed out that smartphones have become indispensable before, during, and after the process of forced migration. Several civil society initiatives have taken up this topic,[4] and some of them even started designing 'integration apps' for newly arrived refugees, adding to existing digital services provided by German cities and the state.[5] For several years, digital infrastructure has become relevant in different aspects of refugee aid worldwide, including education or in camps. 'For many, connectivity has become as critical for survival as food, water, and shelter' is the insight of a UNHCR study (Accenture and UNHCR 2016, 11). In this context, the German Ministry for Economic Collaboration and Development (BMZ) has pointed to the 'unused potentials' of digital media in improving the lives of refugees (Bundesministerium für wirtschaftliche Entwicklung und Zusammenarbeit (BMZ) 2016). At the same time, only a few empirical studies exist to answer questions about the specific digital needs of refugees.

In this chapter, we contribute to an understanding of the role that smartphones play for recently arrived Syrian refugees during and after their process of migration to Germany. Based on qualitative and quantitative data, we shed light on specific forms of 'migrant digitalities' (Trimikliniotis, Parsanoglou, and Tsianos 2015, 3) that enable different forms of participation. In that sense, the smartphone is analysed as a local object that expresses and, at the same time, shapes global relations and transnational migratory movements both into and within Europe. This chapter suggests that smartphones are digital tools that facilitate self-organization, greater autonomy, and increased participation among forced migrants in several ways: *During* the process of migration, they allow information seeking about the trip and the countries of arrival; help in navigating specific routes, thereby avoiding dangers including police, border patrols, and robbers; and aid in staying in touch with friends, family, and other migrants, creating digital travel mates. They can also be lifesavers through emergency call functions and reduce reliance on traffickers. *After* arrival in the country of destination, smartphones enable navigation of the new home area, both in the physical and the figurative sense, as well as various forms of participation. While functions such as translating, staying in touch with loved ones in the home country, or learning German are specific to the needs of newly arrived refugees, usage patterns between migrants and non-migrants increasingly align in Germany, pointing to a veritable post-migrant media use.

PREVIOUS STUDIES ON MOBILE MEDIA AND MIGRATION

Research has for a long time pointed to connectivity between refugees and other migrants through technological and digital means. Steven Vertovec (2004, 219) spoke of mobile-enabled cheap phone calls as 'the social glue of migrant transnationalism' as early as 2004, and Dana Diminescu (2008) has drawn up the image of the 'connected migrant.' These digital and communicative developments are expressions of what migration studies has termed the 'transnational turn' (Bojadžijev and Römhild 2014), whereby notions of fixed cultural entities as well as a 'methodological nationalism' (Beck and Grande 2010)—the idea that societies can only exist as nation-states, and a subsequent analysis falling back upon these 'national containers'—have increasingly been called into question.

While empirical research about the use and impact of mobile media during forced migration is relatively new, over the last few years, several papers have begun to analyse this specific phenomenon in different countries (e.g., Coddington and Mountz 2014; Harney 2013; Wall, Campbell, and Janbek 2015; Witteborn 2015; Gillespie et al. 2016; Accenture and UNHCR 2016; Lim, Bork-Hüffer, and Yeoh 2016; Andrade and Doolin 2016).

Within Germany, different projects have addressed forced migration and integration with and through mobile phones. Most of these were qualitative (Kutscher and Kreß 2015; Fiedler 2016; Karnowski, Springer, and Herzer 2016; Krasnova and AbuJarour 2017), and one draws on a representative quantitative survey (Richter, Kunst, and Emmer 2016). There is also one qualitative project in Austria with comparable research questions (Kaufmann 2016). All projects focused on different stages of migration with a time-based tripartite division: description of media use *before*, *during*, and *after* the process of migration, and a subsequent comparison of these stages, usually showing that 'journey and integration in a hosting society represent two different processes' (Krasnova and AbuJarour 2017, 1796). Furthermore, most of the studies have specific topics, such as identity (Karnowski, Springer, and Herzer 2016); expectations towards Germany (Richter, Kunst, and Emmer 2016); social inclusion in the new society (Krasnova and AbuJarour 2017); media use during the journey (Kaufmann 2016); adolescents (Kutscher and Kreß 2015); or according to the uses-and-gratification approach, deeper searched gratifications (Fiedler 2016). All of them emphasize the importance and evidence of mobile (social) media and connectivity for migration and diaspora communication and self-presentation, as well as the value for integration into the arrival society. By comparison, this chapter focuses on the logistical character of the mobile phone through an actor-focused perspective, thus bringing in a new focus via the concept of logistics. Moreover, this very perspective can show how the phone becomes not just a tool for *integration* into the host society—a theoretical approach that several of the abovementioned studies take—but rather a means for active *participation*. We will come back to this aspect in our conclusions.

METHODOLOGY AND RESEARCH QUESTIONS

Based on an empirical study conducted between January and December 2016 in Berlin—where ninety thousand refugees arrived in 2015 alone (Nolan and Graham-Harrison 2015)—this chapter presents the findings of fifteen qualitative interviews with Syrian refugees as well as a quantitative survey, thus making it the first mixed-methods study on this topic in Germany, to our knowledge. The qualitative interviews were conducted between May and September 2016. Questions focused on the respondents' migration history, their present living circumstances in Germany, and their smartphone usage patterns in their home country, during the trip, and after arrival. The respondents were between 16 and 36 years old (mean age: 28) and came from different educational backgrounds. Seven of them were male, eight female, and all of them had arrived in Germany between August and November 2015. Five interviews were conducted with the help of an Arabic translator, the rest in English. On average, they lasted between 50 and 60 minutes. Pursuing forms of 'digital ethnography' (Pink et al. 2015), we additionally followed relevant Facebook groups and YouTube channels by and for Syrian refugees. We also asked respondents to provide screenshots showing the apps they used and to fill out maps showing their phones' most important usage in different countries (e.g., stages of the migration process). In a second stage of the project, we passed out survey questionnaires to 95 participants (mean age: 30, one-third female, two-thirds male) in two different refugee shelters in Berlin. This was done with the help of an Arabic-speaking research assistant, who addressed potential interview partners, assisted them with unclear questions, and passed out shopping vouchers as a form of a small gratification.[6] These data were gathered in December 2016. Based on our findings in the qualitative interviews, the focus here was on (1) the general usage of the mobile phone, (2) questions about appropriation and assessment of media, and (3) so-called integration apps. These are mobile phone apps that are supposed to help migrants orient themselves in the new society: to better understand local customs and gain access to resources, thus enabling more active participation in the new location. Subsequently, the quantitative data was analysed with the help of SPSS software. Because of the small quantitative sample, we only present descriptive findings in this chapter and no inferential statistics. The qualitative data were fed into the qualitative data analysis software MAXQDA and subsequently coded. While neither the qualitative nor the quantitative interviews are representative, both can be an indicator for current trends within refugee populations in Germany.

Our findings are informed by focusing on the logistics behind media use. Understood as 'the art and science of building networked relations in ways that promote transport, communication, and economic efficiencies' (Mezzadra and Neilson 2013, 12), logistics is more than an economic principle and has in recent years become a useful concept in studying migration (Arnold, Bojadžijev, and Apicella 2018). A focus on logistics enables an understanding of underlying communication networks, usage patterns, and functions that promote refugees' journeys. This focus is also a response to the current 'logistification' of border control (Mezzadra 2017), (i.e., the increased surveillance through digital means in combination with the externalization of European borders in hotspots and the channelling of migrant flows). This 'logistics from above' is answered by refugees with a 'logistics from below' that coordinates processes against these developments.

Key Findings

It is safe to say that smartphones play a key role in contemporary processes of forced migration. In the words of one twenty-four-year-old interview partner, 'The phone is the only way to come here . . . 99 percent you have to have a phone, and internet. Without it? You're lost, you will die!'[7] This importance was also highlighted by all of the abovementioned studies, or as captured in a response reported to Kutschner and Kreß (2015): 'Internet is the same as food.' Furthermore, refugees' mobile media use within the host country does not show significant differences compared to the majority of German society. Younger Syrian migrants in particular use their mobile phones similarly to German youth (for German mobile media statistics, e.g., Koch and Frees 2016), that is, mainly for social coordination, micro-coordination (Ling and Lai 2016)—that is, daily life coordination through mobile phones via chatting, sending photos, and so on—and information seeking, as well as entertainment. As shown in table 7.1, social networks like Facebook, WhatsApp, or Viber are particularly popular among Syrian refugees, in addition to some migration-specific functions, such as language courses, praying apps, or the digital Koran.

Table 7.1. **Regularly used services during all parts of the journey (N = 95). Table constructed by authors.**

Services	Mentions (%)
Messenger (e.g., WhatsApp)	82
Facebook	82
Phone calls	79
Voice messages	70
Maps	69
Reading the news	65
Camera	64
Google search	64
Language course	57
Watching movies and TV shows	57
E-mail	53
Listening to music	52
Koran	45
Games	38
Praying app	38
Photo app (such as Instagram)	36
Online shopping	31
Twitter	20
Online dating	17
Online banking	14
Snapchat	13

Table 7.2.   Most popular apps before, during, and after migration (N = 95). Table constructed by authors.

Ranking	Before Migration	During Migration	After Migration
1	WhatsApp	WhatsApp	WhatsApp
2	Facebook	Maps/location-based services	Facebook
3	Viber	Facebook	Other messenger
4	Other messenger	Viber	Language course/translator
5	Phone call	Phone call	Instagram

Based on previous studies with the threefold division into *before*, *during*, and *after* migration (e.g., Karnowski, Springer, and Herzer 2016; Krasnova and AbuJarour 2017), we also asked about the five most used apps during these different stages. As table 7.2 shows,[8] there are three main differences. First, during migration, location-based functions are more important. Refugees check and send their location often via mobile phones in order to orient themselves and meet each other. Second, after migration, language courses and translator apps appear in the usage patterns, as newcomers want to learn and understand German. In addition, the waiting time for language courses, at the time of writing, often amounted to several months, thus causing a need for self-organized learning. Third, after migration, refugees first started to use Instagram, a social network for pictures. It fits well with some statements from the qualitative interviews, like Kadir's, a twenty-year-old: 'Yeah, [I take pictures] but also not all of the time selfies. Sometimes, I take normal pictures, natural pictures: This is the snow. This is the river. This is the art and everything.' Instagram is a way to show their new lives in the host country to relatives and friends. However, apart from these small changes in usage patterns, there is no general difference between the individual media usage patterns in the host and origin country: The primary mentions of social networks and social messengers during all three stages shows the importance of mobile phones for social cohesion, particularly for young people, in different countries. According to Jensen (2013), the context may change, but the social interaction persists.

Starting from an actor-focused perspective, we categorized the main functions of smartphones as three different forms of 'mobile logistics of migration': *maintenance logistics, coordination logistics*, and *orientation logistics*. These are important in different ways during different stages of the trip. In other words, there is an inherent temporal dimension in terms of which form becomes important at what point.

(a) Maintenance Logistics

Maintenance logistics includes answers to those challenges that arise from the immediate process of migration, which are mainly physical. It includes, first of all, the very basic challenge of protecting the phone against the elements (salt water, sand, rain, etc.). 'I was afraid, because if it falls in the water I'm gonna freak out. . . . So I kept it and put it in plastic bags.' remembers twenty-two-year-old Mohammad. Secondly, the phone needs to be charged on the long journey. Most refugees use external batteries to do this. Arriving in a new village, city, or camp, they report the need to find electricity for recharging. Thirdly, SIM cards need to be found for each new country of transit. Most of our interview partners came along the so-called Balkan Route via Turkey, Greece, Macedonia, Hungary, and Austria and thus 'bought in every country a new SIM card' (Lya, 22). These three areas of maintenance logistics provide the 'groundwork' for maintaining network connections and perpetuating a state of *always on,* even while on a dangerous journey.

(b) Coordination Logistics

In addition to maintenance logistics, coordination logistics is relevant to gain information and support communication on the trip. It provides the digital information needed to navigate the physical environment. Initially, this means navigation in unknown terrain with the help of map apps. While Google Maps was most widely used—'Absolutely, Google Maps I used most,' reports twenty-seven-year-old Zada—others such as maps.me were also deemed useful. Navigation, however, also happened in an interactive fashion, whereby people sent each other the best routes, marked their specific locations, or communicated in Facebook groups about their experiences and how to travel through various countries. Already, the smartphone was used as a tool for participation, albeit in fluctuating circumstances. The digital tool enables a quick change of these circumstances and thus a form of *alterable* participation. Twenty-five-year-old Abdul remembers: 'My cousin communicates with a lot of other people how to go on . . . WhatsApp and using the GPS. And this is the most important thing, of course. And also, we said which city, which area we have to go. So we wrote it in WhatsApp and sent it to the others.' Navigation also becomes a central element in dangerous situations: One interview partner reported losing his brother near the Greek-Macedonian border in the middle of turbulences and used the WhatsApp 'position pin' to locate him in the middle of a big crowd along the border fence. In the most extreme cases, navigation is a matter of life or death, such as in sending distress signals from boats adrift in the Mediterranean Sea.[9]

Second, networking is a key form of coordination logistics on the trip, happening in different and flexible ways. One interview partner, for example, reported travelling with a group of about seventy people in the Greece/Macedonia border regions. This group size provided protection against burglars and alleged organ traffickers. After arriving in Serbia, the group broke up into ten subgroups with five to ten people each because then the central challenge was to take cover from the police, making smaller groups more useful. In both locations, the same people remained networked. The subgroup leaders consistently sent their location via phone to each other, mostly via WhatsApp. Often, leaders were chosen because they had the newest smartphones and the fastest mobile data. What can be observed is a flexible, almost 'just-in-time migration' able to respond to the flexible changes in the border openings and closings that happened in Europe in 2015. The smartphone enabled a constant microcoordination within these situations—in this case, even via transnational realtime communication.

Lastly, coordination logistics takes the form of imparting one's status to and generally communicating with friends and family. Twenty-one-year-old Charda navigated across the Mediterranean with her three younger cousins. Her parents were already in Germany and followed their daughter's trip with the help of the phone in real time, every step of the way: When the motor went out in the little boat Charda and her cousins were on, the family called; when they did not know where to go, her father checked the maps. Charda remembers having successfully crossed the sea: 'When I get to Greece, I had to call everybody that we are safe. We didn't die.' Imparting one's status also means forms of documentation, such as photos and videos, Facebook posts showing which hostel one stayed at, what food one ate, or what island one arrived at.

(c) Orientation Logistics

Finally, forms of orientation logistics become particularly relevant after arrival, where the smartphone becomes 'a window to the world,' as a young woman from Aleppo put it. This includes spatial orientation, even when there is little knowledge of the language and script. Newcomers, however, find creative means. For example, refugees report sending each other photos of the place where they are supposed to meet (e.g., a street corner or a shop front). Others send photos of subway arrival times while standing on a platform to let a friend know they are going to be late. In additional, linguistic orientation becomes a key element. Google Translate helps people translate everyday interactions in real time. It also allows Muslim users to scan food ingredients in supermarkets and translate them instantly to decide if a product is halal or not. Learning German is of particular importance, even before arrival: 'I have an app in Turkey I downloaded for learning languages,' Shadia from Syria remembered. One interview partner compared his language learning apps to the German courses he also attended and concluded: 'Right now I learned in internet more than in school.' Others use YouTube tutorials. Lastly, social orientation is central, mostly in the form of communication with friends and relatives in Germany or in the country of origin. This can sometimes prove to be difficult due to a form of asynchronous digitalization. In Syria, internet or electricity were regularly cut off due to the war, or the devices were not as new as those of the refugees, thus causing compatibility problems. Social orientation with other refugees often happened via self-organized Facebook groups with names such as 'Syrians in Germany,' where people posted German bureaucratic documents and helped in translating or sharing their experiences of how to best react.[10]

DIGITAL AUTONOMY, DIGITAL CITIZENS

Generally, smartphones increase a subjective feeling of autonomy among refugees while coordinating the trip. One Syrian claims: 'Yes it has helped me to be more independent because you can't all the time ask the people, sometimes I need to know by myself to what should I do there. So yeah, the phone has helped me a lot to be independent in my journey.' This indicates independence from other migrants, but also from traffickers. Some of them advertise their services on Facebook, in often short-lived groups with names such as 'Trips to Greece from Izmir.' Sometimes, traffickers present themselves as travel agents, with photos of happy customers safely arriving in the sunset.[11] This advertising, however, also creates systems for comparing and monitoring prices and services. Moreover, there are Facebook groups such as 'Smuggle Yourself to Europe without a Trafficker' that help in navigating part of the trip, particularly the land routes, alone. Not only traffickers, but also others, exploit refugees' vulnerability. For example, when a young woman from Aleppo had to take a taxi in Greece to the Macedonian border, she realized, via her GPS function on her map app, that the driver was taking a longer route, in the opposite direction, and she was able to stop him. In the case of assaults, phones can aid in organizing help: one interview partner reported that, after getting robbed in Hungary, he was able to have his uncle send money via Western Union's mobile money transfer service.

Finally, usage patterns also demonstrate how refugees gain more autonomy towards state agencies or border patrols via information and communications technology (ICT). In September 2015, for example, the Hungarian government wanted to send refugees back to a camp by train, but police officers claimed that they were to be brought to Austria and Germany (Nolan and Graham-Harrison 2015). Those remaining on the platform were able to call and warn the passengers in the already departed train about this misinformation, enabling them to leave the train en route and continue to Austria on foot instead (Brunwasser 2015).

The basic function of increased autonomy via mobile devices continues after arrival. For example, the use of digital platforms opens up possibilities for political organizing, like after the 2015/2016 New Year's Eve in Cologne. That night, large groups of men sexually assaulted women in front of the main train station, with the media mostly accusing refugees and other migrants of these acts. Shortly after that, self-organized Facebook groups such as 'Syrians against Sexism' sprang up, in which several thousand members condemned the attacks against women, and, via the digital platform, organized a real-time rally.[12] Refugees, therefore, used digital technologies and social networks for participating in urban space (Trimikliniotis, Parsanoglou, and Tsianos 2015), reminding us that digital networks are also a form of social practice that inscribes itself into real geographies. Moreover, digital platforms enable forms of participation for newcomers who are not yet part of an established civil society. They help to initiate bottom-up processes of participation, starting from the user and the logistics he or she needs. If *participation is power* (Carpentier 2012), digital platforms help those without citizenship to claim rights and become 'digital citizens' (Isin and Ruppert 2015). Digital means can also help to increase refugees' agency vis-à-vis the state and bureaucracy: at the State Office for Health and Social Affairs (Landesamt für Gesundheit und Soziales, LaGeSo) (the place for initial registrations in Berlin), which became known for having unbearable overcrowding, one woman reported taking photos of the number on display to prove that it really was her turn, after she had been unrightfully rejected despite having a valid number.

To sum up, smartphone use among refugees points to the high level of collective self-empowerment enabled through these devices, resulting in heightened independence from actors such as smugglers, state agencies, or border patrols in various situations. The phone therefore helps to contribute to a certain 'autonomy of migration,' to use an approach from critical migration studies that puts agency centre stage (Mezzadra 2011).

However, the increased use of information technology brings with it certain digitized dangers, which points at systematic constraints to participation attempts, let alone autonomy. The abovementioned logistification and externalization of European borders is largely enabled through digital means. In a general attempt to digitally control refugees, institutions like the UNHCR have been using biometric data to identify refugees for well over a decade (Jacobsen 2015). In Europe, refugees are registered in EURO-DAC, the European fingerprint database, which will possibly be extended to include other biometric identifiers. European expenses for technological border control (drones, olfactory sensors, border patrol robots, etc.) have risen over the last few years (Proctor 2015). Gillespie et al. (2016, 29f.), for example, report that soldiers have asked refugees for Facebook passwords on the Syrian border in order to find out which political side they are on. In Austria, refugees are forced to hand over their mobile phone when applying for asylum; mobile phone data will subsequently be used to verify the applicant's identity (Young-Powell 2017). In Germany, mobile phones are increasingly central for these procedures as well, with new technology enabling the readout of geodata (e.g., locations) for the German Ministry for Migration and Refugees (BAMF). Between September and December 2017 alone, five thousand mobile phone datasets have been read, stored, and kept in a 'data safe' in case individual verifications will be necessary (Schneider 2017). In this context, Vassilis Tsianos and Brigitta Kuster (2010) have spoken about 'Digital Deportability,' meaning the vulnerability and dangers that arise from an increase in digital databases monitoring migrant movements. While the role of smartphones for refugees points to the basic function of increasing autonomy in the process of migration, these digitalized dangers need therefore to be critically monitored as well.

POST-MIGRANT MEDIA USE

The 'connected migrant' (Diminescu 2008) is a reality. Among Syrian refugees arriving in Berlin since 2015, almost everyone had a smartphone and reported that it played a significant role in their migration process. Following Vertovec (2004), the role of cheap phone calls has been replaced by other functions such as messenger services and video calls, making permanent connectivity a 'new social glue of migrant transnationalism.' In the spirit of Arjun Appadurai's approach to material culture, his notion of 'the social life of things' (2013) can be applied to this very object: 'The social life of smartphones' plays a specific role for people on the move. 'Without it, I wouldn't move an inch,' said one interview partner, indicating almost a form of agency on the part of the object, which in turn enables the human's movement and mobility. As the analysis showed, certain uses, such as forming WhatsApp groups to navigate the Balkan Route, or joining Facebook groups to help each other translate German bureaucratic documents, are examples of veritable 'migrant digitalities' (Trimikliniotis, Parsanoglou, and Tsianos 2015, 3), forms of mobile-mediated self-empowerment. At the same time, the determining factor for these usage patterns is not an alleged 'Syrian' or 'Muslim' culture, but is driven by the specific needs created by the situation of (forced) migration and arrival, in other words *situational* needs, not cultural ones. Not surprisingly, the usage patterns of young Syrians are not substantially different from those of young Germans: In our interviews, Syrian refugees not only missed their family in Aleppo, but also their Xbox. They talked about the latest version of computer games like *Need for Speed* or *Call of Duty*. The following screenshots from the interview partners' smartphones illustrate this. Figure 7.1 shows Snapchat and an MP3 Downloader, used for everyday interaction and entertainment. Figure 7.2 shows the dating app Loovoo.[13] Figure 7.3 shows the latest version of Pokemon Go; the young woman had downloaded it in Syria from a US server and brought it via her phone across the Mediterranean even before the version was released in Germany.[14]

When we compare the media use of our sample of young Syrian refugees (with an average age of twenty-eight) with that of young Germans, similar usage patterns are represented in the most used apps (table 7.1): When it comes to media use, a twenty-year-old from Berlin has more in common with a twenty-year-old from Aleppo than with a fifty-year-old from Munich. Both of their daily lives show a high level of mediatization (Krotz 2001),

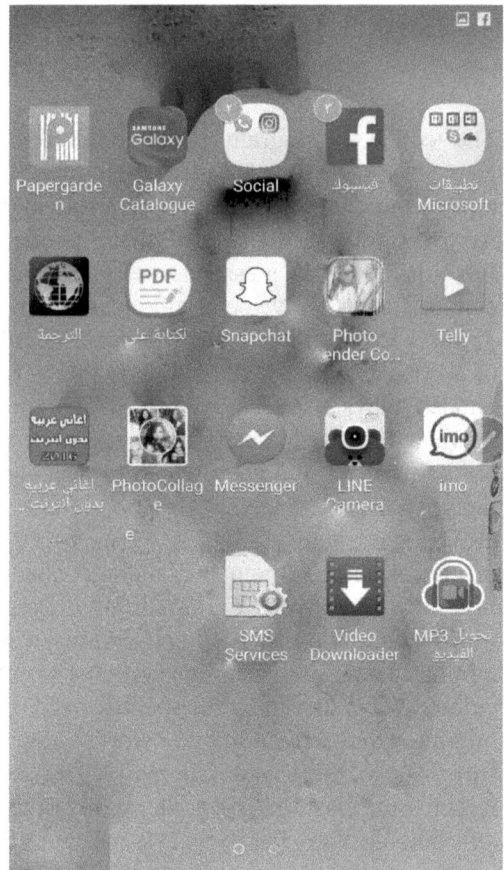

Figure 7.1. Screenshot 1 from an interview partner's phone. Photo by authors.

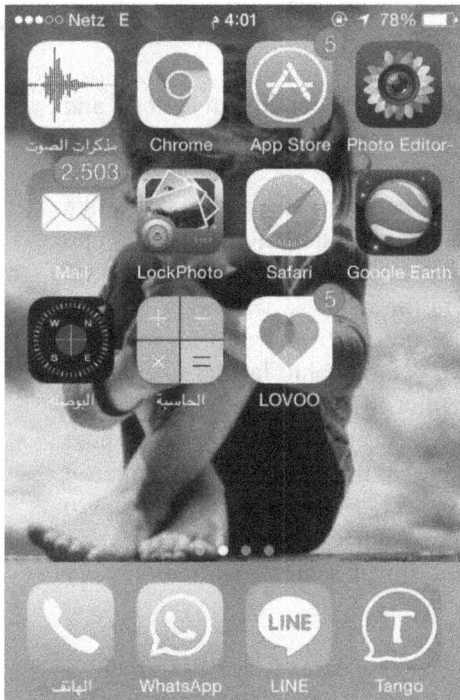

Figure 7.2. Screenshot 2 from an interview partner's phone. Photo by authors.

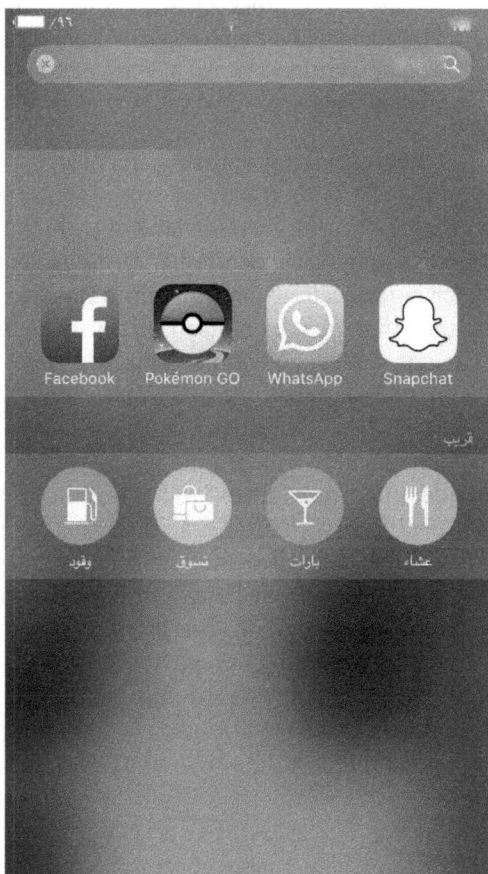

Figure 7.3. Screenshot 3 from an interview partner's phone. Photo by authors.

where mobile media becomes an omnipresent companion for adolescents and young adults. These similarities are an expression of veritable 'post-migrant' (Foroutan 2016) usage patterns. In a country in which about one-fifth of the overall population has a so-called migration background—and in cities like Frankfurt, almost 75 percent of all children under the age of six (Schupp 2015, 158)—identities and lifestyles are increasingly entangled, mixed, and hybridized. The distinction between 'them' and 'us' is becoming blurred, and factors influencing specific media use are much more to be found in subcultural and political affiliations and in demographic factors like age or education.[15] The findings about above-mentioned 'integration apps' emphasize this fact: only 11 of 95 refugees (12 percent) used one or more of these apps. Most did not see a significant use value for their daily life, a scepticism mirrored in international findings by Gillespie et al. (2016, 5), which point to the inefficiencies of many digital resources designed for refugees.[16] Twenty-five-year-old Danyal summarizes his criticism of some apps' unnecessary focus on 'cultural education':

> They give you the information about integration in here. So it's like mostly talking about the cultures, how there are people living here. And when you are in the situation after ten months, nine months, you will see how people, they are living. And you would get used to these kind of groups.

A homogenizing approach focusing on an alleged group identity like 'the refugees' is therefore missing the important aspects. One interview partner explicitly criticizes this label by which he is addressed in Germany. He perceives himself much rather as an involuntarily 'traveller' who was forced to change locations and therefore has specific needs in a new country. Other than that, he sees himself primarily as an IT developer, student, fan of computer games, and so on. This is a good reminder that, while due to specific situational needs we can—and should—analyse the emergence of 'migrant digitalities,' these will change and maybe even cease to exist when the situation changes. Rather than taking 'refugees,' 'Syrians,' or 'Muslims' as given identities, research as well as political intervention needs to take situationally specific usage patterns as their starting point. Finally, our findings illustrate how the phone becomes a means for integration in the host society, as it helps to navigate the challenges of everyday life in terms of bureaucracy, relationships, or navigation. But more than that, the device and its digital platforms enable something much more active: rather than blending into existing societal structures—whether on the move or in the host society—refugees actively participate in and, in turn, alter them. Be it through circumventing borders and finding new routes for arriving or forming networks of mutual support, or for new political actors in the civil society, smartphones have become tools for a participatory logistics from below.

NOTES

1. Between the summer of 2015 and the summer of 2017, about 1.2 million refugees came to Germany, more than ever before in a comparable period in the country's history (Bundesministerium des Innern 2016, 2017; Bundesamt für Migration und Flüchtlinge, 2017). This research project was funded by the Federal Government Commissioner for Migration, Refugees, and Integration as well as by the Federal Chancellery Germany.

2. https://www.facebook.com/permalink.php?story_fbid=271801543276589 &id=100013402368171 (accessed March 22, 2017, page is deleted). For a further media analysis cf. Gillespie et al. (2016, 9).

3. https://www.facebook.com/plugins/post.php?href=https%3A%2F%2Fwww .facebook.com%2Fpermalink.php%3Fstory_fbid%3D1671169523184169%26id %3D100008734126749& (accessed March 22, 2017, page is deleted).

4. Among them, events such as 'Refugee Hackathon' (http://refugeehackathon .de/) or 'Civil Society 4.0—Refugees and Digital Self Organization' (https://www .hkw.de/en/programm/projekte/2016/civil_society_4_0/civil_society_4_0_start.php); or apps/blogs such as 'Arriving in Berlin—A Map made by Refugees' (https://arriv ing-in-berlin.de/), RefugeeHub (http://refhub.de/english/blog/), or the European-wide Refugee Info (https://www.refugee.info/; all accessed March 1, 2018).

5. E.g., 'Ankommen in Deutschland,' an app by, among others, the Federal Office for Migration and Refugees, or with a more regional focus, the app 'Welcome App Germany' (Bundesamt für Migration und Flüchtlinge, 2016; Saxonia Systems AG and Heinrich & Reuter Solutions, 2018).

6. Thank you to Samira Abbas for her help with this project.

7. All quotes are taken from the interview partners in the abovementioned study. All names have been anonymized.

8. The differences in the usage range between tables 7.1 and 7.2 are due to the different character of the questions: In table 7.1, we asked open questions, in table 7.2 closed questions.

9. The activist organization Watch the Med Alarm Phone responds to this function by providing an alarm number to support rescue operations (cf. Stierl 2016).

10. While we focus on the logistics behind the use, there are certainly more functions, including spiritual support provided by apps with names such as 'Islamic Compass.'

11. Cf. (السفر من ازمير الى اليونان Facebook page).

12. Cf. (Wolf 2016; Syrer gegen Sexismus Facebook page).

13. Dating apps have a similar function as for young people from Germany—finding long- and short-term partners. However, Carolin Wiedemann (2016) suggests that the fact that primarily looks are important in some of these apps like

Tinder makes self-representation in social networks easier for young refugees, given that they are often in economically precarious situations and living in a society characterized by racist attitudes—two factors that make finding a partner in real life not necessarily easy.

14. All images have been altered to conceal identities.

15. This is exemplified by the studies undertaken by the Sinus Institute which show the 'hazy relations of everyday reality' (Sinus 2017, translation S.A./S.G, i.e., the fluid borders between different 'migrant milieus' with no causality between an alleged 'culture of origin' and lifestyle/milieu choices).

16. With a small number of exceptions, most of these apps were computed 'top down' from programmers without a migration experience. For an overview of good-practice suggestions for designing digital resources for refugees, see Gillespie et al. (2016, 14ff). Key components of value include that these resources are user centered, secure, and private, accessible, sustainable, trusted, and regularly updated.

Chapter Eight

'It Only Takes Two Minutes'

The So-Called Migration Crisis and Facebook as Civic Infrastructure

Anne Kaun and Julie Uldam

The so-called *migration* crisis in 2015 has led to challenges in migration des-tination countries such as Germany, Sweden, and Denmark. During this time, volunteer-led initiatives provided urgent relief and played a crucial role in meeting the needs of arriving migrants. The work of the volunteers in central train stations and transition shelters was mainly organized with the help of Facebook, both in terms of inward and outward communication. This chapter examines the role of social media for civic participation via studying Swedish volunteer initiatives that emerged in the context of the 'crisis' that reached a peak in 2015. Theoretically, this case study draws on an analytical framework for civic engagement and participation in social media by combining ques-tions of power relations, technological affordances, practices, and discourses. Furthermore, in this chapter, we relate the discussion of civic engagement, participation, and social media to insights from infrastructure studies to theorize the role of Facebook and its implications for volunteer activities. This analysis focuses particularly on temporal affordances of social media in coordinating volunteer work and critically questions the emerging position of Facebook as a civic infrastructure in volunteer organizing.

In 2015, the United Nations Refugee Agency (UNHCR) reported that there were approximately 60 million refugees worldwide (Forsberg 2015). In Sweden, a total of 163,000 people were registered as asylum seekers in 2015. The number of migrants applying for asylum in Sweden reached its peak in November 2015, with almost 40,000 applicants. The same month, Sweden reinstated temporary passport controls at the Danish border, and consequently, these numbers dropped significantly. In November 2016, only around four hundred people applied for asylum in Sweden. These numbers, however, do not tell the stories of long journeys involving risky boat trips, long marches across different countries, and the uncertainty of reaching the destination. They also do not speak of the experience of finally arriving in the new country and the first hours and days spent there. At the same time, these numbers are only indicative of how many refugees reached Sweden in 2015, not of how many actually stayed, since many refugees never registered and considered Sweden to be a transit country on their way to Finland or Norway. Sweden's status as a transit country contributed to the importance of volunteer initiatives to meet the urgent needs of arriving refugees because state institutions argued that they could only support people who officially registered and applied for asylum in Sweden. Strategic transportation hubs such as the central train stations in Malmö and Stockholm became the physical sites of urgent relief primarily where volunteers, predominantly organized through Facebook groups and pages, provided much-needed assistance. Even state officials and municipalities frequently referred arriving migrants to central Facebook groups and pages for urgent help (Statens offentliga utredningar (SOU) 2017, 12).

The groups explored in this chapter share this commonality: Facebook was used as an organizational infrastructure to coordinate their volunteering efforts. The reasons for turning to Facebook can be summarized through one telling quote of one of our informants:

> It only takes like two minutes. The thing that took most time was finding a picture. (Interview 2016-09-16)[1]

This is how the initiator of the group 'We who welcome refugees at Stockholm's central station' describes the initial setting up of the Facebook group. For this young woman, the ease of Facebook in terms of coordination, mobilization, and organization made it an essential infrastructure for her volunteer initiative. Facebook has become part of the everyday life of many Swedes, with 70 percent of internet users visiting the platform, at least from time to time (Findahl and Davidsson 2015). It is therefore not surprising that many people engaged in volunteer refugee activism turned to Facebook as a key platform for coordinating their help efforts. During the interviews that we conducted as part of a larger project on volunteer activism in the context of the so-called migration crisis, it was apparent that Facebook was seen as the only platform where the goals of synchronizing volunteer work and financial donations could be met in a cost- and time-efficient manner.

Now, two years later, organizers commemorate their work of 2015, partly inspired by Facebook's own memory features such as *on that day*. One post by one organizer reminds her followers, friends, and people involved with her Facebook initiative not only of the feelings back then and how the events still have repercussions in her daily life, but also of the entanglement of memories with the Facebook infrastructure:

> Today it has been two years since we started to take care of refugees at Stockholm Central Station. I remember the shock when thousands of people suddenly joined my clumsy little FB-group and through self-organising took care of food, a roof over the head, transport, clothes, legal advice, train tickets and much more for those who came. And how different media appeared on the first day and I had to stand there and speak in TV and to newspapers and other things, completely unprepared and without make-up and in weird clothes, haha. I remember all the love I got from relatives and friends, and today the comments are re-appearing in my 'on-this-day'-feed and warm my heart. (Facebook post, 8 September 2017, shared with friends and tagged people)[2]

Obviously, the situation for migrants in Sweden has changed significantly since 2015, and so have the initiatives to support them. Stricter migration policies led to a steep decline in numbers of arriving migrants. As a result, the initiatives that were set up to provide urgent relief had to rethink their missions. At the same time, the public discourse had changed considerably since the fall of 2015. Initially, individual stories of migrants arriving in Sweden and presenting the lived experience of the 'refugee crisis' were the focus; instead, the discourse now has shifted towards bureaucratic questions on how to handle the influx, which represents a crisis for the Swedish state (Strömbäck 2016).

These shifts and changes over time play a role in this chapter, but rather than asking what has changed in the representation of the refugee crisis, we are interested in the structuring aspects of Facebook as a communication infrastructure for civic engagement and participation. We are drawing on the three fields of infrastructure studies, studies of time and the media, as well as civic engagement research to theorize and empirically investigate the relationship between media infrastructures, on the one hand, and civic engagement and participation, on the other.

CIVIC PARTICIPATION, TEMPORAL AFFORDANCES, AND FACEBOOK AS CIVIC INFRASTRUCTURE IN POST-MIGRANT SWEDEN

Before discussing Facebook's role as civic infrastructure, we need to situate volunteer organizing for migrants within the realm of civic participation. In the early 2000s, a discourse of civic hibernation was prevalent in studies of civic culture, civic engagement, and participation. Young people in particular seemed to be increasingly passive toward politics. However, in the aftermath of the financial crisis starting in 2008, the year 2011 emerged as the year of protest (Kaun 2016) and the 'civic hibernation' of the early 2000s seemed to have ended (Solomon 2011). In reaction to austerity measures implemented to tackle the euro crisis, a wave of civic protests and disobedience washed over Europe. In the United Kingdom, Germany, France, Lithuania, Latvia, and Greece, among others, young and old took to the streets in broad solidarity with economically disenfranchised groups throughout Europe to voice their opinions and contradict the narratives of the 'withdrawn consumer citizen.' These waves of protest have led to rethinking civic culture and participation particularly. In that context, social media seemed to have lowered the threshold for political action. We welcome the re-evaluation of civic participation, but suggest a more nuanced approach that aligns with an emerging field of critical studies of participation and social media (see e.g., Dencik and Leistert 2015).

Our approach of studying civic participation and social media is based on the idea that democracy is not understood in its minimalist expression, which starts and ends with electing representatives, but in its 'maximalist' form, namely, a balanced relationship between representation and participation. Such a balanced relationship reflects the continuous will to broaden participation, while applying a definition of the *political* as being inherent in the *social*. This suggests multidirectional participation and enhances difference and heterogeneity (Carpentier 2011). Based on that understanding and following Peter Dahlgren (2009), we understand civic engagement as a subjective state that is the prerequisite for participation: 'For engagement to become embodied in participation and thereby give rise to civic agency there must be some connection to practical, do-able activities, where citizens can feel empowered' (80). This definition of participation includes community-driven initiatives such as print-shop collectives, community radio, local energy provision, and protest and peace camps such as *Occupy* and *Greenham Common*, but also NGO campaigning and direct action (Baines 2016; Böhm, Spicer, and Fleming 2008; Cammaerts 2009; Feigenbaum, Frenzel, and Mc-Curdy 2013) as well as the forms of participation we focus on in this chapter, namely, volunteering to support arriving migrants. Focusing on volunteering to support arriving migrants allows us to not only capture a specific form of civic participation, but also to explore forms of negotiating the implications of post-migrant societies, namely, the development of ways of living together from bottom up rather than top down.

We define 'volunteering' as a form of participation that requires civic engagement as a subjective state or form of attention to materialize. Elsewhere (Kaun and Uldam 2017; Uldam and Kaun 2017), we have suggested

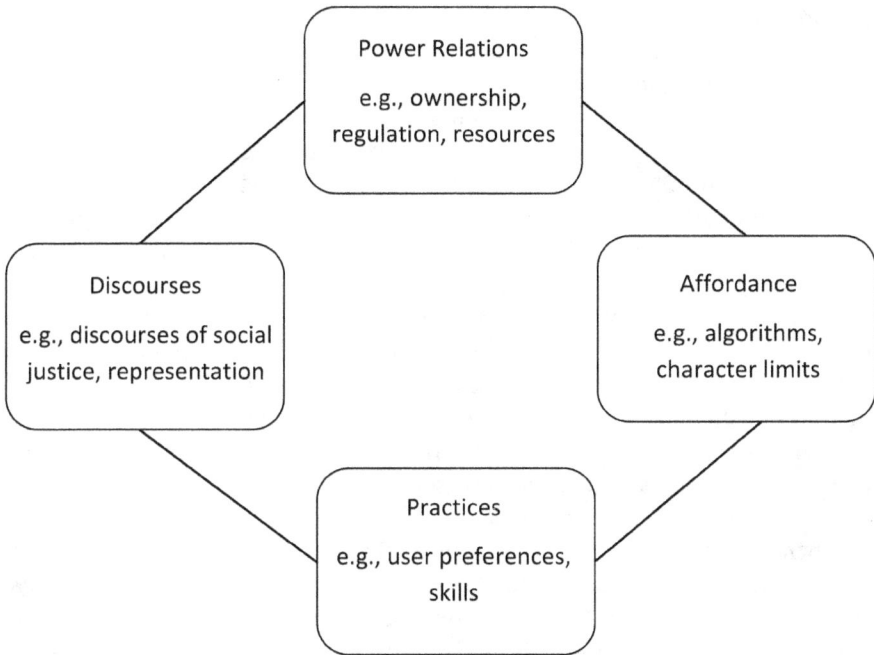

Figure 8.1.   An analytical model of civic participation and social media. Figure constructed by authors.

an analytical model for social media that pays attention to key issues that condition civic engagement and participation. Our aim is to avoid techno-determinism and media-centric focal points. More specifically, the approach we suggest considers the context of civic participation in social media and pays attention to (1) power relations, (2) affordances, (3) practices, and (4) discourses. In doing so, we draw on Nick Couldry's (2012) model of a socially oriented media theory that conceptualizes media in the context of other social institutions that shape our sense of reality and that question the media's overemphasized role in constructing social reality. Similar to Couldry's model, the analytics of social media that we suggest could potentially be applicable to analysing political participation beyond social media, since it is non-media centric (figure 8.1).

In the analytical part of our chapter, we zoom in on temporal affordances—one of the central aspects in our analytical framework for studying social media and civic engagement—of Facebook's communication infrastructure to explore the possibilities and constraints for civic participation. The assumption is that time as an abstract category needs mediation in order to be experienced (Frabetti 2015). Time-mediating technologies, such as calendars, clocks, and diaries, link the individual and lived experience of time to a shared sense of time as well as to temporal cycles (Lash and Urry 1994; Peters 2015). In that sense, the mediation of temporality includes social and political aspects and consequently needs to be considered critically while studying civic engagement. In the remainder of the chapter, we will introduce different layers of temporality that emerge within Facebook as communicative infrastructure for civic engagement and participation.

Our main theoretical starting point is that we should consider Facebook as an emerging civic infrastructure in order to make sense of the central position it has gained for civil society organizing. Infrastructures are commonly understood as 'that which runs "underneath" actual structures—railroad tracks, city plumbing and sewage, electricity, roads and highways, cable wires that connect to the broadcast grid and bring pictures to our TVs. It is that upon which something else rides, or works, a platform of sorts' (Leigh Star and Bowker 2002, 151). Paul Edwards (2003) argues that infrastructures constitute the foundation of modern social worlds by linking macro, meso, and micro scales of temporal, spatial, and social organization. Infrastructures are, hence, 'interrelated social, organizational, and technical components or systems' (Bowker and Leigh Star 1999, 99). Theorists of infrastructures have suggested that these systems are often perceived as taken-for-granted and ready-at-hand. They are mainly invisible until we experience a breakdown, rupture, glitch, or failure. Furthermore, infrastructures are based on large amounts of invisible work that rarely becomes visible. As an approach to study infrastructures, Bowker therefore suggests 'infrastructural inversion' (Bowker and Leigh Star 1999). Similar to reverse engineering, this approach foregrounds going backstage and the importance of looking at infrastructures in the making, as well as moments of disruption as entry points to develop an understanding of these complex underlying systems (Gehl 2014). We here do not aim at inverting or reverse engineering Facebook's infrastructure, but investigate the inherent temporality of the platform while considering moments of emergence, failure, and retooling while coordinating remote supporters and the volunteering work of people on the ground. The understanding of infrastructure that we follow is fundamentally relational. It emerges in the practice and activities of people connected to technical structures. Consequently, we are examining, with Facebook, often considered a black box and invisible infrastructure, without necessarily exploring it in its technical totality (Bucher 2016). That also means that we understand—following among others Julia Velkova (2017)—infrastructuring as a practice that constantly renegotiates infrastructure. In contrast to Velkova's case, which focused on the development of open-source software, our participants have fewer possibilities to influence the overall structure of Facebook as individual users. Instead, the organizers of the initiatives are constantly adapting their ways of using Facebook to the changing context of migration into Sweden, but also in relation to previous failures in using the platform for their work over time.

In the context of social media, Yong-Chan Kim and Sandra Ball-Rokeach (2006) developed a theory of communication infrastructures for community building. Slightly shifting the focus and meaning of infrastructure discussed above, they argue that communication resources such as local newspapers enable storytelling of local communities, which is an essential process in developing and sustaining civic engagement and participation. Hence, we consider Facebook to be a communication infrastructure that constitutes a resource or specific communication opportunity structure for civic engagement. Facebook in turn capitalizes on the adaptation of the platform for civic engagement to further its economic interest through data collection. The business model of Facebook relies heavily on the data gathering to improve targeted advertising and content provision. Hence, the platform is built around principles that increase engagement, such as posts, comments, shares, and likes. These economic aspects can lead potentially to conflicts of interest, complicating the use of Facebook as an infrastructure for civic engagement and political participation, an infrastructure that does not necessarily share the primary focus on civic engagement in pages and groups.

APPROACHING VOLUNTEERING FOR MIGRANTS

For this case study, we combined an analysis of Facebook pages and groups with in-depth interviews with central organizers of key volunteer initiatives in Sweden. The choice of initiatives was based on an analysis of mainstream newspapers. We included organizations that were featured prominently in the reporting. The Facebook pages and groups were monitored over the course of three months, from December 2015 to March 2016. We focused on the main activities of members and moderators as well as the structure of the conversations featured. We also conducted an automated, quantitative analysis of the engagements with posts on the Facebook pages for which—in contrast to groups—analytical tools are available. The practices within the groups were analysed in relation to the more general structure of Facebook, for example differences between Facebook pages and groups. During the interviews, we discussed the findings from the page analysis with the organizers. We interviewed the person who set up the Facebook presence and mainly maintained it throughout the most intense working period. The interview material was then transcribed, and we conducted a theme-based analysis following the categories of our four-dimensional model. The interviews were conducted throughout August until November 2016 and addressed the development of the groups since their inception in 2015. As the number of newly arriving migrants decreased dramatically, the groups had to reconsider their status and, in some cases, change their mission. This is also reflected in their social media practices.

Al Tadamon

The group Al Tadamon—'solidarity' in Arabic—was set up in May 2015 with the aim to provide urgent help for one of the biggest shelters in Sweden, situated in a southern suburb of Stockholm. The group mainly coordinated the collection and distribution of clothes and necessities for the people living in the shelter. In October 2015, the group secured a large room that served as a storage and distribution centre. The Facebook group was mainly used to coordinate the collection of specific products, to collect financial donations, and to invite volunteers to sorting and distribution sessions at the shelter. The group collaborated with the Swedish Migration Agency and partly took responsibility for supplying newly arrived asylum seekers with necessities, which normally is the agency's responsibility. The group still exists, but its clothes shop closed due to the restructuring of the shelter. Most of the residents have been moved either to other shelters in Sweden or to their own apartments. Al Tadamon is currently reconsidering its mission.

Vi som tar emot flyktingar på Stockholms central (Vi som tar emot . . .)/We Who Welcome Refugees at Stockholm's Central Station

This Facebook group was started in September 2015 with the aim of coordinating urgent relief for arriving and transiting migrants in Stockholm's central train station. The group grew rapidly over its first few days, reaching more than seventeen thousand members, and coordinated the collection and distribution of food and clothes, the collection of money to buy tickets for additional travel, transportation to transit shelters, and legal support. The group was initially set up as a public group. Anybody who was added could post and comment on threads. However, this setting was changed after a number of problems with keeping an orderly thread structure occurred. Several other initiatives grew out of this page, including Refugees Welcome Stockholm.

Refugees Welcome Stockholm (RWS)

This group emerged as the main coordinator of relief work at the central train station. Volunteers set up their own transit shelter in a former nightclub and offered help for refugees who needed to rest during their journey through the country and not wanting to register as refugees in Sweden. After the major influx of migrants decreased, when the Swedish borders closed, the group's mission shifted. Currently, the group organizes the community centre Rosa Station (pink station) in the northern part of the city centre of Stockholm, offering language training and social activities. The group is still very active on Facebook and mainly engages in discussions about migration policies. RWS also continues to support protests against the new and stricter migration law that was introduced in the summer of 2016.

Vi gör vad vi kan—We Do What We Can

This initiative was cofounded by playwright and director Paula Stenström Öhman and public relations strategist Petra Kauraisa. Initially, they aimed to collect 500,000 SEK. This money was meant for travel with necessities to Lesvos in Greece to provide urgent relief for migrants arriving there. The initial goal was quickly reached. Overall, the initiative collected almost 11 million SEK and 250 tons of clothes and other non-food items such as shoes, hygiene kits, tents, and sleeping bags. Vi gör vad vi kan emerged as one of the most successful donation campaigns related to the migration crisis in 2015.

Table 8.1. Overview initiatives considered. Table constructed by authors.

Al Tadamon	• Facebook group • Approx. 4,000 members • Served Stockholm's largest shelters distributing clothes and other necessities
Vi som tar emot flyktingar på Stockholms central/We who welcome refugees at Stockholm's central station	• Facebook group • Approx. 17,000 members • Coordinated urgent help at Stockholm's central station (September 2015)
Refugees Welcome Stockholm	• Facebook page • Approx. 11,000 likes • Official organisation with physical centre in Stockholm (Rosa stationen)
Vi gör vad vi kan/We Do What We Can	• Facebook page • Approx. 20,000 likes • collected donations to be distributed in Greece (initially mainly Lesvos) • still raising funds, and ship non-food items (NFI) such as medical supplies to Greece, Iraqi Kurdistan, and Syria

TEMPORAL AFFORDANCES OF FACEBOOK

The organizers of volunteer initiatives whom we have interviewed reacted almost with surprise when we asked them why they turned to Facebook to start their initiative. For them, it was a natural choice, partly related to the speed with which groups and pages are set up and gain visibility. This naturalization of Facebook as a communicative infrastructure for civic initiatives will be analysed through the lens of temporality in the following section. The focus on temporality foregrounds one of the key characteristics of infrastructures, namely providing, in this case temporal, mediation between technological artefacts and human actors. In the material and in relation to previous research on infrastructures, three major tropes emerged: permanent flow, real-timeness, and synchronicity. All three tropes are identified as three interrelated temporal layers emerging within Facebook.

Permanent Flow

The administrator and founder of Al Tadamon emphasizes the need to constantly be active or present within the group, even though the initiative is currently rethinking its mission, since the rescue shelter was closed. She argues:

> It is fairly easy to get a group with many members, but to keep it active is much harder. And this is what you actually want, you don't want to have a dead group with some thousand members, this is little bit the case now. It is a little bit like people gave up, but it is a job to keep the activity up. And this is what you want, you want to have up to 100 likes for a post and this is what we got when we were the most active, like between 200 to 400 per post. (Interview 2016-08-26)

The temporal logic of Facebook is based on its business model, which emphasizes permanent updates, hence creating pressure for the group to constantly upload new content by, for example, sharing success stories or any kind of engagement to remain relevant and thus keep its status as an active group. The alternative is to disappear from the newsfeed and lose the potential visibility with more than four thousand members. In that sense, the exchange and posting of messages is foregrounded rather than the content and mission of the initiative as such. Jodi Dean (2008) has discussed this tendency in social media as contributing to the ideology of communicative capitalism, emphasizing exchange value over use value. This is particularly difficult during the tricky period of reformulating the mission, which created tensions as the administrators confirmed (Kaun and Uldam 2017; Uldam and Kaun 2017). At the same time, the constitutive elements of Facebook as an infrastructure are difficult to change by individual users. For example, the platform does not allow for the adaptation to organizational evolution, an idea captured in the following quote by Al Tadamon's founding member:

> The only thing that I experienced as a constraint was that we started as group and then we had so many members and we realized that it would have been better to have a page instead. . . .We didn't know that we would become an organization with a budget and everything. (Interview 2016-08-26)

The distinction between pages and groups has significant implications in terms of visibility. Since Facebook pages were created mainly with brands and commercial entities in mind, they gain more visibility on the platform; the same is true for open groups. However, since there are potential dangers for both volunteers and migrants connected with visibility in social media, openness was, in some cases, regulated externally. The shelter's management in Stockholm, for example, implemented a strict media protocol, including restricted access for media to the building as well as posts on social media. This had implications for outreach and possibilities to engage broader publics in Al Tadamon's relief work as they were not allowed to post pictures of the building, the clothes shop, or residents in the public group on Facebook. Furthermore, the structure of pages and groups privileges the visibility of administrator posts over posts by members and followers. This asymmetrical visibility establishes another layer in terms of power relations within the platform. It gives voice to the ones who organize relief while marginalizing the voice of the recipients, the refugees, who are also members of these groups. As an organization in transition, Al Tadamon had to decide to either lose more than four thousand members by starting a new page or remain a group, a difficult choice. Finally, Al Tadamon remained a Facebook group, accepting potentially technical difficulties and less visibility by linking to the Facebook group on external websites.

Facebook's infrastructure presents difficulties in adapting to future developments as well as representing the past. As Kaun (Kaun and Stiernstedt 2014) has discussed earlier, Facebook has added some memory features such as 'on that day,' but the platform does not invite engaging with 'old' content, and then only if this leads to new engagement in the form of likes, shares, and comments. The newsfeed and the organization of Facebook groups and pages hardly allow going back in time, at least not very far into the past. In that sense, Facebook encourages and contributes to an experience of immediacy, flow, and presentness. This means that posts that articulated specific needs, but gained, for certain reasons, little to no visibility, have disappeared, unanswered in the Facebook stream.

Real-timeness

Social media platforms have often been heralded for allowing exchanges over vast distances in real-time. This makes it possible to capture behaviour and environmental data as they are happening and allows for immediate response. It has, for example, been argued that Twitter data can be used to detect natural catastrophes such as earthquakes in real-time by analysing user posts and exchanges (Kryvasheyeu et al. 2016). However, there are different stages of real-time-data processing, namely receiving data, processing data, and returning the analysis. Hence, Weltevrede et al. argue that 'media do not operate in real-time, devices and their cultures operate as pacers of real-time' (2014, 127). The authors suggest speaking of real-timeness instead, which foregrounds the production of real-time as part of the platform infrastructure. Suggesting the notion of real-timeness allows us, the authors argue, to take into account the politics of real-time instead of taking it for granted.

When it comes to Facebook's real-timeness in terms of volunteer organizing, we have seen cases where the temporal logics of the platform has created problems for the activists. The Facebook algorithm privileges interaction over recency, which means that posts that trigger new replies gain more visibility, despite their being dated. This has implications for the possibility of coordinating people and efforts to help. Carefully curated threads and posts might be messed up because of comments on older posts that give the impression that these are the most recent and most urgent requests. The curated thread structure (see figure 8.1) was particularly important for the group Vi som tar emot since this was the only way to make a distinction between different needs and areas of work.

Some of the initiatives made a considerable investment both in time and financial resources in producing the feeling of real-timeness when engaging with stakeholders. One of the initiators of Vi gör vad vi kan describes how she and other organizers worked more than full-time with the initiative during peak times. Much of the time invested was dedicated to coordination issues in and through Facebook and Instagram. On Facebook, the initiatives were confronted with numerous inquiries that were pouring in as comments, emails, and private messages. During the most turbulent period, Vi gör vad vi kan hired one person who only took care of communication with stakeholders (mainly donors and potential volunteers) on social media. Similarly, Refugees Welcome Stockholm (RWS) relied on a software package, Relation Desk, to coordinate all Facebook communications, including private messages, comments, and replies to own posts. The software allowed them to forward and distribute messages among different volunteers who were divided into different communication teams. The software also included automated messaging to users trying to get in touch with the group until they could reach out personally. The explicit goal of RWS's communications team was to reply to any engagement on their social media channels as quickly as possible. This professionalized way of handling communications was initially set up by one person who was also responsible for training sessions for new communication volunteers. Similarly, Vi gör vad vi kan engaged a volunteer to handle all Facebook communication, including messages and comments, as well as emails during the initiative's most intense period. The aim was to answer any inquiry as soon as possible, creating a discourse of real-timeness within the organization in relation to their followers.

Synchronicity

In contrast to the notion of real-timeness, which implies immediate capture, processing, and response, synchronicity refers to the coincidence or simultaneity of meaningful events. During the interviews, the organizers of the different volunteer initiatives often referred to the advantages of coordinating people, goods, and money over time and space with the help of Facebook. The coordination of different elements is one of the fundamental functions of infrastructures and therefore is interesting for our discussion (Lash and Urry 1994; Peters 2015). One of the initiators of Vi gör vad vi kan argued, for example, that the majority of exchanges in their social media channels were concerned with logistics. People were wondering how to correctly pack clothes or other things for transport and where exactly to drop them off. However, Facebook contributes to a layering of time that is not always in sync. Digitizing and processing takes time; certain food or clothes that might have been urgently needed at some point might not be required anymore, once the Facebook post gained high visibility in the groups or pages. For example, one post in the group Vi som tar emot . . . urgently requested eggs for one of the stations that provided food for arriving migrants. After the post gained a lot of visibility on the platform, the station was flooded with donations of eggs and had difficulties stopping more deliveries. Our interviewee described the situation as follows:

> We tried to limit the number of different threads within the group. But in between different events people started writing in different threads, like for example one would start writing in the thread on the Mosque and then people started replying to the initial question, but the posts developed into something very general that had nothing to do with the Mosque anymore. Like for example, 'We have a lot of eggs, what should we do with them?' It was just not very easy to guide folk to write in the right place. Everybody is just writing where people have been active the last time. (Interview 2016-09-16)

Consequently, the administrators put extensive efforts into constantly posting updates on what was required and what was not. However, individual posts with certain requests were circulated individually without feedback from people at the station, making synchronization difficult. Hence, the latency of the digital system created smaller and larger problems in terms of synchronizing needs with volunteering commitments.

John Durham Peters (2015) argues that new media are pushing the logistical aspects of media back to centre stage. The perspective of considering media as infrastructures emphasizes understanding them as logistical. In contrast to recording media that have compressed time and transmitting media that have compressed space, logistical media such as Facebook focus on organizing and orienting as they arrange people and things in time and space. They have the job of ordering things and fundamental units (Peters 2015). Peters goes on to analyse classic examples of coordinating and synchronizing people using such things as calendars, clocks, and towers. He argues that calendars, clocks, and towers provide shared temporal and spatial orientations. While calendars and clocks serve primarily for temporal synchronization, towers orient people in space and serve as points of observation and control. Similarly, social networking sites such as Facebook provide an infrastructure of coordinating and orienting people. In contrast to calendars, clocks, and towers, however, Facebook still achieves the status of an unquestioned and seamlessly working infrastructure for organizing people in time and space. The examples of failure in coordination are expressions of this on-going process of claiming the function as a civic infrastructure, while still grappling with characteristics that work against its functionality for civic engagement as exemplified above.

Facebook as Infrastructure for Civic Engagement and Participation in Post-Migrant Societies?

This chapter situated volunteering for arriving migrants in the realm of civic engagement and participation and explored the role of social media for co-ordinating such volunteer work in the Swedish context. Applying a complex analytical model including discourses, power relations, and practices while zooming in on temporal affordance, this chapter examined the ambivalent character of Facebook as it both enables and constraints civic participation. At the same time, Facebook has emerged as a crucial civic infrastructure that takes an important position in coordinating civic participation. We considered this emerging role of Facebook as civic infrastructure through the lens of temporal affordances by scrutinizing volunteer initiatives in the context of the so-called migration crisis of 2015. We discussed the consequences of the tendency of these civic initiatives to rely on an infrastructure that is built according to a specific business model, namely, the exploitation of user engagement in the form of user data (Kaun and Stiernstedt 2014). By focusing on the case of volunteering for migrants, we aimed at showing the practices of infrastructuring. Infrastructuring here is understood as a practice of adaptation and adoption in order to overcome constraints and failures of an infrastructure that is comparatively stable or hard to change by individual users. Instead, users invent small ways to improve infrastructures for their purposes. We discussed, for example, how administrators implemented thread rules to maintain order according to their understanding and needs, despite Facebook's algorithm following other principles. The main finding of our exploration is that volunteer activism on Facebook is characterized by a dynamic interplay between Facebook as an emerging civic infrastructure and practices by users employing the infrastructure for civic participation in slightly unexpected ways. However, the agency and possibilities to alter the platform by users is limited, and we therefore need to critically consider the increasingly dominant position of Facebook when it comes to civic engagement, particularly the specific temporal affordances inherent to the platform that constrain and make civic participation difficult.

NOTES

1. All interviews were conducted in Swedish. Quotes have been translated by the authors.
2. This post was translated from Swedish by the authors and is reproduced with the permission of the informant.

Chapter Nine

Sentiment-Driven Demands and Scenarios for Political Participation in Nativist SNS

Fabian Virchow

For many years, the Dublin Regulation from September 1997 had kept the number of refugees applying for asylum in Germany low. The regulation gave Germany, surrounded by numerous other states, an advantage. The regulation stated that the country in which the asylum seeker first applies for asylum is responsible for either accepting or rejecting the claim. This made countries like Italy and Greece the main destinations of forced migration. From a figure as low as 28,000 applications for asylum in 2008, the number of people claiming protection in Germany under the right to asylum rose steadily, reaching 477,000 in 2015 and 746,000 in 2016 before falling to 223,000 in 2017 (Bundesamt für Migration und Flüchtlinge (BAMF) 2018, 3).

The large number of refugees and the way that German Chancellor Angela Merkel handled the situation (most prominently expressed by her statement, 'We can do it,' on 31 August 2015, after her visit to a refugee camp in Dresden where anti-immigrant protesters had booed her) were just two ingredients of a more complex situation that can best be described as a polarization of German society. On the one hand, in 2015 several million people had welcomed the refugees and extended a helping hand to make arrival a positive experience, but also to provide them with essentials. On the other hand, starting in late summer 2015, a growing number of those living in Germany became more sceptical about the extent of the refugee movement and the possibilities of rapid integration of immigrants and asylum seekers into German society. Those categorically against immigration became more visible and audible, with a growing number of them turning to street demonstrations and violent actions since late 2014. While tabloid and elite media contributed to this development (Jäger and Wamper 2017), key to the overall situation is the idea of a homogenous German people, whose ethnic and cultural core needs to be defended against the 'Other.' This idea is still very much alive and has only recently been fundamentally questioned in the German context. Such nativism can be understood with Hellström and Hervik's definition (2014, 451; but see also Guia 2016, 12, for a list of constitutive elements), according to which nativism

> holds that the nation-state needs to be protected and reserved to members of the national group with the specific aim of consolidating political and cultural homogeneity. Nativist political rhetoric separates between the native and the non-native, by means of demarcating the native culture, including the native people, the native ideas and values, from what is depicted as alien. The rationale behind the nativist message is to propagate that the nation (a distinct territory) belongs to the natives (a distinct 'people').

In contrast to most of post-war Germany, the 2010s witnessed the emergence of a broad range of non-parliamentary nativist groups and right-wing movements (Rehberg, Kunz, and Schlinzig 2016; Virchow 2016a) in addition to a *völkisch* and authoritarian party that ran successfully for parliamentary representation throughout the country, the Alternative für Deutschland (Alternative for Germany, AfD hereafter), currently with ninety-two representatives in the *Bundestag* (German parliament) (Häusler 2016; 2018; Schroeder, Weßels, and Berzel 2018). Political observers and academics have labelled these new political protagonists as 'citizens of anger' (e.g., Benz 2016; Massing 2017) and a 'movement of rage' (Vorländer 2016), thereby emphasizing the role of emotions regarding this phenomenon. Participants in street actions against immigration and refugees have often expressed their deep disappointment in and mistrust of the government in general and of some of its representatives, such as Chancellor Angela Merkel and former Federal Minister of Justice Heiko Maas, in particular. In order to change the situation caused by immigration, which the nativist protagonists consider extremely dangerous for the survival of Germany, they repeatedly called for overthrow and rebellion. While non-parliamentary groups like Patriotische Europäer gegen die Islamisierung des Abendlands (Patriotic Europeans Against the Islamization of the West [PEGIDA]) often declined to questions from the media; they ran their own web pages and social media accounts on platforms such as Facebook in order to serve their audiences.

Using the comments of PEGIDA's Facebook account as empirical material, this chapter explores how people have commented on the latest political developments and events and speak out about political decisions by (particular) state actors and political parties in the government. Furthermore, the analysis focuses on how these comments frame the need for, and propose ways of, political participation and intervention. In doing so, this chapter also seeks to understand what place emotions and sentiment have in the way of demanding particular kinds of political action. Following this introduction, the second section of this chapter offers an overview of the role that emotions play in contentious politics and social movements as a particular kind of political participation. It also outlines the relevance of social network sites (SNS) in nativist and far-right political action and participation. The third section offers some insights into the PEGIDA movement, but also includes a short sketch of the methods and material used for this study. The fourth section presents and discusses the empirical results, while the final section offers some tentative suggestions for further research.

PERSPECTIVES ON POLITICAL PARTICIPATION, EMOTIONS, AND MEDIATIZED NATIVIST MOBILIZATION

Political participation includes different expressions of such participation, ranging from conventional (e.g., elections, political parties) to legal unconventional (e.g., rallies, petitions) to illegal unconventional (e.g., squatting, blockades, wildcat strikes) to illegal and violent expressions (e.g., riots and militant action) (Uehlinger 1988). In the context of media, political participation also includes discussions and interactions between citizens in online forums or in social media; in doing so, any action, even those that might seem to have any deep impact or immediate resonance, becomes an issue of investigation (see Stehling, Thomas, and Kruse's chapter in this volume).

So far, most research on political participation in post-migrant societies has often focused on progressive parties, movements, and individuals (Bukow et al. 2013; Hutter and Kriesi 2013; Gassert 2018). Yet issues such as immigration and interculturalism are not only contested issues in general leading to political action (Rosenberger, Stern, and Merhaut 2018) but are at the very centre of far right and nativist worldviews (Dove 2010; Davidson 2013; Dietrich 2014; Virchow 2017). Called 'restrictionist movements' by Schaeffer (2014), such groups have practiced a wide range of forms of political participation, in general, and contentious politics in particular, with the latter helping to understand the radicalization of movements more clearly (Aminzade et al. 2001).

Historically, research on protest viewed its protagonists as irrational and dangerous masses. Heavily influenced by French social psychologist Gustave Le Bon (1896; 1898), this position assumes that individuals, once they are part of a crowd, lose their personal opinions, values, and beliefs and adopt the mentality of the crowd, yielding to instincts and emotions. While the issue of masses and their role in democracy have remained important (Klein and Nullmeier 1999; Jonsson 2015), the paradigm of the rational political actor who makes decisions according to their individual preferences among the available choices (taking into account all available information and probabilities of events but also potential costs and benefits) became influential in sociology and political sciences from the 1950s onwards (Voss and Abraham 2000). This perspective also became relevant in protest and social movements research (Opp 2013), only to be later questioned and supplemented in the course of the 'emotional turn' in the social sciences and historiography. Over the last twenty years, scholars have returned to emotions as a key to understanding protest and political participation (Jasper 1998; Goodwin, Jasper, and Polletta 2001; Koller 2014).

Emotions in politics and political action play a significant role regarding 'the collective formation of an identity and the adoption of that collective identity by individuals. It can also help explain the durability of a collective identity through the development of emotional bonds' (de Volo 2006, 463; see also Golova 2015). Furthermore, in times of crisis, emotions such as anger and anxiety can be more important in explaining participation in protest than resources, identities, and mobilization networks (Galais and Lorenzini 2017). Additionally, while 'emotions are intense during protests [. . .] meetings also might be emotionally charged, in positive and negative ways, and emotions clearly influence the quality of communication' (della Porta and Giugni 2013, 123). In addition, unpleasant emotions connected to a particular event or development in society can more likely prevent political participation than the lack of information or concern about this particular issue can. In such cases, emotion management includes the refusal to transform knowledge and negative assessment on a particular issue into social and political action (Norgaard 2006). Finally, emotions and the role they play in the political arena should be explored as they are an 'active and highly contested political battleground, where emotional boundaries are actively drawn and redrawn by politicians and political movements' (Kotliar 2016). From that perspective, it should also be taken seriously that emotions in politics are not in the exclusive realm of protesters and social activists, but can also be found on the side of political power (Ost 2004).

Undoubtedly, online technologies have significantly changed political participation, protest, and contentious politics (Dahlgren and Alvares 2013; Sonntag 2013; Tremayne 2014). Sandoval-Almazan and Gil-Garcia (2014) have emphasized that YouTube, Twitter, Facebook, and other social media, among other effects, 'enable faster communications by citizen movements and the delivery of local information to a large audience' (367). Consequently, they might also optimize the recruiting of activists. For example, empirical research has provided evidence about the impact that personalized online networks have when mobilizing for protest events (Tufekci and Wilson 2012; Baek 2015). At the same time, governments also make use of social media when trying to control protest and its outreach (Panagiotopoulos, Bigdeli, and Sams 2014).

Online technologies have enabled right-wing protagonists, too, to form new communicative spaces beyond traditional media (Caren, Jowers, and Gaby 2012; Forchtner, Krzyżanowski, and Wodak 2013; Druxes and Simpson 2015). Karsten Müller and Carlo Schwarz (2018), using data from the AfD Facebook page with over 176,000 posts, more than 290,000 comments, and 500,000 likes by over 93,000 individual users, showed that right-wing anti-refugee sentiment on Facebook predicts violent crimes against refugees in municipalities, compared to otherwise similar municipalities with even higher social media usage. One particular strategy of online discourse of (right-wing) populist politics in Europe and beyond has been identified by Krzyżanowski and Ledin as the 'ongoing civil-to-uncivil shifts in the uncivil society's discursive representations of society and politics' (2017, 577). The strategic discourse of 'uncivil society, under the guise of civil-like "objective opinions" and quasi "facts," has been spreading exclusionary views and thus fuelling uncivil social and political visions resting on discrimination and rejection of diversity' by making extensive use of 'buzzwords/keywords symptomatic of certain opinions and ideologies [. . .] which are only (very) loosely related to occurrences and facts (which in and of themselves are also often dubious)' (ibid.). Uffa Jensen, in his systematic overview of emotions in political contexts, presents the case of an activist of the *völkisch* authoritarian AfD who used his Facebook account to comment on a serious act of violence against a twelve-year-old boy, adding the words, 'Consequences: foreseeable none. About the perpetrator no information. This is the new Germany—I do not like it' (Jensen 2017, 88). Without giving a clear interpretation of the incident, the AfD activist nevertheless refers to topoi such as 'information is held back by the media' and 'The state fails against crime' that are in the very centre of right-wing discourse in German context today. The post was 'liked' by many Facebook users, and a significant number used the 'Angry' button, which the company had introduced late 2015 (ibid., 89–90).

When it comes to right-wing and nativist political actors, the issue of emotions and mediatized nativism is highly relevant. Several authors suggest that groups and individuals belonging to this political spectrum are exploiting and fueling the anxiety that exists in parts of the population in the face of migration and religious plurality (Nussbaum 2012; Wodak 2016), for example by spreading false reports about crimes committed by asylum seekers.

NATIVIST SNS IN PRACTICE

Surprisingly to many observers, several public protests that turned against 'fundamentalist currents of Islam' were organized in Germany, from fall 2014 onwards. A demonstration organized by a group that called itself Hooligans against Salafists (HoGeSa) received great public attention; another group, PEGIDA (explained above), was able to mobilize a sizeable crowd within a few weeks, starting with weekly marches in Dresden of a few hundred that grew to crowds of more than 25,000 in early 2015 (Rehberg, Kunz, and Schlinzig 2016; Virchow 2016a). From May 2016 on, the number of participants reached more than 2,500 only on rare occasions, but the rallies themselves became highly ritualized.

According to the narrative given by PEGIDA's leader Lutz Bachmann, the triggers for starting to organize rallies were clashes between Islamist activists and Kurdish groups in German cities. At PEGIDA's rallies, participants carried a huge banner with the slogan 'Without Violence and United against Faith Wars and Proxy Wars on German Soil.' Urged by many for a statement on its political aims and demands, PEGIDA published a paper on 10 December 2014, addressing nineteen issues. In the statement, PEGIDA demanded, among other things, that refugees should be looked after more efficiently by social workers; that the admission of war refugees and of people fleeing for reasons of religious or political persecution should be acknowledged, as a human duty; and that accommodation of refugees should follow the idea of decentralized housing instead of quartering them in hostels. Further demands addressed the establishment of a European-wide system for distributing refugees, an increase in funds for the police, stricter deportation practices, the introduction of referendum decisions according to the Swiss model, a ban on the delivery of weapons to banned groups like the Kurdish Workers Party, and an end to the public policy for equal chances for men and women. The paper did not at all mention the stereotypically charged term 'Islamisation' (Kerst 2016). In fact, the original statement did not play any real role after its publication. PEGIDA's lead team replaced it shortly afterwards with a paper that focussed on stricter migration and asylum policies, but also contained an anti-EU position combined with pro-Russian sentiments. For the general public, however, the profile of the movement was defined by the racist and anti-Muslim utterances of its most important representatives, made on either the internet or at PEGIDA rallies. The group

claims to promote national values and already has a positive image of Germany in particular and the nation state in general. Germany is seen as an agency of 'humanity' that fulfils a selfless moral mission in granting asylum to refugees. For Pegida, the consequences of this policy include 'foreign infiltration,' as well as so-called 'Muslim parallel societies,' which are seen as dangerous imports of competing moralities. [. . .] According to this logic, the preservation of home through a 'zero tolerance policy' is a self-purpose, ensuring to prevent negative social consequences like poverty and unemployment. (Thran and Boehnke 2015, 178)

While most of the time, PEGIDA representatives did not speak to the media at all (Reuband 2016), the use of social network sites, especially Facebook, was key for the movement to reach out to its followers. PEGIDA started its Facebook account after a meeting on October 10, 2014, calling for a rally on the twentieth of that month. On 23 July 2016, the number of Facebook followers peaked at 205,000, while the most successful rally in terms of number of participants took place on 12 January 2015, when some 25,000 people attended (Amadeu Antonio Stiftung 2016, 37). Dietrich, Gersin, and Herwig (2017, 241) have stressed that PEGIDA's website had a direct link to its Facebook account where the main communication took place and where the above-mentioned papers had been published. In contrast, only a third of PEGIDA supporters, asked in a survey (n = 610), said that they were following PEGIDA's Facebook account (Institut für Demokratieforschung 2016, 24).

So far, there has been limited research on PEGIDA's Facebook account. Until the spring of 2016, the administrators of PEGIDA's Facebook account mainly posted on issues directly linked to the group itself, such as calls for action and media coverage, which also included sharing videos and pictures. On average, postings received some 500 comments, but on certain occasions, such as the *Charlie Hebdo* shootings, comments peaked at nearly 9,200, related to nine posts by PEGIDA admins (ibid., 38).

Facebook is one of the most popular online SNS featuring comments where individuals can express their emotions and opinions via texts, images, and emoticons (Zamani et al. 2014). So far, hardly any qualitative research has been done on PEGIDA's Facebook account. Some have examined the number of posts over time, for the most-used terms and hashtags, respectively, and also whether there are links to other websites (Amadeu Antonio Stiftung 2016). In 2016, the most important German daily newspaper, *Süddeutsche Zeitung*, published an article about PEGIDA's Facebook activities, based on a samples from all posts and comments for the period starting on 28 December 2014, and ending on 31 December 2015 (Munzinger, Rietzschel, and Bendt 2016). During that period, posts and comments peaked in January and in the period of August to October 2015, due to the tangible growth in the anti-immigrant and anti-refugee political climate, respectively. The *Süddeutsche Zeitung* has generously provided its collected data in anonymous form for further evaluation. The empirical part of this chapter investigates a) what kinds of solutions are proposed in posts and comments on PEGIDA's

Facebook page regarding the problems seen as most pressing by the respective authors, and b) what place emotions have in presenting arguments and (de)legitimizing one's own and other protagonists' actions.

Dietrich, Gersin, and Herwig (2017, 246) have explained that automated sentiment analysis (Zamani et al. 2014) faces significant difficulties because it cannot identify ironic and sarcastic tonality, misses the meaning of ambiguous terms and slang, and does not take text environment into account properly. Therefore, manual coding is still the main option. This research is based on a sample of 4,800 comments and posts made by users of PEGIDA's Facebook page during the period mentioned above. The comments were selected randomly from a total of 361,254 comments and posts. Data analysis made use of two set of categories—one on emotions (e.g., rage, fear, hope, frustration, shame, pride), the other on the kind of political action deemed necessary by the author of the comments to bring change to a situation assessed as negative (e.g., leadership change, direct democracy, uprisings [as in 1989]). For matters of space, only selected results can be presented here.

PEGIDA'S EMOTIONALIZED SNS NATIVISM

A first review of the sample of 4,800 SNS comments and posts evenly distributed over the year 2015 revealed that 834 comments and posts had to be excluded from further analysis as they either consisted of mere formalities of speech or would have needed further context for coding.[1] Another 312 comments were URLs only. Those have also been excluded from analysis, but it would be a valuable approach to catalogue the kind of content and style these URLs lead to. An additional 420 comments were clearly posted by opponents and critics of PEGIDA and therefore were also excluded from the sample, ultimately leaving 3,234 comments and posts for the final qualitative content analysis.

The overall results confirm broadly what Stefanowitsch and Flach (2016) have found on the basis of a sample of 1,000 comments from the same unit. The centre of the debate focuses on the idea that a fundamental change in Germany (and in most parts of Europe) is going on, which is labelled as 'Islamization.' This development, that is, the assumption, is driven forward by an alliance, intentionally or not, of the German government, with Chancellor Angela Merkel as the leading figure, in cooperation with Islamic states and supported by mass media. The whole framing is strongly negative. It portrays refugees as fundamentally different and as dangerous and criminal subjects or as the tools of 'background forces.' The PEGIDA movement is mainly portrayed as the saviour, although this fluctuates over time. For example, in

January 2015, many posts and comments expressed great enthusiasm because the Facebook account reached 100,000 followers, but there is also some critical debate regarding the basic document published by PEGIDA, which, according to some of the critics, is not addressing important questions such as the presence of US troops in Germany.

Emotions are overtly expressed in only a relatively small percentage of comments and posts. The following list gives typical examples for the broad range of emotions in the comments and posts:

- *Unease* ('Ich bin Baujahr 50, ich hab mich höchst unwohl gefühlt als ich in meiner letzten WohnStadt weggezogen bin, unter mir Russen, links Albaner, rechts Türken, alles wohnte hier nur keine Deutschen. Ich kam mir fremd im eigen Ort vor.'/'I'm born in 1950, I felt very uncomfortable when I moved away from my last residential city, below me Russians, to the left Albanians, to the right Turks, everyone lived here except Germans. I felt being a stranger in my own place' (2015-01-08T15:16:49).
- *Fear* ('Man traut sich als deutscher nicht mehr raus vor Angst das an der nächsten Ecke vllt wieder ein salafist ist angi hat bodyguards'/'As a German one does not dare to go out, fearing that at the next corner, there is probably a salafist again Angi has bodyguards') (2015-01-10T18:46:22).[2]
- *Rage* ('Alles nur Verbrecher, hoffentlich werden diese Schamrotzer bald aus dem Land gejagt.'/'All just criminals, hopefully, these parasites are soon chased out of the country.') (2015-03-11T17:00:31).
- *Frustration* ('wie kann dieser kretschmann ministerpräsident eines deutschen volkes sein ??? wer verdammt noch mal wählt solche leute— es ist zum kotzen und nicht mehr länger zu ertragen'/'how can this Kretschmann be [minister president] of a German people ??? whoever chooses such people, dammit—this sucks and can no longer be tolerated') (2015-07-16T13:44:24).[3]
- *Hope* ('Pegida bitte nicht aufhören, Ihr seid unsere letzte Chance. Viel Erfolg heute Abend.'/'PEGIDA please do not stop, you are our last chance. Good luck tonight.') (2015-03-02T10:25:56).
- *Admiration* ('Weiter so Pegida! Jeder aufrechte Deutsche bewundert euch für euer Tun.'/'Go on Pegida! Every upright German is admiring you for what you are doing.') (2015-01-03T14:15:27).[4]
- *Pride* ('Man kann stolz sein auf sein Land, ohne das man pleite ist!!!'/'One can be proud of one's country without being broke!!!!') (2015-01-02T11:05:05).[5]
- *Joy* ('Ich habs mir überlegt, ich spende auch. Noch nie hatte ich ein so gutes Gefühl dabei!!/'I thought about it, I also donate. I have never felt so good about it') (2015-01-03T19:29:44).

In general, negative emotions are part of comments on the political situation, the issue of immigration, and asylum, but also on the state of press freedom and the supposed inability or unwillingness of the government to intervene in a way the commentator wants it to act. The more positive emotional expressions nearly all refer to the PEGIDA movement, its dynamics, and the impact it has already or might have in the future. A great number of comments are very enthusiastic about the growth of the movement, especially early in 2015. Several comments referenced current controversies around the PEGIDA phenomenon. For example, the statement above, 'One can be proud of one's country without being broke!!!!,' refers to the discussion about the socioeconomic status of the protestors.

A good number of posts and comments also express the need for action and options for nativist politics. There are a number of suggestions in the posts that refer to different target groups (government, media, refugees, migrants, the left), but also differ according to their timeline, modes of action, and level of violence as well as to the arena of change (e.g., party politics, change of government, system change). In general, the strategic choices commentators make on PEGIA's Facebook account range from some extensions of democratic procedures (albeit for the advantage of a particular political profile) to the idea of changing the very basic rules of the political system. The following quotes are just some examples of the different kinds of strategic options presented in posts and comments on PEGIDA's Facebook page:

- *Increase in pressure based on own strength* ('Über 100000! Mal schaun ob der Hosenanzug am Montag reagiert :-) :-) :-)'/'More than 100,000! Let's see if the suits will react on Monday :-) :-) :-)') (2015-01-03T16:33:54).[6]
- *Immediate authoritarian non-state solution* ('Die liegen schon richtig vor der Wand. Abknallen und fertig . . .'/'They are already right in front of the wall. Pull the trigger and done.') (2015-07-04T13:13:08).
- *Immediate authoritarian state solution* ('Mit der ganzen Härte die das Gesetz zulässt diese gottverdammte Bande ausheben und abschieben !!'/'With all the harshness the law allows, dig out and deport these goddamn gangs!!') (2015-01-15T10:43:31).
- *Short-term party building* ('Lutz Bachmann von Pegida bitttteeee bitttteeee gründe eine Partei, wir brauchen zielstrebige und Volksnahe ehrliche Menschen an der Macht unserer Regierung die das Ohr am Volk am Bürger haben'/'Lutz Bachmann of Pegida pleeeaaase pleeeaaase create a party, we need goal-oriented and people-friendly honest people in power and in government who have an ear for the people, for the citizen') (2015-01-10T17:52:10).

- *Mid-term takeover of government* ('Bis 2017 sollte Pegida eine Partei werden und dann könnt ihr direkt auf Merkels Stuhl sitzen. Das Volk hat genug.Es ist an der Zeit'/'Pegida should become a party by 2017 and then you can sit directly on Merkel's chair. The people have enough. It is time') (2015-07-04T14:40:29).
- *Expansion of direct democracy* ('Das Volk sollte viel mehr entscheiden dürfen. Das nennt man Demokratie !!!!'/'The people should be allowed to decide much more. That's called democracy !!!!') (2015-01-03T13:44:24).
- *Revolt* ('Es wird Zeit das wir Richtung Berlin marschieren, und denen mal Zeigen das die da oben auf einem sehr morschen Holzweg sind'/'It's about time we march towards Berlin, and show them that they up there are on the wrong track') (2015-02-15T12:22:25).
- *System change like 1989* ('Ich bin in Gedanken bei euch.Lasst Euch nicht unterkriegen.PRO PEGIDA!89 haben wirs auch geschafft.'/'I am with you in my thoughts. Do not let it get you down. PRO PEGIDA! 89 we did it too') (2015-03-16T18:11:01).

In many comments and posts, a kind of historic optimism is apparent; its driver is the rapid growth of the PEGIDA movement in late 2014 and early 2015. Comments and posts referring to '1989' or '89' refer to the fall of the Berlin wall in 1989 and subsequent collapse of the German Democratic Republic, a political system that seemed stable but disappeared in a short time period. Such references to the so-called Peaceful Revolution aim at establishing more credibility. At the same time, they keep up members' confidence in the enforceability of a nativist program. Aside from biographical connections to these events in 1989, which some of the PEGIDA protestors might have first-hand experience with, the intention is to profit from a political movement and moment in history that is held in high esteem in large parts of the population.

EMOTIONALIZED NATIVIST RITUAL

In the shadow of a growing number of refugees trying to escape the suffering and dangers of (civil) war, situations of persecutions, and material need, right-wing and nativist actions and political participation have increased across Europe. In Germany, new groups, networks, and political parties such as PEGIDA and the AfD have emerged. They have become subject to wide media coverage, but also perform as media actors off- and online.

It has been argued here that emotions are a key to understanding drivers and dynamics of protest and political participation and that it makes sense to search for traces of them in SNS, which play an increasingly relevant role in day-to-day communications, but especially so for right-wing and nativist protagonists in politics (Happ and Tripps 2017). So far, empirical research has shown that a broad range of (expressions of) emotions are to some extent visible in the comments and posts, when it comes to the issue of political action and the particular kind of participation and intervention particular contributors have in mind. Collins (1990) identified two types of emotions: transient emotions such as joy, embarrassment, fear, and anger, which might have a dramatic and interrupting impact on everyday life, on the one hand. Emotional energy, on the other hand, is a long-term emotional mode that has much more durability. Social movements and political protagonists need to transfer the first type into the second type in order to conserve the energy that is necessary to run long-term campaigns and remain active. Therefore, they need successful ritual interactions. While external observers might assess the decline in attendance at the PEGIDA rallies as a defeat of the movement, the ritual of its (nearly) weekly rallies might still serve the PEGIDA movement. Political participation in its many forms, therefore, is relevant empirically and should further be reflected theoretically in order to discuss it more from a normative point of view.

Political participation in post-migrant societies is not necessarily progressive in the way that it enhances only migrants' and refugees' taking part through them using manifold media. The spectrum of participation as outlined in this book across access, interaction, participation, and collaboration is useful as a heuristic approach, but when it comes to anti-migrant and racist protagonists making use of the broad range of (digital) media to spread their hate, there might be some reservations regarding a positive assessment of an extended level of participation and collaboration of such forces.

NOTES

1. The presentation here partly follows the structure of the interpretation presented by Anatol Stefanowitsch and Susanne Flach (2016) on behalf of the *Süddeutsche Zeitung* in order to allow comparison.

2. Mistakes here and in the following quotes are from the original text. 'Angi' is a reference to Angela Merkel.

3. Winfried Kretschmann is the first ever minister president in a German state who is a member of the Green Party.

4. (2015-01-03T14:15:27) means that the comment was made on 3 January 2015 at 2:15 p.m.

5. The comment refers to the debate about the social status and the socioeconomic situation of participants of PEGIDA rallies.

6. 'Suit' is a reference to Angela Merkel.

Part IV

VOICE AND AGENCY OF MARGINALIZED ACTORS IN POST-MIGRANT SOCIETIES

Chapter Ten

From Niche to Mainstream?

Post-Migrant Media Production as a Means of Fostering Participation

Viktorija Ratković

In discussions of the question of migrant participation in media, the focus for a long time tended to be on mainstream media.[1] Research shows that migrants are vastly underrepresented in mainstream media production, while non-mainstream media, such as alternative media, community media, and/ or ethnic minority media have a long tradition of including migrants (Horz 2014, 133). At the same time, these media tend to be marginalized in the media landscape, as they are understood to be of interest only to specific communities and/or groups. In this chapter, the Austrian magazine *biber* is presented as an example of post-migrant media, as a type of media that highlights ways of combatting marginalization of migrants in media production as well as in non-mainstream media. While post-migrant media are alternative media in the sense that they present alternative representations of everyday life in heterogeneous societies, they mirror the notion that society as a whole can and should be understood as post-migrant. Accordingly—and in contrast to traditional (understandings of) community media and ethnic minority media—they are not produced by members of one particular (ethnic) community for one particular (ethnic) community, but rather by those who have adopted a post-migrant perspective for the post-migrant society as a whole. In order to contextualize *biber*'s position in the Austrian media landscape, this chapter draws on research on the inclusion of migrants in mainstream media production and on non-mainstream media, such as ethnic minority media, which can be positioned as post-migrant media's predecessors. Through this, the chapter elaborates on the media's role in fostering civic cultures. The main focus is post-migrant media production as experienced by the producers of *biber*. By discussing *biber*'s efforts to enable marginalized groups to participate in and through media, the need for and the challenges of the incorporation of the post-migrant perspective in all media are highlighted.

MIGRANTS IN MAINSTREAM MEDIA PRODUCTION: FROM INCLUSION TO PARTICIPATION?

In the German-speaking context, questions of diversity in media are a relatively new field of research (Herczeg 2012, 178). Existing studies on the participation of migrants in media production paint a bleak picture, as migrants in both Germany and Austria and those who are ascribed a migrant background are vastly underrepresented. In 2009, Geißler, Enders, and Reuter found that only 1.2 percent of all journalists working in German newspapers had a migrant background, which means that either they themselves migrated to Germany or that they have at least one parent who did so. Moreover, the authors describe 84 percent of the 1,229 newspapers included in this study as working 'monoethnically' (Geißler, Enders, and Reuter 2009, 91), meaning that they did not employ any journalists with migrant backgrounds. Drawing on the results of this study as well as on those of two others (namely Geißler, Enders, and Reuter 2009 and Oulios 2009), Pöttker claims with some certainty that the percentage of journalists with 'migration experience'[2] working in German media is no higher than 4 to 5 percent (Pöttker 2016, 15). At the same time, 22.5 percent of Germany's inhabitants were either born without a German citizenship and/or have at least one parent for whom this is the case (Statistisches Bundesamt 2017).

In comparison, the situation in Austria is less clear. Two studies conducted in 2012 came to different conclusions. On the one hand, Petra Herczeg (2012) focused on 36 different print media outlets in Austria, including various daily newspapers and magazines, but also the Austrian Press Agency (APA) and the Austrian Broadcasting Corporation (ORF). Based on the responses of these media's editors in chief Herczeg states that, in total, 35 journalists with a migrant background[3] work in these media (the ORF and one newspaper did not provide any numbers). Drawing on the results of a study conducted by Kaltenbrunner et al. (2007), which concluded that 7,100 full-time journalists work in Austria, Herczeg claims that this means that only 0.49 percent of Austrian journalists have a migrant background. At the same time, more than half of the media contacted by Herczeg (55 percent) did not employ any journalists with a migrant background and were thus working 'monoethnically' (Herczeg 2012).

On the other hand, the authors of a survey conducted by the Medien-Servicestelle Neue Österreicher/innen (MNÖ 2012) state that 37 media outlets (12 daily newspapers, 7 magazines, 14 radio stations—2 of these, FM4 and Ö3, are part of ORF—APA, and 3 private TV stations) reported the number of journalists they employ. In total, these media outlets employed 1,716 journalists, out of which 182 (10.6 percent) have international roots. This refers to journalists who were born outside of Austria, have at least one parent who was born outside of Austria, have non-Austrian citizenship, or have a foreign country of origin. Sixty-two of these journalists (3.6 percent) come from Germany, 14 (0.8 percent) from countries belonging to the former Yugoslavia, and 6 (0.35 percent) from Turkey. The authors claim that journalists with a German background are overrepresented because only 2.7 percent of the Austrian population were born in Germany and/or have German citizenship, whereas journalists coming from countries belonging to the former Yugoslavia and Turkey are underrepresented, especially because the ex-Yugoslav community is the second largest, and the Turkish community the third largest immigrant community in Austria.[4] Interestingly, the authors also state that only 5 to 7 percent of the journalists have a migrant background, meaning that they were born outside of Austria and/or have parents who were both born outside of Austria. While no information is given on the number of media outlets that do not employ any non-Austrian journalists, of the authors out of the 37 media outlets reporting their journalists' national background, 22 employ at least one journalist with a German background, while 9 out of the 37 employ only Austrian and German journalists (MNÖ 2012). Although the numbers presented by Herczeg and MNÖ differ vastly, both show that journalists with a migrant background are underrepresented compared to the national average of Austrians with foreign backgrounds. According to Statistik Austria, 22 percent of the Austrian population were either born outside of Austria and/or had/have parents that were not born in Austria (Statistik Austria 2017).

In addition to the national background of journalists in Austria, Geißler, Enders, and Reuter (2009) as well as Herczeg (2012) also explored why migrants are underrepresented in mainstream media production. They came to similar conclusions. Editors claim that individuals with a migrant background tend to lack the necessary qualifications to work as journalists, especially when it comes to having a perfect command of the German language. The overrepresentation of journalists coming from Germany in the Austrian media landscape could thus be because German is their primary language, even though they fall into the category of journalists with a migrant background. At the same time, journalists with a migrant background who find their way into mainstream media often face discrimination. They tend to occupy low positions in the media's hierarchy (Röben 2008, 155), are less often permanently employed than their non-migrant colleagues (Geißler, Enders, and

Reuter 2009), predominantly work in non-prestigious departments (such as reporting on local/regional, society, or lifestyle/entertainment issues), and often are not part of a department at all (105–8). Often, as Oulios states, journalists with a migrant background are assigned topics connected to their migrant background, thus limiting the range of topics they are allowed to report on (Oulios 2009).

While the creation of a diverse media workforce is indeed important and can be measured from data on the inclusion of, for example, migrants in media production, these and similar findings fuel scepticism based on the assumption that the inclusion of migrants in mainstream media necessarily leads to change. On the one hand, the reproduction of problematic representations of migrants is a product of individual gatekeepers' values, as such representations are 'embedded within the production process itself through what appears as a common-sense economic/commercial rationale' (Saha 2016, 46). On the other hand, it is useful to look at the topic of migrants and media through the lens of participation and democratization. If participation is understood as the 'equalisation of power inequalities in particular decision-making processes' (Carpentier 2016a, 72), it is simply not enough to merely include marginalized groups into media production without ensuring that they are involved in crucial decision-making processes. At the same time, and on a much larger scale, media could also play a crucial role in equalizing power relations between migrant and non-migrant members of society, as media can foster civic cultures. *Civic cultures*, as Dahlgren (2011, 103) explains, 'refer to cultural patterns in which identities of citizenship, and the foundations for civic agency, are embedded,' while *civic agency* 'is premised on people being able to see themselves as participants' (102). Accordingly, in order for anyone to be able and willing to participate in the public sphere and political society and thus contribute to a functioning democracy, they must (first) have resources, rights, and chances to develop a civic identity. As for most people, the most fundamental source of their civic identity is probably their received citizenship, understood as 'formal membership as a legitimate, equal, and recognized citizen of the state' (120). However, many migrants and those who are ascribed a migrant background seem to be excluded from what Dahlgren calls 'identities of membership' (119). Nevertheless, even those without formal membership in a certain state can still act as political participants if they are enabled to act as citizens, going beyond just casting a vote in formal elections. Ideally, media should ensure participation of migrants in the media (via including migrants in media production and distributing representations of migrants within the media itself), but also through media by providing migrants 'with the opportunities for mediated participation in public debate and for self-representation in the variety of public spaces that characterize the social' (Carpentier, Dahlgren, and Pasquali 2013, 288). While mainstream media in German-speaking countries today, for the most part, fail to meet either of these challenges, non-mainstream media 'can be seen as a way to redress the power imbalances within the mainstream media' (290). In what follows, one type of non-mainstream media's efforts to enable participation of marginalized groups in as well as through itself are discussed in order to highlight existing challenges and opportunities.

MARGINALIZED MEDIA?
THE CASE FOR POST-MIGRANT MEDIA

As stated above, it is important to note that unlike mainstream media, non-mainstream media, such as community media, alternative media, and/or ethnic minority media, have a long tradition of including migrants (Horz 2014, 133). Different labels for this type of media are sometimes used interchangeably, which shows that a case can be made that these media share many similarities. Community and ethnic minority media tend to be seen as media that are meant to serve a certain community, which is not necessarily in opposition to alternative media's striving to present an alternative to mainstream media. Accordingly, Nico Carpentier states that 'we should not fetishise the many labels attributed to community media, and isolate the different theoretical approaches that these labels represent, but instead combine and respectfully integrate the different approaches to reach a more thorough understanding of community media practices and theories' (Carpentier 2016b, 4).[5] Whereas Carpentier's argument against the fetishization of labels is valid, it is nevertheless important to note that not all alternative and/or community media can be seen as 'ethnic minority media,' even though ethnic minority media could be seen both as alternative and community media. While Matsaganis, Katz, and Ball-Rokeach (2011, 6) define ethnic media as 'media that are produced by and for (a) immigrants, (b) racial, ethnic, and linguistic minorities, as well as (c) indigenous populations living across different countries,' they also state that the term 'ethnic minority media' can be seen as problematic. In some cases, some of those who are labelled a minority are in fact a majority. The terms 'alternative media' and/or 'community media' can be applied to media that are providing certain groups with the opportunity to participate in media production while simultaneously focusing on topics that are not represented in mainstream media. At the same time, research on ethnic community media has to be particularly cautious about not mirroring and thus reinforcing problematic discourses on migration and migrants. Unfortunately, in past research efforts, many problematic aspects are present, for example, when it comes to the terms used to describe this type of media. First, the term 'community' itself can be problematic as the discourse of 'community' can produce essentialized 'ethnic communities' (Bauman 1996), instead of taking into account the diversity and difference within certain 'communities.' In the German-speaking context, this view has contributed to the notion that ethnic minority media are potentially danger-ous; they might, if consumed exclusively, hinder migrants' integration into the majority population (Goldberg 2000, 420). Second, past research efforts tended to use the label 'ethnic media' (Ethnomedien) for ethnic minority me-dia, thus signalling that ethnicity is something only 'Others' have (Weber-Menges 2006; Matsaganis, Katz, and Ball-Rokeach 2011). This perspective omits the fact that most mainstream media can be described as 'ethnic me-dia' as they mainly are produced by white, non-migrant journalists and also mostly target white, non-migrant audiences. Fleras thus makes a case for re-framing mainstream news media '*as if* they were white ethnic media' (Fleras 2016, 23, emphasis in original). Nevertheless, mainstream media are com-monly understood as media that are of interest to everybody, whereas ethnic minority media are seen as only being of interest to particular communities. In contrast, Dreher argues that community media are not necessarily only ad-dressing specific communities, but that 'activities and projects developed by people working with communities subjected to media racism in order to alter or speak back to mainstream news media' should be seen as 'community me-dia interventions' (Dreher 2010, 86). Dreher employs the term 'intervention' in order to 'highlight the change orientation of these activities—they aim not merely for visibility or publicity, but rather to expand, diversify or contest the range and types of representations available' (ibid., 87).

In line with Dreher's argument, I propose a new term for media that are in the tradition of community media, alternative media, and/or ethnic minority media, but at the same time involve different approaches, producers, and audiences: post-migrant media. Post-migrant media are alternative media as they challenge and make visible media power and actively strive to include marginalized groups into media production. At the same time, they aim to produce counter-narratives and alternative representations of migrants and migration. As a result, they intervene in problematic discourses on migra-tion and contribute to the process of negotiating new forms of conviviality in post-migrant societies. Post-migrant media transcend common notions of the term '(ethnic) community' as they are neither produced by members of only one (ethnic) community nor aiming at specific ethnic communities, but at the post-migrant society as a whole. Instead of essentializing migration or a certain so-called ethnic community, they show the differences that ex-ist in every society and within every so-called ethnic community. In doing so, they achieve two seemingly contradictory goals: on the one hand post-migrant media emphasize the experience(s) of migration, while on the other hand they show that migration is not necessarily the most important factor in the lives of migrants and those who are ascribed a migrant background. At the same time, the post-migrant experience is described as one that can provide a sense of community and thus foster civic agency—for migrants, for those who are ascribed a migrant background but also for members of the so-called majority population.

POST-MIGRANT MEDIA PRODUCTION: FOSTERING SUSTAINABILITY AND PROFESSIONALIZATION

Founded in 2006, *biber*[6] is described by its producers as an 'intelligent, critical and stylish' transcultural magazine and the only Austrian magazine reporting directly out of a multi-ethnic community' (*biber* n.d. [a]). It is aimed at what *biber* calls 'new Austrians (Viennese with and without a migration background),' specifically Viennese of the so-called second and third generation as well as at those who appreciate Vienna's cultural diversity. The magazine is published ten times per year; it can be accessed for free at *biber*'s website. Copies are also distributed in 2,700 places in Vienna, and every month 65,000 copies are printed and are read by 179,000 readers (ibid.). *biber*'s readers are mostly young (66 percent are under 30, 86 percent under 40 years) and well educated (ibid.). *biber* is made by 'young, ambitious journalists with Turkish, Bosnian, Serbian, Croatian, Kurdish, Brazilian, Carinthian, Upper Austrian, Slovenian and so forth-ish background' (ibid.), which, as *biber* states, makes authentic reporting possible. Its aim is to reflect and represent the lived diversity in Austria, providing new Austrians with a 'medial identity' and 'emotional home.' It stands for pluralistic tolerance in democratic societies and positions itself against extremist discourses that endanger this diversity (ibid.). *biber* covers a wide range of topics, while mostly using an easy-going and often ironic language. Bright colours and many pictures convey the impression that *biber* is fun and easy to read, as it does not take itself too seriously.

In December of 2017, I conducted an expert interview (following Pfadenhauer 2009) with *biber*'s founder, editor-in-chief, and publisher, Simon Kravagna. Prior to the idea of founding *biber*, Kravagna worked as a journalist himself. He mainly reported on domestic affairs in renowned Austrian daily newspapers and magazines. Kravagna states that even though his mother is German, he is perceived as not having a migrant background, as he was born and raised in Austria. The team that produced the first issue of *biber* consisted of twenty to twenty-five volunteers whom Kravagna found via the noticeboard at the University of Vienna. Initially, he was looking for students with an 'international background,' preferably students from Turkey or the former Yugoslavia. The initial team consisted of university students whose parents and grandparents migrated to Austria as so-called guest workers from Turkey and the former Yugoslavia in the 1960s and 1970s, following the establishment of formal recruitment agreements. Although none of them had any experience in journalism, they all were interested in telling stories they knew from experience but did not see represented in Austrian mainstream media.

Looking back at *biber*'s beginnings, Kravagna states that working with volunteers, which is a common practice in community/alternative media (see Matsaganis, Katz, and Ball-Rokeach 2011, 228), had and still has positive and negative implications. While volunteers tend to be very engaged and committed, they also lack time and experience. Today, the situation is fundamentally different, as the magazine is run by professional journalists with an international background who, according to Kravagna, are paid 'like everybody else.' The editorial staff consists of approximately three full-time employed journalists, one person responsible for organizational aspects, one managing director, a photo editor, and various freelance contributors (photographers, journalists) as well as paid interns.

While achieving sustainability is one of non-mainstream media's biggest challenges, I argue that three interconnected factors enabled *biber*'s evolution and success. First, the magazine presents its readers with a post-migrant perspective and thus fills a growing demand for alternative perspectives on migration. Second, *biber*'s is able to attract advertising partners and important collaborators, thereby securing the magazine's finances. Third, the staff foster professionalization by providing journalism training to diverse target groups. The rest of this chapter explains each of these factors in greater detail.

THE POST-MIGRANT PERSPECTIVE

At the time of *biber*'s founding, as Kravagna states, Austrian mainstream media were mostly ignorant of the concerns that made and make up *biber*'s content. They neither provided the space nor understood topics that were and are of concern to those who have an 'international background.' Kravagna's observation confirms Saha's claim that mainstream media fail to serve non-white (as well as non-indigenous) audiences (Saha 2016). It also describes the German-speaking media landscape in general. For example, Geißler, Enders, and Reuter stated in 2009 that the majority of Germany's editors-in-chief failed to recognize the topic of including migrants in media production as a relevant issue (Geißler, Enders, and Reuter 2009, 88). Ironically, at the same time, migration was an important topic in German-speaking media, but the hegemonic perspective on migration was almost exclusively a non-migrant one. The experiences of those who have 'an additional homeland, an additional language, an additional culture,' as Kravagna puts it, were ignored by mainstream media, thus presenting *biber* as a niche for discussing questions of identity from a post-migrant point of view. In contrast to mainstream media's predominantly negative and stereotypical coverage of migrants, *biber* stressed everyday situations that those who are marked as different encounter (e.g., facing the consequences of speaking a language other than German in public). This provided its writers and readers a platform to discuss personal experiences from their own point of view. By focusing on these kinds of topics, viewpoints, and experiences, *biber* clearly discovered and filled a niche, similar to what is described by Matsaganis, Katz, and Ball-Rokeach:

> [I]nterest in development of hybrid, hyphenated, and conglomerate identities among ethnic minority youth both encourages and is encouraged by the development of ethnic media that reflect these identifications. These shifts in identification can provide opportunities for ethnic media entrepreneurs to develop ethnic media productions in new forms and with new kinds of content that reflect the needs and tastes of youth growing up in an increasingly globalized world. (2011, 261)

While *biber* is primarily produced by those with an 'international background,' the magazine is also directed at those who have no migration experience and is produced in the German language, unlike traditional ethnic community media. Its explicit goal can be described as trying to 'expand, diversify or contest the range and types of representations available' (Dreher 2010, 87), thus making *biber*'s reporting a 'community media intervention' (87), while transcending the meaning of community. The contributors do not share the same ethnicity, but most of them do share the experience of being perceived as non-Austrian and different from the implicit norm. They do not necessarily write from the perspective of a specific ethnic community, but from the perspective of post-migration. Nevertheless, Kravagna states, conflicts between different groups on *biber*'s staff arise at times, for example, when it comes to discussing the wars in the former Yugoslavia or the Kurds' situation in Turkey. As he himself is perceived as Austrian and thus seemingly unbiased, Kravagna sometimes assumes the role of a mediator. In these instances, not being perceived as part of what is commonly understood as an ethnic community is to his advantage, although Kravagna admits that one must be cautious about presuming that those who are unmarked are indeed unbiased and neutral. Accordingly, the 'Austrian standpoint' is continually presented less as a neutral and normal one in *biber*'s reporting, but rather as just as debatable and at times exotic as the views and values that are ascribed to migrant communities (Ratković 2018).

While *biber* is undeniably addressing the needs and interests of those who are ascribed a migration background, Kravagna states that it is not perceived as a 'migration magazine' by what he calls 'the hard-core migrants' community' (e.g., by the conservative members of the Turkish community in Vienna). They, Kravagna claims, are irritated that the staff is made up of journalists with different backgrounds and fail to see anything Turkish in *biber*. Moreover, he states, many see the magazine as too liberal and a 'bobo magazine' that does not represent any community's interests, but instead focuses only on lifestyle topics. In this case, 'bobo' describes a bourgeois-bohemian lifestyle ascribed to those who, on the one hand, claim to hold countercultural and highly tolerant viewpoints, and on the other hand, lead an upper-class, capitalistic lifestyle. In my own research, I have found that *biber* indeed incorporates both aspects. While it presents alternative viewpoints on migration and thus intervenes in problematic discourses on migration, its authors often promote the neoliberal mantra of personal success and perfect lifestyle (Ratković 2018). This combination, I argue, is one of the key factors of *biber*'s success so far. Its producers have managed to cater to an emerging market in a way that makes it attractive to advertising partners and (state) institutions.

FINANCING

As Kravagna admits, being perceived as a 'bobo,' or lifestyle, magazine has helped *biber* secure ads from Austrian companies that see the magazine's target audiences as potential consumers. It is important to note that migrants and those ascribed a migrant background were ignored for a long time by companies selling products. Over the last years, however, Austrian companies, among others in Europe, have become increasingly aware of the buying potential of these target groups. 'Ethnomarketing' uses ethnic characteristics and cultural criteria in order to promote products and services for specific ethnic minorities. Similarly, the post-migrant lifestyle that *biber* promotes can be seen as interconnected with the celebration of an international lifestyle that is enjoyed by those who have the privilege of mobility and not the burden of migration. This is evident in Kravagna's and *biber*'s preference for using the term 'international background' instead of the much more established term 'migration background.' The former seems to carry much more positive connotations. Kravagna also states that in *biber*'s beginnings, representatives of international corporations based in Vienna were in search of a platform that presented positive views on migration that corresponded with their own experiences of working internationally.

More importantly, however, the most crucial aspect of *biber*'s financial success is its being located in Vienna. Kravagna states that Vienna is/was a fertile ground for media as the city, governed by the Social Democratic Party, has spent millions of euros on advertising in all types of media. Also, during *biber*'s beginnings, state and city officials were eager to present Vienna as a multinational city as well as to celebrate diversity. Accordingly, *biber* has a longstanding tradition of cooperating with both Vienna's institutions and Austria's ministries, which translates into advertorials that promote the inclusion of those with a migrant background into Austria's police force, for example. While these collaborations surely can be seen as problematic, as they may hamper a critique of the state and city institutions, Carpentier correctly states that 'community media (and other civil organisations) establish these kinds of linkages with (segments of) the state and the market without necessarily losing their proper identity, and without becoming incorporated and/or assimilated. They are, in other words, not merely counter-hegemonic, but engage with the market and the state' (Carpentier 2016a, 5).

Despite these initial successes, the election of a right-wing government in Austria in 2017 will most likely be damaging for *biber*'s future. Kravagna states that the public perspective on migration has noticeably changed since the arrival of refugees from Arab countries in 2015/2016 in Austria. While multinationalism was beginning to be celebrated during the 1990s, and *biber* was thus able to secure collaborations with important state representatives, migration is once again predominantly being perceived as a problem. This is especially true when it comes to newly arrived refugees from Arab countries whom, as Kravagna says, *biber* is actively striving to include in its production. While the Austrian government is more or less openly hostile towards these refugees, Kravagna thinks that the magazine should continually include the 'newly arrived' on its staff in order to present new perspectives. As *biber*'s success so far has also been based on highlighting outsiders' perspectives, the inclusion of newly arrived refugees might indeed secure its future. Nevertheless, Kravagna also states that in light of current developments, *biber* is planning to rely less on collaborations with state institutions and more on crowdfunding. Crowdfunding can be seen as an example of participation, as it enables people to invest in various types of projects and ventures. Prinzling and Gattermann (2015, 201), based on their study of various crowdfunding campaigns aiming to fund journalistic projects, state that funders of these projects are generally not interested in being actively involved in the production of the journalistic products themselves; however, they believe that crowdfunding not only enables independent journalism, but also media diversity (ibid., 204). Thus, one could argue that funders are not motivated by the wish to participate *in* the media themselves, but by the wish to enable participation *through* media by ensuring that a wide range of opportunities for mediated participation in public debates exists (see Carpentier, Dahlgren, and Pasquali 2013, 288).

TRAINING

As discussed above, one of the main reasons why those with a migrant background remain underrepresented in media production is that migrants allegedly lack the necessary qualifications for journalistic work, as identified by editors of mainstream media. When asked about his experiences working in mainstream media, Kravagna confirmed that those with a migrant background often lack the necessary experience to work at a mainstream newspaper/magazine. In general, as Kravagna states, mainstream media do not take the time to train new staff, but expect everybody to work at a professional level. In order to gain experience, aspiring journalists have to work as unpaid interns. Many of those with a migrant background cannot afford to do so. Also, typical journalism students, Kravagna says, do not have a migrant background. For the most part, their parents are highly educated and are high-income earners who can easily provide for their child's living expenses while they gain the necessary experience working as unpaid interns. Kravagna is also under the impression that the Austrian Universities of Applied Sciences that offer journalism degrees are not interested in fostering diversity in their student body. Accordingly, no one on *biber*'s staff, as Kravagna reports, actually holds a journalism degree (even though all have or are currently obtaining a university degree). To his knowledge, nobody with a journalism degree has ever applied for a job at *biber*.

Although 'most ethnic media rely heavily on the work of volunteers and low-paid staff to put in long hours' (Matsaganis, Katz, and Ball-Rokeach 2011, 228) and editors are forced to play a teaching role, this was only the case during *biber*'s beginnings. Today, Kravagna explains, the journalists working at *biber* are professionals who, for the most part, are not trained on the job. The evolution from a magazine run by volunteers to one made up of professional journalists might seem natural, as those who started as inexperienced volunteers might be expected to naturally turn into professionals by simply doing the job. In reality, there is a high turnover at *biber*, which is mostly a result of poaching by mainstream media. This is often the case in community/alternative/ethnic minority media, as Matsaganis, Katz, and Ball-Rokeach explain. Often, such media are stepping stones for young and talented journalists, while 'this "brain drain" or "poaching,"' however, is more likely to affect large-scale ethnic media organizations with the kind of visibility that allows their journalists to get noticed' (2011, 231). This is very much true for *biber*, which regularly cooperates with Austrian mainstream media, by publishing the same article written by *biber*'s staff, for example. While Kravagna states that these losses are painful for the magazine, he also admits that the situation can be seen as positive, as new journalists are able to join *biber*'s team.

biber has three different training opportunities in place that target three different groups, with the goal to include those who traditionally lack journalistic experience while professionals actually do the work at the same time. The first training program, named 'biber Newcomer,' is aimed at Viennese students fourteen years of age and older. *biber*'s journalists spend a week with a class, providing the students with an opportunity to learn how journalism works. The students then accompany journalists on trips to newspapers, ministries, or companies and attend photography and video workshops. At the end of each week, the students can publish their work on *biber*'s blog.[7] The training is provided free of charge and is sponsored by different companies/institutions (among them the daily newspaper *Heute*, the European Commission, the Austrian Armed Forces, and the Vienna Municipal Education Authority). At the same time, students are involved in the production of two issues of *biber*. Every June and December, a 'biber Newcomer' issue is published. Eighty-five thousand copies of these issues are printed and in part distributed among Viennese schools. (*biber* n.d. [b])

The second program, named 'biber Academy' and founded in 2011, is aimed at eighteen- to twenty-eight-year-olds. The goal is to 'recruit and train the new Austria's future journalism generation' (*biber* n.d. [c]). Those who want to become journalists in order to be able to shape the way the media report about migrants and to improve the ways in which migrants are represented in Austria can apply by describing what they would like to write about. The program consists of a three-month-long basic journalism training program. During the first two months, participants publish their work in *biber*. During the third month, they work at *biber*'s partner media or a press office. Participants are expected to work full time and receive a stipend of 600 euros. Since 2011, sixty participants have completed the training; many of them are now working for Austrian mainstream media and also for various public institutions (e.g., the Austrian Ministry of Foreign Affairs). Some go on to work at *biber* (e.g., Delna Antia, who participated in 2012 and is currently serving as the magazine's deputy editor in chief). The 'biber Academy' is funded by various organizations and companies, among them, the Austrian Federal Railways, the oil and gas company OMV, the Austrian Federal Economic Chamber, and the Austrian Ministry of Foreign Affairs (ibid.).

The third training opportunity/program is aimed at asylum seekers and those granted subsidiary protection in Austria. Starting in March of 2017, *biber* has provided this program's participants with job training named 'Media, Journalism and Communication.' Over the course of four months, participants receive subject-specific German-language training by a professional teacher as well as journalistic training. The goal is to provide participants with an overview of Austria's media landscape and with the opportunity to acquire qualifications necessary for their future careers (e.g., by learning about interview techniques and new/social media). The training is funded by the Vienna Social Fund (*biber* n.d. [d]).

While *biber*'s training programs seem extensive, the goal, as Kravagna states, is not to train hundreds of journalists. Not everybody, Kravagna admits, has to become a journalist, especially as the Austrian media landscape does not provide enough job opportunities. At the same time, it is important to notice that by training participants who go on to work at important companies or institutions, *biber* is extending its network and thus potentially securing future cooperation opportunities and influence. These trainings can also be seen as a means of fostering media literacy when it comes to representations of migrants in mainstream media and thus provide *biber* with potential readers who are looking for alternative representations. Additionally, the trainings offer the magazine an opportunity to stay up to date with new developments and changing migrant communities, while recruiting promising talents at the same time.

While the 'biber Newcomer' program was not designed exclusively for students with a migrant background, 'biber Academy' was originally intended for those who have an 'international background.' Nevertheless, some Austrians without migrant backgrounds applied, which, as Kravagna admits, caused some discussions among *biber*'s staff members. Some argued that those without a migrant background should be able to find other, (paid) internships on their own, but ultimately, it was decided that they should not exclude certain groups based on their origins. Subsequently, participants who do not have a migration background but show interest in *biber*'s topics are also welcome in this program. At the same time, everybody working at *biber* has an 'international background,' and Kravagna states that indigenous Austrians may not feel welcome. They seem to perceive *biber* as a 'migrant medium' that can and maybe should only be produced by those with a migrant background. This is not to say that Austrians without a migrant background are hesitant to write about migration. In mainstream media, the majority of migration topics are covered by those who have no migration experience. The challenge for non-immigrant journalists thus does not lie in writing about migration, but in writing about migration from a post-migrant point of view. While it might seem that only those with a migration background are capable of writing from a post-migrant point of view, I argue that everyone can adopt a critical viewpoint on migration and the representation of migrants that is inherent in a post-migrant perspective. Just as, for example, feminist arguments and perspectives are and should not be limited to cis women, post-migrant arguments and perspectives can be adopted once they have been voiced and elaborated on by those who are currently most affected by existing migration regimes and problematic discourses. The post-migrant perspective is inherently one that accepts heterogeneity, ambivalence, and transformation as key aspects of the everyday experience of all members of society while keeping in mind that power relations, exclusion and inclusion, also play a key role. At the same time, post-migrant media should also incorporate critical non-migrant viewpoints, as those are part of the negotiations about migration processes.

IMPLICATIONS FOR MAINSTREAM MEDIA AND BEYOND

Since the magazine's beginnings, things have changed, as is most obvious from the fact that *biber*'s journalists are often poached by Austrian mainstream media, which at times also publish articles originally written for *biber*. Despite the difficulty that this poaching might represent for *biber* itself, it ultimately leads to migrant voices being represented in mainstream media. Still, the question of how more migrant voices can enter mainstream media remains. So far, *biber* serves as a platform for aspiring journalists to learn the trade and to move on to mainstream media, thus providing mainstream media with a valuable service. While the continuous loss of trained staff is painful for *biber*, the alternative, namely having mainstream media provide in-house training for aspiring journalists from marginalized groups, could hurt *biber* even more. *biber*'s training efforts are a crucial aspect of its success as they strengthen its place in Austria's media landscape and provide the magazine's makers with a growing network of potential supporters. As various Austrian corporations and state institutions fund these training efforts, it is clear that some understanding of the necessity of media and journalism training from a migrant perspective exists. What remains to be seen is whether this understanding will deepen or vanish in the face of growing resentment against refugees and (newly arrived) migrants.

Ultimately, *biber*'s success shows that there is indeed a need and thus a market for alternative representations of migration and for increasing participation of those who are traditionally ascribed a migration background. While market logic might for some be enough of an argument to incorporate diverse and critical perspectives into mainstream media production, it is also important to note that the most relevant argument here is that participation in and through media for diverse groups of people is crucial for democratic civic cultures. Even though strong and loud forces exist which insist that homogeneity and certainty should and can be achieved, the reality is that all societies have always been and will always be characterized by heterogeneity and struggles for participation. While mainstream media often portray (forced) togetherness of (seemingly) diverse groups of people as inevitably problematic, *biber* shows that even though tensions and power imbalances exist, diverse groups of people can actually work with and through conflicts. *biber* is clearly successful in enabling those who are traditionally ascribed a migrant background to participate in *biber*'s production as well as in the production of Austrian mainstream media. At the same time, it also provides its readers the opportunity to participate *through biber*, as it gives room to post-migrant self-representations, opinions, and experiences. Most importantly, however, *biber* portrays even the newly arrived as part of the Austrian society, thus giving them a sense of membership that is crucial to developing their civic agency. This is especially relevant in today's societies which are characterized by people on the move. *biber*'s efforts can thus serve as examples for the ways in which inevitable and constant struggles for participation can be transformed into productive forces that enable new modes of living and working together.

A crucial aspect of the post-migrant perspective in journalism is the need to apply it to all aspects of life and society. This is why it would be interesting to know which positions former *biber*'s journalists occupy in mainstream media and whether their reporting is restricted to migration topics. At the same time, one must keep in mind that participation in media is not restricted to just media output, but also includes organizational decision-making (Carpentier, Dahlgren, and Pasquali 2013, 288). Accordingly—and as existing research on the inclusion of migrants in mainstream media production shows—it is necessary to make sure that those who are trained by *biber* and go on to work in prominent mainstream media are involved in decision-making processes on all levels of media production. Lastly, mainstream media as well as *biber* need to find sustainable ways to encourage those without a migrant background to adopt a post-migrant perspective, ultimately recognizing the fact that they, too, are part of the post-migrant society and thus to act accordingly.

NOTES

1. Acknowledgements: I want to thank Claudia Brunner, Hajnalka Nagy, Daniela Lehner, and Heike Petschnig for their equally critical and encouraging comments on earlier drafts of this chapter.

2. Pöttker uses 'migration experience' and 'migration background' interchangeably, while referring to the definition of 'migration background' of The Federal Statistical Office (Statistisches Bundesamt) which ascribes a migrant background to the following groups: Everyone who migrated to Germany since 1949, who was born in Germany to foreigners, Germans born in Germany with at least one parent who migrated to Germany, or was born in Germany as a foreigner (Statistisches Bundesamt 2012, 6).

3. Herczeg does not provide a definition for the term 'migration background.'

4. No references are given for the numbers on the communities. At the same time, the numbers cannot be corroborated, as Statistik Austria reports on different categories.

5. Carpentier uses the label 'community media' while referring to 'community/ alternative/civil society/rhizomatic media' for reasons of convenience (see Carpentier 2016, 6).

6. The name *biber* was chosen as it carries meaning in German, Serbo-Croatian, and Turkish: while in German, *biber* means 'beaver,' in Serbo-Croatian it means pepper, and in Turkish, chili pepper.

7. See http://www.dasbiber.at/schueler/blog, accessed 9 January 2018.

Chapter Eleven

Beyond Marginalized Voices

Listening as Participation in Multicultural Media

Tanja Dreher and Poppy de Souza

This chapter analyses 'listening' as a crucial mode of media participation for the privileged in response to marginalized voices. Our example is Indigenous Health May Day (#IHMayDay), an annual Twitter event that privileges and amplifies First Nations voices in settler colonial Australia. During this event, non-Indigenous people are invited to participate by listening and amplifying. In this chapter, we extend an interest in media, voice, and participation to the politics of listening as a necessary and undervalued practice for media participation and transformation. Our analysis begins from Foroutan's (2015, 6) observation that national policies of 'integration' place a disproportionate burden on migrant or marginalized communities without an attendant responsibility for the dominant to change. Against a backdrop of resurgent racisms and the state's retreat from official multicultural policies in Australia, First Nations are at the forefront of experiments in the politics of listening. These projects offer specific, situated responsibilities to listen and practices that could be scaled up. The invitation to participate in #IHMayDay by listening signals a clear responsibility for non-Indigenous Australians, and centres First Nations' strengths and voice. However, this politics of listening cannot be adequately understood within European post-migrant frameworks, as the centring of migration obscures rather than transforms the founding dispossession and on-going colonial violence of settler colonial Australia. We, therefore, argue that the foregrounding of colonialism, solidarities, and decolonizing frameworks has much to offer to the emerging scholarship and practice on post-migrant societies.

LISTENING AS PARTICIPATION

The Part IV title, 'Voice and Agency of Marginalized Actors in Post-Migrant Societies,' of this volume indicates that participation in media culture, and in politics, is most commonly understood via metaphors of 'voice' (Couldry 2010). In multicultural societies such as Australia, policies and projects have been developed whereby marginalized communities 'speak up and talk back,' 'find a voice' and share stories. Ensuring 'voice for the voiceless' is a key marker of democracy, social justice, and participatory culture. Only recently has attention shifted to consider 'listening' as an equally vital form of participation in media and politics (O'Donnell, Lloyd, and Dreher 2009). Kate Crawford (2009) provides a compelling argument for considering listening as an active and valuable form of participation in social media in particular. Emerging literature considers listening as the 'other side' of democratic participation (Dreher, McCallum, and Waller 2016) and suggests that listening is the 'key' to 'maximalist' participation (Waller, Dreher, and McCallum 2015). While the concept of 'voice' connects neatly with a familiar understanding of participation as taking part in media production, a focus on 'listening' turns attention to the actors and institutions addressed by marginalized voices and asks questions of receptivity and response (Waller, Dreher, and McCallum 2015; Dreher 2009).

THE LISTENING TURN

The past decade has witnessed increasing calls to bring listening to the forefront in media research, practice, and policy (Burgess 2006; Couldry 2010; Dreher 2009; Husband 2009; Macnamara 2017; O'Donnell, Lloyd, and Dreher 2009; Penman and Turnbull 2012). Theorizations of listening as a political practice stress key features including openness, receptivity, attentiveness, and responsiveness (Bickford 1996; Bassel 2017; Dobson 2014; Fiumara 1990; Lipari 2010; Ratcliffe 2005). Political listening involves 'a little vulnerability' (Coles 2004) and the potential for uncertainty and discomfort, as listening entails the possibility that one might be persuaded or change one's mind (Bickford 1996). The politics of listening thus requires courage (Bickford 1996; Thill 2009) and humility (Ratcliffe 2005; Vice 2010) and a commitment to interdependence rather than the desire for mastery (Bickford 1996; Ratcliffe 2005; Dreher 2009). Attention to the politics of listening thus offers a fresh angle on questions of participation. It shifts the perspective from the voice of the marginalized to questions about the powerful, thereby to some of the focus and responsibility for democratic and just outcomes to media conventions, institutions, and practices (Dreher 2009).

Because much of the literature on the politics of listening has focused on questions of difference, responsibility, and privilege, we argue that this scholarship of listening has much to offer to any analysis of media and participation in post-migrant societies across Europe. Theories of listening can bring questions of responsibility to the fore, given an interest to address the concern that integration policies have placed a disproportionate focus on migrant efforts to adapt and integrate, without an attendant responsibility of those with a 'non-migrant' background to also adapt (Foroutan 2015). A number of authors analyse listening responsibilities or obligations, including Susan Bickford (1996), Roger Silverstone (2013), Krista Ratcliffe (2005), Charles Husband (1996), Cate Thill (2009) and Tanja Dreher (2009a; 2009b). John Downing (2007) has given further focus to Husband's (1996) argument for a 'Right to be Understood,' arguing that constructive cultural change is contingent on engendering 'a sense of obligation to listen' to those historically marginalized from public communication. Dobson (2014) describes political listening as a 'solvent of power,' while Romand Coles (2004) describes social-movement listening practices as 'turning the tables.' For both Dobson (2014) and Kate Lacey (2013), 'listening out' for difference and for voices or opinions that clash with one's own is vital to political life. Taken together, these concepts position listening as a political practice whereby those who are discursively relatively privileged and powerful might participate in transforming media and politics. While much of the literature focuses on individual responsibilities, there is no doubt that responsibilities to listen might also inhere in key democratic institutions (Macnamara 2017; Coleman 2013) and media institutions (Dreher 2009).

LISTENING, PARTICIPATION, AND RESPONSIBILITY IN SETTLER COLONIAL MULTICULTURE

Our work explores the concept of post-migrant societies in the context of Australia, a settler colonial context where Indigenous sovereignty and multiculturalism sit in 'uneasy conversation' (Curthoys 2000). This complicates, but also deepens, our thinking about the responsibility to listen to historically marginalized voices when racialized migrants (non-white/non-Anglo) are both complicit in, and excluded from, the founding logics of the (white) nation and simultaneously victim of, and implicated in, its racial formation through assimilationist, integrationist, and multicultural policies and practices (see

Perera 2005). We suggest that writing from Australia offers a cautionary note as to the possibilities for understanding ourselves as a 'country of migrants' to truly ensure justice, bringing colonialism, privilege, deep inequalities, and institutionalized racisms into the picture.

While 'working through the legacies of departed empire' might indeed be a necessary step to 'developing durable and habitable multiculture' (Gilroy 2006, 27) for post-migrant societies in Britain and Western Europe, the notion of a 'departed empire' does not so easily map onto settler colonial states such as Australia, Canada, the United States, and Aotearoa New Zealand founded on Indigenous dispossession.[1] Indeed, processes of marginalization, as well as possibilities for post-migrant conviviality and participation, work differently in a 'white post-colonizing society' (Moreton-Robinson 2003) where the colonizers/settlers have not gone home and where migrancy and Indigenous dispossession are intimately interlinked. In this context, immigration as a foundational feature of post-migrant societies (Foroutan 2015) is a problematic basis for justice in Australia and beyond, where a countervailing narrative to the 'multicultural success story' is the 'untold story of ongoing oppression of Indigenous peoples' (Bassel 2017, 73).

In an important and strategic move, Avril Bell (2016) rethinks Paul Gilroy's (2004, 2006) seminal work on convivial culture after Empire, looking instead at how conviviality might work in the context of Aotearoa New Zealand and other settler colonial societies with Indigenous populations. She argues that reversing the relationship between 'migrant' and 'settler' cultures works to productively recast white settlers (Pākehā) as the migrant culture and centre its Indigenous Māori population. For Bell, this 'crucial reversal in who is of migrant origin points to ways in which a conviviality that supports everyday decolonization might work somewhat differently in settler society' (Bell 2016, 1171). While we agree with Bell that unsettling and decolonizing relationships and racialized hierarchies are crucial to developing conviviality in settler colonial societies, we are concerned that there are dangers in retaining, even in reversal, the temporal logics of migration and migrancy. It quickly becomes evident that frameworks focusing on negotiations between 'migrant' and 'host' communities can obscure violent exclusions and colonial oppressions as well as smooth over the complexities of entrenched racialized hierarchies. First Nations peoples in settler colonial societies have rightly rejected incorporation into the liberal framework of 'multiculturalism,' refusing the temporal frame that positions them as simply the first in an on-going succession of migrants to be integrated into the multicultural 'melting pot.'[2] As Moran (2017, 215) has noted, Indigenous people have at times resisted 'incorporation within multicultural debates and agendas, asserting instead distinct Indigenous rights and claims in relation to the Australian settler state.'

Building intercultural solidarities that centre Indigenous sovereignty and unsettle dominant narratives of the nation state must begin from an examination of the 'interlocking nature of the processes by which Australia's racialized others were constituted' (Perera 2005, 36). Critically reflecting on her own responsibility as a 'non-Anglo' migrant to Australia, Suvendrini Perera (2005, 37), a Tamil woman from Sri Lanka, makes a compelling case for thinking through the 'possibilities of cross-cultural histories of Indigenous and non-Anglo Australians and their ability to complicate, undermine and decentre the dominant narratives and authority of whiteness in Anglo-Australia.' As Leah Bassel (2017, 80) writes in the Canadian context, narratives of white 'settlers' entering *terra nullius*—the terminology used in international law to describe unoccupied/unclaimed territory, derived from the Latin for 'no man's land'—exclude the 'complex history of racialised migrants in national narratives'; therefore 'speaking and listening from migrant locations can redefine this narrative.'

This necessary and important work, at the intersection of the multicultural and Indigenous, makes clear the pressing need to interrogate the 'sacred ignorance' at the heart of settler colonialism, one which is 'enshrined, sanctioned, blessed, endorsed, [and] affirmed' in the institutions of our society, including media (Perera 2005, 32), and instead take up the responsibility to centre and respect First Nations sovereignty.

In the following section, we analyse a social media intervention developed by Indigenous Australians in order to identify specific practices of listening that might also be applied or adapted for 'multicultural' or 'post-migrant' contexts in Australia and Europe. While #IHMayDay works within an Indigenous/non-Indigenous framework, the practices have relevance for other contexts in which marginalized voices struggle to be heard against dominant narratives. The politics of listening developed here works not on a host-migrant logic, but rather foregrounds principles of solidarity, decolonizing politics, and ally responsibilities. The 'mainstream' or dominant are not asked to offer 'welcome' or acceptance, but rather are invited to shift position and to participate in a decolonizing methodology by practices of listening to and amplifying voices that have been systematically marginalized.

While we focus on an example located in settler colonial Australia, a comparable interest in decolonizing knowledges is increasingly evident within former colonial metropoles as well. Across South Africa, the #RhodesMustFall movement led to campaigns to decolonize universities. It has also inspired a #RhodesMustFall and decolonization movement at Oxford University in the UK. In The Netherlands, scholars and activists seek to bring the long ignored history of the Dutch slave trade to the forefront of public and academic debate. In Germany, claims to reckon with the genocide perpetrated in Namibia have gained some traction. These movements suggest vital opportunities to develop media cultures that are responsive not only to recent migration, but also to the need to destabilize colonial legacies and to unsettle dominant narratives of the nation and belonging. We suggest this requires a necessary double move to democratize *and* decolonize listening practices.

#IHMAYDAY

Indigenous Health May Day (#IHMayDay) is an example of decolonizing media practices. In Australia, Indigenous people use social media at a rate higher than non-Indigenous Australians to 'connect between generations, to connect with culture and to connect with other Indigenous peoples globally' (Carlson 2017). First Nations are also at the forefront of social media interventions, including the strategic use of hashtags (e.g., #Indigenousdads), which explicitly reject 'deficit discourses' with counter-narratives and images of strength and pride. Building on the vibrant and established Indigenous community media sector in Australia, 'the emergence of new platforms like the Twitter account @ IndigenousX, and the innovative use of social media by the National Aboriginal Community Controlled Health Organisation [NACCHO] to disseminate Indigenous health news and to develop networks and influence' (Sweet et al. 2014, 626) are examples of social media interventions that privilege and amplify Indigenous voices. #IHMayDay is part of this burgeoning First Nations resurgence, but what makes the annual event so exciting and innovative is the way it disrupts/intervenes in the 'economies of attention' that shape and mediate how Indigenous people are represented and heard, while simultaneously reimagining/redefining the relationship between listening, participation, and responsibility in its call to action. Beyond asserting a charge of responsibility for non-Indigenous people to participate by listening, the Indigenous organizers of #IHMayDay go further: they invite participants to *listen in very specific ways*, underpinned by decolonizing methodologies.

#IHMayDay is an annual Twitter event developed by Bwgcolman woman Dr Lynore Geia.[3] First held in 2014 and moderated by Geia, it was hosted by Croakey, 'an independent project of social journalism for health' (Croakey 2015). In 2016, Tanja Dreher collaborated with her colleague, Aboriginal woman and associate professor Bronwyn Carlson, to host the 'Twitter day of action' at the University of Wollongong. For fourteen hours, beginning at 7:00 a.m., the #IHMayDay Twitter feed was curated by Dr Lynore Geia, Yorta Yorta woman Summer May Finlay (@SummerMayFinlay), a public health practitioner and researcher, and Bronwyn Carlson. Each hour featured a new guest tweeter, invited by the curating team to contribute their expertise on the 2016 theme of youth and families as well as suicide prevention and to showcase the diversity of Indigenous voices.

#IHMayDay programming prioritizes a strengths-based approach and challenges the 'deficit discourse' that dominates much public discussion, research, and policy-making with regards to First Nations in Australia. Action research and practical interventions increasingly seek to shift the deficit discourse in contexts including education and health. Deficit discourse 'frames and represents Aboriginal identity in a narrative of negativity, deficiency and disempowerment [and] are counter-productive, circular and persistent' (Waller, McCallum, and Gorringe 2018, see also Fforde et al. 2013). Mithaka man, educator, and researcher Scott Gorringe argues that 'when all the thinking, all the conversations and all the approaches are framed in a discourse that sees Aboriginality as a problem, very little positive movement is possible' (Gorringe, 2015, in Waller, McCallum, and Gorringe 2018). In contrast, social journalism projects including #JustJustice, Croakey, and the #IHMayDay Twitter festival explicitly reject the deficit discourse; instead, they foreground a 'strengths-based' approach. This includes privileging Indigenous voices on Indigenous issues, highlighting solutions and successful programs rather than the common framing of entrenched and intractable 'problems,' and prioritizing diverse voices; mainstream media and policy-making routinely feature only a very small, predictable selection of Indigenous spokespeople (McCallum and Waller 2013). Also, contributors to #IHMayDay define 'health' very broadly, and the discussions through the day intersected on jobs, justice, education, health care, mental health, culture, identity, and the mechanisms for change, including proper funding and self-determination (McInerney 2016).

The invitation for non-Indigenous listening as participation draws on Dr Lynore Geia's work on an Aboriginal concept of Dadirri, listening and decolonizing practices (figure 11.1).[4] Tip sheets were circulated for a range of #IHMayDay participants, and non-Indigenous people were encouraged to participate by re-tweeting and listening (figure 11.2). Participants were also asked to pledge to 'fill your feed' with the hashtag #IHMayDay for the entire day (figure 11.3)—a call to critically disrupt the automated ordering and flow of Twitter posts in order to 'crowd out' voices, issues, or threads that might

Lynore K. Geia
@LynoreGeia

Inviting non-Indigenous Twitter friends, please join May 12 #IHMayDay16. Support us thru Listen & RT @MarcTennant

10:01 PM - Apr 20, 2016

💬 2   🔁 17   ♡ 10

Figure 11.1.   @LynoreGeia, 20 April 2016.

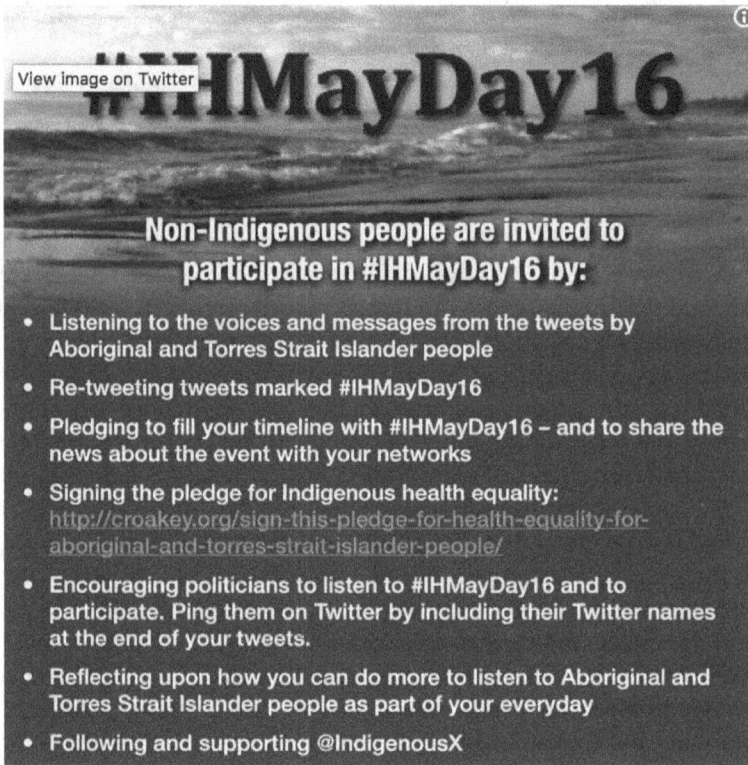

Figure 11.2. #IHMayDay Tip Sheet for non-Indigenous people. Image courtesy of #IHMayDay. Used with the permission of Lynore Geia, Mitchell Ward, and Croakey.

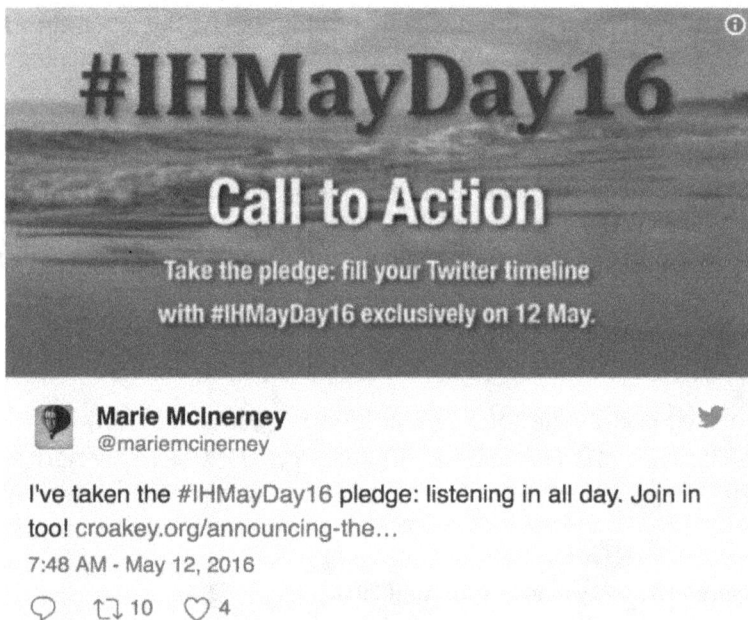

Figure 11.3. @mariemcinerney, 12 May 2016.

normally make up part of the feed in favour of tweets tagged with #IHMay-Day. This encouraged strategic engagement and participation and ultimately led to the hashtag trending nationally on Twitter (Hocking 2016).

The organizers were delighted with the results. Twitter analytics registered almost 65 million impressions, 17,000 tweets, and 2,367 participants. The hashtag #IHMayDay16 trended nationally for two days. The event was profiled on the national NITV program *The Point* and SBS online (Hocking 2016). Political engagement included guest tweeter shifts by federal MP Ken Wyatt and Senator Nova Peris, Twitter engagement by Senators Rachel Siewert and Richard Di Natale (figure 11.4), and an on-campus visit by the local member for Throsby, Steven Jones, streamed live via Periscope and Facebook.

Dr. Lynore Geia welcomed greater engagement by politicians and media with #IHMayDay16, saying 'people are starting to listen a bit more' (in McInerney 2016).

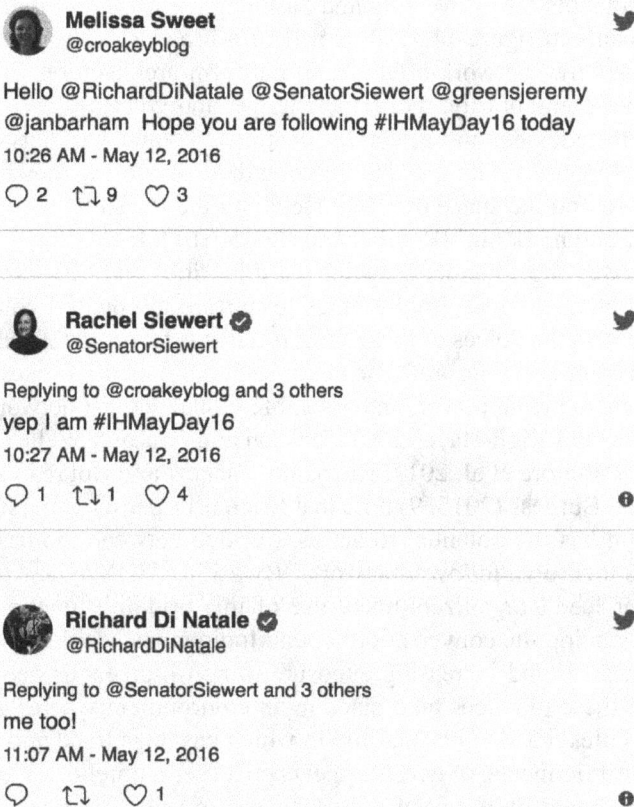

Melissa Sweet
@croakeyblog

Hello @RichardDiNatale @SenatorSiewert @greensjeremy @janbarham Hope you are following #IHMayDay16 today
10:26 AM - May 12, 2016

2   9   3

Rachel Siewert ✓
@SenatorSiewert

Replying to @croakeyblog and 3 others
yep I am #IHMayDay16
10:27 AM - May 12, 2016

1   1   4

Richard Di Natale ✓
@RichardDiNatale

Replying to @SenatorSiewert and 3 others
me too!
11:07 AM - May 12, 2016

     1

Figure 11.4.   @croakeyblog conversation thread, 12 May 2016.

DISCUSSION: A DECOLONIZING POLITICS OF LISTENING

The 2016 #IHMayDay event was on a small scale, but was a practical intervention that developed decolonizing modes of listening, with responsibility for sustained action built into the terms and frames of the event. Indigenous people speak, and non-Indigenous people listen and re-tweet. Listeners privilege and amplify First Nations voices. As a social media intervention, then, it combines a decolonizing framework with a strategic engagement with the affordances of the Twitter platform, specifically the formation of intentional or calculated 'hashtag publics' (Bruns and Burgess 2015) around a coordinated awareness-raising campaign. Listeners participate by pledging to fill their Twitter feeds with #IHMayDay, effectively screening out or tuning out the voices and content that would otherwise routinely be included. This politics of listening is explicitly located in settler-colonial relations of discursive privilege and power and aims to shift narratives and authority. Specific protocols for re-tweeting and hashtagging, as set out in the tip sheet for participants in figure 11.1, form part of a broader strategic intervention that leverages the 'network effects' and platform architectures of Twitter to collectively, if temporarily, redistribute power and voice.

With both indexical and affective functions, Twitter hashtags play a key role in forming, assembling, and mobilizing diverse publics; they hold the potential to 'expand the space of discourse along the lines that they simultaneously name and mark out' (Rambukkana 2015, 161). Increasingly, politically marginalized groups, including racialized minorities and First Nations communities, strategically deploy hashtags to nurture a 'counterpublic community that centers the voices of those most often at the margins' (Jackson 2016, 375). Such counter-publics reframe or contest dominant discourses, open new access points to media power, and assemble global activist networks (Clarke 2017; Duarte and Vigil-Hayes 2017; Jackson and Foucault Welles 2016, 399; Kuo 2016; Latimore et al. 2017; Raynauld, Richez, and Boureau 2018).

Bruns and Burgess (2015, 9) note that 'each user participating in a hashtag conversation has the potential to act as a bridge between the hashtag community and their own follower network.' By asking #IHMayDay participants to 'fill your feed,' organizers make use of this bridging function to enjoin users in extending the conversation around Indigenous health as well as raising awareness of and increasing exposure to non-Indigenous people. At the same time, these practices take place in an environment where 'algorithmic filtering' (Tufekci 2014) plays a role in which hashtags trend and in how the visibility or prominence of tweets appears on a user's timeline.[5] Nevertheless, the explicit frame of re-tweeting-as-listening extends existing hashtagging practices to visually represent an active listening network, an example of the continuing innovation in social media activism by First Nations in Australia.

#IHMayDay founders Lynore Geia and Melissa Sweet have noted that the politics of speaking and listening made explicit by #IHMayDay is 'embedded in decolonizing methodologies' (Geia and Sweet 2014). Decolonizing methodologies are increasingly gaining traction in settler colonial contexts including in the US, Aoetearoa/New Zealand, South Africa, and Australia as a way of engaging First Nations' sovereignty and focusing on the repatriation of land and life in contexts where colonists came to stay and continue to assert state power, and where even the most recent migrants are considered settlers, albeit in different ways (Tuck and Yang 2012). Decolonizing methodologies prioritize Indigenous voices, storytelling, and diversity (Smith 2012; Geia 2012); they privilege 'counter-narratives' in order to 'challenge the status quo in ways that will benefit Indigenous Australian people and communities' (Geia and Sweet 2015, 3).

The argument for Twitter as a 'decolonizing tool' operates in some tension with the political economy critique of the 'colonization of the internet' (Curran, Fenton, and Freedman 2012) and arguments to 'decolonize' the extractive economic relations of digital capitalism focused on data mining and ubiquitous surveillance. However, the decolonizing methodologies underpinning #IHMayDay emphasize alternative epistemologies and ontologies as well as the politics of knowledge and language (Foxwell-Norton, Forde and Meadows 2013; Geia and Sweet 2015; Smith 2012; Tuck and Yang 2012).

IHMayDay cofounders Geia and Sweet (2014, 2) explain that colonization continues to operate 'by excluding Indigenous peoples, by framing them as a problem, and by disrespecting their cultures and knowledges.' In contrast, they find that Twitter enables a wide range of decolonizing practices identified in the literature on decolonization, including:

> Privileging Indigenous Australian voices and listening to these voices in all their diversity; Taking a strengths-based approach; Ensuring proper process, involving relationships and respect; Story-telling in sharing knowledge; Representing Indigenous knowledges and cultures; Practicing reciprocity; Achieving disruption and initiating emancipatory processes—challenging the status quo in ways that will benefit Indigenous Australian peoples and communities. (ibid., 3)

#IHMayDay organizers thus approach Twitter as a 'cyber message stick' whereby Indigenous peoples can 'share messages of survival, resistance and resilience' (Geia and Sweet 2014, 2), as an 'act of self-determination in which Aboriginal and Torres Strait Islander peoples provided strong counter narratives to hegemony' (ibid., 4).

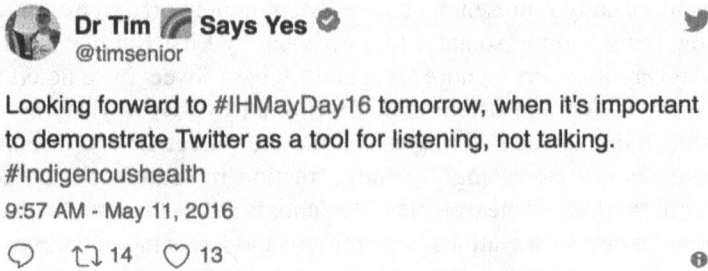

Figure 11.5.   @timsenior, 12 May 2016.

The decolonizing politics of listening at work in #IHMayDay also fore-grounds Susan Bickford's (1996) key category of 'continuations': listeners are asked to encourage others to listen; to seek to embed a politics of listening in their workplaces and organizations; and to 'reflect upon how you can do more to listen to Aboriginal and Torres Strait Islander people as part of your everyday' (see figure 11.2). For Bickford (1996, 170), continuation is understood as a commitment to sustaining the possibility of shared action in the future. Indeed, @timsenior tweeted during #IHMayDay about the importance of 'demonstrating Twitter as a tool for listening,' urging others to critically reflect on how they can engage the platform in different and productive ways (figure 11.5).

Continuation is also vital to 'listening as solidarity,' as theorized by Leah Bassel (2017), an approach in slight contrast to Foroutan's work on the same category. While Foroutan (2015) looks to Canada as a leading example of a 'post-migrant' society, with its motto of 'unity in diversity,' her focus on how such a model might apply to Europe overlooks the complexities of the settler-colonial context, in particular how this motto raises discomfort for First Nations Canadians. Bassel, in contrast, examines the difficult work of developing solidarities between 'No Border' migrant-justice activists and First Nations resurgence movements in Canada. In this context, a continuing politics of listening emerges as the key demand of First Nations activists:

> At the reclamation site, some settler activists came and wanted to fight the po-lice. They yelled, threw things and egged the other side on, getting our people all worked up. We have to live there. Remember, no white people were arrested in that raid but 50 of our people have been charged. If they want to help, they have to listen, take direction and stick around. (Doreen Silversmith in Amadahy 2008, quoted in Bassel 2017, 76)

Here, listening is a practice that requires shifting position, relinquishing au-thority, and sticking with hard conversations as much as attention to specific narratives. Clemencia Rodriguez (2011), for example, has argued that in conflict situations, citizens' media that are 'performative' are more effective than citizens' media that are 'informative.' That is, citizens' media are most significant when enabling participants and audiences to 'perform' peace, rather than when disseminating information or messages about peace. Following this line of argument, #IHMayDay can be seen as a significant opportunity to 'perform' a politics of listening as solidarity, or to decolonize listening, as much as significant 'content.'

LISTENING AS PARTICIPATION BEYOND 'POST-MIGRANT' FRAMEWORKS

How might we register First Nations' calls to set the terms and frames of participation in a multicultural settler society? Having outlined a 'decolonizing' politics of listening as participation in settler colonial Australia, we now turn to identify some of the key characteristics of 'listening as solidarity' that might extend thinking on European 'post-migrant' societies beyond existing frameworks.

We are wary of the term 'post-migrant,' even as we appreciate the aim to move beyond 'integration' frameworks. In a settler colonial context such as in Australia, claims to 'unity in diversity' and celebrating 'a nation of migrants' are rightly critiqued for obscuring the highly uneven and racialized prospects of migration and whitewash on-going colonial violence. For example, in Australia and elsewhere, we see contemporary increases in business and skilled migration while simultaneously, militarized border regimes in former Australian colonial territories keep asylum seekers in offshore detention camps; in other words, there is a celebration of multiculturalism while racisms are entrenched (cf. Gilroy 2004; 2006) and First Nations dispossession and disadvantage continues. We ultimately seek conceptual frameworks and political practices that address this twin dynamics of nation states which celebrate diversity while also institutionalizing racism.

Against this backdrop, we are inspired by Foroutan's (2015, 6) aim to develop alternatives to national policies of 'integration,' with a focus on the responsibility for the dominant to change. Drawing on examples of 'decolonizing' listening or listening as solidarity, we identify four specific practices that might shift some responsibility for change from marginalized or migrant communities to the dominant or 'mainstream.'

First, we note that the politics of listening is located and contextual. Rather than a general obligation to listen, listening as participation is a responsibility for those who are relatively discursively privileged in the context of specific histories and contemporary politics that produce hierarchies of voice and attention. If, as this section of the book suggests, voice and agency of marginalized actors are crucial in post-migrant societies, then the participation and responsibilities of the dominant might be best understood as a politics of listening. This requires making explicit the specific and located hierarchies of voice and (in)attention and requires change among those people and institutions that are normalized in narrations of the nation, signalling a shift from speaking to listening.

Secondly, the example of #IHMayDay suggests practices of privileging and amplifying oppressed or marginalized voices. In the context of media and multiculturalism, this could involve giving priority to the voices of refugees and asylum seekers whose futures are at the centre of national debates; yet they are very rarely able to set the agenda or to speak on their own terms. This practice also entails a deliberate relinquishing of control or divestment of power by those in privileged positions in order to privilege other voices.

Thirdly and relatedly, listening as participation as part of a politics of solidarity requires tuning out dominant discourses of deficit or deviance, giving over narrative power and in turn supporting practices of self-determination. Just as #IHMayDay diverts attention from the all-too-familiar frame of Indigenous dysfunction and despair, a politics of listening more broadly would 'listen out' for strengths, agency, and expertise among communities that have been marginalized as deficient or threatening, including migrant and refugee communities.

Finally, listening as participation for more democratic media and for more just futures requires practice and commitment to continuation. This is a sustained commitment to listening that aims to maintain possibilities for shared action in the context of deep difference and inequalities. In this sense, listening as participation is not simply an end in itself, but rather a vital step in processes for social transformation (Dreher 2017b; Thill 2015).

Overall, then, we argue for a need for the discursively privileged not only to adapt, but also to actively listen out, and to decentre and destabilize privileged voices and narratives.

TOWARDS A POLITICS OF LISTENING AS PARTICIPATION IN MULTICULTURAL MEDIA

Our brief discussion here offers some suggestions for understanding listening as a crucial form of participation in media culture; it still leaves much scope for further theorizing and debate. While we have focused on individual participation via listening in #IHMayDay, there is no doubt that media institutions also facilitate and shape the politics of listening in various ways (Dreher 2009). In developing institutional strategies and responsibilities for listening, and in scaling up from examples such as #IHMayDay, we stress the need not simply to expand but rather to destabilize and transform entrenched understandings of 'nation.' This might include decentring privileged whiteness in order to make space for marginalized voices, and dislodging comfortable assumptions of national origins and belonging, in other words, unsettling 'hosts' rather than merely integrating migrants. Listening offers a vital framework to focus on powerful institutions and privileged actors and to highlight practices of solidarity and decolonization. Together, listening practices of privileging and amplifying marginalized voices and tuning out colonial narratives hold the potential to contribute to more just and democratic media.

NOTES

1. This may also ring true for parts of Scandinavian Europe where Indigenous Sámi dispossesion and struggles for traditional hunting and fishing rights are ongoing.

2. The sleight of hand here is that the 'first' in 'First Nations' is compulsorily redefined in a way that rejects the ontological primacy of Indigenous peoples and is instead recast as the first in a succession of migrations to the lands on which the nation state has been formed.

3. In keeping with our own commitment to decolonizing methodologies, we endeavour to follow the self-identification protocols of First Nations, including by naming scholars who identify as Bwgcolman (north-eastern Queensland), Yorta Yorta (north-eastern Victoria and south-eastern NSW), and Mithaka (south-western Queensland).

4. Dadirri, a practice of inner, deep listening or 'tuning in,' comes from the Ngan'gikurunggurr and Ngen'giwumirri languages of the First Nations peoples of the Daly River region in northern Australia. See West et al. (2012, 1582–90).

5. Since 2016, Twitter has used an algorithm-defined timeline to which tweets appear in a user's feed, based on a number of signals. This feature is set up as opt-in by default, but can be turned off so tweets display in reverse-chronological order.

Chapter Twelve

Doing Memory and Contentious Participation

Remembering the Victims of Right-Wing Violence in German Political Culture

Steffen Rudolph, Tanja Thomas, and Fabian Virchow

In 2012, City officials argued that the 'Mölln Speech' should not be too political. We could not accept this because obviously, the arson attack was a political crime. That is why the 'Mölln speech' is a political, an anti-Fascist speech [. . .]. Since then, we organize the 'Mölln speech in Exile' and go to different cities. I did not expect this, but we receive a lot of resonance [. . .], and we also demonstrated that the victims and families are able to organize their very own commemoration event. [. . .] Even more importantly, we empowered other affected persons to organize their own commemoration events, we empowered them to speak up, to show in public, and to fight against racism. (Interview with Ibrahim Arslan 2018)

On 23 November 1992, two neo-Nazis set fire to the home of a migrant family in Mölln, a small town in Germany's most northern state, and murdered fifty-one-year-old Bahide Arslan, ten-year-old Yeliz Arslan, and fourteen-year-old Ayşe Yılmaz. Several other family members were badly injured. Ibrahim Arslan, then seven years old, survived. Today, he has become a public advocate for victims of right-wing violence. In an interview conducted by students of media studies at the University of Tübingen,[1] he talked about the annual commemoration ceremony that had been organized mainly by Mölln's city officials. Until 2012, these officials had accepted that the Arslan family and an activist group working under the title 'Freundeskreis im Gedenken an den rassistischen Brandanschlag von Mölln 1992' (Friends in remembrance of the racist arson attack of Mölln 1992) were actively participating in the annual commemoration events.

In 2013, however, the 'Möllner Rede' (Mölln Speech), regularly given by Ibrahim Arslan during these events, was cancelled from the official commemoration events of the city of Mölln. In response to this, the Arslan family

Figure 12.1. 'Mölln Speech in Exile' at HAU Hebbel am Ufer, Berlin, 19 November 2017. *Source:* Massimo Perinelli.

and their friends launched the 'Möllner Rede im Exil' (Mölln Speech in Exile), which has been held in different cities over the years. Meanwhile, a blog started announcing the annual ceremonies and documenting the speeches, but also providing an archive and information on other initiatives that are involved in memory work, or as we call it, 'doing memory' around right-wing violence.

This 1992 incident in Mölln is just one of many cases of deadly right-wing violence in post-war Germany in which the question of remembrance—whether and how—turned out to be controversial. In general, attention for victims of right-wing violence has gained ground since late 2011, after the uncovering of the neo-Nazi group Nationalsozialistischer Untergrund (National Socialist Underground [NSU]) that killed nine migrants and a police officer and carried out bombings that have hurt many more (Karakayalı et al. 2017; Virchow 2016b).

In this chapter's first section, we outline different theoretical approaches in order to understand the relevance of remembering as part of the political culture in a given country but also as a potential way of contentious participation around issues of belonging and recognition. These include perspectives from research on political culture, on memory, and on recognition, but also on issues such as voice and listening. The second section provides a concise overview of the dimensions of right-wing violence in post-war Germany by defining this phenomenon and retracing its history and dynamics. We will show that right-wing violence has no systematic place in the self-image of post-war Germany, but has been depoliticized and individualized for most of the time, similar to racism. The third section is devoted to empirical research on the concept of doing memory and offers a detailed case study of Mölln. In the fourth and final section, we discuss our empirical results in light of our theoretical discussion and outline some ideas on future research in this field.

DOING MEMORY AS A PERFORMATIVE PRACTICE EMBEDDED IN POLITICAL CULTURE

Research on political culture has made its breakthrough with the comparative study of the political cultures of several countries by Gabriel A. Almond and Sidney Verba (Almond and Verba 1963; Hooghe 2011). Since then, most studies on political culture mainly refer to attitudes, opinions, and values of the inhabitants within a given country, focused on its specific history and its day-to-day political, economic, and social developments. As Welzel (2009, 299) has pointed out, political culture is about 'the psychological dimension of political systems, including all politically relevant beliefs, values, and attitudes.' In fact, different kinds of culture can be distinguished, such as elite and mass cultures; local, regional, and national cultures; and also the subcultures of particular groups. As given populations defined by spatial, organizational, or identification boundaries are of special interest, data from surveying individuals, mainly via face-to-face and telephone polling, are aggregated in order to end up with representative surveys. Such kinds of research make up a large part of the field of political culture research.

Yet many have criticized the fact that face-to-face and telephone polling, by nature, does not provide in-depth knowledge about people's belief systems or produce deeper insights into individuals' thought patterns, their origin, and their transformation or changeability. In order to better understand the complex process of how belief systems and thought patterns are formed, Karl Rohe (1987; 1994) broadened the approach to studying political cultures by adding a historical-hermeneutical perspective. He suggested that next to attitudes, perceptions should be investigated in order to get a real idea of the political culture of a given society; he argued that perceptions are situated much more deeply in society than just attitudes. This chapter borrows the conceptualization of political culture, offered by Karl Rohe and Andreas Dörner (1990, 24), as a 'historically grown, collectively shared, for the most part self-evident and therefore mostly unconscious "design for political living" that navigates the perception, thinking, feeling, and indirectly also the behaviour of political actors' (translated by the authors).

Following Trutz von Trotha (1995), German sociologists Thomas Herz and Michael Schwab-Trapp have applied the concept of 'basic narrative' to political culture research in general and to the analysis of post-war German society and the onset of racist violence in the early 1990s in particular (Herz 1996; Herz and Schwab-Trapp 1997). The idea of a 'basic narrative,' as they propose, is key to understanding the political culture of a society; the 'basic narrative' is the one construction of a society's history and culture that contains the dominant and legitimizing constructions of the past. It is, therefore, an infallible point of reference in the conflicts surrounding the construction of the past and the shaping of the present. According to Herz and Schwab-Trapp, the core of the 'basic narrative' of post-war Germany refers to the Nazi regime: how it came to power, what crimes it committed, and what lessons were learned once it was defeated. In the mid-1990s, Herz sketched out this basic narrative:

> One day, the German people saw themselves confronted with the Nazis. The Nazis established a totalitarian and despotic regime. It was a state of arbitrariness and injustice. There was resistance to this regime because the German people had been misled. The Germans were in fact a 'community' suffering. This is especially true for the soldiers. They fought for their homeland and not for the Nazis. One means of stabilizing the system was economic success, at least until the beginning of the war. After the war, the Germans successfully dealt with the Nazi past. They have learned from the past. The economic miracle and the welfare state have helped to build a stable society. The Federal Republic is a pluralistic and open society. The extermination of European Jewry was a crime, but the expulsion of the Germans was also a crime. Other countries also have war criminals. There is no collective guilt, only collective responsibility. The Germans made reparation to the Jewish people and sentenced the criminals. Suffering from the Nazi past is part of Jewish but not of German fate. (Herz 1997, 251; translated by the authors)

On closer inspection, a 'basic narrative' consists of a number of 'short stories' and 'small narratives' which, depending on the topic, pick up particular aspects and reference those aspects back to the overall story. This differentiation of the 'basic narrative' into several miniature narratives suggests a microscopic approach. As the basic narrative is hegemonic, but at the same time challenged by competing narratives, there are on-going conflicts about continuity and change of the 'basic narrative' on different levels of society. Such conflicts might be more local (e.g., about renaming a street bearing the name of a former Nazi [Frese and Weidner 2018]); they might be regional (e.g., about former Nazis as elected governing officials [Klausch 2013]); or they might be on the national level (e.g., the Bitburg controversy when in 1985 German Chancellor Helmut Kohl and US President Ronald Reagan met at the graves of World War II soldiers, including those of former Waffen SS members [Hartman 1986; Hallet 2005]).

Changes to a country's basic narrative can have wide-ranging cultural, legal, and political consequences. The unification of the two German states and the wave of racist violence in the early 1990s led to the restriction of the fundamental right to asylum, one of the institutionalized lessons learned from the Nazi past. The change of the 'basic narrative' cannot be traced in detail in this chapter. Above all, public memory of the crimes committed by the Nazi regime has intensified and expanded since the end of World War II. In many cases, civil society initiatives took action to remember victims of the Holocaust, to establish sites of commemoration, and to elucidate the involvement of a great number of Germans in the Holocaust. Also, in laborious 'recognition fights' (Tümmers 2011), a growing number of victim groups who sought justice for crimes committed against them by the Nazi regime were at least to some extent financially compensated (Borggräfe 2014).

Both post-war German states claimed to have learnt from the Nazi past, albeit in different ways (Danyel 1995; Kannapin 2005; Hammerstein 2017). Both states developed a particular way of remembering the historical situation that brought the Nazis to power, but also what caused World War II, what crimes Germans committed across Europe, what happened during the Holocaust, and what ended the war. Both 'basic narratives' had in common that racism and antisemitism should not have any place in society. The former German Democratic Republic (GDR) denied the existence of such ideological formations (or even worse, structures beyond the attitudes of individuals) in principle (Waibel 2016). People identified as holding racist or Nazi views were sentenced for being enemies of the socialist order. The Federal Republic of Germany (FRG), actually in negotiations with the GDR, bought out several individuals sentenced for this reason for being held as 'political prisoners.' The GDR's secret service did not take the phenomenon of a growing extreme-right youth scene more seriously until the late 1980s and still tried to deny any political dimension to this movement and labelled them hooligans instead (Wagner 2014). In the FRG, extreme-right groups and acts of racist and antisemitic violence were more visible. However, in hegemonic discourse, these phenomena were either relegated to the past or dismissed as being outside the nation-state (Attia 2014). Racist violence was either depoliticized or pathologized (Herz 1996) instead of being understood as a contemporary expression of racism that was still alive in post-war Germany. In many cases, victims of racist attacks were portrayed as the actual perpetrators, and the experiences and perspectives of those affected by racism and right-wing violence remained largely silenced.

For many decades after the end of World War II, the vast majority of German society did not (want to) listen to the stories told by migrants about racist discrimination and violence. Ironically, there is a lot of situated knowledge in migrant communities about racism (Perinelli 2017, 155ff.), which the majority of the German population ignores or denies. This ignorance or denial is part of a much larger strategy of keeping migrants and their contributions to society invisible and of discouraging 'ethnic minorities from participating in the public sphere on issues that concern them' (de Wit and Koopmans 2005, 69). In fact, until the beginning of the twenty-first century, hegemonic media and political discourse did not acknowledge that Germany had become an immigration society. Consequently, they also did not respect and recognize the perspectives and knowledge of millions of German people of colour or people of colour living in Germany. To this day, for example, there is no museum that commemorates the history of immigration to Germany, despite a constant influx of immigrants before and since World War II. Although Germany is undeniably a diverse country, as witnessed by the visibility of different racial and ethnic groups, history and memory are rarely linked with migration or to immigrants as significant protagonists, especially their contribution to social justice and workers' rights (Motte and Ohliger 2004). Media production that aims at improving the visibility of migrants is often somewhat dismissively labelled 'ethnic' or 'ethnic minority media' (see Ratković's chapter in this volume), thus emphasizing their lack of relevance for the majority of the population. Today, very little research is conducted on diversity in the newsrooms and in journalism, and journalists who are familiar with ethnic minorities are a tiny minority of only 2 to 3 percent.[2] In sum, these examples show that diversity among the population is rarely made visible and, consequently, not recognized. In this context, we refer to main paradigms of recognition theory as outlined by Nancy Fraser and Axel Honneth (2003) and Judith Butler (2009b) to stress how important recognition is in the context of political and cultural representation and participation. Butler emphasizes the relevance of visual experience and social visibility that is organized by normative frames that 'work to differentiate the lives we can apprehend from those we cannot' (Butler 2009b, 3). She conceptualizes (social) visibility as being constituted by recognition whereby it becomes a problem for those who have been expelled from the structures and procedures of political representation. Accordingly, there is a 'differential distribution of recognizability' across different social positions (Willig 2012, 140). In this sense, visibility means becoming visible as a recognizable subject, and this means coming into existence (Butler 2001, 593). From such a perspective, only the recognizable subject is able to participate in meaning production, to raise their voice, and to be active in societal debates. However, as Nancy Fraser and Axel Honneth have pointed out, these opportunities also depend on the availability of resources. Her theory of recognition encompasses the idea of redistribution as a prerequisite of 'participatory parity' (Fraser and Honneth 2003, 54).

The concepts of visibility and recognition guide our analysis about whose experiences are perceived and whose knowledge is listened to when assessing antisemitism and racism in general, but also in the process of doing memory on acts of right-wing violence.

We conceptualize doing memory as a performative process (Fischer-Lichte and Lehnert 2000, 14) instead of just archiving and securing pasts that have come to an end and became static. Taking 'doing memory' as a performative and conflictual process that constitutes, stages, re-stages, and steadily modifies its subject also brings in dimensions of changeability and of power, as the various protagonists involved in acts of doing memory on a particular issue have varying power resources (Gerbel et al. 2005, 15). Following Meike Penkwitt's (2006) conceptualization of remembering along the lines of doing gender, the concept of doing memory includes the idea that individual acts of remembering are affected by hegemonic discourse and collective memory, and that collective memory originates through concrete acts of remembrance. Finally, we should be aware of the fact that such acts of remembrance are part of creative developments in which 'situated knowledge production' (Haraway 1988) takes place. That also means that current acts of remembering necessarily position themselves towards earlier cases of doing memory and towards the 'truth(s)' and materializations earlier acts of remembrance have made visible and relevant.

RIGHT-WING VIOLENCE AND THE
MANY DIMENSIONS OF DOING MEMORY

Right-wing violence in post-war Germany is not a recent phenomenon. Students who went to the streets in the early 1950s opposing the screening of films by antisemitic director Veit Harlan were attacked verbally and physically by right-wing activists. Anticommunist groups like the paramilitary 'Technical Service' of the League of German Youth prepared to kill leaders of the Social Democratic Party and the Communist Party. German nationalists took part in bombings in the 1960s aimed at bringing self-determination to South Tyrol, a region in northern Italy bordering Austria that had become part of Italy at the end of World War I, despite the protests of a sizeable German-speaking population. Small, right-wing terrorist groups emerged from the late 1960s onwards in response to the failure of extreme-right parties at the ballot box, but more importantly, in reaction to developments that these groups read as destroying the German homeland. The most important one was the Neue Ostpolitik (New East Policy), which included the final recognition of the rivers Oder and Neisse as the German-Polish border by the FRG and the loss of former German territories in Eastern Europe, but mostly addressed issues of immigration and asylum.

A massive rise of racist violence took place in the early 1990s. Along with having physical attacks on people of colour on a daily basis in the streets and in their homes across the country, locations such as Mölln, Solingen, Hoyerswerda, and Rostock became known worldwide as sites of racist killings or racist mass violence. When a two-thirds majority of the German parliament substantially limited the fundamental right to asylum in 1993, the level of violence decreased, but the extreme right and other racist groups believed the parliament's decision to be the result of their campaign and violence and saw their political manoeuvres confirmed as successful action models (Prenzel 2012; Kleffner and Spangenberg 2016). More than twenty years later, right-wing violence rose to unprecedented levels when racist groups and individuals tried to stop refugees from coming to and staying in Germany, by means of threat, intimidation, and violence.

The extent of right-wing violence is controversial. While state authorities list the number of people killed by right-wing violence since 1990 as 83, watchdog groups and quality newspapers speak of significantly more than 150 victims, with a significant number remaining unreported. In fact, there are several dozen more victims from the pre-1990 period (Brausam 2018; Radke and Staud 2018). For many years, most of the victims had been forgotten by the general public, and only a few of them were actively remembered. In cities like Mölln and Solingen, more or less regular acts of remembrance kept the violent past alive, mostly because the racist acts of deadly violence in these cities in 1992 and 1993, respectively, hit headlines all over the world and had become synonymous for the spreading right-wing violence in the early 1990s.

In November 2011, the general public was made aware of a right-wing terror group under the name National Socialist Underground (NSU). Two of its members committed suicide as a result of a police search, and a third member set fire to the apartment they lived in. From 1998 to 2011, the group had killed nine migrants and a female police officer, was responsible for fifteen robberies, and executed three bomb attacks. The discovery of the group led to several parliamentary investigation committees (Virchow 2014) and a lawsuit against five neo-Nazis before the Munich Higher Regional Court lasting from May 2013 to July 2018 and fostered a previously not seen debate on the level of right-wing violence and racism in German society.

When German Chancellor Angela Merkel announced in February 2012 that the background of the killings and bomb attacks would be cleared up without restrictions, many observers remained sceptical in the face of file removals by intelligence agencies and wondered how substantial this investigation would indeed turn out to be (von der Behrens 2018). This growing public attention also resulted in several German states verifying if violent deaths were connected to right-wing extremist motives (Feldmann et al. 2018). As a result, official statistics had to be corrected.

In fact, victims of the bomb attacks, family members of those murdered by the NSU, migrant groups, and a broad network of anti-Fascist and antiracist activists were able to run a campaign of contentious participation (Kim 2011; Tarrow 2015) to bring attention to the NSU complex. This happened via unofficially renaming streets in several German cities with the names of the victims of the NSU, fighting for official renaming, producing up to thirty theatre plays (Brod 2018), publishing of memories written by relatives of the victims of the NSU, releasing documentaries, and so on. These are great examples of doing memory that aim at recognizing the victims of the attacks as victims of racist violence and overcoming secondary victimization by police, prosecutors, and media.

Overall, the NSU case led to a growing awareness of the level of rightwing violence and racism in German society. In addition to doing memory related to the victims of the NSU, acts of doing memory related to other victims

Figure 12.2.   Doing memory on the victims of the NSU. Protest march, Munich, 11 July 2018. *Source:* Fabian Virchow.

of right-wing violence emerged and became more relevant. For example, in Hamburg, activists turned to a case of a racist murder from 1980. In that year, neo-Nazis had killed two Vietnamese refugees, a crime that had largely been forgotten. Now, there are regular acts of doing memory related to the deaths of Nguyễn Ngọc Châu and Đỗ Anh Lân. Also, largely forgotten groups of victims of right-wing violence such as homeless people are now remembered more systematically. As we will show below with regard to Mölln, the NSU case has also increased the willingness of city representatives to clearly and publicly recognize and name right-wing violence.

MÖLLN—CONTESTED MEMORY OF A RACIST ATTACK

The racist attack in Mölln on the night of 23 November 1992 was one of the most horrible acts of right-wing violence after the unification of the two German states. Today, the city is in the same category as other infamous places such as Rostock-Lichtenhagen, Hoyerswerda, and Solingen. On the day after the arson attack in Mölln, spontaneous demonstrations against racism took place in the city and the neighbouring county town of Ratzeburg, gathering more than six thousand people. At the end of the week, major protests were organized in various cities in northern Germany such as Kiel and Lübeck, the latter being close to Mölln. Hamburg, an hour away from the crime scene, was the host of the main memorial services; twenty thousand people attended the funeral march. Norbert Blüm, then Federal Minister of Labour and Social Affairs, and Klaus Kinkel, then Federal Minister for Foreign Affairs, served as the two most highly ranked representatives of the German government. Helmut Kohl, German Chancellor from 1982 to 1998, did not participate in the memorial ceremony for the victims at Hamburg; his spokesman slightingly spoke of what he termed 'condolence tourism.'

The most prominent reactions to the Mölln attacks among German's civil society were the so-called Lichterketten demonstrations—chains of people silently holding candles against racism. The first took place in Munich and became the city's biggest post-war demonstration, with over four hundred thousand people attending. Being a gentle form of protest, Lichterketten demonstrations gained widespread popularity all over Germany. They brought together people who had never participated in any political rally before. It is estimated that between November 1992 and the end of January 1993, almost three million people joined in this kind of protest (Chung 2017, 153f.).

While civil society was impressive in protesting against intolerance and racism, this protest attitude was not reflected among policy-makers. On the contrary, the Christian Democratic Party, the Christian Social Union, and the Social Democrats fundamentally recast the right of asylum in order to limit immigration. The attacks of Mölln took place at a time when reports of violence by right-wing extremists in Germany were the order of the day, and conservative politicians tried to blame the victims. In a process of scapegoating, the sheer presence of migrants was construed as the very cause for racist violence. Therefore, German citizens, as it was implied, needed to be protected against their own violent reactions towards this presence of migrants, and the solution became to radically restrict migration to Germany.

Although the public has, overall, condemned the racist attacks all over Germany, and annual commemorations have taken place in Mölln since then, the city still struggles with its past. In this part, we will focus on two examples of doing memory as an on-going conflictual process that involves different protagonists shaping and re-shaping what is commemorated, who gets recognition, what artefacts are involved, and what kind of relationships are established. Building upon the distinction of participation and collaboration introduced in chapter 1 of this volume, we argue that there is a slight shift towards the latter over time. In other words, doing memory related to the arson attacks in Mölln can be summarized as a move from merely silencing the victims to forms of partial participation, and ultimately to moments of collaboration, facilitated especially by digital media.

THE RENAMING OF A STREET—
A CITY STRUGGLING WITH ITS PAST

The first controversy around the memorialization of the Mölln attack dates back to the immediate years after the attack and revolves around the recognition of victims by embedding their story in the city's history and memory. Permanent visibility is the key here, as commonly done by monuments, memorial plaques, murals, and the dedication of streets or public places. Here, the renaming of a street to commemorate the murdered victims, especially Bahide Arslan, is at the centre of this controversy.

One year after the attack, the city of Cologne, almost 500 kilometres (approximately 310 miles) southwest of Mölln, renamed one of its streets Bahide-Arslan-Straße, in a part of the city with a significant migrant population. As a result, the Green Party proposed a similar gesture at the meeting of Mölln's city council in the fall of 1994. The Green Party chose a short, unnamed stretch of a street from the reconstructed house of the arson attack at Mühlenstraße to the city's park, stretching no more than 200 yards, and proposed naming it Bahide Arslan Gang. Yet the city council decided on the name Lohgerbergang. Acknowledging the immediate past of the arson attack and recognizing the victims was not an option. Instead, the city council chose to remember some medieval craftsmen who supposedly had lived there—with 'Lohgerber' meaning bark tanners. This form of 'invented tradition' appeared to be the more appropriate alternative among the city council's majority. Following this decision, the issue of remembering the attack on the migrant home was silenced in Mölln for nearly twenty years.

Meanwhile, the city council of Kiel, the capital of the federal state to which Mölln belongs, decided unanimously in 1997 to name a public square after Bahide Arslan. Two years later, marking the seventh anniversary of the deadly attack, the 'Bahide-Arslan-Platz' was inaugurated in the district of Gaarden-Ost. Similar to Cologne, this is a neighbourhood in Kiel with a high migrant population. Together with the renaming, a public artwork was installed. The granite sculpture of a boat hull by local artist Ben Siebenrock is an invitation to commemorate and reflect on the topic of migration.

It was not until 2012 that the street renaming issue regained momentum in Mölln. With the beginning of the 2010s, the family of the victims became more visible at the annual commemoration events in Mölln. This coincided with an overall shift of memory on right-wing violence that was the result of NSU's unmasking in November 2011 and an increased usage of digital media such as blogs and social media by political activist groups. In 2012, at the twentieth anniversary of the attacks, Faruk Arslan, the son of Bahide Arslan, father of Yeliz Arslan and uncle of Ayşe Yılmaz, spoke out in favour of renaming the Lohgerbergang after his mother. Also, local activists organized a demonstration under the slogan 'reclaim and remember' and organized a first symbolic renaming of the street. The street sign of that passage was pasted over with the name Bahide Arslan. This intervention, supporting the demands of the family, was repeated a year later—now with the symbolic addition of Yeliz-Arslan-Straße and Ayşe-Yılmaz-Straße. At the yearly commemoration event, the brother of Ayşe Yılmaz, Servat Yılmaz, requested that three streets be renamed after the victims. The city council, now under considerable pressure by activists and the Arslan family through their increasing visibility and with the intent to change the name of the passage, finally decided to rename the small Lohgerbergang as Bahide-Arslan-Gang in April 2014, even though the decision was not unanimous.

But things became complicated again. After renaming the passage, no information was added to the name on the street sign. As a result, activists temporarily added a plate in almost the same colour above the street sign that included Bahide Arslan's year of birth and death, her occupation, and, most importantly, the fact that her death was a result of a racist arson attack. Again, only after this contentious doing memory by activists supporting the demands of the family, particularly the information that the attack on Bahide Arslan was racially motivated, the city of Mölln ultimately installed an official sign with the requested information a year later.

While this first conflict was structured around the struggle for permanent visibility in the city of Mölln, which its officials only granted after a long period of resistance, the second dispute revolved around the annual event of commemoration.

STRUGGLING FOR COLLABORATION

In the immediate years after the racist attack, the events surrounding the anniversary were mainly organized by the local initiative Miteinander leben (Living together), a group of people that teamed up in Mölln as a reaction to the attack. Their intention was to form an association that would foster intercultural learning, respect, and tolerance. Part of their activity had been a silent vigil on the twenty-third of each month. Although this act of doing memory ended half a year later due to lack of support by the citizens of Mölln, the group kept on organizing the main annual commemoration events in Mölln until the late 1990s. While, during the first years, city officials remained mostly passive during the annual commemoration, the city of Mölln began taking a more active part around the year 2000. In 2010, it finally became the sole organizer when Miteinander leben restructured its activities away from the annual event.

In a turn to current societal issues from a mere retrospective view of the racist attack, the city invented the so-called Mölln Speech in 2009 as a main part of the commemoration event. The first speech was given by the prolific journalist Andreas Speit, who has written extensively about the extreme right, that very year, and by Imran Ayata, cofounder of the migrant network Kanak Attack, two years later. In 2012, the city of Mölln invited the Arslan family to take an active role in shaping the commemoration. However, things did not get off to a good start. For example, the family proposed Beate Klarsfeld, the famous investigator of Nazi crimes and perpetrators, as the annual speaker, but this suggestion was somewhat controversial for many city officials. Additionally, when the victims and survivors of the racist attack criticized the official commemoration in Mölln during the event (especially their role as mere extras, the lack of a genuine victims' perspective, and the deficiency of support), conflicts quickly became overt. City officials repudiated that critique and declined further cooperation. Consequently, the Arslan family started to organize alternative events supported by the association 'Friends in remembrance of the racist arson attack of Mölln 1992.'

One of the events that was organized by this collaboration was a silent vigil in front of the house of the deadly arson attack; this act of doing memory is neither part of the official agenda of the city of Mölln, nor mentioned in the official program. The most prominent of this alternative commemoration is the Mölln Speech in Exile. Taking place at various cities in Germany over the last years, these exile speeches are mostly hosted by cultural institutions that invite victims and relatives to organize the commemoration with the help of supporters. These events gained particular attention and publicity via blogs and social media. They are not only used to remember the arson attack in Mölln, but also serve as places of solidarity among and with people affected by racism. At these events, there are usually many other victims of racist attacks present (e.g., the relatives and families of Burak Bektaş, Oury Jalloh, and the victims of the NSU murders). They provide an opportunity for victims and family members to voice their perspective, to get support and recognition, and to face a public that is eager to listen and learn. Furthermore, there is a notable use of digital media by activists and the 'Friends in remembrance of the racist arson attack of Mölln 1992' to organize events and protests and to publish as well as archive announcements, texts, and audio-visual material of these events, thereby linking acts of doing memory on- and offline. This is further supplemented by an intense networking between different initiatives that are doing memory related to right-wing violence with the result of increasing visibility.

While the memory of the arson attack of Mölln was long dominated by a local hegemony of commemoration practices and by the official remembrance of mainstream society, the Arslan family and supporting activists made the victims' perspective the key element in their activism. Their activities go far beyond the official ceremonies in Mölln, which, although continually emphasizing the importance of remembrance, seem to be more focused on the recovery of the city's reputation by avoiding naming racism as the root cause of the attack in 1992. As a result, the victims' perspective is marginalized in Mölln, and they are only granted participation if it fits into the official frame of commemoration.

On the contrary, events like the Mölln Speech in Exile or the 'unofficial' silent vigil are forms of collaboration. People like the activists of the 'Friends in remembrance of the racist arson attack of Mölln 1992' and associated initiatives are fostering bonds and connections by using digital media in order to shape the future of a post-migrant society that is aware of racist violence. Questioning one's own resources and privileges, they take the perspective of the victims, their stories, and their traumas as a starting point around which to plan commemorative activities.

Even though the official commemorative activities in Mölln are mostly non-collaborative, at least the city's invitation to the Arslan family to be part of the commemoration events is a partial form of participation. They were offered the possibility to speak, to voice their demands, and even at times to decide who should participate in the events. However, this only worked until conflict and divergent conceptions started to emerge. The moment the victims and their relatives began to critique the city's official commemoration, the city questioned and curtailed their participation. Participation and collaboration differ, as we argue, in their way they relate to recognition. While participation has a bias towards incorporating different voices into a given setting and is therefore likely to sanction inconvenient divergences, collaboration implies the openness to change one's positions due to the voices and stories of others. While participation grants recognition, collaboration calls relations of recognition into question. By addressing resource-based hierarchies as well as by listening to the voices of the victims and the marginalized, collaboration is a quintessential part of convivialist futures.

RE-VISIONING THE BASIC NARRATIVE:
VOICE AND LISTENING AS PREREQUISITES

Acts of collaborative remembering and forgetting as contested practices are intimately interwoven with individual and societal recognition of experiences, social positions, and rights. Although acts of collaborative remembrance are often conflictual, they have the potential to open up diverse opportunities for sharing equal political and social rights as the basis for living together in heterogeneous societies. In terms of memory practices of violent, racist attacks discussed in this chapter, it is key that victims of right-wing violence and those affected by racism become participatory actors and collaborative performers of doing memory.

The struggle is to make positions such as the multifaceted practice of criticizing racism, for which the controversies in Mölln are just an example and which refer to the long history of racist violence in Germany, an essential element of a revised 'basic narrative.' A 'politics of listening' as proposed by Dreher (2009) and the sharing of power (Digoh-Ersoy 2017) are essential here. They are supported by a doing memory that draws on new media practices enabling victims of racist violence to tell their stories on their own terms and initiate collaboration (Bassel 2017). One of the challenges is to speak out in order to oppose any form of racist 'complicit silence' (Assmann 2016, 157). Another one is to listen, which is not only about giving a voice to the marginalized, but to structurally question the standards of recognition, privileges, and institutions that regulate who can be heard, what can be said, and what can be remembered.

NOTES

1. The students' work resulted in a webdocumentary: http://www.doing-memory .de/#TP3_Audio4_Defensive_oder_Offensive_.

2. https://www.grimme-lab.de/2017/05/25/vielfalt-foerdern-migranten-im-jour nalismus/.

Chapter Thirteen

Memorialization, Participation, and Self-Representation

Remembering Refugeedom in the Cypriot Village of Dasaki Achnas

Nico Carpentier

In 1974, the inhabitants of Achna, all of them Greek Cypriots, were forced to flee their village.[1] Their refuge, Dasaki Achnas, in a nearby British military base became their new and permanent home. This new village on the base thus created a post-migratory situation, even though the migration was forced, and was coupled with the traumatic experience of displacement.

This chapter focuses on how the villagers memorialized these events and how their memorialization materialized in the Panagia Trachias Church Memorial in the early 2000s. More particularly, the case study will analyse the participatory components of the memorial's construction, where the community, represented by the mayor and the Community Council, engaged in negotiations with the artist Pampos Mihlis, and resisted the critical suggestions of the Cypriot Advisory Monuments' Committee.

Theoretically, the chapter is positioned in a political studies approach towards participation, which defines participation as the equalization of power relations (Carpentier 2016a). Participation is seen as localized, contextualized by its grounding in particular field(s), and as an object of political struggles about its intensity and outcomes. Moreover, inspired by a combination of discourse theory, new materialism, and assemblage theory, participation is seen as an entanglement of discourses and materials (Carpentier 2017).

Based on this theoretical positioning, the following two questions emerge in relation to the Panagia Trachias Church Memorial. First, how did the community mimetically represent its trauma and suffering through the memorial, which is embedded in nationalist and religious discourses that are closely aligned with the hegemonic representations of the twentieth-century military confrontations, resulting in the division of the island (often referred to as the 'Cyprus Problem')? Second, how participatory was the construction process of the memorial?

THE CYPRUS PROBLEM AND ITS MEMORALIZATION

In the twentieth century, Cyprus suffered from a series of violent conflicts. In 1955, EOKA (the National Organization of Cypriot Fighters), a right-wing Greek-Cypriot organization, launched a guerrilla war against the British colonizers, driven by Greek nationalism and with *enosis* (the unification of Cyprus with the Greek state) as one of its main objectives. This independence war antagonized substantial parts of the Greek-Cypriot and Turkish-Cypriot populations, but also the Left and the Right. Consequently, soon after the island's independence in 1960, the violence continued, with severe intercommunal fighting in 1963/1964 and 1967/1968. The Turkish Cypriots, less than 20 percent of the total population of Cyprus, were forced to withdraw into a series of enclaves that were turned into military strongholds. In 1974, when the Greek military junta, supported by right-wing Cypriots, initiated a coup against the (Greek-Cypriot) president and archbishop Makarios III, Turkey invaded the island, resulting in the defeat of the coup, the fall of the Greek junta, the Turkish occupation of about one-third of the island, and the almost total segregation of the Greek-Cypriot and Turkish-Cypriot communities. While in the 1960s, most of the refugees were Turkish Cypriots, after 1974, 160,000 to 200,000 Greek Cypriots were forced to flee the north (Cockburn 2004, 65; Sant Cassia 2005, 22; Gürel, Hatay, and Yakinthou 2012, 8–10). From the south, between 40,000 and 50,000 Turkish Cypriots fled to the north (Tesser 2013, 114). As all negotiations have failed to unite the island, Cyprus is still divided. The internationally recognized Republic of Cyprus governs in the south, while the Turkish Republic of Northern Cyprus, which is financially supported and only recognized by Turkey, controls the north.

The violent confrontations in Cyprus in the second half of the twentieth century have left their mark on the Cypriot landscape, not only because of the physical buffer zone that cuts across the entire island. Memorials and commemoration sites are also very visible parts of the nationalist assemblage, spread all over the island. On the basis of a mapping project in the south of Cyprus, Karaiskou (2014, 20) refers to 'nearly six hundred memorials spread over an approximate 5,750 square kilometers of the island's southern portion (an average of one monument per ten square kilometers).' In most cases, these memorials and commemoration sites are part of the (post-)antagonist nationalist assemblage, with materialities that invite a reading that supports the heroism and sacrifice of Cypriots and that celebrates the military victories of EOKA in the south (during the independence war) and of Turkey in the north (in 1974). In the south, they commemorate the defeat and losses of the Greek-Cypriot community (in 1974).

When we focus on the southern part of Cyprus, I have argued in earlier publications (Carpentier 2014; 2018a; 2018b)[2] that the independence-war memorials are materializations of the hegemonic nationalist discourse, based on nodal points such as freedom and liberation, justice, unity, and heroism. The emphasis on self-sacrifice and suffering, which supports the notion of heroism, forms a significant nodal point of this hegemony, as each contestation or nuance would inevitably undermine the very meaningfulness of self-sacrifice. The 1974-related memorials share a number of characteristics with the independence-war memorials, but there is also a structural difference. From a Greek-Cypriot point of view, 1974 was a significant moment of loss. This is also reflected in the memorializations of 1974 (in the south). They no longer celebrate the victory, but demonstrate and serve as reminders of the loss the Greek-Cypriot community has suffered. The female figure plays a particular symbolic role here. While female figures are also present in the independence memorials, often as goddesses of victory, the female figures in the 1974 memorials have been transformed into suffering mothers.[3]

Nevertheless, there are two crucial nuances to be made. With the last lethal upsurges of violence dating from 1996, Cyprus has entered the stage of post-antagonist nationalism, where the Cypriot elites (and part of the population) still identify with the antagonistic nationalist discourses, but where the hegemonic force of these discourses has severely been weakened, and their centrality in everyday life has decreased. This also translates into how these statues and monuments feature in everyday Greek-Cypriot life, and become neutralized by the banality that surrounds them. This cold-shouldering is reinforced even more by the tourist industry that exposes the statues to the often-disinterested gazes of tourists. A second, and even more important nuance, is that despite the omnipresence of statues and memorial sites that support the hegemonic discourse, statues inviting alternative or counter-hegemonic readings have appeared, even though they remain rare. The statues that support an alternative or counter-hegemonic discourse, for instance, provide visibility to the Turkish-Cypriots in southern Cyprus, or express support for peace and diversity. This is enabled by the capacity of individuals or private local organizations to erect statues themselves, even though the government of the Republic of Cyprus, for instance, also acted to significantly stimulate such statuary by encouraging local governments to spend 1 percent of their annual budget on art (Karaiskou 2013).

COMMUNITY PARTICIPATION AND SELF-REPRESENTATION

The case study in this chapter focuses on how a rural community constructed a memorial to commemorate its traumatic displacement in the mid-1970s. Community participation played a significant role in this process, as the different groups within the village aligned themselves with the project and collectively resisted the outside attempts of the Cypriot state to alter the project. This implies that participation took place at two levels. First, the villagers participated in the development and construction process of the memorial, partially through their elected representatives, but also more directly. Second, as the village's public space is also regulated externally, the Dasaki Achnas villagers engaged with the Republic of Cyprus on the state level, which we can also see as a participatory process, even if the villagers took so much control that it is hardly still appropriate to label this component 'participatory.'

Nevertheless, as a first step, it is important to clarify what the concept of participation means here. As I have argued before, the literature on participation, including media and participation, has produced many different positions (see, e.g., Jenkins and Carpentier 2013 and Allen et al. 2014 for two fairly recent media-related debates).[4] Arguably, two main approaches to participation can be distinguished in these debates: a sociological approach and a political (studies) approach (see also Lepik 2013).[5]

The sociological approach defines participation as taking part in particular social processes, a definition which casts a very wide net. In this approach, participation includes many (if not all) types of human interaction, in combination with interactions with texts and technologies. Power is not excluded from this approach, but remains one of the many secondary concepts to support it. One example of how participation is defined in this approach is Melucci's (1989, 174) definition, when they say that participation has a double meaning: 'It means both taking part, that is, acting so as to promote the interests and the needs of an actor as well as belonging to a system, identifying with the "general interests" of the community.' This sociological approach results, for instance, in labelling consumption as participatory because consumers are taking part in a culture of consumption and are exercising consumer choices (Lury 2011, 12). Also, in the context of sports, the label of 'participation' is used, as exemplified by Delaney and Madigan's (2009) frequent use of the participation concept in their introduction to the sociology of sports. We can find a similar approach in what is labelled 'cultural participation,' where participation is defined as individual art (or cultural) exposure, attendance, or access, in some cases complemented by individual art (or cultural) creation.

In practice, this implies that the concept of participation is used for attending a concert or visiting a museum.

In contrast, the political approach produces a much more restrictive definition of participation, which refers to the equalization of power inequalities in particular decision-making processes (see Carpentier 2011). Participation then becomes defined as the equalization of power relations between privileged and non-privileged actors in formal or informal decision-making processes. For instance, in the field of democratic theory, Pateman's (1970) *Participation and Democratic Theory* is highly instrumental in showing the significance of power in defining participation; it can be seen as a key illustration of the political approach towards participation. Also, in the field of urban planning, Arnstein (1969, 216), in her seminal article 'A Ladder of Citizen Participation,' links participation explicitly to power, saying 'that citizen participation is a categorical term for citizen power.'

The political approach also allows emphasizing that participation itself is an object of struggle, and that different ideological projects (and their proponents) defend different participatory intensities. More minimalist versions of participation tend to protect the power positions of privileged (elite) actors, to the detriment of non-privileged (non-elite) actors, without totally excluding the latter. In contrast, more maximalist versions of participation strive for a full equilibrium between all actors (which protects the non-privileged actors). Here, it is important to emphasize the notion of privilege and the idea that participation is always and necessarily corrective: A participatory process corrects a more general societal power imbalance, where actors who have different power positions in society enter into a process where this power imbalance is (partially) addressed and equalized. Or, to put things differently, participation, as a concept, does not apply to situations where actors who have equal power positions interact and co-decide.

These struggles over participatory intensities do not remain restricted to a more abstract societal level; on the contrary, they enter into the micro levels of participatory processes, very much in line with Foucault's (1978) micro analytics of power. At these micro levels, actors struggle for the equalization of power relations, or, in contrast, for the centralization of decision-making powers. Although maximalist-participatory processes can strengthen and empower non-privileged actors and place them in a more egalitarian position with privileged actors, there is, of course, no certainty that all non-privileged actors necessarily benefit in equal ways, or that non-privileged actors would not (ab)use participatory processes to then, in turn, centralize power and exclude (what once were) privileged actors.

THE DASAKI ACHNAS MEMORIAL
AS A COMMUNICATIVE ASSEMBLAGE

Fleeing their village after the second phase of the Turkish Army invasion in 1974, the inhabitants of the Greek-Cypriot village of Achna sought refuge in the nearby British base, the Dhekelia British Sovereign Base Area. Protected by the base, they erected a provisional tent village, only a few hundreds of metres south of Achna.[6] Unable to return to their old village, now located in the Turkish Republic in Northern Cyprus, and used as a Turkish-Cypriot military camp, a new Achna was built, called Dasaki Achnas. At first, this new village was a tent camp, as Demetris Mattolis, one of the interviewees and a member of Dasaki Achnas's Community Council, describes. In response to the question of how long he lived in tents, he said: 'Six months, seven. From August to September, until early '75. Then came the huts—a wooden construction, with sheets on top of the ceilings—and around the '80s, '82, the first houses were built. That is, the state gave the land together with small financial help.' The village continued to exist and now still has about two thousand inhabitants.

In the early 2000s, the Panagia Trachias Church Memorial was built on the main square of the village. This memorial is one of the many that refer to the intense cultural trauma (Sztompka 2000) of the 1950s, 1960s, and 1970s, where a very large proportion of both Greek-Cypriot and Turkish-Cypriot

Figure 13.1.   The village of Dasaki Achnas. Photo by author.

populations became refugees in their own country. To study this memorial, in particular the participatory dimensions of the construction process as a struggle, a case study approach (Yin 1994) was used, gathering relevant data about the memorial through an extensive site visit. This visit allowed to photographically document the memorial and its surroundings, conduct ten interviews with nine Dasaki Achnas inhabitants,[7] and transcribe/capture the minutes from the meetings of the Advisory Monuments' Committee with representatives of the Ministry of Education and Culture and the District Administration of Famagusta (among others).[8] Qualitative textual analysis (Silverman 2006) was then used to analyse the collected material.

The Panagia Trachias Church Memorial was designed by the Dasaki Achnas–born artist Pambos Michlis and under the initiative of the communist then-mayor of Dasaki Achnas, Georgios Tsiapis. The construction process took a considerable amount of time—Community Council member Mattolis mentions eight to ten years—and financial resources. Kyprianos Pitsillos, the Secretary of the Community Council, estimated a cost of one hundred thousand Cypriot pounds.[9] As former-mayor Tsiapis mentions, when explaining the slow pace, the lengthy timeline and the amount of funding are related: 'But the main reason for the delay was economic, economic reasons.' Financing came from, according to a long-time employee of the Community Council Michalis Anastasiou, 'the Communist [Party], the EOKA Historical Memory Museum, I think, and the Community Council.'

Figure 13.2.   The Panagia Trachias Church Memorial in Dasaki Achnas. Photo by author.

The memorial is centrally located on the main village square, and consists of two main (integrated) architectural components. The west side of the memorial is a (refugee) tent in reinforced cement, representing several large tent sheets strapped to the floor with ropes. The east side of the memorial represents a church, with a church bell tower, topped with a cross. In the interview with Community Council Secretary Pitsillos, he emphasized that the building is a memorial, and not a church, even if it—architecturally and historically—references a church:[10]

> There is a misunderstanding, which is that it is a church. It is not a church, it is a monument. There is a huge difference between a church and a monument. It is a monument that was made for refugees. There, the reason people confuse it, is because at the place where the monument was constructed, there was a tent, which was [then] used as a church. [. . .] After that, a stone church was built, and then the monument was built. And because [these earlier constructions] were there, they confuse it for a church. It is a monument, not a church, and when you come to see it, it has nothing to do with a church—the churches we know. The fact that it was given the name of Saint Demetrius gives this symbolism. Because Saint Demetrius is the patron saint of the refugees. It is a combination, but it is not a church. And I stress it. It's a monument. I want this world to know, not to speak of a church. (Interview with Kyprianos Pitsillos)

When entering the memorial, which has to be done from the tent-side, the visitor encounters three groups of statues. Facing the entry is a group of nine people, each of them only half present, with closed eyes. Mattolis describes these statues as follows: 'At the entrance there are some sculptures that seem to be the world who hurts and suffers from the invasion and from the loss of their relatives.' Some of them hold photographs of their loved ones, cut in two. This statue group is (also) a reference to the missing, those who disappeared in the 1960s and 1970s, and whom the Greek-Cypriot community believed for a very long time, against all better judgement, to be still alive, with this hope being fed by nationalist propaganda. Photographs of Greek-Cypriots holding up photographs of the missing, in a very similar pose to the memorial statue group, belong to the most iconic representations of the Cyprus Problem and the human suffering and despair it has caused for the families involved. The second statue that visitors encounter when making their way in is that of a dead elderly woman, lying on the floor, with her hand on her chest and her head tilted back. In one of the interviews with the artist, who also made the sculptures, he talks about how he made this statue after the image of his mother:

> The woman who is dead at the entrance has come out to be my mother by chance. When I was working to make this statue, the few days I worked on it I began to discover that I was constantly feeling my mother's arms. Embraced by

my mother. And I feel that this sculpture came out of my flesh. And my mother looks terrified and the first time my sister came to see it, she cried. (Interview 1 with Pambos Michlis)

The third statue group, positioned more inside of the memorial, represents a mother with child. Both are asleep, with the head of the child resting on the lap of the mother. The floor is rocky, and the mother is holding a flower and a candle in one hand (interview 2 with Pambos Michlis), and caressing the head of the child with her other hand.

Figure 13.3.   Holding the missing. Photo by author.

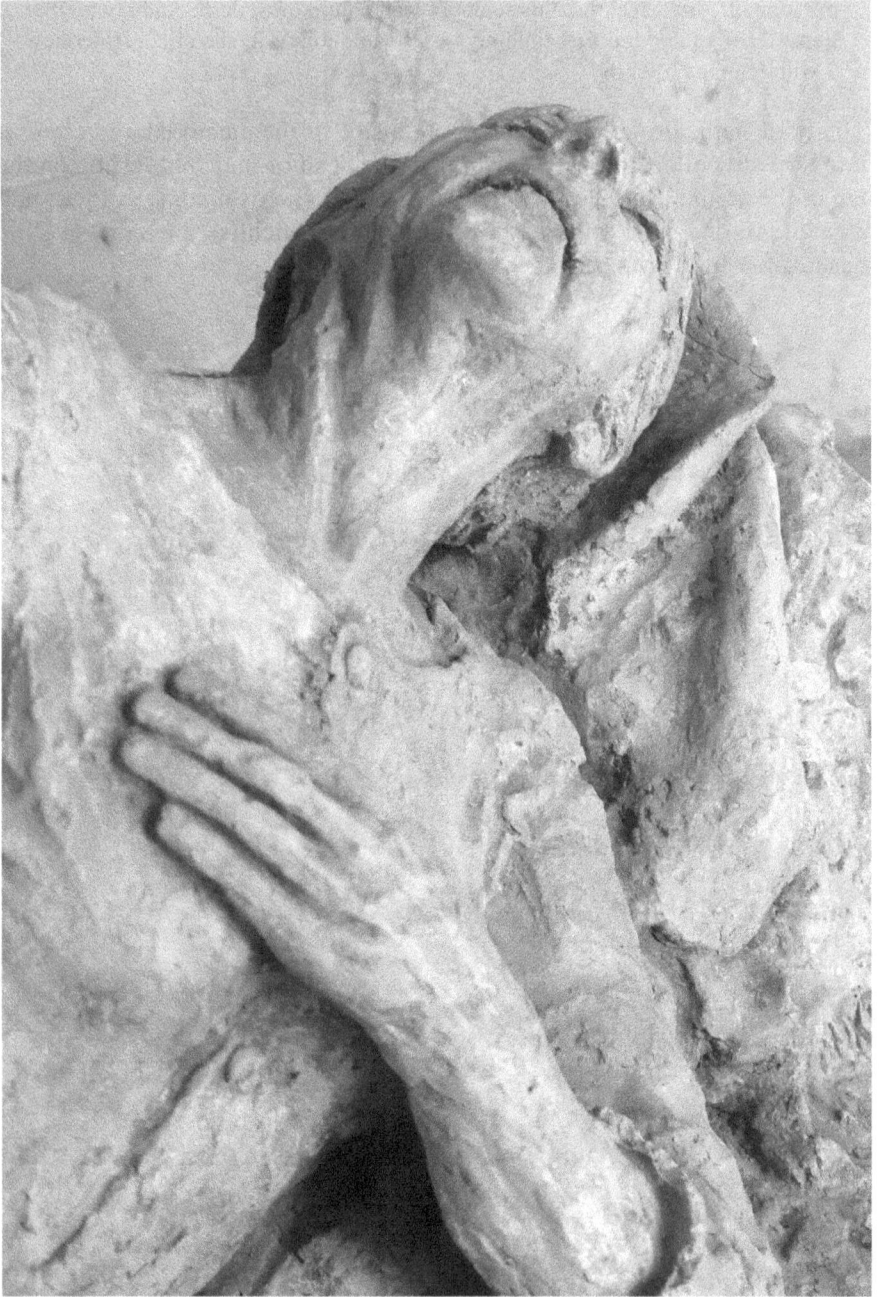

Figure 13.4. The dead mother. Photo by author.

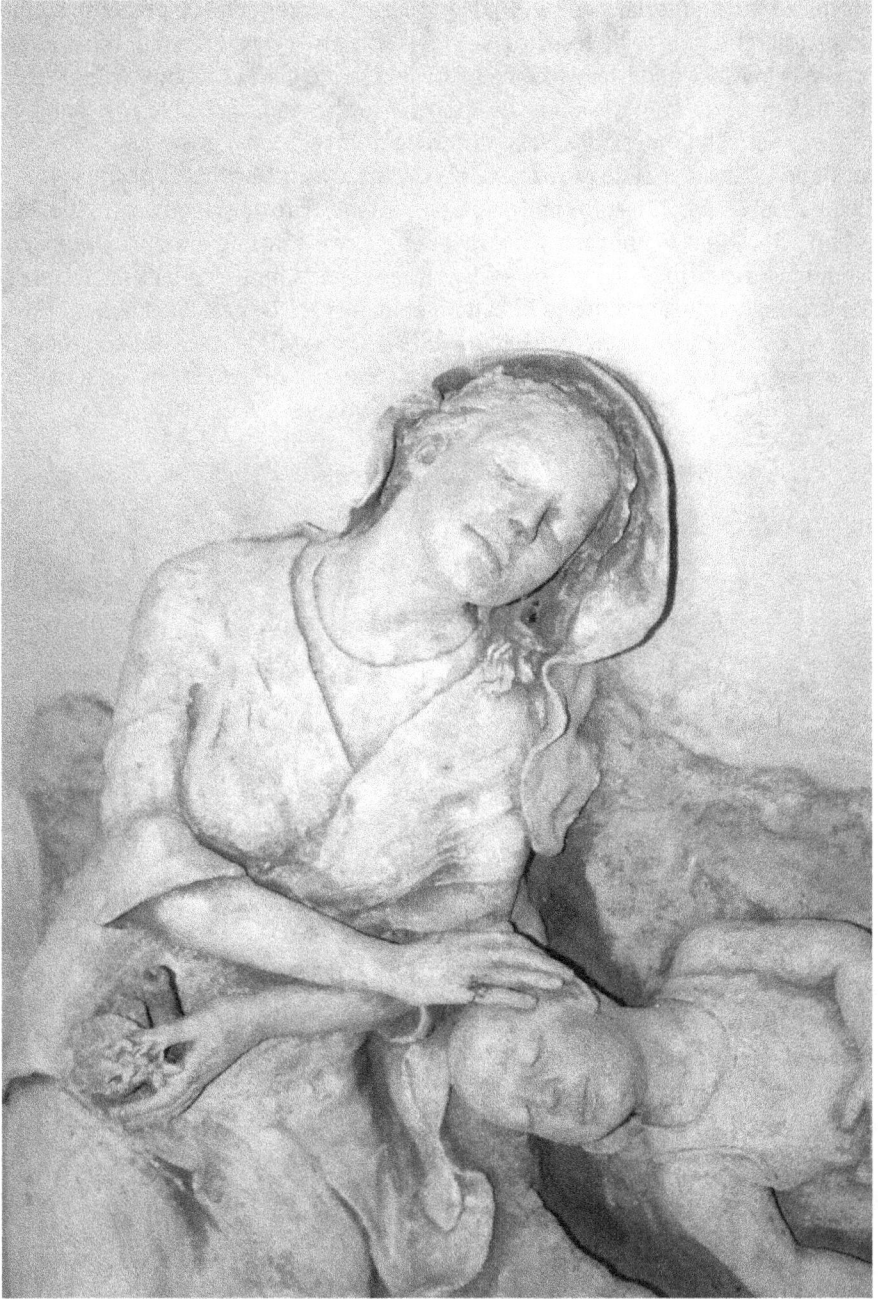

Figure 13.5. Mother with child. Photo by author.

Inside the memorial, we can find a chapel-like interior with a table that contains a large cross with Jesus on it, flanked by two other figures, most likely the Virgin Mary and Mary Magdalene. Next to the table is a book with an icon on its cover, an icon customarily referring to the saint that gives his name to the church. This interior is very different from what the artist had originally designed, but for financial reasons, his design was never realized (Interview 2 with Pambos Michlis). Behind the table, a long narrow window provides the room with light. Within the window opening, we can find small sculptures of about ten roped-in birds. In one of the proposal texts for the memorial, the artist describes the birds and the architectural elements on the east side in the following terms: 'Birds, together with the window, the skylight, the roof and the bell tower symbolize the hope for freedom, the resilience of human beings, and their belief' (Proposal Pambos Michlis, appendix Minutes 21/9/2001).

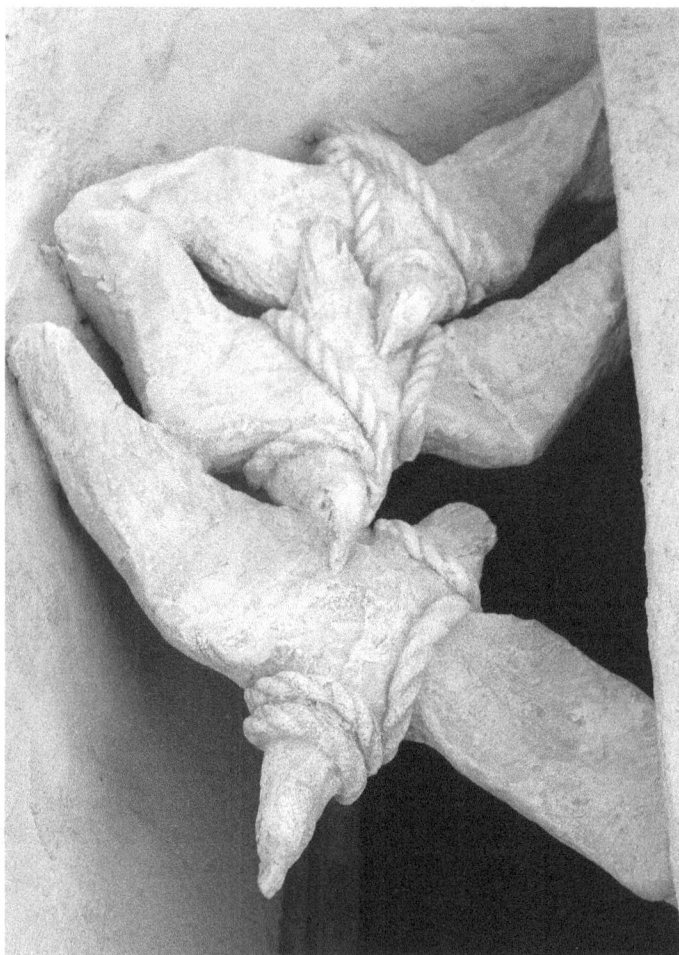

Figure 13.6.   Birds of freedom. Photo by author.

Figure 13.7. The altar from behind. Photo by author.

Figure 13.8.   The bell tower. Photo by author.

Figure 13.9. The statue of Yiasoumis K. Theodosiou. Photo by author.

Some of the surrounding buildings and structures provide a significant context for the memorial. Very close to the east side of the memorial, we can find another statue, representing Yiasoumis K. Theodosiou, a young villager and EOKA fighter who was killed in 1958, during the Cypriot independence war, when placing mines in the area.[11] On both sides of his bust, large flagpoles bear the Greek colours and fly the Greek flag. This memorial was 'commissioned by the private committee for Yiasoumis Theodosiou memorial, the

Figure 13.10. Greek flags at the Yiasoumis Association building. Photo by author.

nationalist Achna Union and the Cooperative Bank of Achna.'[12] Across the street, the large Yiasoumis Association building looks out on the square. This building, painted white and blue, has these inscriptions on the front: 'Youth of nationalist beliefs of Dasos Achnas' and 'Nationalist Unions of Yiasoumis.' A bit more to the east, still next to the square, we can find the village's Communist Party (AKEL) building.

The memorial is a discursive-material assemblage that becomes meaningful through a series of discourses; at the same time, it invites becoming aligned with these discourses. In particular, there is a strong emphasis on Greek-Cypriot suffering, loss, heroic coping, hope, and redemption, but also on remembering the violent events from the 1950s, 1960s, and 1970s that caused this suffering and loss (one of the famous Greek-Cypriot slogans is *Dhen Xechno*—I do not forget). These events are articulated through an antagonistic nationalism that, for decades, has been constructing the Turkish-Cypriots (and the Turks) as enemies who are responsible for the suffering of the Greek Cypriots and for blocking those solutions to the Cyprus Problem that the Greek-Cypriot community perceive as just. Also, the Orthodox religious discourse and the aesthetics of mimesis are strongly present. These discourses fed into the construction of the memorial and legitimated its construction from the very beginning, as well as the mobilization of the many different materials that now constitute the memorial.

At the same time, the memorial invites activating these discourses, acting as their material condensation and as a reminder of the village's cultural trauma, communicating this trauma to the villagers, and even more so, to visitors, as Mattolis explains: 'For us who live it every day, it does not make us feel so much, but for some strangers who are coming for the first time and see it, it is something impressive.' But also the future generations need to be made aware of the suffering of their parents and grandparents:

> Something needed to be done there to symbolize, we said, because after 40 years new generations must have something [for them] to know what has been happening. Because we who lived it, okay, we knew. But children now in the elementary school, who are 5, 6, 10 years old, . . . When you bring them here to the square and tell them that this thing symbolizes the tent that their parents or grandparents lived in. (Interview with Demetris Mattolis)

The memorial is also contextualized through its location on the village square, within close proximity of the EOKA memorial and the building of a nationalist organization. In addition, the villagers actively use the memorial to ritualistically commemorate their loss, as Lambros Papaioannou, the priest of Dasaki Achnas, answers in relation to a question about the existence of these gatherings: 'Yes, every year. Every year we come here and the crowd gathers [. . .]. And so, on that Sunday we come and remember here. With a parade of all residents and students.'

REPRESENTING THE TRAUMA: PARTICIPATIONS 1

The memorial is a material reminder of the village's cultural trauma of displacement, and its construction was characterized by several participatory components. One crucial participatory component was grounded in the logic of representative democracy, where the elected village leadership is mandated, via a participatory process, to take the initiative. Community Council member Mattolis emphasizes the democratic mandate of the Community Council as follows: 'The members of the Community Council, who were elected by the community, were not appointed by anyone. They were elected members of the Community Council, together with the president of the community.'

In the case of the Panagia Trachias Church Memorial, the then-mayor Tsiapis has been credited for launching the idea of constructing a 'real' monument. To use his own words: 'And then I made the suggestion [. . .] to make a monument that is related to the church that served the inhabitants of the community in the first years after the invasion.' The village's Community Council, however, took the first initiative to memorialize the village's trauma, and the council's civil engineer created the first design (Interview with Georgios Tsiapis). Mayor Tsiapis then convinced the Council to become more ambitious and commission a monument, as Kyprianos Pitsillos, secretary of the Community Council, explains:

The space there initially began as a square formation, to then become a small chapel, with a tile [. . .] to symbolize the refugees. The idea was the Community Council's. Then, then, the then communist [mayor], Mr. Tsiapis, raised the idea that what had been prefabricated did not symbolize anything, nor was it remarkable, and we had to make a monument, which also has the glory to the community but also really symbolizes all the events. The initial idea came from Mr. Tsiapis, whom the council members accepted and considered [to be] right. (Interview with Kyprianos Pitsillos)

Once the decision was made to construct a memorial, 'a contest has been announced but no one was interested in taking part' (Interview 1 with Pambos Michlis). Instead, the artist, Pambos Michlis, who was born in the village but later moved to Limassol (Interview 2 with Pambos Michlis), was invited to submit a design: 'Afterwards, however, when we said that we would do something good, we assigned the work—after we told him about our idea—to Pambos Michlis, who is a remarkable artist and a villager' (Interview with

Georgios Tsiapis). Michlis himself describes this part of the process, and the dialogue with the Community Council members, in the following terms:

> The day I left the council and came home [. . .], the next morning I decided to make a plan, with a free hand, to see if anything could really happen there. And what you see today, came out. It was a 35–40 minute chalk design—I still have some photo of it—and it's just what you see today. Designed with chalks. It is the first thing that was designed. (Interview 1 with Pambos Michlis)

In this initial phase, we can see the collaboration between the Community Council and the artist. Council member Mattolis describes this stage as follows: 'Oral ideas were given to him, he made a mixture of the thoughts he had from the community and his own thoughts—for sure, as an artist, he had ideas too' (Interview with Demetris Mattolis). Council Secretary Pitsillos also described the collaboration and negotiation with the artist, when discussing the monument's mock-up: 'When Mihlis made the mock-up, some opinions were expressed about details. But before the artist had designed it, he had listened to the ideas of the council. The artist [. . .] designed something that we all liked. There was no radical change [comparing the design with the actual monument]' (Interview with Kyprianos Pitsillos).

In addition to the participatory process between the artist and community members during the early planning stages, popular support for the construction of the memorial has been high, and its evaluation afterwards positive. All interviewees confirmed their support, and the support of other villagers, for the memorial. A rather telling response to the question 'Did you hear from someone being disappointed [about the memorial]?' came from civil engineer Giorgos Stylianou: 'No. I did not hear such nonsense from anyone.' Support also features in the story that Council Secretary Pitsillos tells, with quite some pride, about a ministerial visit: 'One day, at a visit by the Minister of Education and Culture, he saw it and immediately stopped because it impressed him. He ordered to give us money. They did; it was 6,000 Euros' (Interview with Kyprianos Pitsillos).

THE STRUGGLE WITH, AND EXCLUSION OF, THE 'OUTSIDE': PARTICIPATIONS 2

The Dasaki Achnas public space has been regulated by several actors, and not only by the Dasaki Achnas Community Council. Former mayor Tsiapis as well as the village's civil engineer Stylianou emphasize that both provincial authorities and the British base had to grant permission for the memorial to be constructed. These permits were produced without many problems; the real struggle was with the Advisory Monuments' Committee of the Ministry of Education and Culture. This committee, which only had an advisory capacity, focused more on the architecture of the memorial. Its interventions were seen as interference, and there was no constructive dialogue between the Advisory Monuments' Committee on the one hand and the Community Council and the artist on the other. The voices of the Advisory Monuments' Committee, experts in diverse relevant fields, were met with resistance and blocked from the decision-making process. In other words, the participation of the Advisory Monuments' Committee was not desired.

The minutes of the meetings show the attempts of the Advisory Monuments' Committee to alter the design of the memorial. In particular, the bell tower received severe criticism from the Advisory Monuments' Committee. During the 21 September 2001 meeting it was even suggested to remove it from the design (Minutes 21/9/2001). In addition, the Advisory Monuments' Committee articulated a list of eight critiques and suggestions during this meeting. One of these items is worded rather strongly: 'The artist's intention to construct a hill for the placement of the subject is rejected' (Minutes 21/9/2001). Another item that is featured on this list, the heavy rooftop construction, was discussed during the second meeting, on 25 June 2002, where one member of the Advisory Monuments' Committee, 'Mr. Anastasiades [from Aristotle University], recommended the construction of the tile roof with other, lighter materials (epoxy and stainless steel) to completely eliminate static dangers, but also because it is a more flexible material that can produce the shapes and form required for [the memorial] to function and [to be] aesthetically correct' (Minutes 25/6/2002). The minutes also capture the response from 'the civil engineer and the artist,' who, in unison, 'while not rejecting the idea, gave assurances that all the above will apply to the construction materials they propose themselves' (Minutes 25/6/2002).

When we turn to the perspective of the village (and its political representatives) and the artist, we can find a much more combative attitude. They vehemently rejected the suggestions from the Advisory Monuments' Committee. The former mayor Tsiapis summarizes this by pointing out that the memorial copies the original design: 'It copies the maquette, magnifies the maquette' (Interview with Georgios Tsiapis). The artist also describes his refusal to implement the requested changes, and he does so in the following terms: 'These members asked for some changes and some comments they have made, which I irrevocably did not accept. I told them "or it will be as I want it, or as you will. Then you will confuse me and I will not be able to create"' (Interview 1 with Pambos Michlis). The following long quote, from an interview with the former mayor, describes the Community Council's similarly combative position:

—No matter how strange you look, it's all about the greatness of free thinking. We did not get into moulds. No one came to tell us, 'you know, you will make a monument and we will give you money, you have to enter these moulds.' We did what we thought to be right—and the artist. That's why something went out [. . .] and that's why I think the community of Achna feels proud to have this monument.

—There was no committee from the Ministry of Culture and Education . . .?

—[. . .] some committee came in to . . . But they want you to get into some moulds that will dictate you and make the monument inside those moulds.

—How many times did they come?

—I think 1–2 times.

—And their point of view?

—They looked. They realized we were not going to follow the course they wanted [. . .]. I think we have rightly done what we thought was right—and the artist—and I think that this monument will eventually gain glamor, either pan-Cyprian or even global. (Interview with Georgios Tsiapis)

A second actor who was not allowed (much) access to the decision-making process of the memorial's construction was the construction company. The artist mentions how he maintained being involved during the construction process: 'I alone decided about everything, up to the last detail. Up to the clay . . . the cement when it [. . .] was flying over the monument, I was present' (Interview 1 with Pambos Michlis). Moreover, the artist resisted changes implemented by the construction company, thereby positioning the company in a purely executing role: 'I have never accepted any changes. The company had made changes and the moulding had been changed terribly, which I did not accept and I used great effort to bring the monument back to the shape of the maquette. If you photograph both the model and the monument, you will see that they are the same two things' (Interview 1 with Pambos Michlis).

VOICES FROM WITHIN THE COMMUNITY: PARTICIPATIONS 3

Most of the interviewees argue at great length that the political decisions of the Community Council (and the artist) gained unanimous support from the village's inhabitants, and that there was no disagreement within the community. Only after quite some insisting do interviewees mention that there were dissonant voices within the village. The Community Council Secretary Pitsillos mentions issues regarding the desirability of the memorial and uses the majority argument to legitimate the decision: 'Some were critical because they considered it unnecessary. But it is important that the majority accepted it and liked it.' Council member Mattolis also refers to the discussion about the functionality of the memorial: 'Some reservations may have been about whether it would become a church or a monument. But ultimately the decision was [to construct a monument]' (Interview with Demetris Mattolis).

The location of the memorial, close to the Yiasoumis K. Theodosiou memorial, also raised some concern. The artist himself was quite hesitant when it came to placing these two monuments in close proximity: 'I did not agree to go so close to the other monument for aesthetic reasons. [. . .] They did not want that. They wanted to see it. To be on the road, [and to be able to] see it. And for it to be exactly where the church-pantry was' (Interview 1 with Pambos Michlis). Anastasiou, an employee of the Community Council, also refers to the location debate when he describes the politics of the nationalist group: 'They [the nationalists] simply did not want it to be there because they thought they might lose the [Yiasoumis K. Theodosiou] monument. You know? This is my personal opinion' (Interview with Michalis Anastasiou). But interestingly, other interviewees still deny the existence of the debate about the location: 'No, for this work, I do not think there was any reaction or anything, because it does not affect. . . . Because the Yiasoumis monument is also part of the whole square design' (Interview with Demetris Mattolis).

It is, in particular, the artist who highlights the disagreements within the political representation, for instance, when he points out that 'There was no criticism of the artistic proposal I made there, [nothing] negative. But there were political demands' (Interview 1 with Pambos Michlis). During both interviews, Michlis expressed his irritation with the financial constraints, the demands from the Community Council about additions to the memorial after it had been built, and the politics within the village. He argues, also referring to the location debate, that 'there was a problem between the two main parties in the village. Others said no, others said yes, others said, "it will not be there" and it has become a hustle that has lasted until today [. . .]—as they are divided into two groups, what happens often in the villages—to be half, half instead' (Interview 1 with Pambos Michlis).

PARTICIPATION AND TRAUMA—A CONCLUSION

In general, this case study demonstrates the complexities of participatory practices. On one level, the Community Council represented the village, as they gained their mandate through a participatory moment (elections) and through exercising a form of democratic leadership. Moreover, the interviews show the extensive popular support for the memorial among Dasaki Achnas inhabitants, who feel that this communicative assemblage speaks to the outside world what *they* want it to say. Nevertheless, this apparent consensus is not complete, even if it took quite some probing during the interviews to bring these diverging opinions to the surface. This only shows that homogeneity is actively maintained and performed, but that cracks in this 'consensual front' do exist, and they can be made visible. Still, participation is not necessarily equated with consensus, but arguably requires agonistic ways (Mouffe 2013) to resolve these conflicts in ways that are acceptable to all involved. In the case of the memorial construction, this seems to have been the case.

A more troubling component of this participatory analysis is how the village closed its borders (at least symbolically) and firmly kept the Advisory Monuments' Committee out of the decision-making process. The alliance between the Community Council, mayor, and artist was quite strong and allowed for the exclusion of the experts from the Advisory Monuments' Committee. Even though participatory processes require a re-articulation of the privileged actors' identities, their almost total exclusion might be seen as going too far, tapping into a more populist version of participatory ideology, which is grounded in the elimination of the establishment/elite.

In explaining this strong desire to communicate about one's 'own' suffering, but also the exclusionary practices that restricted the participatory processes, we should take the depth of Dasaki Achnas's cultural trauma into account. It is an exceptional situation when an entire village is forced to move a few hundred meters, into a military base, which is territory that is still an integral part of Great Britain. It is reminiscent of the copy of the empire that Jorge Luis Borges (1975) describes in his one-page short story 'On Exactitude in Science.' Despite the minimal distance in space and in time, which renders this an undesired post-migratory situation, the cultural trauma is still experienced most intensely. This trauma provided the motivation and strength to the village to communicate the trauma to itself and to visitors, to protect the homogeneity of the village's position towards the memorial, and to monopolize the participatory-communicative process by excluding as many external voices as possible.

The exclusions were a way to protect the village's desire to express its own suffering, but this comes at a cost, as the interconnection of suffering across the island, even with their 'own' Greek-Cypriot community in other villages and towns, is made difficult. Of course, and this comes as no surprise, given the history of the Cyprus Problem, the interconnection of suffering with other communities, in particular with the Turkish-Cypriot community, is completely absent as well. Here, we can observe the limits of participatory logics, when a cultural trauma produces a disconnection of the participatory process from (the broad articulation) of key values, such as universal human rights, social justice, and care for the other.

NOTES

1. The Greek alphabet is not used here, to make the text more accessible. Also, for Cypriot cities, and for Cyprus itself, the English name is used.

2. This chapter reuses texts from these three publications.

3. Very rarely do we see a grieving father figure, as in the *Memorial for the Missing* in Dali; in most cases, it is the mother who plays the central role.

4. This argument has been, in particular, developed in the article 'Beyond the Ladder of Participation' (Carpentier 2016a). The next paragraphs originate from this article.

5. These two labels refer to the dominant use of participation in these academic fields. This does not imply that this dominant use is exclusive, and that these fields are homogeneous. The political studies approach towards participation will be abbreviated as the political approach, for reasons of brevity.

6. See http://www.prio-cyprus-displacement.net/default.asp?id=538.

7. These nine interviews were with: Michalis Anastasiou (employee of the Community Council since 1993), Maria Lysandrou (inhabitant), Demetris Mattolis (member of the Community Council for the last seventeen years and president of the Cultural Association of the village), Pambos Michlis (artist of the memorial), Lambros Papaioannou (Dasaki Achnas priest), Kyprianos Pitsillos (secretary of the Community Council), Giorgos Stylianou (Dasaki Achnas civil engineer), Georgios Tsiapis (former mayor of Dasaki Achnas), and Nikos Vasilas (Dasaki Achnas mayor from 2017). The interviewer was in all but one case Andrea Christofi. The second interview with Pambos Michlis was done by Nico Carpentier. Interview translations (from Greek) were done by Angeliki Boubouka, while Vaia Doudaki helped with the translation of the minutes. Also thanks to Angeliki Gazi for her appreciated help.

8. These minutes were collected in the framework of the Public Art of Cyprus project (http://publicart.ouc.ac.cy/). I want to thank Vicky Karaiskou for making them available to me.

9. Cyprus joined the EU in 2004, and the Eurozone in 2008. Before 2008, the Cypriot pound was the currency of the Republic of Cyprus.

10. A bit more to the southeast, we can find the Church of Saint Marina and Archangel Michael. As Maria Lysandrou, one of the inhabitants of the village explains: 'So, the square ended with the monument there, which is the centre of the village, and the church was built just below, serving the village properly' (Interview with Maria Lysandrou).

11. http://myweb.cytanet.com.cy/iaae5559/biographies/hadzitheodosiou.htm (in Greek).

12. http://publicart.ouc.ac.cy/?p=363.

Afterword

Who, With Whom, and Where?

Nick Couldry

Media research has out-scaled, to use a US term. It no longer just studies how people 'read' media texts, or make particular texts to be read: it studies everything they do, feel, work on together in relation to the 'field' of media, understanding 'media' here to mean the expanded domain of interfaces that human beings have with large-scale infrastructures for the circulation of meaning, from films to photo-exchange platforms. In doing this, media research no longer claims exclusive dominion over a field called 'media,' but seeks to grasp media as a set of productive relations within a much larger space of power: economic and social, civic and political, cultural and ecological (media research aspires to be non-media-centric).

On the face of it, media research could not be better placed to address the relations between media (in this multiply extended sense) and one of the most important global transformations of the early twenty-first century: the increasing flow of people across national borders under pressures and forces that are wholly or largely not of their making. Digital migrant studies becomes a paradigmatic site of investigation, and this book brings together many fine examples of its latest thinking.

Taking that achievement as the starting-point, I want in these final reflections to ask: 'Is this enough?' Is this book's role to be a summation, an at least temporary resting-point along the path towards a synthetic understanding of migrants' uses of digital media? Or rather, do the book's complexities, the tensions and inescapable incompletenesses they suggest, point to a still larger set of questions that media research—indeed the citizens who make up the network of today's media researchers—must confront in thinking about the increasingly fractured societies in and between which such migration is taking place?

The book's organizing concept of 'participation' foregrounds these tensions: Who is part of what and, if we acknowledge that any political and societal 'whole' is necessarily exclusionary as well as inclusionary (Isin 2002), who can *not* be part of what? And who or what constructs the relation of part to whole, given that the term 'participation' literally means the act of making (or being made) oneself a part of some whole? Any idea of democracy requires some notion of a 'whole,' a demos that captures somehow the totality of human relations deemed relevant to a particular territory of decision-making. But what and where is the demos today? How should we think about the relation between the conditions under which a digital demos is formed (where and between what points?)[1] and the conditions under which people, whether migrating or not, live their everyday lives?

In 2004, at the height of neoliberal politics (the pomp of George W Bush in Washington, DC. and Tony Blair in London), I wrote down some reflections on what, if anything, could still be salvaged, by way of contestation against prevailing neoliberal norms, from the tradition of cultural studies. The piece was called 'In the Place of a Common Culture, What?,' echoing Raymond Williams's once-resonant notion of a common culture. In that article, I foregrounded the problems of locating democratic politics, and politics' *paradoxical* relation to the solidarities built by people *through* communication. I cited among other theorists Jean-Luc Nancy and his notion of an 'inoperative community,' a community sustained only through the *absence* of the rhetorical operations of reification, on which conventional notions of community depend: 'It is the work that the community does not do and it is not that forms community. . . . Community is made of what retreats from it' (1991, xxxix, quoted in Couldry 2004). The tensions on which Nancy's notion is folded are still relevant today, as we will see. But the answers that I provided in the rest of the article were, I must admit, entirely focussed on the UK political scene and its own gaps and fissures.

Clearly such a national focus is inadequate today as a way of grasping the wider problem. We know this *not* because we possess a coherent framework for analysing the conditions for democratic politics comprehensively on a transnational scale, but because we see, in country after country, parallel eruptions *and disruptions* of democratic engagement, often around similar issues: economic austerity, social justice, defensive populism, migration, and threats to employment security from many things other than migration.

This book is important because of its resolutely transnational framing of the question of who participates in media and, through that, in democracy, and on what terms? So, to repeat my question from 2004, but more bluntly and with more urgency: 'Who, with whom, and where?' What *is* the role of media practice in the configuration or decomposition of democratic politics today, as concerns, in particular, migrant populations and their claims to political recognition?

LIMITS AND POTENTIALS

The essays in this collection cover very well both sides of how to evaluate what media offer to migrant populations, particularly populations on the move between nations. They explain how digital platforms underpin possibilities of new civic culture, make possible an entirely different logistics of movement by individuals and families between countries, support perhaps even a social infrastructure for migrants on the move and their anxiously waiting loved ones, and enable different practices of activism and memorialization. Through multiple media, different representations of community and democratic entitlement—or just human life itself—are made to circulate, different modes of *self*-representation, new forms of voice even.

But we hear also in these chapters about limits: the precarity of migrants, their vulnerability, as Radha Hegde reminds us, to the continual vilification from settled populations and their shadow relation to the forces not of movement, but of national integration (Peter Dahlgren's chapter). These forces hugely complicate what counts as 'collaboration' in the space of contemporary media. As Anne Kaun and Julie Uldam remind us, the new flows and potentials of social media platforms come with costs and limitations, based in the commercial incentives on which those platforms are based. Yes, Facebook may open a channel which facilitates a certain experience of liveness between migrants on the move, but it also makes less usable pathways of memory and possibilities for holding onto people's past on those same platforms.

Where then—apart from trying to make as balanced a summation as possible of both limits and potentials of migrant media and respecting how they play out variously under different political and cultural conditions—where can we go next in thinking about media and the conditions for expanding political inclusion? How can we, as media researchers, make more specific our contribution to Nancy Fraser's (2005) agenda of confronting not just political injustices in their recognizable forms but also the underlying *meta*-political injustice: the conditions which block human beings from even being considered as those to whom issues of justice are relevant in a particular territory? For it is questions of meta-political injustice—the deepest justice of exclusion from political membership itself, through or in spite of media—that this book raises.

LIVING TOGETHER UNDER CONDITIONS
OF ACCELERATED CIRCULATION

Underlying the arguments of the book's chapters is, I suggest, a conceptual tension that it would be good to make explicit. On the one hand, there are, as Brigitte Hipfl notes, new possibilities of conviviality, the conditions under which we successfully live *with*, that is, live *in* a shared space with, each other.[2] On the other hand, there is 'circulation,' the accelerated circulation not just of people, but of messages, images, representations, emotions, new processes of passing-*through*. Movement-'through' generates encounters, comings-together in a place which may, or very often may not, generate a place positive for mutual recognition and so the beginnings of democratic process.

Sometimes imaginative movement—the unsettling effect of hearing accounts of others or indeed taking the risk of giving one's own account to others, whether in dialogue or through cultural forms such as film and the visual arts—can do the work of challenging a place that is too settled and making it open to new relations, new possibilities of movement-through.

It should be clear however that these relations between 'in' and 'through'—or more concretely between *convivencia* and circulation—are ambivalent, unstable, and uncertain in their political and social consequences. Fabian Virchow in his chapter cites the notion of *un*civil society from the sociolinguists Krzyżanowski and Ledin (2017). *Accelerated circulation* of text, image and the transmissible effects of text and image (often called 'affect') does not obviously increase the chances of civility. Quite the opposite: unless much further work of repair and reconstruction is done, it likely increases the chances of incivility, a disturbing of the norms that enable us to live together yet also apart (that Erving Goffman (1966) called 'civil indifference'). Civil indifference may be a well-known feature of healthy cities, but in this book it is not established urban spaces we are mainly discussing, but other zones of encounter: the nation's physical border and, even more difficult to grasp, the space of digital encounters online.

How should we start to think about the architecture of digital spaces, from the point of view of trying to ensure they are healthy ecologies, not toxic ones? How do we conceptualize the invasion of online spectacle's pressures into everyday media activity, the spectacle not just of the border,[3] but of the everyday online encounter with those we barely know?

From this perspective, the key issue in the investigations of digital migrant studies is not agency, still less empowerment. For the potential for agency and empowerment of some sort, from somewhere, in a mediated space of accelerated circulation and encounter can be taken for granted. The issue instead is civility. However under digital conditions (the differently configured social space-time of deep mediatization (Couldry and Hepp 2016) can civility between physically distant people be achieved and how?

How, to recall Thomas Hobbes, can a new state of nature (but this time technologically enabled) of all-against-all be avoided? What digital architectures do we need to make civility at scale even possible so that the idea of digital civic cultures become not a chimaera but a living breathing possibility that we can sustain and share?

These, I suggest, are the questions which this important book leaves us with. Answering them will be the work of a new book at least, or perhaps a new discipline for which as yet we lack a name.

NOTES

1. For interesting reflections from a decade ago, see Bohman 2007.
2. As Hipfl notes, drawing on Wise and Noble (2016), the Spanish word *convivencia* is more vivid and broad in its implications than conviviality.
3. De Genova (2013), mentioned in several chapters.

Bibliography

Accenture and UNHCR. 2016. 'Connecting Refugees: How Internet and Mobile Connectivity Can Improve Refugee Well-Being and Transform Humanitarian Action.' https://www.accenture.com/t20160913T012423__w__/us-en/_acnmedia/PDF-30/Accenture-Connecting-Refugees.pdf.

Adloff, Frank. 2015. 'Immer im Takt bleiben? Zu einer konvivialistischen Affektpolitik.' In *Konvivialismus. Eine Debatte*, edited by Frank Adloff and Volker M. Heins, 71–83. Bielefeld: Transcript.

Adloff, Frank, Sérgio Costa, Ina Kerner, and Andrea Vetter. 2016. 'For a Politics of Conviviality.' *futureswewant.net*. Published July 8, 2016. http://futureswewant.net/adloff-costa-kerner-vetter-conviviality.

Agamben, Giorgio. 1995. 'We Refugees.' Translated by Michael Rocke. *Symposium* 49 (2): 114–19. https://doi.org/10.1080/00397709.1995.10733798.

Agamben, Giorgio. 1998. *Homo Sacer: Sovereign Power and Bare Life*. Stanford, CA: Stanford University Press.

Ager, Alastair, and Alison Strang. 2008. 'Understanding Integration: A Conceptual Framework.' *Journal of Refugee Studies* 21 (2): 166–91. https://doi.org/10.1093/jrs/fen016.

Ahmed, Sara. 2004. *The Cultural Politics of Emotion*. New York: Routledge.

Ai Weiwei, dir. 2017. *Human Flow*. Germany/USA/China/Palestine: 24 Media Production Company/AC Films/Ai Weiwei Studio/Ginger Ink and Halliday Finch/Green Channel/HighLight Films/Human Flow/Maysara Films/Optical Group Film and TV Productions/Participant Media/Redrum Production/Ret Film.

Ai Weiwei. 2018. 'The Refugee Crisis Isn't About Refugees. It's About Us.' *The Guardian*, 2 February 2018. Accessed 21 July 2018. https://www.theguardian.com/commentisfree/2018/feb/02/refugee-crisis-human-flow-ai-weiwei-china.

Al Alawi, Walaa, dir. 2015. *The Girl, Whose Shadow Reflects the Moon*. Accessed 20 July 2018. http://anotherkindofgirl.com/walaa#/id/i10983910.

Alencar, Amanda. 2017. 'Refugee Integration and Social Media: A Local and Experiential Perspective.' *Information, Communication & Society.* https://doi.org/10.10 80/1369118X.2017.1340500.

Al Hariri, Muna, dir. 2015. *Dreams Without Borders.* Accessed 20 July 2018. http:// anotherkindofgirl.com/muna#/id/i10747115.

Allen, Danielle, Moya Bailey, Nico Carpentier, Natalie Fenton, Henry Jenkins, Alexis Lothian, Jack Linchuan Qiu, Mirko Tobias Schaefer, and Ramesh Srinivasan. 2014. 'Participations: Dialogues on the Participatory Promise of Contemporary Culture and Politics. Part 3: Politics.' *International Journal of Communication* 8 (Forum): 1129–51. http://ijoc.org/index.php/ijoc/article/view/2787/1124.

Almond, Gabriel A., and Sidney Verba. 1963. *The Civic Culture. Political Attitudes and Democracy in Five Nations.* Princeton, NJ: Princeton University Press.

Amadahy, Zainab. 2008. 'A Roundtable on Relationship-Building in Indigenous Solidarity Work.' Retrieved from https://indyclass.files.wordpress.com/2008/09/ e2809clisten-take-direction-and-stick-around1.pdf.

Amadeu Antonio Stiftung. 2016. *Peggy war da! Gender und Social Media als Kitt rechtspopulistischer Bewegungen.* Berlin: AAS.

Aminzade, Ronald R., Jack A. Goldstone, Doug McAdam, Elizabeth J. Perry, William H. Sewell Jr., Sidney Tarrow, and Charles Tilly. 2001. *Silence and Voice in the Study of Contentious Politics.* Cambridge: Cambridge University Press.

Andrade, Antonio Diaz, and Bill Doolin. 2016. 'Information and Communication Technology and the Social Inclusion of Refugees.' *MIS Quarterly* 40 (2): 405–16. https://doi.org/10.25300/MISQ/2016/40.2.06.

Another Kind of Girl Collective. n.d. 'Another Kind of Girl Collective.' Accessed 20 July 2018. http://anotherkindofgirl.com/#/id/i11551491.

Another Kind of Girl Collective. n.d. 'About the Collective.' Accessed 22 July 2018. http:/anotherkindofgirl.com/about-the-workshops.

Appadurai, Arjun. 1996. *Modernity at Large. Cultural Dimensions of Globalization.* Minneapolis: University of Minnesota Press.

Appadurai, Arjun. 2006. *Fear of Small Numbers: An Essay on the Geography of Anger.* Durham, NC: Duke University Press.

Appadurai, Arjun. 2013. *The Social Life of Things: Commodities in Cultural Perspective.* 11th ed. Cambridge: Cambridge University Press.

Appadurai, Arjun. 2016. 'Aspirational Maps: On Migrant Narratives and Imagined Future Citizenship.' *Eurozine.* Accessed 12 July 2018. https://www.eurozine.com/ aspirational-maps/?pdf.

Appiah, Kwame Anthony. 2006. *Cosmopolitanism: Ethics in a World of Strangers.* New York: Norton.

Arnold, Sina, Manuela Bojadžijev, and Sabrina Apicella. 2018. 'Logistik und Migration. Eine integrierte Perspektive für die empirischen Kulturwissenschaften.' In *Grounding Logistics*, Special issue of Berliner Blätter, Ethnologische und Ethnographische Beiträge, edited by Sina Arnold, Manuela Bojadžijev, and Sabrina Apicella. Berlin: Panama Verlag. Forthcoming.

Arnstein, Sherry R. 1969. 'A Ladder of Citizen Participation.' *Journal of the American Institute of Planners* 35 (4): 216–24.

Assmann, Aleida. 2016. *Formen des Vergessens*. Göttingen, Germany: Wallstein.

Attia, Iman. 2014. 'Rassismus (nicht) beim Namen nennen.' *Aus Politik und Zeitgeschichte* nos. 13–14 (March): 8–14. https://www.bpb.de/shop/zeitschriften/apuz/180868/rassismus-und-diskriminierung.

Back, Les, Shamser Sinha, with Charlynne Bryan. 2012. 'New Hierarchies of Belonging.' *European Journal of Cultural Studies* 15 (2): 139–54. https://doi.org/10.1177/1367549411432030.

Back, Les, and Shamser Sinha. 2016. 'Multicultural Conviviality in the Midst of Racim's Ruins.' *Journal of Intercultural Studies* 37 (5): 517–32. https://doi.org/10.1080/07256868.2016.1211625.

Baek, Young Min. 2015. 'Political Mobilization Through Social Network Sites: The Mobilizing Power of Political Messages Received from SNS Friends.' *Computers in Human Behavior* 44 (March): 12–19. https://doi.org/10.1016/j.chb.2014.11.021.

Baines, Jess. 2016. 'Engaging (Past) Participants: The Case of Radicalprintshops. org.' In *Innovative Methods in Media and Communication Research*, edited by Sebastian Kubitschko and Anne Kaun, 17–35. Basingstoke, UK: Palgrave Macmillan. https://doi.org/10.1007/978-3-319-40700-5_2.

Bal, Mieke, and Miguel A. Hernández-Navarro. 2011. Introduction to *Art and Visibility in Migratory Culture*, by Mieke Bal and Miguel A. Hernández-Navarro, 9–20. Amsterdam: Rodopi.

Balibar, Etienne. 2002. *Politics and the Other Scene*. Translated by Christine Jones, James Swenson, and Chris Turner. London: Verso.

Bargetz, Brigitte. 2009. 'The Politics of the Everyday: A Feminist Revision of the Public/Private Frame.' In *Reconciling the Irreconcilable*, edited by I. Papkova, Vienna: IWM Junior Visiting Fellows' Conferences, Vol. 24. Accessed 2 August 2018. http://www.iwm.at/publications/5-junior-visiting-fellows-conferences/vol-xxiv/the-politics-of-the-everyday/.

Baricelli, Michele. 2013. 'Collected Memories statt kollektives Gedächtnis: Zeitgeschichte in der Migrationsgesellschaft.' In *Handbuch Zeitgeschichte im Geschichtsunterricht*, edited by Markus Furrer and Kurt Messmer, 89–118. Schwalbach am Taunus, Germany: Wochenschau-Verlag.

Bassel, Leah. 2017. *The Politics of Listening*. London: Palgrave Macmillan.

Bauder, Harald. 2008. 'Media Discourse and the New German Immigration Law.' *Journal of Ethnic and Migration Studies* 34 (1): 95–112. https://doi.org/10.1080/13691830701708783.

Bauman, Gerd. 1996. *Contesting Culture: Discourses of Identity in Multi-Ethnic London*. Cambridge: Cambridge University Press.

Baym, Nancy K. 2015. *Personal Connections in the Digital Age*, 2nd ed., Cambridge, UK: Polity Press.

Beck, Ulrich. 2002. 'The Cosmopolitan Perspective: Sociology in the Second Age of Modernity.' In *Conceiving Cosmopolitanism: Theory, Context and Practice*, edited by Steven Vertovec and Robert Cohen, 61–85. Oxford: Oxford University Press.

Beck, Ulrich, and Edgar Grande. 2010. 'Jenseits des Methodologischen Nationalismus Außereuropäische und Europäische Variationen der Zweiten Moderne.' *Soziale Welt* 61 (3/4): 187–216.

Behdad, Ali. 2005. *A Forgetful Nation: On Immigration and Cultural Identity in the United States.* Durham, NC: Duke University Press.

Bell, Avril. 2016. 'Decolonizing Conviviality and "Becoming Ordinary": Cross-Cultural Face-to-Face Encounters in Aotearoa New Zealand.' *Ethnic and Racial Studies* 39 (7): 1170–86. https://doi.org/10.1080/01419870.2015.1103883.

Benhabib, Seyla. 2006. *Another Cosmopolitanism: Hospitality, Sovereignity, and Democratic Iterations.* Edited by Robert Post. New York: Oxford University Press.

Benson, Rodney. 2002. 'The Political/Literary Model of French Journalism: Change and Continuity in Immigration News Coverage, 1973–1991.' *Journal of European Area Studies* 10 (1): 49–70. https://doi.org/10.1080/14608460220148437.

Benson, Rodney. 2013. *Shaping Immigration News: A French-American Comparison.* Cambridge: Cambridge University Press.

Benz, Wolfgang (ed.). 2016. *Fremdenfeinde und Wutbürger: Verliert die demokratische Gesellschaft ihre Mitte?* Berlin: Metropol.

Berry, Mike, Inaki Garcia-Blanco, and Kerry Moore. 2015. *Press Coverage of the Refugee and Migrant Crisis in the EU: A Content Analysis of Five European Countries.* Report Prepared for the United Nations High Commission for Refugees. Cardiff School of Journalism, Media and Cultural Studies. Accessed 12 April 2018. http://www.unhcr.org/56bb369c9.html.

Bhattacharyya, Gargi. 2008. *Dangerous Brown Men: Exploiting Sex, Violence and Feminism in the War on Terror.* New York: Zed Books.

biber n.d. (a) 'Über uns.' Accessed 9 January 2018. http://www.dasbiber.at/%C3% BCber-uns.

biber n.d. (b) 'biber Newcomer.' Accessed 9 January 2018. http://www.dasbiber.at/ redaktion-2-go.

biber n.d. (c) 'Akademie mit scharf.' Accessed 9 January 2018. http://www.dasbiber .at/akademie-mit-scharf.

biber n.d. (d) 'Praxis-Training "Medien, Journalismus & Kommunikation" für Asylberechtigte.' Accessed 9 January 2018. http://www.dasbiber.at/blog/medien -training-fuer-asylwerber-wien.

Bickford, Susan. 1996. *The Dissonance of Democracy: Listening, Conflict, and Citizenship.* Ithaca, NY: Cornell University Press.

Bigo, Didier. 2002. 'Security and Immigration: Toward a Critique of the Governmentality of Unease.' *Alternatives: Global, Local, Political* 27 (1): 63–92. https://doi .org/10.1177/03043754020270S105.

Block, Sharon. 2001. 'Rape and Race in Colonial Newspapers, 1728–1776.' *Journalism History* 27 (4): 146–55.

Böhm, Steffen, André Spicer, and Peter Fleming. 2008. 'Infra-political Dimensions of Resistance to International Business: A Neo-Gramscian Approach.' *Scandinavian Journal of Management* 24 (3): 169–82. https://doi.org/10.1016/j.sca man.2008.03.008.

Bohman, James. 2007. *Democracy across Borders.* Cambridge, MA: MIT Press.

Bojadžijev, Manuela, and Regina Römhild. 2014. 'Was kommt nach dem "transnational turn"? Perspektiven für eine kritische Migrationsforschung.' In *Vom Rand ins Zentrum: Perspektiven einer kritischen Migrationsforschung,* Berliner

Blätter, Ethnographische und ethnologische Beiträge, Heft 65, edited by Manuela Bojadžijev, Katrin Amelang, Beate Binder, Alexa Färber, and Labor Migration, 10–24. Berlin: Panama Verlag.

Boltanski, Luc. 1999. *Distant Suffering: Morality, Media and Politics.* Translated by Graham Burchill. Cambridge: Cambridge University Press.

Borges, Jorge Luis. 1975. *A Universal History of Infamy.* Translated by Norman Thomas de Giovanni. Harmondsworth, UK: Penguin Books.

Borggräfe, Henning. 2014. *Zwangsarbeiterentschädigung. Vom Streit um 'vergessene Opfer' zur Selbstaussöhnung der Deutschen.* Göttingen, Germany: Wallstein.

Boulila, Stefanie C., and Christiane Carri. 2017. 'On Cologne: Gender, Migration and Unacknowledged Racisms in Germany.' *European Journal of Women's Studies* 24 (3): 286–93. https://doi.org/10.1177/1350506817712447.

Bowker, Geoffrey, and Susan Leigh Star. 1999. *Sorting Things Out: Classification and Its Consequences.* Cambridge, MA: MIT Press.

Brausam, Anna. 2018. 'Todesopfer rechter Gewalt seit 1990.' *Opferfonds-cura.de.* Published 9 May 2018. http://www.opferfonds-cura.de/todesopfer-rechter-gewalt/.

Breckenridge, Carol A., Sheldon Pollock, Homi K. Bhabha, and Dipesh Chakrabarty. 2002. *Cosmopolitanism.* Durham, NC: Duke University Press.

Brod, Anna. 2018. 'Theater erzählen den NSU. Persönliche und gesellschaftliche Krisen auf der Bühne.' In *Krisen erzählen*, edited by Irmtraud Hnilica, Thomas Wortmann, and Iuditha Balint. Forthcoming. Würzburg, Germany: Königshausen & Neumann.

Brooks, Xan. 2017. 'Ai Weiwei: "Without the Prison, the Beatings, What Would I Be?"' *The Guardian*, 17 September 2017. Accessed 21 July 2018. https://www.the guardian.com/film/2017/sep/17/ai-weiwei-without-the-prison-the-beatings-what -would-i-be.

Bruns, Axel, and Jean Burgess. 2015. 'Twitter Hashtags from Ad Hoc to Calculated Publics.' In *Hashtag Publics: The Power and Politics of Discursive Networks*, edited by Nathan Rambukkana, 13–28. New York: Peter Lang.

Brunwasser, Matthew. 2015. 'A 21st-Century Migrant's Essentials: Food, Shelter, Smartphone." *New York Times*, 25 August 2015. Retrieved from https://www .nytimes.com/2015/08/26/world/europe/a-21st-century-migrants-checklist-water -shelter-smartphone.html.

Bucher, Taina. 2016. 'Neither Black Nor Box: Ways of Knowing Algorithms.' In *Innovative Methods in Media and Communication Research,* edited by Sebastian Kubitschko and Anne Kaun, 81–98. Basingstoke, UK: Palgrave Macmillan. https:// doi.org/10.1007/978-3-319-40700-5_5.

Bukow, Wolf-Dietrich, Markus Ottersbach, Sonja Preissing, and Bettina Lösch. 2013. *Partizipation in der Einwanderungsgesellschaft.* Wiesbaden, Germany: Springer VS.

Bundesamt für Migration und Flüchtlinge (BAMF). 2016. 'Ankommen (3.0).' (Mobile application Software) Retrieved from http://ankommenapp.de/APP/EN/ Startseite/startseite-node.html.

Bundesamt für Migration und Flüchtlinge (BAMF). 2017. 'Das Bundesamt in Zahlen 2016,' 24 August 2017. Retrieved from http://www.bamf.de/SharedDocs/Anlagen/ DE/Publikationen/Broschueren/bundesamt-in-zahlen-2016.html?nn=9121126.

Bundesamt für Migration und Flucht (BAMF). 2018. *Aktuelle Zahlen zu Asyl (6/2018)*. Nürnberg, Germany: BAMF.

Bundeskanzleramt. n.d. 'HELP-Service for Foreign Citizens.' Accessed 11 April 2018. https://www.help.gv.at/Portal.Node/hlpd/public/content/26/Seite.260430.html.

Bundesministerium des Inneren. 2016. '890.000 Asylsuchende im Jahr 2015,' 30 September 2016. Retrieved from http://www.bmi.bund.de/SharedDocs/Presse mitteilungen/DE/2016/09/asylsuchende-2015.html.

Bundesministerium des Innern. 2017. '90.389 Asylsuchende im ersten Halbjahr 2017,' 7 July 2017. http://www.bmi.bund.de/SharedDocs/Pressemitteilungen/ DE/2017/07/asylantraege-juni-2017.

Bundesministerium für wirtschaftliche Zusammenarbeit und Entwicklung (BMZ). 2016. 'Entwicklung trifft Entwickler bei ICT4Refugees-Konferenz,' 31 May 2016. http://www.bmz.de/20160531-1.

Burgess, Jean. 2006. 'Hearing Ordinary Voices: Cultural Studies, Vernacular Creativity and Digital Storytelling.' *Continuum* 20 (2): 201–14.

Butler, Judith. 1993. *Bodies That Matter. On the Discursive Limits of 'Sex.'* London: Routledge.

Butler, Judith. 2001. 'Eine Welt, in der Antigone am Leben geblieben wäre.' Interview with Judith Butler by Carolin Emcke and Martin Saar. *Deutsche Zeitschrift für Philosophie* 49 (4): 587–99. https://doi.org/10.1524/dzph.2001.49.4.587.

Butler, Judith. 2004. *Precarious Life: The Powers of Mourning and Violence*. London: Verso.

Butler, Judith. 2009a. 'Performativity, Precarity and Sexual Politics.' *AIBR. Revista de Antropología Iberoamericana* 4 (3): i–xiii. https://doi.org/10.11156/ aibr.040305.

Butler, Judith. 2009b. *Frames of War: When Is Life Grievable?* New York: Verso.

Butler, Judith. 2012. *Parting Ways: Jewishness and the Critique of Zionism*. New York: Columbia University Press.

Butler, Judith, and Gayatri Chakravorty Spivak. 2007. *Who Sings the Nation State? Language, Politics, Belonging*. London: Seagull Books.

Cammaerts, Bart. 2009. 'Community Radio in the West: A Legacy of Struggle for Survival in a State and Capitalist Controlled Media Environment.' *International Communication Gazette* 71 (8): 635–54. https://doi.org/10.1177/1748048509345057.

Cammaerts, Bart, Alice Mattoni, and Patrick McCurdy. 2013. 'Introduction: Mediation and Protest Movements.' In *Mediation and Protest Movements*, edited by Bart Cammaerts, Alice Mattoni, and Patrick McCurdy, 1–20. Bristol: Intellect.

Cammaerts, Bart, Brooks DeCillia, João Magalhães, and César Jimenez-Martínez. 2016. *Journalistic Representations of Jeremy Corbyn in the British Press: From Watchdog to Attackdog*. Academic Report on Journalistic Representations of Jeremy Corbyn. Department of Media and Communications, London School of Economics and Political Science. Accessed 12 April 2018. http://www.lse.ac.uk/media-and -communications/assets/documents/research/projects/corbyn/Cobyn-Report.pdf.

Campani, Giovanna. 2001. 'Migrants and Media: The Italian Case.' In *Media and Migration: Constructions of Mobility and Difference*, edited by Russell King and Nancy Wood, 38–52. London: Routledge.

Caren, Neal, Kay Jowers, and Sarah Gaby. 2012. 'A Social Movement Online. Stormfront and the White Nationalist Movement.' In *Media, Movements, and Political Change*, edited by Jennifer Earl and Deana A. Rohlinger, 163–93 Bingley, UK: Emerald.

Carleheden Mikael, Carl-Göran Heidegren, and Rasmus Willig. 2012. 'Recognition, Social Invisibility, and Disrespect.' *Distinktion: Journal of Social Theory* 13 (1): 1–3. https://doi.org/10.1080/1600910X.2012.648734.

Carlson, Bronwyn. 2017. 'Why Are Indigenous People Such Avid Users of Social Media?' *theguardian.com*. Published 27 April 2017. http://www.theguardian.com/commentisfree/2017/apr/27/why-are-indigenous-people-such-avid-users-of-social -media.

Carpentier, Nico. 2009. 'Participation Is Not Enough: The Conditions of Possibility of Mediated Participatory Practices.' *European Journal of Communication* 24 (4): 407–20. https://doi.org/10.1177/0267323109345682.

Carpentier, Nico. 2011. *Media and Participation: A Site of Ideological-Democratic Struggle*. Bristol, UK: Intellect.

Carpentier, Nico. 2012. 'The Concept of Participation. If They Have Access and Interact, Do They Really Participate?' *Fronteiras—estudos midiáticos* 14 (2): 164–77. https://doi.org/10.4013/fem.2012.142.10.

Carpentier, Nico. 2014. 'Beeldenstrijd in Cyprus: Het Problematische Herdenken van een Conflictueus Verleden.' *nY* 24: 129–68.

Carpentier, Nico. 2015. 'Differentiating Between Access, Interaction and Participation.' *Conjunctions: Transdisciplinary Journal of Cultural Participation* 2 (2): 7–28. https://doi.org/10.7146/tjcp.v2i2.23117.

Carpentier, Nico. 2016a. 'Beyond the Ladder of Participation: An Analytical Toolkit for the Critical Analysis of Participatory Media Processes.' *Javnost—The Public* 23 (1): 70–88.

Carpentier, Nico. 2016b. 'Community Media as Rhizome: Expanding the Research Agenda.' *Journal of Alternative and Community Media* (1): 4–6. https://joacm.org/index.php/joacm/article/view/847/735.

Carpentier, Nico. 2017. *The Discursive-Material Knot: Cyprus in Conflict and Community Media Participation.* New York: Peter Lang Publishing.

Carpentier, Nico. 2018a. 'Deconstructing Nationalist Assemblages: A Visual Essay on the Greek Cypriot Memorials Related to Two Violent Conflicts in 20th Century Cyprus.' *Communicazioni Sociali* 2018 (1): 33–49.

Carpentier, Nico. 2018b. 'Iconoclastic Controversy in Cyprus: The Problematic Rethinking of a Conflicted Past.' In *Cyprus and Its Conflicts: Representations, Materialities and Cultures*, edited by Vaia Doudaki and Nico Carpentier, 25–54. New York: Berghahn Books.

Carpentier, Nico, and Peter Dahlgren (eds). 2011. 'Interrogating Audiences: Theoretical Horizons of Participation.' Special Issue. *Communication Management Quarterly: Časopis za upravljanje komuniciranjem* 6 (21).

Carpentier, Nico, and Peter Dahlgren. 2011. 'Introduction: Interrogating Audiences: Theoretical Horizons of Participation.' *Communication Management Quarterly: Časopis za upravljanje komuniciranjem* 6 (21): 7–12.

Carpentier, Nico, Peter Dahlgren, and Francesca Pasquali. 2013. 'Waves of Media Democratization: A Brief History of Contemporary Participatory Practices in the Media Sphere.' *Convergence: The International Journal of Research into New Media Technologies* 19 (3): 287–94. https://doi.org/10.1177/1354856513486529.

Caviedes, Alexander. 2015. 'An Emerging "European" News Portrayal of Immigration?' *Journal of Ethnic and Migration Studies* 41 (6): 897–917. https://doi.org/10.1080/1369183X.2014.1002199.

Chin, Rita. 2017. *The Crisis of Multiculturalism in Europe: A History*. Princeton, NJ: Princeton University Press.

Chouliaraki, Lilie. 2006. *The Spectatorship of Suffering*. London: Sage Publications.

Chouliaraki, Lilie. 2008a. 'The Mediation of Suffering and the Vision of a Cosmopolitan Public.' *Television & New Media* 9 (5): 371–91. https://doi.org/10.1177/1527476408315496.

Chouliaraki, Lilie. 2008b. 'The Symbolic Power of Transnational Media. Managing the Visibility of Suffering.' *Global Media and Communication* 4 (3): 329–51. https://doi.org/10.1177/1742766508096084.

Chouliaraki, Lilie, Myria Georgiou, and Rafal Zaborowski. 2017. *The European 'Migration Crisis' and the Media: A Cross-European Press Content Analysis*. Project Report. Department of Media and Communications, London School of Economics and Political Science. Accessed 12 April 2018. http://www.lse.ac.uk/media-and-communications/assets/documents/research/projects/media-and-migration/Migration-and-media-report-FINAL-June17.pdf.

Chouliaraki, Lilie, and Pierluigi Musarò. 2017. 'The Mediatized Border: Technologies and Affects of Migrant Reception in the Greek and Italian Borders.' *Feminist Media Studies* 17 (4): 535–49. https://doi.org/10.1080/14680777.2017.1326550.

Chouliaraki, Lilie, and Rafal Zaborowski. 2017. 'Voice and Community in the Refugee Crisis: A Content Analysis of News Coverage in Eight European Countries.' *International Communication Gazette* 79 (6–7): 1–23. https://doi.org/10.1177/1748048517727173.

Christensen, Miyase, and Andrè Jansson. 2015. *Cosmopolitanism and the Media. Cartographies of Change*. New York: Palgrave Macmillan.

Chung, C.K. Martin. 2017. *Repentance for the Holocaust: Lessons from Jewish Thought for Confronting the German Past*. London: Cornell University Press.

Clarke, Kamari Maxine. 2017. 'Rethinking Sovereignty Through Hashtag Publics: The New Body Politics.' *Cultural Anthropology* 32 (3): 359–66. https://doi.org/10.14506/ca32.3.05.

Cockburn, Cynthia. 2004. *The Line: Women, Partition and the Gender Order in Cyprus*. London: Zed Books.

Coddington, Kate, and Alison Mountz. 2014. 'Countering Isolation with the Use of Technology: How Asylum-Seeking Detainees on Islands in the Indian Ocean Use Social Media to Transcend Their Confinement.' *Journal of the Indian Ocean Region* 10 (1): 97–112. https://doi.org/10.1080/19480881.2014.896104.

Cohen, Jean, and Andrew Arato. 1992. *Civil Society and Political Theory*. Cambridge, MA: MIT Press.

Coleman, Stephen. February 2013. 'The Challenge of Digital Hearing.' *Journal of Digital and Media Literacy* 2 (1): 3. http://www.jodml.org/2013/02/01/challenge-of-digital-hearing.

Coles, Romand. 2004. 'Moving Democracy: Industrial Areas Foundation Social Movements and the Political Arts of Listening, Traveling, and Tabling.' *Political Theory* 32 (5): 678–705.

Collins, Randall. 1990. 'Stratification, Emotional Energy, and the Transient Emotions.' In *Research Agendas in the Sociology of Emotions*, edited by Theodore D. Kemper, 27–57. Albany: State University of New York Press.

Cooper, Anthony, Chris Perkins, and Chris Rumford. 2014. 'The Vernacularization of Borders.' In *Placing the Border in Everyday Life*, edited by Reece Jones and Corey Johnson, 15–32. Surrey, UK: Ashgate.

Corpus Ong, Jonathan. 2009. 'The Cosmopolitan Continuum. Locating Cosmopolitanism in Media and Cultural Studies.' *Media, Culture, Society* 31 (3): 449–66. https://doi.org/10.1177/0163443709102716.

Couldry, Nick. 2004. 'In the Place of a Common Culture, What?' *Review of Education, Pedagogy and Cultural Studies* 26: 1–19. [Reprinted in Couldry, Nick. 2016. *Listening Beyond the Echoes: Media, Ethics and Agency in an Uncertain World*. Boulder, CO: Paradigm Press.]

Couldry, Nick. 2009. 'Rethinking the Politics of Voice.' *Continuum: Journal of Media and Cultural Studies* 23 (4): 579–82. https://doi.org/10.1080/10304310903026594.

Couldry, Nick. 2010. *Why Voice Matters: Culture and Politics After Neoliberalism*. Los Angeles: Sage Publications.

Couldry, Nick. 2012. *Media, Society, World: Social Theory and Digital Media Practice*. Cambridge, UK: Polity Press.

Couldry, Nick, and Andreas Hepp. 2016. *The Mediated Construction of Reality*. Cambridge, UK: Polity Press.

Crawford, Kate. 2009. 'Following You: Disciplines of Listening in Social Media.' *Continuum: Journal of Media and Cultural Studies* 23 (4): 525–35. https://doi.org/10.1080/10304310903003270.

Croakey. 2015. 'About #IHMayDay.' *Croakey* (blog), 25 October 2015. https://croakey.org/about-ihmayday.

Curran, James, Natalie Fenton, and Des Freedman. 2012. *Misunderstanding the Internet*. London: Routledge.

Curthoys, Ann. 2000. 'An Uneasy Conversation: The Multicultural and the Indigenous.' In *Race, Colour and Identity in Australia and New Zealand*, edited by John Docker and Gerhard Fisher, 21–36. Sydney: UNSW Press.

Dahlberg, Lincoln. 2014. 'The Habermasian Public Sphere and Exclusion: An Engagement with Poststructuralist-Influenced Critics.' *Communication Theory* 24 (1): 21–41. https://doi.org/10.1111/comt.12010.

Dahlgren, Peter. 2000. 'The Internet and the Democratization of Civic Culture.' *Political Communication* 17 (4): 335–40. https://doi.org/10.1080/10584600050178933.

Dahlgren, Peter. 2009. *Media and Political Engagement: Citizens, Communication, and Democracy*. Cambridge: Cambridge University Press.

Dahlgren, Peter. 2013. *The Political Web: Participation, Media, and Alternative Democracy.* Basingstoke, UK: Palgrave Macmillan.

Dahlgren, Peter. 2016. 'Moral Spectatorship and Its Discourses: The "Mediapolis" in the Swedish Refugee Crisis.' *Javnost—The Public* 23 (4): 382–97. https://doi.org/10.1080/13183222.2016.1247332.

Dahlgren, Peter, and Claudia Alvares. 2013. 'Political Participation in an Age of Mediatisation.' *Javnost—The Public* 20 (2): 47–65.

Danyel, Jürgen. 1995. *Die geteilte Vergangenheit. Zum Umgang mit Nationalsozialismus und Widerstand in beiden deutschen Staaten.* Berlin: Akademie-Verlag.

Davidson, Neil. 2013. 'Right-Wing Social Movements: The Political Indeterminacy of Mass Mobilisation.' In *Marxism and Social Movements*, edited by Colin Barker, Laurence Cox, John Krinsky, and Alf Gunvald Nilsen, 277–97. Leiden, NL: Brill.

Dean, Jodi. 2008. 'Communicative Capitalism: Circulation and the Foreclosure of Politics.' In *Digital Media and Democracy*, edited by Megan Boler, 101–21. Cambridge, MA: MIT Press.

De Genova, Nicholas. 2013. 'Spectacles of Migrant "Illegality": The Scene of Exclusion, the Obscene of Inclusion.' *Ethnic and Racial Studies* 36 (7): 1180–98. https://doi.org/10.1080/01419870.2013.783710.

Dekker, Rianne, and Godfried Engbersen. 2014. 'How Social Media Transform Migrant Networks and Facilitate Migration.' *Global Networks—A Journal of Transnational Affairs* 14 (4): 401–18. https://doi.org/10.1111/glob.12040.

Delaney, Tim, and Tim Madigan. 2009. *The Sociology of Sports: An Introduction.* Jefferson, NC: McFarland.

Delanty, Gerard. 2006. 'The Cosmopolitan Imagination: Critical Cosmopolitanism and Social Theory.' *The British Journal of Sociology* 57 (1): 25–47. https://doi.org/10.1111/j.1468-4446.2006.00092.x.

Delanty, Gerard, and Baogang He. 2008. 'Cosmopolitan Perspectives on European and Asian Transnationalism.' *International Sociology* 23 (3): 323–44. https://doi.org/10.1177/0268580908088893.

de Leeuw, Marc, and Sonja van Wichelen. 2012. 'Civilizing Migrants: Integration, Culture and Citizenship.' *European Journal of Cultural Studies* 15 (2): 195–210. https://doi.org/10.1177/1367549411432029.

della Porta, Donatella, and Marco Giugni. 2013. 'Emotions in Movements.' In *Meeting Democracy. Power and Deliberation in Global Justice Movements*, edited by Donatella della Porta and Dieter Rucht, 123–51. Cambridge: Cambridge University Press.

Dencik, Lina, and Oliver Leistert. 2015. Introduction to *Critical Perspectives on Social Media and Protest*, by Lina Dencik and Oliver Leistert, 1–12. London: Rowman and Littlefield International.

de Volo, Lorraine Bayard. 2006. 'The Dynamics of Emotion and Activism: Grief, Gender, and Collective Identity in Revolutionary Nicaragua.' *Mobilization* 11 (4): 461–74. https://doi.org/10.17813/maiq.11.4.q21r3432561l21t7.

de Wit, Thom Duyvene, and Ruud Koopmans. 2005. 'The Integration of Ethnic Minorities into Political Culture: The Netherlands, Germany and Great Britain Compared.' *Acta Politica* 40 (1): 50–73. https://doi.org/10.1057/palgrave.ap.5500096.

Dickerson, Caitlin. 2017. 'How Fake News Turned a Small Town Upside Down.' *New York Times*, 26 September 2017. https://www.nytimes.com/2017/09/26/maga-zine/how-fake-news-turned-a-small-town-upside-down.html.

Dietrich, David R. 2014. *Rebellious Conservatives: Social Movements in Defense of Privilege*. New York: Palgrave Macmillan.

Dietrich, Nico, Enrico Gersin, and Alan Herweg. 2017. 'Analysemöglichkeiten der Online-Kommunikation auf Social Network Sites am Beispiel PEGIDA und Face-book.' In *Muslime, Flüchtlinge und Pegida*, edited by Wolfgang Frindte and Nico Dietrich, 235–66. Wiesbaden, Germany: Springer VS.

Dietze, Gabriele. 2016. 'Ethnosexismus. Sex-Mob-Narrative um die Kölner Sylvester-nacht.' *Movements, Journal for Critical Migration and Border Regime Studies* 2 (1). http://movements-journal.org/issues/03.rassismus/10.dietze—ethnosexismus.html.

Digoh-Ersoy, Laura. 2017. 'Schwarze Geschichte(n) in Deutschland erinnern. Rassis-muskritische Bildung als Empowermentarbeit.' In *Antisemitismus, Rassismus und das Lernen aus Geschichte(n)*, edited by Anne Broden, Stefan E. Hößl, and Marcus Meier, 98–108, Weinheim, Germany: Beltz/Juventa.

Diker, Eleni. 2017. 'Social Media and Migration.' Vienna: Political and Social Research Institute of Europe. Accessed 10 October 2017. Retrieved from http://ps-europe.org/social-media-and-migration.

Diminescu, Dana. 2008. 'The Connected Migrant: An Epistemological Manifesto.' *Social Science Information* 47 (4): 565–79. https://doi.org/10.1177/0539018408096447.

Dines, Nick, Nicola Montagna, and Vincenzo Ruggiero. 2015. 'Thinking Lampedusa: Border Construction, the Spectacle of Bare Life and the Productivity of Migrants.' *Ethnic and Racial Studies* 38 (3): 430–45. https://doi.org/10.1080/01419870.2014 .936892.

Dobson, Andrew. 2014. *Listening for Democracy: Recognition, Representation, Rec-onciliation*. Oxford: Oxford University Press.

Dove, April Lee. 2010. 'Framing Illegal Immigration at the U.S.-Mexican Border: Anti-Illegal Immigration Groups and the Importance of Place in Framing.' In *Research in Social Movements, Conflicts and Change*, edited by Patrick G. Coy, 199–237. Bingley, UK: Emerald.

Downing, John. 2007. 'Grassroots Media: Establishing Priorities for the Years Ahead.' *Global Media Journal: Australian Edition* 1 (1): 1–16.

Dreher, Tanja. 2009. 'Listening Across Difference. Media and Multiculturalism Be-yond the Politics of Voice.' *Continuum: Journal of Media and Cultural Studies* 23 (4): 445–58. https://doi.org/10.1080/10304310903015712.

Dreher, Tanja. 2010. 'Speaking Up or Being Heard? Community Media Interventions and the Politics of Listening.' *Media, Culture & Society* 32 (1): 85–103. https://doi .org/10.1177/0163443709350099.

Dreher, Tanja. 2017a. 'Social/Participation/Listening: Keywords for the Social Im-pact of Community Media.' *Communication Research and Practice* 3 (1): 14–30. https://doi.org/10.1080/22041451.2016.1273737.

Dreher, Tanja. 2017b. 'Listening—A Normative Framework for Transforming Media, Democracy and Marginalization.' In *Media and Citizenship: Between*

Marginalisation and Participation, edited by Anthea Garman and Herman Wasserman, 16–33. Pretoria: HSRC Press.

Dreher, Tanja, Kerry McCallum, and Lisa Waller. 2016. 'Indigenous Voices and Mediatized Policy-Making in the Digital Age.' *Information, Communication & Society* 19 (1): 23–39. https://doi.org/10.1080/1369118X.2015.1093534.Drüeke, Ricarda, and Katharina Fritsche. 2015. 'Geflüchtete in den Medien—Medien für Geflüchtete.' *Medien Journal* (4): 12–18.

Druxes, Helga, and Patricia Anne Simpson (eds). 2015. *Digital Media Strategies of the Far Right in Europe and the United States.* Lanham, MD: Lexington.

Duarte, Marisa Elena, and Morgan Vigil-Hayes. 2017. '#Indigenous: A Technical and Decolonial Analysis of Activist Uses of Hashtags Across Social Movements.' *MediaTropes* 7 (1): 166–84.

Edwards, Michael. 2014. *Civil Society,* 3rd ed. Cambridge, UK: Polity Press.

Edwards, Paul N. 2003. 'Infrastructure and Modernity: Force, Time, and Social Organization in the History of Sociotechnical Systems.' In *Modernity and Technology,* edited by Thomas J. Misa, Philip Brey, and Andrew Feenberg, 185–226. Cambridge, MA: MIT Press.

Ekman, Joakim, and Erik Amnå. 2012. 'Political Participation and Civic Engagement: Towards a New Typology.' *Human Affairs* 22 (3): 283–300. https://doi.org/10.2478/s13374-012-0024-1.

Emilson, Erik Örjan. 2009. 'Recasting Swedish Historical Identity.' Gothenburg, Sweden: Gothenburg University, CERGU. Accessed 24 June 2018. Retrieved from http://hdl.handle.net/2077/20229.

Enrado, Patty. 2017. 'LUNAFEST Filmmaker Laura Doggett: Creating a Space for Girls to Express Their Stories Through Film. Accessed 24 June 2018. Retrieved from https://patch.com/california/berkeley/lunafest-filmmaker-laura-doggett-creating-space-girls-express-their-stories.

Entman, Robert M. 1993. 'Framing: Toward Clarification of a Fractured Paradigm.' *Journal of Communication* 43 (4): 51–58. https://doi.org/10.1111/j.1460-2466.1993.tb01304.x.

Espahangizi, Kijan, Sabine Hess, Juliane Karakayalı, Bernd Kasparek, Simona Pagano, Mathias Rodatz, and Vassilis S. Tsianos. 2016. 'Rassismus in der postmigrantischen Gesellschaft. Zur Einleitung.' *Movements. Journal for Critical Migration and Border Regime Studies* 2 (1): 9–23.

European Journalism Observatory. 2015. 'Research: How Europe's Newspapers Reported The Migration Crisis.' *European Journalism Observatory—EJO.* Published 9 November 2015. http://en.ejo.ch/research/research-how-europes-newspapers-reported-the-migration-crisis.

Facebook Page السفر من ازمير الى اليونان n.d. In Facebook (personal page). https://bit.ly/2mzeTeo.

Fanon, Frantz. 1952. *Black Skin, White Masks.* Translated by Richard Philcox. New York: Grove Press.

Feigenbaum, Anna, Fabian Frenzel, and Patrick McCurdy. 2013. *Protest Camps.* London: Zed Books.

Feldmann, Dorina, Michael Kohlstruck, Max Laube, Gebhard Schultz, and Helmut Tausendteufel. 2018. *Klassifikation politisch rechter Tötungsdelikte—Berlin 1990 bis 2008*. Berlin: Universitätsverlag der TU.

Fforde, Cressida, Lawrence Bamblett, Ray Lovett, Scott Gorringe, and Bill Fogarty. 2013. 'Discourse, Deficit and Identity: Aboriginality, the Race Paradigm and the Language of Representation in Contemporary Australia.' *Media International Australia* 149 (1): 162–73.

Fiedler, Anke. 2016. 'Information to go: Kommunikation im Prozess der Migration am Beispiel syrischer und irakischer Flüchtlinge auf ihrem Weg nach Deutschland.' *Global Media Journal—German Edition* 6 (1). http://www.globalmediajournal.de/de/2016/07/21/information-to-go-kommunikation-im-prozess-der-migration-am-beispiel-syrischer-und-irakischer-fluchtlinge-auf-ihrem-weg-nach-deutschland.

Findahl, Olle, and Pamela Davidsson. 2015. 'Svenskarna och internet' [The Swedes and the Internet]. Accessed 24 July 2018. Retrieved from: https://www.iis.se/docs/Svenskarna_och_internet_2015.pdf.

Finnegan, William. 2006. 'New in Town: The Somalis of Lewiston.' *New Yorker*, 11 December 2006, 46–58.

Fischer-Lichte, Erika, and Gertrud Lehnert. 2000. 'Der Sonderforschungsbereich "Kulturen des Performativen."' *Paragrana. Internationale Zeitschrift für historische Anthropologie* 9 (2): 9–19.

Fiumara, Gemma Corradi. 1990. *The Other Side of Language: A Philosophy of Listening*. London: Routledge.

Fleras, Augie. 2016. 'Theorizing Minority Misrepresentations. Reframing Mainstream Newsmedia as If White Ethnic Media.' In *Media and Minorities. Questions on Representation from an International Perspective*, edited by Georg Ruhrmann, Yasemin Shooman, and Peter Widmann, 21–38. Göttingen, Germany: Vandenhoeck & Ruprecht.

Forchtner, Bernhard, Michał Krzyżanowski, and Ruth Wodak. 2013. 'Mediatisation, Right-Wing Populism and Political Campaigning: The Case of the Austrian Freedom Party (FPÖ).' In *Media Talk and Political Elections in Europe and America*, edited by Andrew Tolson and Mats Ekström, 205–28. Basingstoke, UK: Palgrave Macmillan.

Foroutan, Naika. 2015. 'Unity in Diversity: Integration in a Post-Migrant Society.' *Policy Brief—Focus Migration*, no. 28. http://m.bpb.de/gesellschaft/migration/kurzdossiers/205290/integration-in-a-post-migrant-society.

Foroutan, Naika. 2016. 'Postmigrantische Gesellschaften.' In *Einwanderungsgesellschaft Deutschland*, edited by Ulrich Brinkmann and Martina Sauer, 227–54. Wiesbaden, Germany: Springer VS. https://doi.org/10.1007/978-3-658-05746-6_9.

Foroutan, Naika. 2018a. 'Was will eine postmigrantische Gesellschaftsanalyse?' In *Postmigrantische Perspektiven: Ordnungssysteme, Repräsentationen, Kritik*, edited by Naika Foroutan, Juliane Karakayalı, and Riem Spielhaus, 269–99. Frankfurt, Germany: Campus Verlag.

Foroutan, Naika. 2018b. 'Die postmigrantische Perspektive: Aushandlungsprozesse in pluralen Gesellschaften.' In *Postmigrantische Visionen: Erfahrungen—Ideen—Reflexionen*, edited by Marc Hill and Erol Yıldız, 15–27. Bielefeld, Germany: Transcript.

Forsberg, Ulrika. 2015. '60 miljoner på flykt—den högsta siffran någonsin.' [60 Million Refugees—The Largest Number Ever]. *Sverigeforunhcr.se*, last modified 16 June 2015. Accessed 30 April 2018. https://sverigeforunhcr.se/blogg/60-miljoner-pa-flykt-den-hogsta-siffran-nagonsin.

Foucault, Michel. 1978. *History of Sexuality. Part 1: An Introduction.* New York: Pantheon Books.

Foucault, Michel. 1986. 'Of Other Spaces.' *Diacritics* 16 (1): 22–7. https://doi.org/10.2307/464648.

Foxwell-Norton, Kerrie, Susan Forde, and Michael Meadows. 2013. 'Land, Listening and Voice: Investigating Community and Media Representations of the Queensland Struggle for Land Rights and Equality.' *Media International Australia* 149 (1): 150–61.

Frabetti, Federica. 2015. *Software Theory: A Cultural and Philosophical Study.* London: Rowman and Littlefield International.

Franquet Dos Santos Silva, Miguel, Svein Brurås, and Ana Beriain Bañares. 2018. 'Improper Distance: The Refugee Crisis Presented by Two Newsrooms.' *Journal of Refugee Studies.* https://doi.org/10.1093/jrs/fex045.

Fraser, Nancy. 2005. 'Reframing Global Justice.' *New Left Review* no. 36: 69–90.

Fraser, Nancy, and Axel Honneth. 2003. *Redistribution or Recognition? A Political-Philosophical Exchange.* London: Verso.

Freedman, Estelle. 2015. *Redefining Rape: Sexual Violence in the Era of Suffrage and Segregation.* Cambridge, MA: Harvard University Press.

Frese, Matthias, and Marcus Weidner (eds). 2018. *Verhandelte Erinnerungen. Der Umgang mit Ehrungen, Denkmälern und Gedenkorten nach 1945.* Paderborn, Germany: Schöningh.

Fuchs, Christian (2014) *Social Media: A Critical Introduction.* London: Sage Publications.

Gajjala, Radhika. 2014. 'Women and Other Women: Implicit Binaries in Cyberfeminism.' *Communcation and Critical/Cultural Studies* 11 (3): 288–92. https://doi.org/10.1080/14791420.2014.926241.

Galais, Carol, and Jasmine Lorenzini. 2017. 'Half of Loaf Is (Not) Better Than None: How Austerity-Related Grievances and Emotions Triggered Protest in Spain.' *Mobilization* 22 (1): 77–95. https://doi.org/10.17813/1086-671X-22-1-77.

Gassert, Philipp. 2018. *Bewegte Gesellschaft. Deutsche Protestgeschichte seit 1945.* Stuttgart, Germany: Kohlhammer.

Gay, Roxane. 2016. 'Who Gets to Be Angry?' *New York Times.* Accessed 27 July 2018. https://www.nytimes.com/2016/06/12/opinion/sunday/who-gets-to-be-angry.html.

Gehl, Robert W. 2014. *Reverse Engineering Social Media: Software, Culture, and Political Economy in New Media Capitalism.* Philadelphia: Temple University Press.

Geia, Lynore, and Melissa Sweet. 2015. '#IHMayDay: Showcasing Indigenous Knowledge and Innovation.' *Proceedings of the 13th National Rural Health Conference.* 24–27 May, Darwin, Northern Territory, Australia. http://www.ruralhealth.org.au/13nrhc/images/paper_Geia,%20Lynore.pdf.

Geißel, Brigitte. 2004. *Konflikte und Definitionen in der genderorientierten und Mainstream-Partizipationsforschung. Ein Literaturüberblick.* Discussion Paper Nr. SP IV 2004–403. WZB Berlin. http://nbn-resolving.de/urn:nbn:de:0168-ssoar-118137.

Geißler, Rainer, Kristina Enders, and Verena Reuter. 2009. 'Wenig ethnische Diversität in deutschen Zeitungsredaktionen.' In *Massenmedien und die Integration ethnischer Minderheiten in Deutschland,* edited by Rainer Geißler and Horst Pöttker, 79–117. Bielefeld, Germany: Transcript.

Gelles, David. 2016. 'For Helping Immigrants, Chobani's Founder Draws Threats.' *New York Times,* 31 October 2016. https://www.nytimes.com/2016/11/01/business/for-helping-immigrants-chobanis-founder-draws-threats.html?_r=0.

Georgiou, Myria. 2018. 'Does the Subaltern Speak? Migrant Voices in Digital Europe.' *Popular Communication* 16 (1): 45–57. https://doi.org/10.1080/15405702.2017.1412440.

Gerbel, Christian, Manfred Lechner, Dagmar C.G. Lorenz, Oliver Marchart, Vrääth Öhner, Ines Steiner, Andrea Strutz, and Heidemarie Uhl (eds). 2005. *Transformationen gesellschaftlicher Erinnerung. Zur 'Gedächtnisgeschichte' der Zweiten Republik.* Vienna: Turia + Kant.

Gillespie, Marie, Lawrence Ampofo, Margaret Cheesman, Becky Faith, Evgenia Iliadou, Ali Issa, Souad Osseiran, and Dimitris Skleparis. 2016. *Mapping Refugee Media Journeys: Smartphones and Social Media Networks.* The Open University/France Médias Monde. Accessed 10 October 2017. Retrieved from http://www.open.ac.uk/ccig/sites/www.open.ac.uk.ccig/files/Mapping%20Refugee%20Media%20Journeys%2016%20May%20FIN%20MG_0.pdf.

Gilroy, Paul. 2004. *After Empire: Melancholia or Convivial Culture?* London: Routledge.

Gilroy, Paul. 2005. *Postcolonial Melancholia.* New York: Columbia University Press.

Gilroy, Paul. 2006. 'Multiculture in Times of War: An Inaugural Lecture Given at the London School of Economics.' *Critical Quarterly* 48 (4): 27–45. https://doi.org/10.1111/j.1467-8705.2006.00731.x.

Glick Schiller, Nina, and Noel B. Salazar. 2013. 'Regimes of Mobility Across the Globe.' *Journal of Ethnic and Migration Studies* 39 (2): 138–200. https://doi.org/10.1080/1369183X.2013.723253.

Goffman, Erving. 1966. *Behavior in Public Places.* New York: Free Press.

Gohl, Christopher. 2015. 'Ethik der digitalen Kollaboration.' In *Digitale Politikvermittlung,* edited by Mike Friedrichsen and Roland A. Kohn, 215–30. Wiesbaden, Germany: Springer.

Goldberg, Andreas. 2000. 'Medien der Migrant/innen.' In *Interkulturelle Literatur in Deutschland. Ein Handbuch,* edited by Carmine Chiellino, 419–35. Stuttgart, Germany: Metzler Verlag.

Golden Girls Filmproduktion. n.d. Pressemappe, *Tomorrow You Will Leave.* 11 April 2018. http://www.tomorrowyouwillleave.com/images/Pressemappe_TYL.pdf.

Golova, Tatiana. 2015. 'Emotional Constructions of Identities in Protest Spaces.' In *Protests as Events: Politics, Activism and Leisure,* edited by Ian R. Lamond and Karl Spracklen, 231–51. London: Rowman and Littlefield.

Golshan, Tara. 2016. 'Donald Trump Introduced Us to "Angel Moms." Here's Why They Matter.' *Vox*, 1 September 2016. https://www.vox.com/2016/9/1/12751434/donald-trump-angel-moms-explained.

Goodwin, Jeff, James M. Jasper, and Francesca Polletta (eds). 2001. *Passionate Politics. Emotions and Social Movements*. Chicago: University of Chicago Press.

Götz, Irene. 2016. 'Mobility and Immobility: Background of the Project.' In *Bounded Mobilities: Ethnographic Perspectives on Social Hierarchies and Global Inequalities*, edited by Miriam Gutekunst, Andreas Hackl, Sabine Leoncini, Julia Sophia Schwarz, and Irene Götz, 9–11. Bielefeld, Germany: Transcript.

Grittmann, Elke, and Tanja Thomas. 2017. 'Visibility, Voice and Encounter in Cosmopolitan Online Communication: Rethinking Cultural Citizenship in Post-Migrant Societies.' In *(Mis)understanding Political Participation: Digital Practices, New Forms of Participation and the Renewal of Democracy*, edited by Jeffrey Wimmer, Cornelia Wallner, Rainer Winter, and Karoline Oelsner, 213–28. New York: Routledge Taylor & Francis Group (Routledge Studies in European Communication Research and Education, 13).

Guia, Aitana. 2016. 'The Concept of Nativism and Anti-Immigrant Sentiments in Europe.' EUI Working Papers 2016/20. San Domenico di Fiesole: European University Institute.

Gürel, Ayla, Mete Hatay, and Christalla Yakinthou. 2012. *An Overview of Events and Perceptions: Displacement in Cyprus—Consequences of Civil and Military Strife, 5*. Oslo: Peace Research Institute Oslo (PRIO).

Habring, Johanna. 2016. 'Der Migrant im Kopf.' *Migrazine, online magazin von migrantinnen für alle* (1): n.p. http://www.migrazine.at/artikel/der-migrant-im-kopf.

Haddad, Emma. 2007. 'Danger Happens at the Border.' In *Borderscapes: Hidden Geographies and Politics at Territory's Edge*, edited by Prem Kumar Rajaram and Carl Grundy-Warr, 119–36. Minneapolis: University of Minnesota Press.

Halberstam, Judith. 1993. 'Imagined Violence/Queer Violence: Representation, Rage, and Resistance.' *Social Text* 37 (winter): 187–201. https://doi.org/10.2307/466268.

Hall, Stuart. 1997. 'The Spectacle of the Other.' In *Representation: Cultural Representations and Signifying Practices*, edited by Stuart Hall, 225–97. London: Open University and Sage Publications.

Hallet, Theo. 2005. *Umstrittene Versöhnung. Reagan und Kohl in Bitburg 1985*. Erfurt, Germany: Sutton.

Hammerstein, Katrin. 2017. *Gemeinsame Vergangenheit—getrennte Erinnerung? Der Nationalsozialismus in Gedächtnisdiskursen und Identitätskonstruktionen von Bundesrepublik Deutschland, DDR und Österreich*. Göttingen, Germany: Wallstein.

Happ, Samantha, and Felix Tripps. 2017. '"Ich bin ja kein Nazi, aber . . ."—Diskursstrategien rechtspopulistischer Propaganda in Facebook. Eine Analyse von Facebook-Posts und Kommentaren der AfD und NPD im Kontext der Flüchtlingsdebatte.' *Kommunikation.medien* 8: 1–27. https://doi.org/10.25598/JKM/2017-8.4.

Haraway, Donna. 1988. 'Situated Knowledges: The Science Question in Feminism and the Privilege of Partial Perspective.' *Feminist Studies* 14 (3): 575–99. http://www.jstor.org/stable/3178066.

Harney, Nicholas. 2013. 'Precarity, Affect and Problem Solving with Mobile Phones by Asylum Seekers, Refugees and Migrants in Naples, Italy.' *Journal of Refugee Studies* 26 (4): 541–57. https://doi.org/10.1093/jrs/fet017.

Hartman, Geoffrey H. 1986. *Bitburg in Moral and Political Perspective*. Bloomington: Indiana University Press.

Hasinoff, Amy Adele. 2014. 'Contradictions of Participation: Critical Feminist Interventions in New Media Studies.' *Communication and Critical/Cultural Studies* 11 (3): 270–72. https://doi.org/10.1080/14791420.2014.926242.

Häusler, Alexander (ed.). 2016. *Die Alternative für Deutschland. Programmatik, Entwicklung und politische Verortung*. Wiesbaden, Germany: Springer VS.

Häusler, Alexander (ed). 2018. *Völkisch-autoritärer Populismus. Der Rechtsruck in Deutschland und die AfD*. Hamburg, Germany: VSA.

Hegde, Radha Sarma. 2011. *Circuits of Visibility: Gender and Transnational Media Cultures*. New York: New York University Press.

Hegde, Radha Sarma. 2016. *Mediating Migration*. Cambridge, UK: Polity Press.

Held, David. 2010. *Cosmopolitanism: Ideal and Realities*. Cambridge, UK: Polity Press.

Hellström, Andreas, and Peter Hervik. 2014. 'Feeding the Beast: Nourishing Nativist Appeals in Sweden and in Denmark.' *Journal of International Migration and Integration* 15 (3): 449–67. https://doi.org/10.1007/s12134-013-0293-5.

Herczeg, Petra. 2012. 'Geschlossene Gesellschaft: Über Diversität in den Medien, Journalismus und Migration.' In *Migration und Integration—wissenschaftliche Perspektiven aus Österreich*, edited by Julia Dahlvik, Heinz Fassmann, and Wiebke Sievers, 177–92. Vienna: Vienna University Press.

Hermes, Joke. 2005. *Re-Reading Popular Culture*. Malden, MA: Blackwell Publishing.

Herz, Thomas. 1996. 'Rechtsradikalismus und die "Basiserzählung." Wandlungen in der politischen Kultur Deutschlands.' In *Rechtsextremismus. Ergebnisse und Perspektiven der Forschung*, edited by Jürgen W. Falter, Hans-Gerd Jaschke, and Jürgen R. Winkler, 485–501. Opladen, Germany: Westdeutscher Verlag.

Herz, Thomas. 1997. 'Die "Basiserzählung" und die NS-Vergangenheit. Zur Veränderung der politischen Kultur in Deutschland.' In *Umkämpfte Vergangenheit. Diskurse über den Nationalsozialismus seit 1945*, edited by Thomas Herz and Michael Schwab-Trapp, 249–65. Opladen, Germany: Westdeutscher Verlag.

Herz, Thomas, and Michael Schwab-Trapp. 1997. *Umkämpfte Vergangenheit. Diskurse über den Nationalsozialismus seit 1945*. Opladen, Germany: Westdeutscher Verlag.

Hill, Marc, and Erol Yıldız. 2018. *Postmigrantische Visionen: Erfahrungen—Ideen— Reflexionen*. Bielefeld, Germany: Transcript.

Hipfl, Brigitte. 2016. 'Import Export—Explorations of Precarity in European Migratory Culture.' In *Postcolonial Transitions in Europe,* edited by Sandra Ponzanesi and Gianmaria Colpani, 191–208. Lanham, MD: Rowman & Littlefield.

Hocking, Rachael. 2016. '#IHMayDay16 Gets Indigenous Health Trending on Twitter.' *Sbs.com*. Published 12 May 2016. http://www.sbs.com.au/nitv/nitv-news/article/2016/05/12/ihmayday16-gets-indigenous-health-trend-twitter.

Holzberg, Billy, Kristina Kolbe, and Rafal Zaborowski. 2018. 'Figures of Crisis: The Delineation of (Un)deserving Refugees in the German Press.' *Sociology* 52 (3): 534–50. https://doi.org/10.1177/0038038518759460.

Honneth, Axel. 2007. *Disrespect: The Normative Foundations of Critical Theory.* Cambridge, UK: Polity Press.

Hooghe, Marc. 2011. 'Political Culture.' In *21st Century Political Science: A Reference Handbook*, edited by John T. Ishiyama and Marijke Breuning, 201–9. Thousand Oaks, CA: Sage Publications.

hooks, bell. 1995. *Killing Rage: Ending Racism.* New York: Henry Holt.

Horsti, Karina. 2016. 'Visibility without Voice: Media Witnessing Irregular Migrants in BBC Online News Journalism.' *African Journalism Studies* 37 (1): 1–20. https://doi.org/10.1080/23743670.2015.1084585.

Horsti, Karina. 2017a. 'Digital Islamophobia: The Swedish Woman as a Figure of Pure and Dangerous Whiteness.' *New Media and Society* 19 (9): 1440–57. https://doi.org/10.1177/1461444816642169.

Horsti, Karina. 2017b. 'Witnessing the Experience of European Bordering: Watching the Documentary *Under den samme himmel* in an Immigration Detention Centre.' *International Journal of Cultural Studies.* Online First. https://doi.org/10.1177/1367877917743606.

Horz, Christine. 2014. *Medien—Migration—Partizipation. Eine Studie am Beispiel iranischer Fernsehproduktion im Offenen Kanal.* Bielefeld, Germany: Transcript.

Husband, Charles. 1996. 'The Right to Be Understood: Conceiving the Multi-ethnic Public Sphere.' *Innovation: The European Journal of Social Science Research* 9 (2): 205–15.

Husband, Charles. 2009. 'Between Listening and Understanding.' *Continuum* 23 (4): 441–43.

Hutter, Swen, and Hanspeter Kriesi. 2013. 'Movements of the Left, Movements of the Right Reconsidered.' In *The Future of Social Movement Research: Dynamics, Mechanisms, and Processes*, edited by Jacquelien van Stekelenburg, Conny Roggeband, and Bert Klandermans, 281–98. Minneapolis: University of Minnesota Press.

Institut für Demokratieforschung. 2016. *Büchse der Pandora? PEGIDA im Jahr 2016 und die Profanisierung rechtspopulistischer Positionen.* Göttingen, Germany: Institut für Demokratieforschung

International Centre for Migration Policy Development. 2017. *How Does the Media on Both Sides of the Mediterranean Report on Migration? The Ethical Journalism Network for EUROMED Migration IV.* Accessed 12 April 2018. https://www.icmpd.org/fileadmin/2017/Media_Migration_17_country_chapters.pdf.

Isin, Engin. 2002. *Being Political: Genealogies of Citizenship.* Minneapolis: University of Minnesota Press.

Isin, Engin F., and Evelyn Ruppert. 2015. *Being Digital Citizens.* London: Rowman & Littlefield.

Jackson, Sarah J. 2016. '(Re)Imagining Intersectional Democracy from Black Feminism to Hashtag Activism.' *Women's Studies in Communication* 39 (4): 375–79.

Jackson, Sarah J., and Brooke Foucault Welles. 2016. '#Ferguson Is Everywhere: Initiators in Emerging Counterpublic Networks.' *Information, Communication & Society* 19 (3): 397–418. https://doi.org/10.1080/1369118X.2015.1106571.

Jacobs, Ben, and Alan Yuhas. 2016. 'Somali Migrants Are "Disaster" for Minnesota, Says Donald Trump.' *The Guardian*, 7 November 2016. http://www.theguardian.com/us-news/2016/nov/06/donald-trump-minnesota-somali-migrants-isis.

Jacobsen, Katja Lindskov. 2015. 'Experimentation in Humanitarian Locations: UN-HCR and Biometric Registration of Afghan Refugees.' *Security Dialogue* 46 (2): 144–64. https://doi.org/10.1177/0967010614552545.

Jäger, Margarete, and Regina Wamper (eds). 2017. *Von der Willkommenskultur zur Notstandsstimmung. Der Fluchtdiskurs in deutschen Medien 2015 und 2016.* Duisburg, Germany: DISS.

Jasper, James M. 1998. 'The Emotions of Protest: Affective and Reactive Emotions In and Around Social Movements.' *Sociological Forum* 13 (3): 397–424. https://www.jstor.org/stable/684696.

Jenkins, Henry, and Nico Carpentier. 2013. 'Theorizing Participatory Intensities: A Conversation About Participation and Politics.' *Convergence: The International Journal of Research into New Media Technologies* 19 (3): 265–86. https://doi.org/10.1177/1354856513482090.

Jensen, Klaus Bruhn. 2013. 'What's Mobile in Mobile Communication?' *Mobile Media & Communication* 1 (1): 26–31. https://doi.org/10.1177/2050157912459493.

Jensen, Uffa. 2017. *Zornpolitik.* Berlin: Suhrkamp.

Jibawi, Khaldiya, dir. 2015. *Another Kind of Girl.* Accessed 20 July 2018. http://anotherkindofgirl.com/khaldiya#/id/i10983912.

Jonsson, Stefan. 2015. *Masse und Demokratie.* Göttingen, Germany: Wallstein.

Kaase, Max. 1992. 'Vergleichende Politische Partizipationsforschung.' In *Vergleichende Politikwissenschaft. Ein einführendes Studienbuch,* edited by Dirk Berg-Schlosser and Ferdinand Müller-Rommel, 145–60. Opladen, Germany: Leske + Budrich.

Kaltenbrunner, Andy, Matthias Karmasin, Daniela Kraus, and Astrid Zimmermann. 2007. *Der Journalisten-Report: Österreichs Medien und ihre Macher. Eine empirische Erhebung.* Vienna: Facultas.

Kannapin, Detlef. 2005. *Dialektik der Bilder. Der Nationalsozialismus im Film. Ein Ost-West-Vergleich.* Berlin: Karl Dietz Verlag.

Karaiskou, Vicky. 2013. 'Particularities of Commemoration in the Republic of Cyprus.' 1 August 2018. Retrieved from http://publicart.ouc.ac.cy/?p=4975.

Karaiskou, Vicky. 2014. 'Visual Narrations in Public Space: Codifying Memorials in Cyprus.' *The International Journal of Social, Political, and Community Agendas in the Arts* 8 (2): 15–26.

Karakayalı, Juliane, Çağrı Kavheci, Doris Liebscher, and Carl Melchers (eds). 2017. *Den NSU-Komplex analysieren. Aktuelle Perspektiven aus der Wissenschaft.* Bielefeld, Germany: Transcript.

Karnowski, Veronika, Nina Springer, and Julia Herzer. 2016. '"I Was More of a Real Person. Now I'm Always on My Smartphone." Syrian Refugees' Use of Their

Mobile Phones in and to Manage Their Journey to Europe.' Presentation at *ECREA Pre-Conference: Media and Migration*, Prague, 7–9 November 2016.

Kaufmann, Katja. 2016. 'Wie nutzen Flüchtlinge Ihre Smartphones auf der Reise nach Europa? Ergebnisse einer qualitativen Interview-Studie mit syrischen Schutzsuchenden in Österreich.' *SWS-Rundschau* 3 (56): 319–42.

Kaun, Anne. 2016. *Crisis and Critique: A History of Media Participation.* London: Zed Books.

Kaun, Anne, and Fredrik Stiernstedt. 2014. 'Facebook Time: Technological and Institutional Affordances for Media Memories.' *New Media and Society* 16 (7): 1154–68. https://doi.org/10.1177/1461444814544001.

Kaun, Anne, and Julie Uldam. 2017. '"Volunteering Is Like Any Other Business": Civic Participation and Social Media.' *New Media and Society.* Online first. https://doi.org/10.1177/1461444817731920.

Käte Hamburger Kolleg/Centre for Global Cooperation Research (KHK/GCR21). 2014. *Convivialist Manifesto: A Declaration of Interdependence* (Global Dialogues 3). Duisburg, Germany. https://doi.org/10.14282/2198-0403-gd-3.

Kerst, Benjamin. 2016. 'Islamisierung.' In: *Handbuch rechtsextremer Kampfbegriffe*, edited by Bente Gießelmann, Robin Heun, Benjamin Kerst, and Fabian Virchow, 144–61. Schwalbach am Taunus, Germany: Wochenschau-Verlag.

Khosravi, Shahram. 2010. *The 'Illegal Traveler: An Auto-Ethnography of Borders.* New York: Palgrave Macmillan.

Kim, Sun-Chul. 2011. 'Participation, Contentious.' In *International Encyclopedia of Political Science*, edited by Bertrand Badie, Dirk Berg-Schlosser, and Leonardo Morlino, vol. 6. Los Angeles: Sage Publications.

Kim, Yong-Chan, and Sandra J. Ball-Rokeach. 2006. 'Civic Engagement From a Communication Infrastructure Perspective.' *Communication Theory* 16 (2): 173–97. https://doi.org/10.1111/j.1468-2885.2006.00267.x.

Kirchick, James. 2016. 'The Disgusting Breitbart Smear Campaign Against the Immigrant Owner of Chobani.' *The Daily Beast*, 2 September 2016. https://www.the-dailybeast.com/the-disgusting-breitbart-smear-campaign-against-the-immigrant-owner-of-chobani.

Kirkwood, Steve, Andy McKinlay, and Chris McVittie. 2013. 'They're More Than Animals: Refugees' Accounts of Racially Motivated Violence.' *British Journal of Social Psychology* 52 (4): 747–62. https://doi.org/10.1111/bjso.12007.

Klausch, Hans-Peter. 2013. *Braune Spuren im Saar-Landtag. Die Die NS-Vergangenheit saarländischer Abgeordneter.* Saarbrücken, Germany: Die Linke im Landtag.

Klayman, Alison, dir. 2012. *Ai Weiwei Never Sorry.* US: Expressions United Media, MUSE Film and Television, Never Sorry.

Kleffner, Heike, and Anna Spangenberg (eds). 2016. *Generation Hoyerswerda.* Berlin: be.bra Verlag.

Klein, Ansgar, and Frank Nullmeier (eds). 1999. *Masse—Macht—Emotionen. Zu einer politischen Soziologie der Emotionen.* Opladen, Germany: Westdeutscher Verlag.

Koch, Wolfgang, and Beate Frees. 2016. 'Dynamische Entwicklung bei mobiler Internetnutzung sowie Audios und Videos.' *Media Perspektiven* 9: 418–37.

Kohler, Manfred. 2017. 'Austrian Public Opinion in the "Refugee Crisis."' In *Migration in Austria*, edited by Günter Bischof and Dirk Rupnow, 257–70. New Orleans: University of New Orleans Press and Innsbruck University Press.

Koller, Christian. 2014. 'Soziale Bewegungen: Emotion und Solidarität.' In *Theoretische Ansätze und Konzepte der Forschung über soziale Bewegungen in der Geschichtswissenschaft*, edited by Jürgen Mittag and Heike Stadtland, 403–22. Essen, Germany: Klartext.

Kotliar, Dan M. 2016. 'Emotional Oppositions: The Political Struggle over Citizen's Emotions.' *Qualitative Sociology* 39 (3): 267–86. https://doi.org/10.1007/s11133-016-9334-7.

Krasnova, Hanna, and Safa'a AbuJarour. 2017. 'Understanding the Role of ICTs in Promoting Social Inclusion: The Case of Syrian Refugees in Germany.' In *Proceedings of the 25th European Conference on Information Systems (ECIS)*, 1792–1806. Guimarães, Portugal, 5–10 June 2017.

Krotz, Friedrich. 2001. *Die Mediatisierung kommunikativen Handelns: der Wandel von Alltag und sozialen Beziehungen, Kultur und Gesellschaft durch die Medien*. Wiesbaden, Germany: Westdeutscher Verlag.

Kryvasheyeu, Yury, Haohui Chen, Nick Obradovich, Esteban Moro, Pascal Van Hentenryck, James Fowler, and Manuel Cebrian. 2016. 'Rapid Assessment of Disaster Damage Using Social Media Activity.' *Science Advances* 2 (3). https://doi.org/10.1126/sciadv.1500779.

Krzyżanowski, Michał, and Per Ledin. 2017. 'Uncivility on the Web. Populism in/ and the Borderline Discourses of Exclusion.' *Journal of Language and Politics* 16 (4): 566–81. https://doi.org/10.1075/jlp.17028.krz.

Kuo, Rachel. 2016. 'Racial Justice Activist Hashtags: Counterpublics and Discourse Circulation.' *New Media & Society* 20 (2): 495–514. https://doi.org/10.1177/1461444816663485.

Kutscher, Nadia, and Lisa-Marie Kreß. 2015. 'Internet ist gleich mit Essen. Empirische Studie zur Nutzung digitaler Medien durch unbegleitete minderjährige Flüchtlinge.' Universität Vechta. Retrieved from https://images.dkhw.de/filead min/Redaktion/1.1_Startseite/3_Nachrichten/Studie_Fluechtlingskinder-digitale_ Medien/Studie_digitale_Medien_und_Fluechtlingskinder_Langversion.pdf.

Kutscher, Nadia, and Lisa-Marie Kreß. 2018. 'The Ambivalent Potentials of Social Media Use by Unaccompanied Minor Refugees.' *Social Media + Society* 4 (1): 1–10. https://doi.org/10.1177/2056305118764438.

Kyriakidou, Maria 2009. 'Imagining Ourselves Beyond the Nation? Exploring Cosmopolitanism in Relation to Media Coverage of Distant Suffering.' *Studies in Ethnicity and Nationalism* 9 (3): 481–96. https://doi.org/10.1111/j.1754-9469.2009.01062.x.

Lacey, Kate. 2013. *Listening Publics: The Politics and Experience of Listening in the Media Age*. Cambridge, UK: Polity Press.

Laclau, Ernesto, and Chantal Mouffe. 2001. *Hegemony and Socialist Strategy: Towards a Radical Democratic Politics*, 2nd ed. London: Verso.

Landsberg, Alison. 2004. *Prosthetic Memory: The Transformation of American Remembrance in the Age of Mass Culture*. New York: Columbia University Press.

Lash, Scott, and John Urry. 1994. *Economies of Signs and Space.* London: Sage Publications. http://dx.doi.org/10.4135/9781446280539.

Latimore, Jack, David Nolan, Margaret Simons, and Elyas Khan. 2017. 'Reassembling the Indigenous Public Sphere.' *Australasian Journal of Information Systems* 21 (0): 1–15. https://doi.org/10.3127/ajis.v21i0.1529.

Lazaridis, Gabriella. 2015. *International Migration into Europe: From Subjects to Abjects.* Basingstoke, UK: Palgrave Macmillan.

Le Bon, Gustave. 1896. *The Crowd. A Study of the Popular Mind.* Auckland, NZ: Floating Press.

Le Bon, Gustave. 1898. *The Psychology of Peoples.* New York: Palgrave Macmillan.

Leigh Star, Susan, and Geoffrey Bowker. 2002. 'How to Infrastructure.' In *Handbook of New Media: Social Shaping and Consequences of ICTs*, edited by Leah A. Lievrouw and Sonia Livingstone, 151–62. London: Sage Publications. http://dx.doi.org/10.4135/9781446211304.n13.

Lepik, Krista. 2013. 'Governmentality and Cultural Participation in Estonian Public Knowledge Institutions.' Unpublished PhD thesis, University of Tartu Press. http://dspace.utlib.ee/dspace/bitstream/handle/10062/32240/lepik_krista_2.pdf?sequence=4.

Lesage, Julia. 1988. 'Women's Rage.' In *Marxism and the Interpretation of Culture*, edited by Cary Nelson and Larry Grossberg, 419–28. Chicago: University of Illinois Press.

Les Convivialistes. 2014. 'Abridged Version of the Convivialist Manifesto: Declaration of Interdependence.' Accessed 3 July 2018. http://www.lesconvivialistes.org/abriged-version-convivialist-manifesto.

Lester, Libby, and Simon Cottle. 2009. 'Visualizing Climate Change: Television News and Ecological Citizenship.' *International Journal of Communication* 3: 920–36. https://ijoc.org/index.php/ijoc/article/view/509.

Leurs, Koen, and Sandra Ponzanesi. 2018. 'Connected Migrants. Encapsulation and Cosmopolitanization.' *Popular Communication* 16 (1): 4–20. https://doi.org/10.1080/15405702.2017.1418359.

Leurs, Koen, and Kevin Smets. 2018. 'Five Questions for Digital Migration Studies: Learning from Digital Connectivity and Forced Migration in(to)Europe.' *Social Media + Society* 4 (1): 1–16. https://doi.org/10.1177/2056305118764425.

Libell, Henrik Pryser, and Catherine Porter. 2018. 'From Norway to Haiti, Trump's Comments Stir Fresh Outrage.' *New York Times*, 11 January 2018. https://www.nytimes.com/2018/01/11/world/trump-countries-haiti-africa.html.

Lim, Sun Sun, Tabea Bork-Hüffer, and Brenda SA Yeoh. 2016. 'Mobility, Migration and New Media: Manoeuvring Through Physical, Digital and Liminal Spaces.' *New Media & Society* 18 (10): 2147–54. https://doi.org/10.1177/1461444816655610.

Lindell, Johan. 2014. 'Cosmopolitanism in a Mediatized World: The Social Stratification of Global Orientations.' Karlstad University Studies, no. 23. Karlstad: Fakulteten för humaniora och samhällsvetenskap, Medie- och kommunikationsvetenskap, Karlstads universitet. http://urn.kb.se/resolve?urn=urn:nbn:se:kau:diva-31782.

Ling, Rich, and Chih-Hui Lai. 2016. 'Microcoordination 2.0: Social Coordination in the Age of Smartphones and Messaging Apps.' *Journal of Communication* 66 (5): 834–56. https://doi.org/10.1111/jcom.12251.

Linklater, Andrew. 2007. 'Distant Suffering and Cosmopolitan Obligations.' *International Politics* 44 (1): 19–36. https://doi.org/10.1057/palgrave.ip.8800156.

Lipari, Lisbeth. 2010. 'Listening, Thinking, Being.' *Communication Theory* 20 (3): 348–62. https://doi.org/10.1111/j.1468-2885.2010.01366.x.

Longazel, Jamie. 2016. *Undocumented Fears: Immigration and the Politics of Divide and Conquer in Hazelton, Pennsylvania.* Philadelphia: Temple University Press.

Lorde, Audre. 1984. *Sister Outsider: Essays and Speeches.* Trumansburg, NY: Crossing Press.

Loshitzky, Yosefa. 2006. 'Journeys of Hope to Fortress Europe.' *Third Text* 20 (6): 745–54.

Luibhéid, Eithne. 2002. *Entry Denied: Controlling Sexuality at the Border.* Minneapolis: University of Minnesota Press.

Lury, Celia. 2011. *Consumer Culture.* Cambridge, UK: Polity Press and New Brunswick, NJ: Rutgers University Press.

Macnamara, Jim. 2017. 'Toward a Theory and Practice of Organizational Listening.' *International Journal of Listening* 32 (1): 1–23.

Marciniak, Katarzyna. 2006. 'Immigrant Rage: Alienhood, "Hygienic" Identities, and the Second World.' *Differences: A Journal of Feminist Cultural Studies* 17 (2): 33–63. https://doi.org/10.1215/10407391-2006-002.

Marciniak, Katarzyna. 2013. 'Legal/Illegal: Protesting Citizenship in Fortress America.' *Citizenship Studies* 17 (2): 260–77. https://doi.org/10.1080/13621025.2013.780754.

Marciniak, Katarzyna. 2014. 'Pedagogy of Rage.' In *Immigrant Protest: Politics, Aesthetics, and Everyday Dissent*, edited by Katarzyna Marciniak and Imogen Tyler, 121–43. New York: SUNY Press.

Marciniak, Katarzyna. 2017. '"Opening a Certain Poetic Space": What Can Art Do for Refugees?' *Media and Migration.* Special Issue of *Media Fields Journal* 12. http://mediafieldsjournal.org/.

Marciniak, Katarzyna, and Bruce Bennett. 2018. 'Aporias of Foreignness: Transnational Encounters in Cinema.' *Transnational Cinemas* 9 (1): 1–12. https://doi.org/10.1080/20403526.2018.1478371.

Marciniak, Katarzyna, and Imogen Tyler. 2014. 'Introduction: Immigrant Protest: Noborder Scholarship.' In *Immigrant Protest. Politics, Aesthetics, and Everyday Dissent*, by Katarzyna Marciniak and Imogen Tyler, 1–21. New York: SUNY Press.

Marcus, Jane. 1988. *Art and Anger: Reading Like a Woman.* Columbus: Ohio State University Press.

Marks, Laura U. 2000. *The Skin of the Film: Intercultural Cinema, Embodiment, and the Senses.* Durham, NC: Duke University Press.

Massing, Peter. 2017. *Wutbürger.* Schwalbach am Taunus, Germany: Wochenschau-Verlag.

Massumi, Brian. 2015. *Politics of Affect*. Cambridge, UK: Polity Press.

Matsaganis, Matthew D., Vikki S. Katz, and Sandra J. Ball-Rokeach. 2011. *Understanding Ethnic Media: Producers, Consumers, and Societies*. Thousand Oaks, CA: Sage Publications.

Mazzara, Federica. 2016. 'Subverting the Narrative of the Lampedusa Borderscape.' *Crossings: Journal of Migration & Culture* 7 (2): 135–47. https://doi.org/10.1386/cjmc.7.2.135_1.

McCallum, Kerry, and Lisa Waller. 2013. 'The Intervention of Media Power in Indigenous Policy-Making.' *Media International Australia* 149 (1): 139–49. https://doi.org/10.1177/1329878X1314900115.

McGregor, Elaine, and Melissa Siegel. 2013. 'Social Media and Migration Research.' Maastricht: Maastricht University, School of Governance/United Nations University, UNI_MERIT Working Papers Series. Accessed 24 June 2018. Retrieved from http://www.www.merit.unu.edu/publications/working-papers/?year_id=2013.

McInerney, Marie. 2016. 'IHMAYDAY16—Another Huge Day of Immersion and Wider Engagement on Indigenous Health.' *Croakey* (blog), 6 June 2016. https://croakey.org/ihmayday16-another-huge-day-of-immersion-and-wider-engagement-on-indigenous-health.

McMahon, Laura. 2012. *Cinema and Contact: The Withdrawal of Touch in Nancy, Bresson, Duras, and Denis*. London: Legenda.

Medien-Servicestelle Neue Österreicher/innen (MNÖ). 2012. 'JournalistInnen mit Migrationshintergrund: Neue Zahlen.' *medienservicestelle.at*. Accessed 9 January 2018. http://medienservicestelle.at/migration_bewegt/2012/11/21/neue-zahlen-zu-journalistinnen-mit-migrationshintergrund.

Meer, Nasar, Tariq Modood, and Ricard Zapata-Barrero. 2016. *Multiculturalism and Interculturalism: Debating the Dividing Lines*. Edinburgh: Edinburgh University Press.

Mejias, Sam, and Shakuntala Banaji. 2017. *UK Youth Perspectives and Priorities for Brexit Negotiations*. Department of Media and Communications, London School of Economics and Political Science. Accessed 12 April 2018. http://www.lse.ac.uk/media@lse/research/ABetterBrexitforYoungPeople/A%20Better%20Brexit%20for%20Young%20People.pdf.

Melucci, Alberto. 1989. *Nomads of the Present: Social Movements and Individual Needs in Contemporary Society*. Edited by John Keane and Paul Mier. London: Hutchinson Radius.

Mezzadra, Sandro. 2011. 'The Gaze of Autonomy: Capitalism, Migration and Social Struggles.' In *The Contested Politics of Mobility: Borderzones and Irregularity*, Routledge Advances in International Relations and Global Politics, vol. 87, edited by Vicki Squire, 121–42. London: Routledge.

Mezzadra, Sandro. 2017. 'Digital Mobility, Logistics, and the Politics of Migration.' *Spheres. Journal for Digital Cultures* (4): 1–4. http://spheres-journal.org/digital-mobility-logistics-and-the-politics-of-migration.

Mezzadra, Sandro, and Brett Neilson. 2013. *Border as Method, or, the Multiplication of Labor*. Durham, NC: Duke University Press.

M.I.A, dir. 2016. *Borders*. Video, 4:42. Posted by Miavevo. Accessed 20 July 2018. https://www.youtube.com/watch?v=r-Nw7HbaeWY.

Modood, Tariq. 2013. *Multiculturalsim*, 2nd ed. Cambridge, UK: Polity Press.

Moeller, Susan D. 1999. *Compassion Fatigue: How the Media Sell Disease, Famine, War and Death*. New York: Routledge.

Mokre, Monika. 2015. 'Solidarität oder Hilfsbereitschaft?' *Migrazine, online magazin von migrantinnen für alle* (1): n.p. http://www.migrazine.at/artikel/solidarit-t -oder-hilfsbereitschaft.

Moore, Martin, and Gordon Ramsay. 2017. *UK Media Coverage of the 2016 EU Referendum Campaign*. Centre for the Study of Media, Communication and Power, Policy Institute at King's College, London. Accessed 12 April 2018. https://www .kcl.ac.uk/sspp/policy-institute/CMCP/UK-media-coverage-of-the-2016-EU-Refer endum-campaign.pdf.

Moran, Anthony. 2017. 'Aboriginal and Multicultural Imaginaries: Tensions, Accommodations, Reconciliation.' In *The Public Life of Australian Multiculturalism*, 207–40. Cham, CH: Palgrave Macmillan.

Moreton-Robinson, Aileen. 2003. 'I Still Call Australia Home: Indigenous Belonging and Place in a White Postcolonizing Society.' In *Uprootings/Regroundings: Questions of Home and Migration*, edited by Sarah Ahmed, 23–40. Oxford, UK: Berg Publishing.

Motte, Jan, and Rainer Ohliger (eds.). 2004. *Geschichte und Gedächtnis in der Einwanderungsgesellschaft. Migration zwischen historischer Rekonstruktion und Erinnerungspolitik*. Essen: Klartext Verlag.

Mouffe, Chantal. 2013. *Agonistics: Thinking the World Politically*. London: Verso.

Müller, Karsten, and Carlo Schwarz. 2018. 'Fanning the Flames of Hate: Social Media and Hate Crime.' Available at SSRN. https://ssrn.com/abstract=3082972 or http://dx.doi.org/10.2139/ssrn.3082972.

Mulvey, Gareth. 2013. 'In Search of Normality: Refugee Integration in Scotland.' Scottish Refugee Council. Accessed 24 June 2018. Retrieved from http://www .scottishrefugeecouncil.org.uk/assets/5790/final_report.pdf.

Munzenrieder, Kyle. 2016. 'Artist Olek Covers Two Homes in Hot Pink Crochet.' *W* magazine, 5 September 2016. https://www.wmagazine.com/story/artist-olek -covers-two-homes-in-hot-pink-crochet.

Munzinger, Hannes, Antonie Rietzschel, and Hauke Bendt. 2016. 'Pegida auf facebook. Hetze im Sekundentakt.' *Süddeutsche Zeitung*, 3 February 2016. https:// www.sueddeutsche.de/politik/ein-jahr-pegida-pegida-auf-facebook-hetze-im -sekundentakt-1.2806271.

Murphy, Tom. 2015. 'Refugee Crisis: M.I.A.'s Powerful Protest Song and Video.' *Humanosphere*, 29 December 2015. http://www.humanosphere.org/basics/2015/12/ refugee-crisis-m-s-powerful-song-video/.

Naficy, Hamid. 2001. *An Accented Cinema. Exile and Diasporic Filmmaking*. Princeton, NJ: Princeton University Press.

Nail, Thomas. 2015. *The Figure of the Migrant*. Stanford, CA: Stanford University Press.

Nail, Thomas. 2016. 'A Tale of Two Crises: Migration and Terrorism after the Paris Attacks.' *Studies in Ethnicity and Nationalism* 16 (1): 158–67. https://doi.org/10.1111/sena.12168.

Nancy, Jean-Luc. 1991. *The Inoperative Community*. Minneapolis: University of Minnesota Press.

Nancy, Jean-Luc. 2000. *Being Singular Plural*. Translated by Robert D. Richardson and Anne E. O'Byrne. Stanford, CA: Stanford University Press.

Nayeri, Dina. 2017. 'The Ungrateful Refugee: "We Have no Debt to Repay."' *The Guardian*, 4 April 2017. https://www.theguardian.com/world/2017/apr/04/dina-nayeri-ungrateful-refugee.

New York Times. 2017. 'Transcript of Donald Trump's Immigration Speech.' 1 September 2017. https://www.nytimes.com/2016/09/02/us/politics/transcript-trump-immigration-speech.html.

Nichols, Bill. 2001. *Introduction to Documentary*. Bloomington: Indiana University Press.

Nolan, Dan, and Emma Graham-Harrison. 2015. 'Hungarian Police and Refugees in Standoff after Train Returns to Camp.' *The Guardian*, 4 September 2015. https://www.theguardian.com/world/2015/sep/03/hungary-train-diverts-refugees-back-to-camp.

Norgaard, Kari Marie. 2006. '"People Want to Protect Themselves a Little Bit": Emotions, Denial, and Social Movement Nonparticipation.' *Sociological Inquiry* 76 (3): 372–96. https://doi.org/10.1111/j.1475-682X.2006.00160.x.

Noveck, Beth Simone. 2009. *Wiki Government: How Technology Can Make Government Better, Democracy, and Citizens More Powerful*. Washington, DC: Brookings Institution Press.

Nowicka, Magdalena, and Steven Vertovec. 2014. 'Convivialities.' Special Issue. *European Journal of Cultural Studies* 17 (4).

Nussbaum, Martha. 2012. *The New Religious Intolerance: Overcoming the Politics of Fear in an Anxious Age*. Cambridge, MA: Belknap Press of Harvard University Press.

Nyers, Peter. 2015. 'Migrant Citizenship and Autonomous Mobilities.' *Migration, Mobility & Displacement* 1 (1): 23–39. https://journals.uvic.ca/index.php/mmd/article/view/13521/4414.

O'Donnell, Penny, Justine Lloyd, and Tanja Dreher. 2009. 'Listening, Pathbuilding and Continuations: A Research Agenda for the Analysis of Listening.' *Continuum* 23 (4): 423–39. https://doi.org/10.1080/10304310903056252.

OECD/European Union. 2015. *Indicators of Immigrant Integration 2015: Settling In*. Paris: OECD Publishing. http://dx.doi.org/10.1787/9789264234024-en.

Olivieri, Domitilla. 2016. 'Diasporic Proximities: Spaces of "Home" in European Documentary.' *Transnational Cinemas* 7 (2): 135–50. https://doi.org/10.1080/20403526.2016.1217626.

Opp, Karl-Dieter. 2013. 'Rational Choice Theory and Social Movements.' In *The Wiley-Blackwell Encyclopedia of Social and Political Movements*, vol. 3, edited by David A. Snow, Donatella della Porta, Bert Klandermans, and Doug McAdam, 1051–58. London: Blackwell.

Orgad, Shani. 2012. *Media Representation and the Global Imagination.* Cambridge, UK: Polity Press.

Ost, David. 2004. 'Politics as the Mobilization of Anger: Emotions in Movements and in Power.' *European Journal of Social Theory* 7 (2): 229–44. https://doi .org/10.1177/1368431004041753.

Oulios, Miltiadis. 2009. 'Weshalb gibt es so wenig Journalisten mit Einwanderungshintergrund in deutschen Massenmedien? Eine explorative Studie.' In *Massenmedien und die Integration ethnischer Minderheiten in Deutschland*, edited by Rainer Geißler and Horst Pöttker, 119–44. Bielefeld, Germany: Transcript.

Panagiotopoulos, Panagiotis, Alinaghi Ziaee Bigdeli, and Steven Sams. 2014. 'Citizen-Government Collaboration on Social Media: The Case of Twitter in the 2011 Riots in England.' *Government Information Quarterly* 31 (3): 349–57. https://doi .org/10.1016/j.giq.2013.10.014.

Pantti, Mervi, and Markus Ojala. 2018. 'Caught between Sympathy and Suspicion: Journalistic Perceptions and Practices of Telling Asylum Seekers' Personal Stories.' *Media, Culture and Society*, online first, February. https://doi .org/10.1177/0163443718756177.

Papadopoulos, Dimitris, and Vassilis S. Tsianos. 2013. 'After Citizenship: Autonomy of Migration: Organisational Ontologoy and Mobile Commons.' *Citizenship Studies* 17 (2): 178–96. https://doi.org/10.1080/13621025.2013.780736.

Pateman, Carole. 1970. *Participation and Democratic Theory.* Cambridge: Cambridge University Press.

Penkwitt, Meike. 2006. 'Einleitung "Erinnern und Geschlecht."' *Freiburger Frauen-Studien* 19: 1–26.

Penman, Robyn, and Sue Turnbull. 2012. 'From Listening . . . to the Dialogic Realities of Participatory Democracy.' *Continuum* 26 (1): 61–72.

Perera, Suvendrini. 2005. 'Who Will I Become? The Multiple Formations of Australian Whiteness.' *Australian Critical Race and Whiteness Studies Association Journal* 1: 30–39.

Perinelli, Massimo. 2017. 'Situiertes Wissen vs. Korrumpiertes Wissen. Warum die migrantische Perspektive in die Wissenschaft gehört. Und der Verfassungsschutz raus.' In *Den NSU-Komplex analysieren*, edited by Julian Karakayalı, Çağrı Kahveci, Doris Liebscher, and Carl Melchers, 145–62. Bielefeld, Germany: Transcript.

Peters, John Durham. 2015. *The Marvellous Clouds: Towards a Philosophy of Elemental Media.* Chicago: University of Chicago Press.

Pfadenhauer, Michaela. 2009. 'At Eye Level: The Expert Interview—A Talk Between Expert and Quasi-expert.' In: *Interviewing Experts*, edited by Alexander Bogner, Beate Littig, and Wolfgang Menz, 81–97. New York: Palgrave Macmillian.

Pfoser, Paula. 2012. 'Mama Illegal und die Verantwortung der Journalist_innen. Publikumsgespräch.' https://www.youtube.com/watch?v=bsTTKSoohfk. 28 May 2018.

Phelphs, Jerome. 2017. 'Why Is So Much Art about the "Refugee Crisis" So Bad?' *opendemocracy.net.* Last modified 11 May 2017.

Phillips, Whitney, and Ryan M. Milner. 2017. *The Ambivalent Internet: Mischief, Oddity, and Antagonism Online.* Cambridge, UK: Polity Press.

Pink, Sarah, Heather A. Horst, John Postill, Larissa Hjorth, Tania Lewis, and Jo Tacchi. 2015. *Digital Ethnography: Principles and Practice*. Los Angeles: Sage Publications.

Pollock, Griselda. 2006. 'Migratory Aesthetics: Further Thoughts by way of a Postscript.' AHRC Centre for Cultural Analysis, Theory & History. *Leeds.ac.uk*. Accessed 28 May 2018. http://www.leeds.ac.uk/cath/ahrc/events/2006/0111/post script.html.

Ponzanesi, Sandra, and Verena Berger. 2016. 'Introduction: Genres and Tropes in Postcolonial Cinema(s) in Europe.' *Transnational Cinemas* 7 (2): 111–17. https://doi.org/10.1080/20403526.2016.1217641.

Ponzanesi, Sandra, and Koen Leurs. 2014. 'On Digital Crossings in Europe.' *Crossings: Journal of Migration & Culture* 5 (1): 3–22. https://doi.org/10.1386/cjmc.5.1.3_1.

Ponzanesi, Sandra, and Marguerite Waller. 2012. 'Introduction.' In *Postcolonial Cinema Studies*, edited by Sandra Ponzanesi and Marguerite Waller, 1–16. London: Routledge.

Pöttker, Horst. 2016. 'Mehr Vielfalt im Journalistenberuf—wie lässt sich das gesellschaftspolitische Ziel erreichen?' In *Migranten als Journalisten? Eine Studie zu Berufsperspektiven in der Einwanderungsgesellschaft*, edited by Horst Pöttker, Christina Kiesewetter, and Juliana Lofink, 11–20. Wiesbaden: Springer.

Prenzel, Thomas. 2012. *20 Jahre Rostock-Lichtenhagen. Kontext, Dimensionen und Folgen der rassistischen Gewalt*. Rostock: Universität Rostock.

Prinzling, Marlis, and Gattermann, Carolin. 2015. 'Finanziert! Journalismus, den die Crowd kauft. Eine Studie zu Crowdfunding als Finanzierungsmöglichkeit von Journalismus.' In *Schnittstellen (in) der Medienökonomie*, edited by Sven Pagel, 188–212. Baden-Baden: Nomos.

Proctor, Keith. 2015. 'Europe's Migrant Crisis: Defense Contractors Are Poised to Win Big.' *Fortune*, 10 September 2015. http://fortune.com/2015/09/10/europe -migrant-crisis-defense-contractors.

Puar, Jasbir. 2007. *Terrorist Assemblages: Homonationalism in Queer Times*. Durham, NC: Duke University Press.

Radke, Johannes, and Toralf Staud. 2018. 'Todesopfer rechter Gewalt in Deutschland seit der Wiedervereinigung.' *Tagesspiegel.de*. Published 27 September 2018. https://www.tagesspiegel.de/politik/interaktive-karte-todesopfer-rechter-gewalt-in -deutschland-seit-der-wiedervereinigung/23117414.html.

Rambukkana, Nathan. 2015. 'From #RaceFail to #Ferguson: The Digital Intimacies of Race-Activist Hashtag Publics.' *The Fibreculture Journal* 194 (26): 160–89. https://doi.org/10.15307/fcj.26.194.2015.

Ratcliffe, Krista. 2005. *Rhetorical Listening: Identification, Gender, Whiteness*. Carbondale: Southern Illinois University Press.

Ratković, Viktorija. 2018. *Postmigrantische Medien. Die Magazine biber und migrazine zwischen Anpassung, Kritik und Transformation*. Bielefeld, Germany: Transcript.

Ratnam, Niru. 2016. 'Ai Weiwei's Aylan Kurdi Image is Crude, Thoughtless, and Egotistical.' *The Spectator*, 1 February 2016. https://blogs.spectator.co.uk/2016/02/ ai-weiweis-aylan-kurdi-image-is-crude-thoughtless-and-egotistical.

Rattansi, Ali. 2011. *Multiculturalism: A Very Short Introduction*. Oxford: Oxford University Press.

Raynauld, Vincent, Emmanuelle Richez, and Katie Boudreau Morris. 2018. 'Canada Is #IdleNoMore: Exploring Dynamics of Indigenous Political and Civic Protest in the Twitterverse.' *Information, Communication & Society* 21 (4): 626–42.

Rehberg, Karl-Siegbert, Franziska Kunz, and Tino Schlinzig (eds). 2016. *PEGIDA—Rechtspopulismus zwischen Fremdenangst und 'Wende'-Enttäuschung? Analysen im Überblick*. Bielefeld, Germany: Transcript.

Reuband, Karl-Heinz. 2016. 'Außenseiter oder Repräsentanten der Mehrheit? Selbst- und Fremdwahrnehmung der Teilnehmer von PEGIDA-Kundgebungen.' In *PEGIDA—Rechtspopulismus zwischen Fremdenangst und 'Wende-Enttäuschung? Analysen im Überblick*, edited by Karl-Siegbert Rehberg, Franziska Kunz, and Tino Schlinzig, 165–87. Bielefeld, Germany: Transcript.

Richard, Sylvain. 2009. 'Arash T. Riahi's For a Moment of Freedom.' *Arts & Opinion* 8 (4): n.p. http://www.artsandopinion.com/2009_v8_n4/foramomentof freedom.htm.

Richter, Carola, Marlene Kunst, and Martin Emmer. 2016. 'Aus der Forschungs- praxis: Flucht 2.0—Erfahrungen zur Befragung von Flüchtlingen zu Ihrer mobilen Mediennutzung.' *Global Media Journal—German Edition* 6 (1). http://www .globalmediajournal.de/2016/07/20/flucht-2-0-zur-forschung-mituber-fluchtlinge -und-ihre-mediennutzung.

Röben, Bärbel. 2008. 'Migrantinnen in den Medien. Diversität in der journalistischen Produktion—am Beispiel Frankfurt/Main.' In *Medien—Diversität—Ungleichheit. Zur medialen Konstruktion sozialer Differenz*, edited by Ulla Wischermann and Tanja Thomas, 141–59. Wiesbaden, Germany: VS Verlag.

Robertson, Alexa. 2010. *Mediated Cosmopolitanism*. Cambridge, UK: Polity Press.

Rodriguez, Clemencia. 2011. *Citizens' Media Against Armed Conflict: Disrupting Violence in Colombia*. Minneapolis: University of Minnesota Press.

Rohe, Karl. 1987. 'Politische Kultur und der kulturelle Aspekt von politischer Wirklichkeit. Konzeptionelle und typologische Überlegungen zu Gegenstand und Fragestellung Politischer Kultur-Forschung.' In *Politische Kultur in Deutschland. Bilanz und Perspektiven der Forschung*, edited by Dirk Berg-Schlosser and Jakob Schissler, 39–49. Opladen, Germany: Westdeutscher Verlag.

Rohe, Karl. 1994. 'Politische Kultur: Zum Verständnis eines theoretischen Konzepts.' In *Politische Kultur in Ost-und Westdeutschland*, edited by Oskar Niedermayer and Klaus von Beyme, 1–21. Opladen, Germany: Leske + Budrich.

Rohe, Karl, and Andreas Dörner. 1990. "Von der Untertanenkultur zur "Partizipa- tionsrevolution"? Kontinuität und Wandel politischer Kultur in Deutschland.' *Politische Bildung* 23 (3): 18–33.

Rome, Philip Willan. 2017. 'Gang Rape Fuels Italian Anger at Migrants.' *The Times*, 4 September 2017. https://www.thetimes.co.uk/article/gang-rape-fuels-italian -anger-at-migrants-lg0mgwmqp.

Römhild, Regina. 2017. 'Beyond the Bounds of the Ethnic. For Postmigrant Cultural and Social Research.' *Journal of Aesthetics & Culture* 9 (2): 69–75. https://doi.org/ 10.1080/20004214.2017.1379850.

Rosenberger, Sieglinde, Verena Stern, and Nina Merhaut (eds). 2018. *Protest Movements in Asylum and Deportation*. Cham, CH: Springer International.

Rupnow, Dirk. 2017. 'The History and Memory of Migration in Post-War Austria: Current Trends and Future Challenges.' In *Migration in Austria*, edited by Günter Bischof and Dirk Rupnow, 37–65. New Orleans: University of New Orleans Press and Innsbruck University Press.

Sabsay, Leticia. 2012. 'The Emergence of the Other Sexual Citizen: Orientalism and the Modernisation of Sexuality.' *Citizenship Studies* 16 (5–6): 605–23. https://doi.org/10.1080/13621025.2012.698484.

Saha, Anamik. 2016. 'From the Politics of Representation to the Politics of Production.' In *Media and Minorities: Questions on Representation from an International Perspective*, edited by Georg Ruhrmann, Yasemin Shooman, and Peter Widmann, 39–49. Göttingen, Germany: Vandenhoeck & Ruprecht.

Sandoval-Almazan, Rodrigo, and J. Ramon Gil-Garcia. 2014. 'Towards Cyberactivism 2.0? Understanding the Use of Social Media and Other Information Technologies for Political Activism and Social Movements.' *Government Information Quarterly* 31 (3): 365–78. https://doi.org/10.1016/j.giq.2013.10.016.

Sant Cassia, Paul. 2005. *Bodies of Evidence: Burial, Memory and the Recovery of Missing Persons in Cyprus*. New York: Berghahn Books.

Sauer, Birgit. 2016. 'Veranderung, Ausschluss und Selbstvergewisserung.' *MO Magazin für Menschenrechte* 43: 8–9. https://www.sosmitmensch.at/dl/NrsqJlmJKoLJqx4KJK/MO43_MAGAZIN_kl.pdf.

Saxonia Systems AG and Heinrich & Reuter Solutions (Heires). 2018. 'Welcome App Germany (2.0.0.8)' (Mobile application Software). Retrieved from https://play.google.com/store/apps/details?id=de.welcome_app_concept.welcome2germany.

Sayad, Abdelmalek. 2004. *The Suffering of the Immigrant*. Translated by David Macey. Cambridge, UK: Polity Press.

Schaeffer, Robert K. 2014. *Social Movements and Global Social Change: The Rising Tide*. Lanham, MD: Rowman and Littlefield.

Scheibelhofer, Paul. 2016. 'Repräsentationen fremder Männlichkeit und die restriktive Bearbeitung der 'Flüchtlingskrise.' *migrazine, online magazin von migrantinnen für alle* (1): n.p. http://www.migrazine.at/artikel/repr-sentationen-fremder-m-nnlichkeit-und-die-restriktive-bearbeitung-der-fl-chtlingskrise.

Schiefer, Karin. 2007. 'Arash T. Riahi: For a Moment, Freedom—Interview.' *austrianfilms.com*. Accessed 11 April 2018. http://www.austrianfilms.com/news/cn/bodyarash_t_riahi_for_a_moment_freedom_-_interviewbody.

Schneider, Jens. 2017. 'Im Asyl-Netz.' *Süddeutsche Zeitung*, 7 December 2017, 6.

Schroeder, Wolfgang, Bernhard Weßels, and Alexander Berzel. 2018. 'Die AfD in den Landtagen: Bipolarität als Struktur und Strategie—zwischen Parlaments- und, Bewegungs'-Orientierung.' *Zeitschrift für Parlamentsfragen* 49 (1): 91–110. https://doi.org/10.5771/0340-1758-2018-1-91.

Schunck, Reinhard. 2014. *Transnational Activities and Immigrant Integration in Germany. International Perspectives on Migration*. Berlin: Springer. https://doi.org/10.1007/978-3-319-03928-2.

Schupp, Patrick. 2015. 'Frankfurter Integrations- und Diversitätsbericht 2011–2014.' Ein Bericht des Amts für multikulturelle Angelegenheiten. Frankfurt am Main. Retrieved from https://www.vielfalt-bewegt-frankfurt.de/sites/default/files/amka -integration-v1-final-ansicht_0.pdf.

Seeßlen, Georg. 2016. 'Kino und Migration—Auf der Flucht.' *epd-film.de*. Published 18 January 2016. https://www.epd-film.de/themen/kino-und-migration-auf-der-flucht.

Sharma, Devika, and Frederik Tygstrup. 2015. Introduction to *Structures of Feeling. Affectivity and the Study of Culture*, edited by Devika Sharma and Frederik Tygstrup, 1–19. Berlin: de Gruyter.

Sharpe, Jenny. 1991. 'The Unspeakable Limits of Rape: Colonial Violence and Counter-Insurgency.' *Genders* 10: 25–46. https://doi.org/10.5555/gen.1991.10.25.

Silverman, David. 2006. *Interpreting Qualitative Data: Methods for Analysing Talk, Text and Interaction.* London: Sage Publications.

Silverstone, Roger. 2013. *Media and Morality: On the Rise of the Mediapolis.* Cambridge, UK: Polity Press.

Simic, Charles. 1999. 'Refugees.' In *Letters of Transit: Reflections on Exile, Identity, Language, and Loss*, edited by André Aciman, 115–35. New York: The New Press.

Sinus. 2017. 'Informationen zu den Sinus Milieus.' http://www.sinus-institut .de/fileadmin/user_data/sinus-institut/Dokumente/downloadcenter/Sinus_Mi lieus/2017-01-01_Informationen_zu_den_Sinus-Milieus.pdf.

Smith, Linda Tuhiwai. 2012. *Decolonizing Methodologies: Research and Indigenous Peoples.* London: Zed Books.

Sobchack, Vivian. 2004. *Carnal Thoughts: Embodiment and Moving Image Culture.* Berkeley: University of California Press.

Soguk, Nevzat. 2007. 'Border's Capture: Insurrectional Politics, Border-Crossing Humans, and the New Political.' In *Borderscapes: Hidden Geographies and Politics at Territory's Edge*, edited by Prem Kumar Rajaram and Carl Grundy-Warr, 283–308. Minneapolis: University of Minnesota Press.

Solomon, Clare. 2011. 'We felt liberated.' In *Springtime: The New Student Rebellions,* edited by Clare Solomon and Tania Palmieri, 11–16. London: Verso.

Somaini, Francesco. 2018. 'Who Wrote This? The Role of Bylines in News Coverage of Immigrants and Refugees.' *Journal of Applied Journalism and Media Studies* 7 (1): 153–76. https://doi.org/10.1386/ajms.7.1.153_1.

Sonntag, Karlheinz. 2013. *E-Protest: neue soziale Bewegungen und Revolutionen.* Heidelberg: Universitätsverlag Winter.

Sontag, Susan. 2003. *Regarding the Pain of Others.* London: Hamish Hamilton.

Spivak, Gayatri Chakravorty. 1985. 'Can the Subaltern Speak? Speculations on Widow Sacrifice.' *Wedge* 7–8: 120–30.

Spivak, Gayatri Chakravorty. 1988. 'Can the Subaltern Speak?' In *Marxism and the Interpretation of Culture*, edited by Cary Nelson and Lawrence Grossberg, 271–313. Urbana: University of Illinois Press.

Squire, Vicki. 2015. *Post/Humanitarian Border Politics between Mexico and the US: People, Places, Things.* London: Palgrave Macmillan. https://doi.org/10 .1057/9781137395894.

Statens offentliga utredningar (SOU). 2017. *Att ta emot människor på flykt* [To Receive Refugees]. Stockholm: Elanders.

Statistik Austria. 2017. Migration & Integration. Zahlen. Daten. Indikatoren 2017. Vienna.

Statistik Austria. 2017. 'Bevölkerung mit Migrationshintergrund nach Bundesländern (Jahresdurchschnitt 2016).' *statistik.at.* Last modified 22 March 2017. https://www.statistik.at/web_de/statistiken/menschen_und_gesellschaft/bevoelkerung/be voelkerungsstruktur/bevoelkerung_nach_migrationshintergrund/033241.html.

Statistisches Bundesamt. 2017. "Bevölkerung mit Migrationshintergrund um 8,5% gestiegen.' *destatis.de.* Accessed 9 January 2018. https://www.destatis.de/DE/PresseService/Presse/Pressemitteilungen/2017/08/PD17_261_12511pdf.pdf?__blob=publicationFile.

Steadman, Ryan. 2016. 'Ai Weiwei Receives Backlash for Mimicking Image of Drowned 3-Year-Old Refugee.' *Observer Culture*, 1 February 2016. http://observer.com/2016/02/photo-of-ai-weiwei-aping-drowned-refugee-toddler-draws-praise-ire/.

Stefanowitsch, Anatol, and Susanne Flach. 2016. *Auswertung von Userkommentaren auf der offiziellen Facebook-Seite von PEGIDA, Januar bis Dezember 2015.* Berlin: Freie Universität Berlin.

Stierl, Maurice. 2016. 'A Sea of Struggle—Activist Border Interventions in the Mediterranean Sea.' *Citizenship Studies* 20 (5): 561–78. https://doi.org/10.1080/13621 025.2016.1182683.

Strand, Torill. 2010. 'The Making of a New Cosmopolitanism.' *Studies in Philosophy and Education* 29 (2): 229–42. https://doi.org/10.1007/s11217-009-9161-3.

Strang, Alison, and Alastair Ager. 2010. 'Refugee Integration: Emerging Trends and Remaining Agendas.' *Journal of Refugee Studies* 23 (4): 589–607. https://doi.org/10.1093/jrs/feq046.

Strömbäck, Jesper. 2016. 'Hur skildrar medierna flyktingkrisen?' [How Do the Media Report About the Refugee Crisis?]. Paper Presented at the Mediemötet 2016, Göteborg, SE.Suffee, Zak. 2015. 'United Kingdom: How Journalism Plays Follow-my-leader with Rhetoric of Negativity.' In *Moving Stories: International Review of How Media Cover Migration,* edited by Aidan White, 39–44. London: Ethical Journalism Network.

Sweet, Melissa A., Patricia Dudgeon, Kerry McCallum, and Matthew D. Ricketson. 2014. 'Decolonising Practices: Can Journalism Learn From Health Care to Improve Indigenous Health Outcomes?' *The Medical Journal of Australia* 200 (11): 626–27.

Syrer gegen Sexismus. n.d. In Facebook (fan page). https://www.facebook.com/pg/SyrerGegenSexismus/about/?ref=page_internal.

Sztompka, Piotr. 2000. 'Cultural Trauma: The Other Face of Social Change.' *European Journal of Social Theory* 3: 449–66.

Tarrow, Sidney. 2015. "Contentious Politics.' In *The Oxford Handbook of Social Movements*, edited by Donatella Della Porta and Mario Diani, 86–107. Oxford: Oxford University Press.

Terkessidis, Mark. 2015. *Kollaboration.* Frankfurt/M.: Suhrkamp.

Tesser, Lynn M. 2013. *Ethnic Cleansing and the European Union: An Interdisciplinary Approach to Security, Memory and Ethnography.* Basingstoke, UK: Palgrave Macmillan.

The Economist. 2017. "Migrants with Mobiles." *Economist.com.* Print edition. Published 17 February 2017. Accessed 24 June 2018. http://www.economist.com/news/international/21716637-technology-has-made-migrating-europe-easier-over-time-it-will-also-make-migration.

The Economist Intelligence Unit. 2008. *The Role of Trust in Business Collaboration: An Economist Intelligence Unit Briefing Paper Sponsored by Cisco Systems.* Accessed 1 August 2018. https://graphics.eiu.com/upload/cisco_trust.pdf.

Thill, Cate. 2009. 'Courageous Listening, Responsibility for the Other and the Northern Territory Intervention.' *Continuum* 23 (4): 537–48.

Thill, Cate. 2015. 'Listening for Policy Change: How the Voices of Disabled People Shaped Australia's National Disability Insurance Scheme.' *Disability & Society* 30 (1): 15–28.

Thompson, Rachel. 2016. 'Syrian and Ukrainian Refugees Worked Together to Create a Symbol of Hope.' *Mashable*, 7 September 2016. https://mashable.com/2016/09/07/refugees-crochet-house/#3kcXBtnNLqq1.

Thran, Malte, and Lukas Boehnke. 2015. 'The Value-based Nationalism of Pegida.' *Journal for Deradicalization* 3 (summer): 178–209.

Ticktin, Miriam. 2008. 'Sexual Violence as the Language of Border Control: Where French Feminist and Anti-immigrant Rhetoric Meet.' *Signs: Journal of Women in Culture and Society* 33 (4): 863–89. https://doi.org/10.1086/528851.Tomlinson, John. 1999. *Globalization and culture.* Chicago: University of Chicago Press.

Tremayne, Mark. 2014. 'Anatomy of Protest in the Digital Era: A Network Analysis of Twitter and Occupy Wall Street.' *Social Movement Studies* 13 (1): 110–26. https://doi.org/10.1080/14742837.2013.830969.

Trimikliniotis, Nicos, Dimitris Parsanoglou, and Vassilis S. Tsianos. 2015. *Mobile Commons, Migrant Digitalities and the Right to the City.* London: Palgrave Macmillan. https://doi.org/10.1057/9781137406910.

Trinh T. Minh-ha, dir. 1983. *Reassemblage: From Firelight to the Screen.* US: Jean-Paul Bourdier, DVD.

Trinh T. Minh-ha. 1989. *Woman, Native, Other. Writing Postcoloniality and Feminism.* Bloomington: Indiana University Press.

Trinh T. Minh-ha. 2011. *Elsewhere, within Here: Immigration, Refugeeism, and the Boundary Event.* London: Routledge.

Tsianos, Vassilis, and Juliane Karakayalı. 2014. 'Repräscntationspolitik in der postmigrantischen Gesellschaft.' *APuZ Aus Politik und Zeitgeschichte* 64 (13-14/2014): 33–39.

Tsianos, Vassilis, and Brigitta Kuster. 2010. 'Border Crossings. Transnational Digital Networks, Migration and Gender.' http://www.mignetproject.eu/wp-content/uploads/2012/10/MIGNET_Deliverable_6_Thematic_report_Border_crossings.pdf.

Tuck, Eve, and K. Wayne Yang. 2012. 'Decolonization Is Not a Metaphor.' *Decolonization: Indigeneity, Education & Society* 1 (1): 1–40.

Tufekci, Zeynep. 2014. 'What Happens to #Ferguson Affects Ferguson.' *The Message* (blog), 14 August 2014. https://medium.com/message/ferguson-is-also-a-net -neutrality-issue-6d2f3db51eb0.

Tufekci, Zeynep, and Christopher Wilson. 2012. 'Social Media and the Decision to Participate in Political Protest: Observations from Tahrir Square.' *Journal of Communication* 62 (2): 363–79. https://doi.org/10.1111/j.1460-2466.2012.01629.x.

Tümmers, Henning. 2011. *Anerkennungskämpfe. Die Nachgeschichte der nationalsozialistischen Zwangssterilisation in der Bundesrepublik.* Göttingen, Germany: Wallstein.

Turner, Bryan S. 2006. 'Citizenship and the Crisis of Multiculturalism.' *Citizenship Studies* 10 (5): 607–18. https://doi.org/10.1080/13621020600955041.

Tyler, Imogen. 2013. *Revolting Subjects: Social Abjection and Resistance in Neoliberal Britain.* London: Zed Books.

Tyler, Imogen. 2017. 'The Hieroglyphics of the Border: Racial Stigma in Neoliberal Europe.' *Ethnic and Racial Studies* 41 (10): 1783–1801. https://doi.org/10.1080/0 1419870.2017.1361542.

Uehlinger, Hans-Martin. 1988. *Politische Partizipation in der Bundesrepublik.* Opladen, Germany: Westdeutscher Verlag.

Uldam, Julie, and Anne Kaun. 2017. 'Towards a Framework for Studying Political Participation in Social Media.' In *(Mis)Understanding Political Participation: Digital Practices, New Forms of Participation and the Renewal of Democracy,* edited by Jeffrey Wimmer, Cornelia Wallner, Rainer Winter, and Karoline Oelsner, 181–95. New York: Routledge.

van Dijck, José. 2013. *The Culture of Connectivity: A Critical History of Social Media.* Oxford: Oxford University Press.

Vaughan-Williams, Nick. 2015. *Europe's Border Crisis: Biopolitical Security and Beyond.* Oxford: Oxford University Press

Velkova, Julia. 2017. 'Repairing and Developing Software Infrastructures: The Case of Morevna Project in Russia.' *New Media and Society,* online first. https://doi .org/10.1177/1461444817731922.

Vertovec, Steven. 2004. 'Cheap Calls: The Social Glue of Migrant Transnationalism.' *Global Networks* 4 (2): 219–24. https://doi.org/10.1111/j.1471-0374.2004.00088.x.

Vertovec, Steven, and Robin Cohen. 2002. *Conceiving Cosmopolitanism: Theory, Context and Practice.* Oxford: Oxford University Press.

Vertovec, Steven, and Susanne Wessendorff. 2010. *The Multiculturalism Backlash: Discourses, Policies and Practices.* Abingdon, UK: Routledge.

Vice, Samantha. 2010. 'How Do I Live in This Strange Place?' *Journal of Social Philosophy* 41 (3): 323–42.

Virchow, Fabian. 2014. 'Der "NSU" und der staatliche Sicherheitsapparat im Lichte der parlamentarischen Untersuchungsausschüsse und Kommissionen.' *Neue Kriminalpolitik* 26. Jg (2): 140–52.

Virchow, Fabian. 2016a. 'PEGIDA: Understanding the Emergence and Essence of Nativist Protest in Dresden.' *Journal of Intercultural Studies* 37 (6): 541–55. https://doi.org/10.1080/07256868.2016.1235026.

Virchow, Fabian. 2016b. *Nicht nur der NSU—Eine kleine Geschichte des Rechtsterrorismus in Deutschland.* Erfurt, Germany: Landeszentrale für politische Bildung Thüringen.

Virchow, Fabian. 2017. 'Post-Fascist Right-Wing Social Movements.' In *The History of Social Movements in Global Perspective: A Survey*, edited by Stefan Berger and Holger Nehring, 619–46. London: Palgrave Macmillan.

Vis, Farida, and Olga Goriunova. 2015. *The Iconic Image on Social Media: A Rapid Research Response to the Death of Aylan Kurdi.* Visual Social Media Lab December 2015. Accessed 12 April 2018. https://research.gold.ac.uk/14624/1/KURDI%20REPORT.pdf.

Vliegenthart, Rens, and Conny Roggeband. 2007. 'Framing Immigration and Integration: Relationships Between Press and Parliament in the Netherlands.' *International Communication Gazette* 69 (3): 295–319. https://doi.org/10.1177/1748048507076582.

von der Behrens, Antonia. 2018. *Kein Schlusswort. Nazi-Terror, Sicherheitsbehörden, Unterstützernetzwerk. Plädoyers im NSU-Prozess.* Hamburg: VSA.

von Hilgers, Lisa. n.d. 'Einen Augenblick Freiheit. Materialien zu einem Film von Arash T. Riahi.' Herausgegeben von Filmladen Filmverleih Wien, *kinomachtschule.at.* Accessed 11 April 2018. http://www.kinomachtschule.at/data/augenblickfreiheit.pdf.

von Trotha, Trutz. 1995. 'Political Culture, Xenophobia and the Development of the Violence of the Radical Right in the Federal Republic of Germany.' *Crime, Law and Social Change* 24 (1): 37–47. https://doi.org/10.1007/BF01297656.

Vorländer, Hans. 2016. *PEGIDA. Entwicklung, Zusammensetzung und Deutung einer Empörungsbewegung.* Wiesbaden, Germany: Springer VS.

Voss, Thomas, and Martin Abraham. 2000. 'Rational Choice Theory in Sociology: A Survey.' In *The International Handbook of Sociology*, edited by Stella R. Quah and Arnaud Sales, 50–83. London: Sage Publications.

Wagner, Bernd. 2014. *Rechtsradikalismus in der Spät-DDR.* Berlin: Edition Widerschein.

Waibel, Harry. 2016. 'Rassismus in der DDR.' *Zeitschrift des Forschungsverbundes SED-Staat* 39: 111–30.

Wall, Melissa, Madeline Otis Campbell, and Dana Janbek. 2015. 'Syrian Refugees and Information Precarity.' *New Media & Society* 19 (2): 240–54. https://doi.org/10.1177/1461444815591967.

Waller, Lisa, Tanja Dreher, and Kerry McCallum. 2015. 'The Listening Key: Unlocking the Democratic Potential of Indigenous Participatory Media.' *Media International Australia* 154 (1): 57–66.

Waller, Lisa, Kerry McCallum, and Scott Gorringe. 2018. 'Resisting the Truancy Trap: Indigenous Media and School Attendance in "Remote" Australia.' *Postcolonial Directions in Education* 7(2): 122–47.

Walters, William. 2011. 'Foucault and Frontiers: Notes on the Birth of the Humanitarian Border.' In *Governmentality: Current Issues and Future Challenges*, edited by Ulrich Bröckling, Susanne Krasmann, and Thomas Lemke, 138–64. New York: Routledge.

Washington Post. 2015. 'Full Text: Donald Trump Announces a Presidential Bid.' 16 June 2015. https://www.washingtonpost.com/news/post-politics/wp/2015/06/16/full-text-donald-trump-announces-a-presidential-bid.Weber-Menges, Sonja. 2006. 'Die Entwicklung der Ethnomedien in Deutschland' In *Integration durch Massenmedien. Medien und Migration im internationalen Vergleich*, edited by Rainer Geißler and Horst Pöttker, 121–45. Bielefeld, Germany: Transcript.

Weinstock, Daniel M. 2007. 'Liberalism, Multiculturalism, and the Problem of Internal Minorirties.' In *Multiculturalism and Political Theory,* edited by Anthony Simon Laden and David Owen, 244–64. Cambridge: Cambridge University Press.

Weltevrede, Esther, Anne Helmond, and Caroline Gerlitz. 2014. 'The Politics of Real-Time: A Device Perspective on Social Media Platforms and Search Engines.' *Theory, Culture & Society* 31 (6): 125–50. https://doi.org/10.1177/0263276414537318.

Welzel, Christian. 2009. 'Political Culture.' In *The SAGE Handbook of Comparative Politics*, edited by Todd Landman and Neil Robinson, 299–319. London: Sage Publications.

West, Roianne, Lee Stewart, Kim Foster, and Kim Usher. 2012. 'Through a Critical Lens: Indigenist Research and the Dadirri Method.' *Qualitative Health Research* 22 (11): 1582–90.

White, Aidan. 2015. *Moving Stories: International Review of How Media Cover Migration.* Ethical Journalism Network, London. Accessed 12 April 2018. https://ethicaljournalismnetwork.org/wp-content/uploads/2016/09/moving-stories-ejn.pdf.

Wickström, Mats. 2013. 'Conceptual Change in Postwar Sweden: The Marginalization of Assimilation and the Introduction of Integration.' In *Debating Multiculturalism in the Nordic Welfare States,* edited by Peter Kivisto and Östen Wahlbeck, 110–39. Basingstoke, UK: Palgrave Macmillan.

Wiedemann, Carolin. 2016. 'Integration mit Tinder. Wegwischen und ankommen.' *Frankfurter Allgemeine Zeitung*, 20 May 2016. http://www.faz.net/aktuell/feuilleton/integration-mit-tinder-wegwischen-und-ankommen-14233956.html.

Wien Museum. 2004. 'Gastarbajteri. 40 Jahre Arbeitsmigration. Eine Ausstellung der Initiative Minderheiten und des Wien Museums.' Accessed 11 April 2018. http://www.wienmuseum.at/de/aktuelle-ausstellungen/ansicht/gastarbajteri40-jahre-arbeitsmigrationeine-ausstellung-der-initiative-minderheiten-und-des-wien.html.

Williams, Raymond. 1978. *Marxism and Literature*. Oxford: Oxford University Press.

Willig, Rasmus. 2012. 'Recognition and Critique. An Interview with Judith Butler.' *Distinktion. Scandinavian Journal of Social Theory* 13 (1): 139–44. https://doi.org/10.1080/1600910X.2012.648742.

Wimmer, Jeffrey, Cornelia Wallner, Rainer Winter, and Karoline Oelsner. 2018. Introduction to *(Mis)understanding Political Participation: Digital Practices, New Forms of Participation and the Renewal of Democracy*, edited by Jeffrey Wimmer, Cornelia Wallner, Rainer Winter, and Karoline Oelsner, 1–13. New York: Routledge Taylor & Francis Group (Routledge Studies in European Communication Research and Education, 13).

Wise, Amanda. 2016. 'Convivial Labour and the "Joking Relationship": Humour and Everyday Multiculturalism at Work.' *Journal of Intercultural Studies* 37 (5): 481–500. https://doi.org/10.1080/07256868.2016.1211628.

Wise, Amanda, and Greg Noble. 2016. 'Convivialities: An Orientation.' *Journal of Intercultural Studies* 37 (3): 423–31. https://doi.org/10.1080/07256868.2016.1213786.

Witteborn, Saskia. 2015. 'Becoming (Im)perceptible: Forced Migrants and Virtual Practice.' *Journal of Refugee Studies* 28 (3): 350–67. https://doi.org/10.1093/jrs/feu036.

Wodak, Ruth. 2016. *Politik der Angst. Zur Wirkung rechtspopulistischer Diskurse.* Vienna: Edition Konturen.

Wolf, Christian. 2016. 'Flüchtlinge stellen sich gegen Sexismus.' *WDR*, 16 January 2016. https://www1.wdr.de/nachrichten/rheinland/syrer-demonstration-koeln-100.html.

Yıldız, Erol. 2015. 'Postmigrantische Perspektiven. Aufbruch in eine neue Geschichtlichkeit.' In *Nach der Migration. Postmigrantische Perspektiven jenseits der Parallelgesellschaft*, edited by Erol Yıldız and Marc Hill, 19–36. Bielefeld, Germany: Transcript.

Yin, Robert K. 1994. *Case Study Research: Design and Methods.* Thousand Oaks, CA: Sage Publications.

Young-Powell, Abby. 2017. 'Asylum Seekers Will Have to Hand Over Cash and Phones, Austria's New Coalition says.' *The Telegraph*, 18 December 2017. http://www.telegraph.co.uk/news/2017/12/18/austrian-far-right-sworn-government-amid-protests.

Zaborowski, Rafal, and Myria Georgiou. 2016. 'Migration Crisis? Try Crisis in the European Press.' *Open Democracy*. Last modified 13 May 2017. https://www.opendemocracy.net/rafal-zaborowski-myria-georgiou/refugee-crisis-try-crisis-in-european-press.

Zamani, Nur Azmina Mohamad, Siti Z.Z. Abidin, Nasiroh Omar, and M.Z.Z. Abiden. 2014. 'Sentiment Analysis: Determining People's Emotions in Facebook.' *Proceedings of the 13th International Conference on Applied Computer and Applied Computational Science*: 111–16.

Žižek, Slavoj. 1994. *Metastases of Enjoyment: Six Essays on Woman and Causality.* London: Verso.

Index

About the Contributors

Arjun Appadurai is Paulette Goddard Professor of Media, Culture, and Communication at New York University. He is also Professor of Anthropology and Globalization at The Hertie School of Governance in Berlin. He is an internationally recognized scholar of globalization and media, of the cultural dimensions of economic development and of struggles over national and transnational identity. His primary areal specialty is South Asia. He is the author of numerous books and articles on migration, transnational dynamics, sovereignty and media. His most recent book is *Banking on Words: The Failure of Language in the Age of Derivative Finance* (2015). He has a forthcoming book (co-authored) on Failure, with Polity Press.

Sina Arnold is a Postdoctoral Research Associate at the Center for Research on Antisemitism at the Technische Universität Berlin and member of the Berlin Institute for Integration and Migration Research (BIM) at the Humboldt-Universität Berlin, Germany. Her research focuses on antisemitism and racism in post-migrant societies and social movements, nationalism and (post-) national identity, and logistics and migrant digitalities. She most recently co-edited *Grounding Logistics—Ethnographische Zugriffe auf Logistik, Migration und Mobilität*. Special Issue of: *Berliner Blätter. Ethnologische und Ethnographische Beiträge* (2018).

Nico Carpentier is Professor in Media and Communication Studies at the Department of Informatics and Media of Uppsala University, Sweden. In addition, he holds two part-time positions, those of Associate Professor at the Communication Studies Department of the Vrije Universiteit Brussel (VUB— Free University of Brussels, Belgium) and Lecturer at the Charles University in Prague (Czech Republic). His latest monograph is *The Discursive-Material Knot: Cyprus in Conflict and Community Media Participation* (2017).

Nick Couldry is a sociologist of media and culture. He is Professor of Media Communications and Social Theory at the London School of Economics and Political Science. He is the author or editor of thirteen books including *The Costs of Connection: How Data colonizes Human Life and Appropriates it for Capitalism* (with Ulises Mejias, 2019), *The Mediated Construction of Reality* (with Andreas Hepp, 2016), *Media, Society, World: Social Theory and Digital Media Practice* (2012) and *Why Voice Matters: Culture and Politics After Neoliberalism* (2010).

Peter Dahlgren is Professor Emeritus at the Department of Communication and Media, Lund University, Sweden. His recent work has addressed the internet and political participation, examining civic identities and engagement. Active in European academic networks, he has also been a visiting scholar at several universities.

Poppy de Souza is an interdisciplinary researcher based at the Griffith Centre for Social and Cultural Research, Griffith University, Brisbane, Australia. Her doctoral thesis *Beyond Voice Poverty* explored the politics and political economies of voice, from the intersecting vantage points of speech, listening, and recognition. Poppy currently contributes to projects in the areas of Indigenous leadership and political participation, listening and media justice, and ethnic community media.

Tanja Dreher is an ARC Future Fellow, UNSW Scientia Fellow, and Associate Professor in Media at the University of New South Wales in Sydney, Australia. Tanja's research focuses on the politics of listening in the context of media and multiculturalism, Indigenous sovereignties, feminisms, and anti-racism. Her work has been published in *Media, Culture & Society, Information, Communication & Society* and *Continuum*. Tanja is also working on a monograph, *Listening across Difference: Media beyond the Politics of Voice*.

Stephan Oliver Görland is Lecturer and Researcher for Communication & Media Studies at the Institute for Media Research at the University of Rostock (IMF), Germany, and Associate Member at the Berlin Institute for Integration and Migration Research (BIM), Germany. He studied Communication Science, Psychology, Law, and Political Science in Vienna from 2006 to 2011 and is now a PhD candidate at the IMF. His research topics are mobile media, organization of time through media, migration and media use, and research methods. His current research focuses on mobile media usage in 'in-between-situations.'

Radha S. Hegde is Professor in the Department of Media, Culture, and Communication at New York University. She is the author of *Mediating Migration* (2016), editor of *Circuits of Visibility: Gender and Transnational Media Cultures* (2011), and co-editor of the *Handbook of the Indian Diaspora* (2018). She is also the co-editor of the journal *Feminist Media Studies*.

Brigitte Hipfl is Associate Professor of Media Studies at the Department of Media and Communication Studies at the University of Klagenfurt, Austria. Her research interests are media and gender, subject formations, the affective labour of media, and postcolonial Europe. Among her recent publications is a book co-edited with Kristín Loftsdottír and Andrea L. Smith, *Messy Europe— Crisis, Race, and Nation-State in a Postcolonial World* (2018).

Anne Kaun is Associate Professor in Media and Communication Studies at Södertörn University, Sweden. Her research is concerned with media and political activism and the role of technology for political participation in the current media ecology from a historical perspective. In 2016, she published her book *Crisis and Critique*.

Merle-Marie Kruse is Research Associate in the project *Agonistic Engagement in Post-Migrant Societies*, funded by the German-Israeli Foundation for Scientific Research and Development (GIF) and situated at the Institute of Media Studies, Eberhard Karls University, Tübingen, Germany. Her research interests include media and civic engagement, researching and rethinking the 'political' in media cultures, popular culture and national identity, cultural studies, and discourse analysis. In her PhD project, she explores young people's negotiations of the 'political' in mediatized everyday lives.

Katarzyna Marciniak, Professor of Transnational Studies in the English Department at Ohio University in the US, specializes in transnational cinemas and the discourses of immigration and foreignness. As Research Fellow, she is affiliated with the Department of English Studies, University of South Africa. With Anikó Imre and Áine O'Healy, she is Series Editor of *Global Cinema*, and her most recent publication is *Teaching Transnational Cinema: Politics and Pedagogy* (2016).

Viktorija Ratković is Senior Scientist at the Centre for Peace Research and Peace Education at the Department of Educational Science, Alpen-Adria-Universität Klagenfurt, Austria. Her research interests include media and migration, peace and conflict studies, and cultural studies.

Steffen Rudolph is Research Assistant in the project 'Doing Memory on Right-wing Violence in Mediated Public Spheres' at the Eberhard Karls

University, Tübingen, Germany. His research interests encompass cultural memory studies, sociology of arts and culture, social inequality, digital divide research, social change, and cultural studies. In his PhD project, he focused on digital media and social inequalities.

Miriam Stehling is Postdoctoral Researcher at the Institute of Media Studies at the Eberhard Karls University, Tübingen, Germany. Her research interests include media audiences, media, participation, and protest as well as cultural and gender media studies. Her current research examines forms of feminist hashtag activism.

Tanja Thomas is Professor of Media Studies with a focus on transformations in Media Cultures at the Eberhard Karls University, Tübingen, Germany. Her research interests include critical media and cultural theory, cultural media studies, feminist theory, and gender media studies. Her current research projects focuses on doing memory on right-wing violence in mediated public spheres, and on media and protest by and against refugees in Israel and Germany.

Julie Uldam is Associate Professor in the Department of Communication & Arts at Roskilde University, Denmark. Her research explores the role of media in relation to civic engagement and forms of citizenship. She is the co-author of *Civic Engagement and Social Media—Political Participation beyond Protest* (2015).

Fabian Virchow is Professor of Political Science with a focus on social theory and theories of collective action at the Düsseldorf University of Applied Sciences, Germany. His research interests and publications focus on the history, ideology, and political practice of right-wing parties and movements, political culture research in general, and the place of military issues in political culture in particular. His most recent research is on the history of far-right media and on doing memory on right-wing violence as contentious politics.

Rafal Zaborowski is Lecturer in Digital Culture in the Department of Digital Humanities, King's College London. Rafal has co-led the Migration and the Media project (2016–2018) at the London School of Economics, which analysed European media representations of migrants and refugees. In his current work, Rafal is interested in the issues of voice and media framing of crises and events. More broadly, Rafal is interested in media audiences, focusing especially on social practices of listening and generational engagements with music media.